Living a Muslim Life

Inside Islamic Culture and Spirituality

John Herlihy

Ansar Books

Living a Muslim Life:
Inside Islamic Culture and Spirituality

All rights reserved.
No part of this book may be used or reproduced
in any manner without written permission,
except in critical articles and reviews.

Copyright © 2015 John Herlihy
Ansar Books
Miami, Florida USA
All rights reserved.
ISBN-13: 978-0692403624
ISBN-10: 0692403620

Dedication

To All Seekers of Truth

-- Other Works --
by John Herlihy

In Search of the Truth

The Seeker and the Way

Veils and Keys

Modern Man at the Crossroads

Near and Distant Horizons

Borderlands of the Spirit

Wisdom's Journey

The Essential René Guénon (ed.)

Journeys with Soul

Wisdom of the Senses

Islam for our Time

Holy Qur'an: An Intimate Portrait

Feathers in the Dust

Contents

Preface: Islam For Our Time

PART ONE: TRADITIONAL WORLDVIEW

1.1 Religion and Tradition in Context
1.2 Traditional vs. Scientific Knowledge
1.3 The Question of Origins
1.4 The Sources of Knowledge
1.5 The Islamic Worldview

PART TWO: THE WORLD RELIGIONS

2.1 Individual Religions in Context
2.2 Judaism: The Way of the Law
2.3 Christianity: The Way of Love
2.4 Islam: The Way of Return
2.5 The Eastern Religions

PART THREE: HISTORICAL CONTEXT

3.1 Pre-Islamic Arabia
3.2 The Descent of the Qur'an
3.3 The Compilation of the Book
3.4 The Impact of the Qur'an
3.5 The Love of the Prophet

PART FOUR: ISLAM AND SCIENCE

4.1 Islamic Science as Sacred Science
4.2 The Qur'an and Science
4.3 Islamic Classification of Knowledge
4.4 Islamic Scholars in History
4.5 Islamic Contributions to Science

PART FIVE: FOUNDATION AND PILLARS

5.1 The Mystery and Certitude of Faith
5.2 To Witness and Surrender
5.3 Tribute to the Illuminated Book
5.4 The Art of Qur'anic Recitation
5.5 Human Consciousness Rising

PART SIX: SPIRITUAL LIFE

6.1 Dreams of a Forgotten Spirituality
6.2 Spiritual Disciplines
6.3 The Significance of Prayer
6.4 The Rigors of the Fast
6.5 Ramadhan Nights in Madinah
6.6 Journey of Our Time

PART SEVEN: THE HIGHER FACULTIES

7.1 The Logic of Reason
7.2 The Light of the Intellect
7.3 The Modes of Intelligence
7.4 The Cave of the Heart
7.5 The Power of Communication

PART EIGHT: SACRED PSYCHOLOGY

8.1 Integral Anthropology
8.2 The Spiritual Emotions
8.3 Sacred Psychology
8.4 The Paradox of Free Will
8.5 Wisdom of the Senses

PART NINE: ETHICS AND MORALITY

9.1 Living the Ethical Life of Islam
9.2 Ethics Thru History
9.3 Modern Ethics
9.4 Islamic Ethics
9.5 The Individual Virtues

Epilogue: Crisis and Challenge

Acknowledgements
Biographical Note
Index

Preface

Islam For Our Time

The discerning and well-informed reader may well wonder why the world needs another introduction to Islam when a cursory review of the books now available with online booksellers will immediately reveal a wide range of works on every aspect of Islam as a religious framework, including books on the historical development of the religion, its relationship—hostility or rivalry as the case may be—to Christianity, a presentation of the basic tenets of the religion, such as the five pillars or the articles of faith, the political and social implications of its doctrines, the evolution and development of Islamic science, or the philosophical underpinnings of the teachings of the religion.

What is lacking across this spread of literary offerings is a book on Islam that reveals the inner experience of the Muslim life, the soul and spirit of the religion, rather than the facts, the doctrines, the history, the schools of thought, the academic treatises on philosophy and theology, or the claims of exclusivity against other religions. Is there a book that addresses the phases of the moon regarding our transient faith in the world of the spirit? Is there a book that examines the moods of the heart and the seasons within the soul as we come to terms with the mystery of our true humanity, including the autumn melancholy of frayed hopes and empty despair, the winter of our discontent with ourselves, the spring of hope in a renewed sense of spirituality, and the summer of fulfillment in a life destiny that reaches its full potential in the courage and certainty that the religion instills within the aspiring soul?

Living a Muslim Life seeks to portray a religion born in the wonder and miracle of revealed words the world had never heard before, with a message that would be recited on the tongue, tucked away in the mind for safe-keeping, and revered within the heart as the sacred speech of the Supreme Being; a religion that unites the entire body and its five senses into one sublime sense, to become Nature's watchmen with a vision that transcends the physical world and absorbs the world of the spirit through every faculty and pore of the body. We have endeavored to expose Islam as a religion that reminds us that we need God in today's anti-spiritual, materialistic and secular world with its technological edge, theory of evolution and vision of progress within an earthly paradise that the modern scientific worldview sets forth as the ultimate end of the human endeavor to reach beyond itself.

Our aim in writing this book is to characterize Islam as a religion that touches the heart as well as the mind, and a philosophy of life that clarifies the universal mysteries that perennially elude our full understanding of ourselves and our world; a religion whose calligraphy of words whispers secrets that touch the strings of our hearts with their inspiration and insight; a religion that offers an experience fused with the incense and perfume of an elevated sense of spirituality that invades our inner senses, leaving us misty-eyed with a sense of longing for the Beloved that can be found within the cave of the heart as well as the deepest recesses of the night sky. We hope to clarify some of the misunderstandings that continue to distort the image of Islam in the public consciousness, oftentimes through mass media outlets that try to encapsulate the broad field and incredible depth of the religion into a thimble-full of attitudes that have the power to tilt the axis of understanding in the wrong direction about the inner world of Islam, with its focus on tolerance, equality, inclusiveness and completeness found within its traditional worldview.

This work is intended for multiple audiences. Firstly, we hope to present Islam in a positive light for those individuals interested in having a better understanding of its teachings, given the extent of the present-day misconceptions of its true nature and purpose perpetuated daily in the mass media around the world. Secondly, many people, especially young people and students, have expressed a renewed interest in Islam as a dynamic force in today's world, a religion whose community of followers number in the billions of practitioners. Obviously, it is in the interest of people generally to more fully understand its core teachings and unique coloration, so that it can find its place within the family of the truly great, global spiritual traditions of the modern era. Islam is not just a patchwork quilt of antiquated verses and sayings that do not address the needs of people today, together with the issues and questions that form the sustaining web of our future world. It is indeed a religion uniquely suited for the challenges of our time.

Our journey through the traditional world of Islamic culture and spirituality commences in Part One with some reflections on the idea of the worldview as the background and framework of universal questions, universal mysteries if you will, that confront us every day of our lives. Part Two places Islam in context within the family of the major religious and spiritual traditions of the present-day, followed in Part Three by a depiction of pre-Islamic Arabia at the time when there was a sudden intrusion of the other-worldly into the reality of this world with a descent of knowledge from the Divine to the human that took the form of revelation, or sacred speech of God. Part Four identifies Islamic science as a "sacred science" based on the philosophy of revelation from a Supreme Being and introduces the idea of the classification of knowledge within the Islamic context, especially during the Golden Years of the Islamic Middle Ages when the individual Islamic sciences not only flourished, but also provided the basis and framework for the development of modern science that commenced during the time of the European Renaissance.

Parts Five and Six provide opportunities to explore the foundation and spiritual life within the Islamic cultural and spiritual framework, the so-called traditional world of Islamic spirituality in the book's sub-title. In Part Seven, we deal with the true significance of the key human faculties, explaining the relationship of reason and intelligence with the heart knowledge that informs the emotions. In Part Eight, we reflect on the idea of a sacred psychology of humanity and how it may affect people's perception of self. Psychology today plays an important role in understanding human identity and in monitoring the behavioral trends that come to make up the actions of our lives during the modern era. Finally, Part Nine deals with morality and ethics—ancient, traditional, modern, and Islamic—in order to highlight and place in context the importance of ethics and morality in today's world, an environment well grounded in materialism, secularism, and egoism masquerading as a courageous, humanitarian individualism without the foundation of traditional ethics that once grounded people within a traditional setting and modes of moral behavior.

Muslims themselves may be interested in reading a prosaic introduction of their religion by someone such as myself, a convert to the religion, who has come in from the cold so to speak, from outside the religion and the community of the faithful, with a different angle of vision from those who were born into the religion. Young Muslims spend many hours from a very early age learning the body of knowledge and spiritual practices based on the *Sunnah*, which is comprised of the Qur'an and *Hadith* or sayings of the Prophet that are still available in their original form for the benefit of contemporary Muslims. They learn Qur'anic recitation together with the strict rules of pronunciation (*tajwid*) and memorization, and the comprehensive rules of *adab* or cultural behavior and good manners that govern all aspects of social and private domestic life within the Islamic domain.

In addition, young Muslims spend their school years learning the prayers, the rituals, and the spiritual disciplines that govern Islamic spiritual life, and they are thoroughly grounded in the life of the Prophet and his companions, including the historical record of what they underwent and suffered during the early days of Islam when the Qur'an itself was still in various stages of descent and the complete dogma and ritual practices not yet firmly established. They are well versed in the early history of the rise and spread of Islam across the Islamic crescent that extends now from the Maghreb, the land of the setting sun, the dense jungles of Malaysia and the Malay archipelago of Indonesia, to the Great Wall of China. One could say that there is really no stone unturned with regard to what the average Muslim knows about his or her religion. However, much of this information is passed on to young Muslims either as theoretical knowledge or as rote practice that has been learned by example in family life and through habit and repetition. When is the kernel exposed inside the husk for them? How is the nut broken open and who nurtures this exposure to the higher realities?

The Muslims of today need to respond to the challenge of 14 centuries ago and listen to the call of the Prophet Muhammad (PBUH)[1], that there is one truth, one reality, one God who has communicated this knowledge through the descent of a revelation, that there is one final messenger, the seal of all the prophets (*al-khatim al-anbiya*), who has proclaimed this perennial truth for future generations across time, who himself exemplifies the way of return and represents the essence of the religion through his thoughts and actions. We know these facts to be the hallmark and banner of the religion; but what does it mean in today's modern and technologically advanced society and how do we incorporate a life of spirituality into our lives in a busy, modern world? How do we as Muslims, especially young Muslims discovering themselves and newly entering into the mainstream of life, find the balance between the traditional worldview and values that Islam offers within a well-defined setting of philosophy, history, culture, science and religious thinking with the modern, secular, rational and purely humanistic approach to life that we find predominant throughout the rest of the modern world, based on the modern, scientific worldview which suggests that humanity themselves are the sole measure against which the values and norms of life are established?

Needless to say, this notion of a purely physical reality as the sole reality runs counter to the spirit of Islam that lays claim to revealed, indeed universal knowledge that falls off the edge of matter and illuminates the vista beyond the physical horizon to reveal an integrated and unified Reality within our comprehension and grasp. As we sleep, do we sometimes form questions on our lips during the night, seeking in vain for an answer to the interrogatives what – how – when – where? Then, upon awakening, what do we see but the same thing that Henry David Thoreau saw in the 19th century as he woke up, none other than "…dawning Nature, in whom all creatures live, looking in at my broad windows with serene and satisfied face, and no question on *her* lips."[2]

Let us awaken every morning to become Nature's watchmen once again, ready to answer the questions that confront us every day of our lives, not by talking in our sleep in shadowy dreams, but living a Muslim life that becomes the true reality of our world. In pursuing a life of spirituality, let us awaken every day like Nature herself, with no question on our lips, only the reality of a conscious awakening to the great spiritual realities that lie within us and around us, in the sunrise and snow, in the glow worm and the bee, in the diamond and the dew, and in the hearts and souls of humanity, a reality that is living, luminous.

---

[1] An acronym PBUH here stands for "blessings and peace upon him", an epithet the traditions (*hadith*) encourage the Muslims to use when the name of the Prophet is invoked, out of respect and love for his memory. A spoken reference is made in Arabic; for simplicity's sake while remaining faithful to the traditional convention, the acronym will be used throughout this work following reference to the Prophet Muhammad (PBUH).

[2] Henry David Thoreau, *Walden* (Boston: Beacon Press, 1997), p. 165.

PART ONE

Traditional Worldview

1.1 Religion and Tradition in Context

Religion has many shades and colors, like a house with many floors and rooms. Its walls contain history and future promise, dogma and rituals, spiritual disciplines and ethical valuations, not to forget the sinners and saints who mingle together within its four walls. Its framework has sects and schools of thought, commandments to follow and customs to take part in. Like all fine houses, it is well placed with a garden whose setting provides a spiritual and universal context to its order and functioning. We know the meaning of our own personal religion, whether it be Islam, Christianity, or one of the other world religions. But what is the meaning of religion as such, and how are we to understand its full meaning and significance within the framework of our lives? All Muslims know that they take part in, and embrace whole-heartedly, the Religion of Islam as their religion by birth and spiritual inheritance; but what does this legacy mean to them and how does the individual Muslim fulfill its true mandate? Is it an empty house with creaking stairs and a leaky roof, or is it a vibrant, living presence whose open doors and windows give fresh air and light to the meaning of their lives as it is intended to do?

    Religion has the power to hover over us like a giant of some mythic fairy tale, uplifting trees by the roots and climbing a magical beanstalk in some distant land, set among floating clouds and mountain peaks. It terrorizes us with its demands of obedience and the curse of damnation, and challenges us with the power of our own free will to surrender to God and the promise of eternal life of the soul in paradise. Like a ghost in the night, a rainbow in the mist, or a mirage in the desert, we cannot put our finger on its mysterious presence. Somehow it escapes the glare of too much light and the rational scrutiny of the five senses. We rely on the intuition of our sixth sense to use the context and framework that the religion provides us, to move through life with a sense of place and belonging within a universe that does not fully explain itself. The religion encourages us to use the inner faculties and five outer senses that we do have to make our way through life and fulfill the mandate of the human condition. Its ghostly presence pres in our lives demands a testimony of faith (*shahadah*) to transcend the limitations of the physical world in order to reveal a world of inner experience with the power to transform lives and change destinies; yet, through a trick of mind, this entire world of the "unknown" and the "unseen" (*al-ghaib*) can escape us if we close ourselves off to the miraculous possibilities that religion offers.

Young Muslims by and large still appreciate the vast legacy that Islam brings to the table of their lives and they still instinctively believe in the precepts and dogmas of the religion. Unlike their Western counterparts, they still quietly preserve the instinctive faith that serves as the spark of all religious commitment and spirituality; but they may not fully know the true value of their religion within the broader context of what is called the perennial philosophy in which all the great world religions take part. There is a sacred theme of unity that runs as a golden thread through the fabric of all the world religions, including the ancient wisdoms of Hinduism, Taoism and Buddhism of the Far East, together with the religions "of the book" that include Judaism, Christianity and Islam. This theme of oneness (*tawhid*) is none other than the existence of a Supreme Being and a Universal Intelligence, a Presence that is Transcendent and Absolute, what Islam identifies as the Outward, the Inward, and the Friend among the ninety-nine names of God in the Islamic tradition. Call it what you will, the belief in a Universal Creator that sustains and guides the universe cuts across religion as such and forms the foundation and cornerstone to its meaning and significance.

The Religion of Islam understands very well its place within the universal scheme of things. While it is very prescriptive with clear dogmas, specific laws, and well identified rituals and spiritual disciplines that constitute its own angle of vision and approach, it also identifies its role within the universal application of religion and connects into a broader system of metaphysical principles that transcend the individual religious forms. Islam understands itself as the primordial religion (*al-din al-hanif*), according to the Qur'an, because it is based on the unique doctrine of Unity that lies at the heart of the universe, as well as within the framework of the natural order. To complement what lies at the heart of the universe, humanity has been given a "human nature", a primordial nature (*fitrah*) in Qur'anic terminology, an original and pure human nature that they bear deep within their own soul as the essence of their being, a nature that makes them not only uniquely human, but also uniquely spiritual beings.

Similarly, Islam is considered to be the last of the great world religions both in its form and in its character. The Prophet Muhammad (PBUH), is identified in the Qur'an as the "seal of the prophets", and this is emphasized at the end of his mission with the descent of the final verse of the Qur'an that states dramatically:

'Today, I have perfected your religion for you, completed my favor upon you, and have chosen for you surrender (*islam*) as your religion." (5:3) It is none other than the religion of surrender (*islam*) that is the cornerstone of the first, primordial religion, bringing to full circle, with its universal theme of unity, the entire progression of the formal religious experience back to the original primordial point out of which the universe was born. Before Islam was a formalized religion with a capital "I", cast within the stone of a fixed and ritualized community of worshippers with a professed history and an accepted body of dogma and laws, it was a community of men and women whose minds had been captured by the essence of what would later become sealed by the details of the religion and its formal practice. That essence is none other than the great witnessing in Islam, the *shahadah*, that seized the mind and hearts of the Companions of the Prophet with its incisive knowledge of the One and the clear path of return to the Source to internalize this knowledge through surrender (*islam*) and worship (*ibadah*).

The concept of religion, its original source and reason for existence, finds its origin and validity in the descent of a revelation from the Divine Being to the human creature. The actual form of the religion, and its entire structure and framework, is born out of a direct communication, a Word or *Logos*, in which the Supreme Being identifies Himself as the true reality and the only reality worthy of our worship and praise. Every religious form builds its supporting tradition—social, cultural or otherwise—from the bedrock of a direct revelation that lays out in detail the essential knowledge of God and all that relates to the human response to that knowledge. This revelatory knowledge speaks directly to the human faculties and senses. Then the inner faculties and five senses process this knowledge and set the scene within the mind and heart for the development of human excellence (*ihsan*) over the course of a lifetime. As knowledge from the Divine Realm, universal revelation substantiates each of the individual religious forms with its knowledge of universal existence and the metaphysical principles that underlie all of existence. As such, the main significance of revelation lies in the fact of its "Word of God" quality, taking part as it does in the character of absoluteness, from sacred laws, to rites and rituals, to the importance of sacred symbols and myths and to the efficacy of the spiritual disciplines, all of which contain blessing (*barakah*) for Muslims, as well as knowledge that is absolute and beyond human argument.

The meaning of the word "religion", in the Islamic context, goes beyond the concept of revelation as the descent of knowledge from the Divine to the human as point of departure and source of the religion. The English word "religion", in Arabic *al-dīn*, does little justice to the full significance of the word's meaning in Arabic, because the concept of *al-dīn* in Islam is less formal and more practical than one finds within the English context for the word "religion". The Arabic *dīn* signifies a way of life that adheres to a sacred norm in which the entire life is molded to become a way of being, in addition to being a way of knowledge that commences with the descent of the Book and the inscription of the pen on the heart of the Muslims, echoing the very first verse, in the form of a direct command, to descend into the mind and heart of the Prophet in the cave of Mt. Hira: "Read (recite) in the name of thy Lord Who created." (96:1) To that end, what the Muslims call the Sunnah comprises not only the verses and laws and entreaties of the Holy Qur'an; but also the sayings of the Prophet, compiled a century or more after his death, that perpetuate his attitudes, his behavior and virtually his way of life. The Prophet himself represents the supreme example of a human being who was the receptacle and instrument of the sacred verses, wrapped in the words and harmonious energy of the Holy Spirit.

Obviously, we need the individual form of a specific religion to make our way in this world. Indeed, a particular religion provides not only the destination in the form of fulfillment, salvation, and ultimately the peace of the Paradise; but also the way to arrive at that destination. What is the good of knowing where we want to go and profess to believe in a body of knowledge that promises blessing, happiness and peace, if we do not know how to arrive at that self-professed goal? Young people today do not need convincing about the importance of being on top of their game, of being clever and skilled at what they need to accomplish, particularly what they want from "this world". There are enough examples in the professional and entertainment world in the form of Superman, Spiderman, or other super-heroes with special powers, to impress upon today's young people the importance of having goals and being successful and powerful in the world. There are ample stories of entrepreneurs like Bill Gates, a high-tech nerd who dropped out of college to become the richest man in the world, to attest to the fact that people now know that they need to develop themselves, to empower themselves with a fully developed skill set, in order to raise their mind and will power so that they can transcend their own limitations and be successful in life.

The question is: How can these fundamental insights that are self-evident to the young and old of today be accomplished, not only in this life, but within the context of a greater, inner journey into the soul and spirit of humanity across the life of our time? We cannot just run through fields with our shoes off or desire to float upon clouds and expect to arrive at the true destination that is built into the human condition. The great gift of Islam is that it provides the Muslims with the means to reach beyond themselves and achieve transcendence within the human condition. This transcendence means an escape from their own weaknesses and limitations through the inner *jihad al-nafs*, or battle of the mind, heart, and soul, the ability to rise above themselves to higher level of consciousness through the remembrance of God every moment of their lives, and to achieve a high level of virtue through application of the principles of the religion in their actions and lives. The great s*hahadah,* or testament of faith in Islam, is not just a formula, but an inner truth that shapes and colors every moment of a Muslim life.

It is not so much what we believe as Muslims, but rather how we can internalize and give meaning to the knowledge of the religion that we say we believe in through our actions and lives. It is not the ritual acts of prayer and fasting and the other duties that make Muslims what they are any more than the shell makes a walnut what it is. The spiritual rites are the ritual foundation to the religion that attempt to remember and uphold the religious truths through a scaffolding of rites and rituals that are intended to raise the spiritual consciousness of the person through acts of daily remembrance. We should not say that I am Muslim because I pray and fast and have made the *hajj*. These things are between you and God whose effectiveness depends on their level of sincerity and commitment, especially the fast, for who knows but God whether a person has truly abstained from food and drink during the daylight hours. If being a Muslim means being a member of a club whose clubhouse contains all the tomes of literature that describe the knowledge of God, then we can close the door of this house and confine ourselves within some small box for all the benefit we would take by mouthing empty words that sit in a book on the shelf. That is not what the great sheikhs, walis and spiritual poets of the past have left behind as a legacy of the spiritual life. What they have left behind to follow is the manner of being Muslim, the "how" and not the "what" of a Muslim life, through actions that contain their own truth, through intentions that have the backing of the divine will, through surrender that meets the moment of the divine command and through virtue that contains its own light and that shines forth from the human face to light the way.

This is the true meaning of the Islamic *din*. As one of the family of the great and revealed world religions, the Religion of Islam adds its own particular perspective to the history of formal religious unfolding by highlighting once again the supreme principle of unity (*tawhid*) expressed in the first of the two statements of the *shahadah* that there is "no god but God". Secondly, Islam emphasizes the importance of commitment to the singular Islamic path in the second of the two statements of the *shahadah*, namely that "Muhammad (PBUH) is His Messenger". As such, Islam's unique angle of vision rests with the polarity "knowledge and action", or alternatively "faith and surrender", or yet again "law and way". As Muslims, young people need to understand the unique position that Islam now plays in highlighting the true meaning of religion as such, a religion worthy both of the world's attention and capable of leading people into the future of themselves and their true destiny.

In summary, Islam identifies itself with the primordial religion that always existed since the symbolic time of Adam and the Golden Era. Islam is also considered the final religion and "seal" of all the previous religions. According to the Qur'an, it recognizes and accepts the chain of prophets and religions that have preceded it. In fact, the *hadith* refer to over 186,000 prophets that have come to humanity over the ages. It could also be called the "natural religion" insofar as it is the religion of proto-nature (*al-din al-fitrah*). In other words, the religion is in the nature of things and identifies the true nature of both man and the natural order as a condition of "surrender". The Oneness of the Absolute is revealed in the natural order and in the heart of humanity as the "primordial message" that lies within the very heart of the universe. This is the true meaning and significance of Islam as a religion within the broader concept of religion "as such", as a principle of unfolding spiritual life in the knowledge of God expressed and realized within the *ummah* (community) of Islam as a living tradition.

Any betrayal in preserving a way of life that reflects the very spirit of *din*, understood in the Islamic worldview as an elaborate and well specified way of life with precepts, dogmas, and modes of action to give it shape and coloration, runs the risk of a self-betrayal in the way Muslims understand themselves and their place in the world. As bearers of the banner of Islam, they set the example that needs to be upheld like a banner in the wind, the standard for a way of living and of being that reflects the traditional knowledge and the universal truth set forth in the Qur'an. The individual religion of Islam and the universal prototype of Religion as such come together in the silhouette of man against the light of the distant horizon. Islam has bestowed a powerful gift upon the Muslims; a gift that they themselves can bear and bring to fruition in their encounter with themselves and the world.

1.2 Traditional vs. Scientific Knowledge

The two prevailing, modern-day worldviews of traditional and modern scientific knowledge, like two great ships the size of behemoths, are floating through the waters of our time with the expressed purpose of taking us to the ultimate destination of human destiny within a universal framework that not only make sense to people generally, but that are supposedly true to reality. Regrettably, they are on a collision course with each other that could have devastating consequences for humanity. In the absence of a clearly defined concept of religion in the modern world that is understandable and makes sense to people, the concept of knowledge itself has undergone a gradual shift of seismic proportions that we need to understand in order to address its inevitable consequences upon our lives.

A fracture, a crack, indeed a Grand Canyon is in the making that has slowly developed over time, leading into what we now call the modern–and sometimes post-modern--world of science and technology, of evolution and progress, with a hedge toward materialism that promises to lead humanity to success and happiness. Whether this modern-day split in the fabric of life's understanding widens or narrows will depend largely upon the extent of our collective perception of what knowledge truly is and how we apply that knowledge to our lives. No one now needs convincing of the importance of knowledge itself, especially in today's competitive world where education is the key to a successful career and a prosperous life. However, the question remains to haunt our modern-day consciousness: What do we mean by the word knowledge itself that leads us to believe so strongly in its limitless possibilities, and what are the sources of knowledge that we believe so completely in its absolute certitude?

Since the 17th century, the advance of modern science has proclaimed a universe whose laws are open to discovery through human reason and an emerging scientific methodology. This new evolving science sought, in the uncompromising words of one of its earliest exponents, Francis Bacon, "not to imagine or suppose, but to *discover* what nature does or may be made to do."[3] Similar to the traditional point of view, the modern, scientific mind is concerned with the imponderable mysteries of existence, and has sought to equip present and future generations with a long list of provable, objective, and thus convincing facts that may well serve humanity in the interests of truth. What modern science discovers, however, must not be at the expense of the truth and the reality that lies at the heart of all existence, as well as the heart of humanity, a truth that is proclaimed by all the great world traditions.

The grand divide between modern science and traditional knowledge is everywhere apparent from their methods of study and their angle of approach to the pursuit of knowledge of the Reality (*al-Haqq*) as a fundamental goal of humanity. The method of scientific research is outwardly directed, while the pursuit of traditional knowledge is directed inwardly. Modern science finds its basis in observation and deduction from sense data, together with the theories and facts that emerge from the pursuit of the scientific method, using the faculty of reason and the five senses as the sole instruments of verification of an objective reality. Religion finds its source of knowledge and inspiration in revelation and the human ability to understand the truth through the intellect which then discriminates between truth and error through the use of intelligence, followed by realization and internalization of that truth through spiritual experience. The focus of science is on the physical manifestations within nature, while the focus of religion and its supporting traditions is on human nature (*fitrah*), striving to understand the workings of the inner nature of humanity and attempting to grow beyond the limiting horizon of the earthly condition. Science is knowledge and its application within the physical world; religion is knowledge and transcendence of self within the metaphysical world.

Religion begins with the descent of revelation that unveils the mystery of the Divinity and speaks of the unity of the cosmos as a manifestation of the Principle of the One from which everything originates and outwardly flows. Science begins with faith in its own assumptions and proceeds with the accumulation and analysis of data through the scientific method of observation (the five senses and human reason [*al-aql*]). It constructs an unfinished mosaic of fragmented facts, figures, and formulas and speaks of patterns, tendencies, and possibilities; but it categorically refuses to refer to metaphysical principles that transcend the human order unless they are verifiable within manifested nature. The modern worldview does not admit of an inner message or profess an inherent meaning and purpose to the natural order of the universe. We could ask the reason for this adamant attitude against the unseen (*al-ghaib*); but an answer may break apart the myth of the independence of modern science and the absolute quality of its methods and point of view that repudiates everything that

---

[3] Loren Eiseley, *The Unexpected Universe*, New York: Harcourt Brace Jovanorich, Inc., 1969, p. 27.

transcends it by declaring it unproved and thus unsubstantiated according to its own rigid criteria.

Ultimately, knowledge must reflect the whole; reality must be a manifestation of an organic and holistic reality; the universe must be what it is, namely an ordered and harmonious totality that we see outwardly reflected in the harmony and lawfulness of the celestial spheres. The elements found in the natural order must be related to the whole, partly in order to understand their meaning and purpose, and partly to preserve the integrity of their own individual integrity which relies on the harmony and balance of the Whole. "The science of our time knows how to measure galaxies and split atoms, but it is incapable of the smallest investigation beyond the sensible world, so much so that outside its own self-imposed but unrecognized limits it remains more ignorant than the most rudimentary magic."[4] Modern science presents a vast accumulation of detailed knowledge which no one could hope to grasp in its totality, partly because modern science does not accept a perspective of totality that satisfies its demand for physical proof, and partly because the accumulated facts simply do not add up to a complete and unified theory in the scientific sense, a totality and a unity (*al-tawhid*) in the Islamic sense of the term.

If the traditional knowledge of metaphysics lacks sufficient proof from the scientific point of view, then it could be affirmed that from the metaphysical perspective, modern science lacks significance and the means of achieving a comprehensive meaning to the facts it uncovers that would amount to a universal cosmology regarding the origin and fate of the universe. It is not worth gathering together an extensive body of knowledge of the physical world, only to lose the essential knowledge of the soul of man and the Spirit of God as an unwanted consequence of the accumulated discoveries of physical nature. It is not worth the sacrifice of a traditional knowledge that belongs to a higher order of understanding with the power of unifying the multiplicity of all knowledge and of unifying the wide diversity of the manifested world into a single Whole, for the sake of an analytic knowledge that knows everything about the facts of the universe, but that understands nothing about the significance and meaning of the universal and metaphysical truths.

The prevailing attitudes of modern science have not always been the established standard in earlier, more traditional societies. In addition, science has not always been modern. History portrays western science as having gone through a far more traditional era when the meaning of the term "science" itself reflected the metaphysical and spiritual roots of knowledge that found its ultimate source in the sacred scriptures of the various religions, an essential knowledge that addresses the grand questions of humanity, including the questions of origin, destiny, and final end of humanity within the context of the universe as we know it. The traditional sciences were considered "a knowledge, which, while not pure

---

[4] Frithjof Schuon, *In the Tracts of Buddhism*, tr. Marco Pallis, London: Unwin Paperbacks, 1989, p. 40.

metaphysics, is traditional, that is, related to metaphysical principles, and though a science in the sense of organized knowledge of a particular domain of reality, it is not divorced from the immutability which characterizes the principial order."[5] In this regard, knowledge draws its doubt or its certitude from the acceptance of the principle of revelation as the ultimate source of the essential knowledge. The tradition of a pursuing science of the physical laws of the universe was left to the relatively lower-level understanding of science as we know it in the modern world.

Another notable difference between traditional knowledge and modern science lies in the meaning of their application in life. Modern science applies its knowledge to the benefit and enhancement of the quality of life on the physical, practical, and sensorial levels of experience. This is not surprising since it is only interested in the physical plane of existence as the sole expression of true reality. The traditional sciences, on the other hand, understand themselves to be applications of a metaphysical doctrine that gains entrance to a different order of reality and integrates this knowledge into a unity through synthesis and full integration into a person's behavior and action. Thus, the way a person is provides a direct reflection of the way he/she acts and behaves. The traditional sciences prepare the way for a higher expression of the essential knowledge and offers a pathway leading toward that knowledge.

In today's world, scientists describe the universe in terms of two basic theories, relativity and quantum mechanics, considered to be the two great intellectual achievements of the twentieth century. The theory of relativity now dominates the field of astronomy by describing the force of gravity and the large-scale structure of the universe. Quantum mechanics, on the other hand, deals with phenomena on very small scales within the quantum world. Not surprisingly, astronomy as the macrocosmic field of the infinitely large[6] and quantum physics as the microcosmic field of the infinitely small[7] are beginning to create cracks of denial in the wall of scientific truth that has always accompanied the scientific attitude concerning higher levels of reality. The findings of both astronomy and physics have begun to hint at the possibility of domains that are actually "trans-physical", domains that virtually transcend the purely physical plane of existence.

The sciences of physics and astronomy also point to another astounding insight: They both contain their own distinct worlds and suggest the possibility of more undisclosed insights that are different from anything we perceive directly with our senses; as such they seem to follow their own distinct laws. We live

---

[5] S.H.Nasr, *The Need for a Sacred Science*, Albany, NY: SUNY Press, 1993, p. 95.

[6] The general theory of relativity describes the force of gravity and the large-scale structure of the universe, sizes on a scale as large as a multiplicity of millions (1 with twenty four zeros after it) miles, which is the size of the observable universe.

[7] Quantum mechanics deals with phenomena on extremely small scales, such as a millionth of a millionth of an inch, leading to a technology of the miniscule that we now call nanotechnology.

between two worlds, the one macro and the other micro in dimension and orders of magnitude, just as from the traditional point of view, we live in the continuum of time within the envelope of eternity. As regards the linear progress of time, time's continuum seems directional and timely, moving forward at a rate that coincides with the ticking of a metronome and the beating of our hearts. Outside the linear progress of time, time's continuum seems like a pause between two eternities, a single breath of humanity that has had its moment only to fall back into the ocean of the Spirit. Our lives are but fragments, a parenthesis that opens the envelope of the space/time continuum and closes out the eternal now. Between the infinitely large and infinitely small worlds of astronomy and physics lies the meso-world of the intelligible and the understandable, the meso-world of everyday phenomena. This middle land is reminiscent of the "middle way" of Islam. We experience directly a meso-world with our senses and are expected to follow the middle way, a path that not only reflects the reality of the natural order in which nature is beautiful because it symbolizes and reflects beauty, but also because the middle way represents the way of measure and balance that we hope to achieve in our lives as a reflection of the Islamic principles.

For centuries, western science has insisted on observing the natural order directly while, at the same time, it has systematically refused to believe in anything that was perceived indirectly, from behind a symbol or a veil as it were, such as the truths of the traditional world that were perceived indirectly through myth, symbols, and metaphor. It wanted to find its truth in the atoms and molecules of every drop of water and every grain of sand. Now, however, with the discoveries of quantum physics, modern science has turned a corner, only to arrive at a kind of black hole in its study of the physical universe. It has discovered to its surprise that matter cannot always be substantiated and form cannot always be visualized. In fact, modern science is now reaching beyond its traditional domain of the physical world into areas that are difficult to imagine even for scientists, much less visualize or listen to for verification through the senses. For example, physicists are forced to ask themselves: Is a neutron a particle or a wave? Physicists no longer know since it behaves as both a particle and a wave and its behavior is characterized by unpredictability.

In the traditional perspective, people were accused of believing, without coming to a true understanding of the physical world around them. With regard to some of the latest findings of quantum physics, scientists find themselves understanding their theories, but without actually believing them, because they point towards border areas into which science has been forbidden to venture. "The normal reaction to a first exposure to relativity is: 'I think I understand it; I just don't believe it.' Normally it takes a physicist about five years of contact with the ideas before he feels comfortable with them – not because they are complex or obscure, but just terribly strange."[8] Now quantum and astro-physics are exploring the frontiers of these borderlands with an intensity and thoroughness

---

[8] Robert March, *Physics for Poets* (New York: McGraw-Hill, 1970), p. 128.

that it always brings to its investigations, and these scientific disciplines are beginning to make some startling discoveries and some inescapable realizations that could possibly lead to a breakthrough in the way the traditional and modern scientific worldviews interact with each other.

The time has come to reflect within ourselves about the interrelatedness and unity that scientists are slowing beginning to discover within the basic elements of the phenomenal world. The time has come to use the great achievements of modern science, together with traditional knowledge, to provide a consistency of perspective and philosophical depth to the knowledge that is being made available to people during this time period. We need to leave behind with finality all preconceived notions concerning the unknown mystery, in order to open ourselves to the full view of a new and unexplored horizon that begins within humanity as a realization that the origin and final end are one and the same. The aim of knowledge is not the discovery of some ultimate proof that will prove all our scientific theories to the detriment of metaphysical knowledge. The aim of knowledge is but a return to the Origin of all things which lie at the heart of humanity, within the nucleus of the atom, and at the Absolute Center of the universe. To have knowledge of our origins and final end is to know from where we originate and therefore the destination to which we will ultimately return, the end being only part of a greater cycle where the end returns to the beginning to reunite with its origin.

Whether it is the recent findings of modern science in the fields of biology, chemistry and physics that have revolutionized the entire intellectual framework of our time and enriched the storehouse of modern knowledge as never before, or the wide diversity and profound scope of the traditional knowledge whose fullness reaches down from Heaven to enrich the earth and whose broad base of influence spans across all races and cultures, one thing must become clear. The deeper a modern and contemporary person explores either the rational or intuitive perspective, the more that person must realize the existence of a unique similarity of aim and purpose between the two contemporary paradigms of knowledge. A bridge of opportunity is beginning to emerge that may span the divide that exists between scientific and traditional knowledge that would be too important for us to ignore.

Science needs a perennial philosophy of universal truths in order to substantiate the facts and the findings that it uncovers on the physical plane of manifestation, and in order to give them accessibility and meaning to the people of our time. Traditionally, the world religions, and the religion of Islam in particular, have accomplished this feat with considerable success by offering a sacred philosophy of life and practical wisdom to help fulfill life's purpose in a manner that is comprehensible to everyone. The science we envision would have to be a "sacred science" rather than an exclusively "empirical science" such as we have now, a science that holds the door open to permit the higher, metaphysical realities to reveal themselves within the natural order as the universal principles that they truly are.

Neither science nor religion can continue into the new millennium as islands unto themselves. Nor can either modern science or the great world religions suffer a fatal compromise at the expense of the other perspective. The world cannot afford to lose either the incredible quality or depth of the traditional knowledge or the incredible precision, accuracy and range of the knowledge of modern science. They both need to integrate themselves into a comprehensive theory of knowledge that the adherents of these two perspectives would be willing to believe in and act upon. Each perspective needs to exhibit a new consciousness that complements the incredible breadth of knowledge and possibility that these valid and alternative fields of vision encompass. They both need to be inclusive rather than exclusive, inviting dialogue and exchange between related fields of interest to bridge their differences and frames of reference. It is not for nothing that the Messenger of Islam is quoted as having said: "Seek knowledge[9] (of science), even unto China," which was a form of Arab hyperbole to suggest that the knowledge of science was so important one should seek it even unto "the ends of the earth". No doubt, the Prophet of Islam was thinking of traditional knowledge that finds its source in the headwaters of revelation that flowed into him, then to his companions and ultimately into the world we now live in.

1.3 The Question of Origins

Every system of knowledge that aspires to being a worldview with the power to capture the minds and hearts of a mass population needs to address and come to terms with the question of origins. The question of origins is a perennial one that will not go away and its unresolved mystery continues to haunt the modern psyche of humanity, no matter how adept scientists have become at extricating the secrets that lie sequestered within the bedrock of the natural order. No matter how determined their efforts to lay claim once and for all to a definitive discovery that would resolve the secret of origins, and no matter how far we have come in discovering what happened during what modern science calls the "initial singularity" of the Big Bang that initiated the beginning of the universe, scientists never quite arrive at the source of the universal story whose mythical telling would reveal the true origin of humanity, of existence, and of the universe itself.

Our search for true origins leads us back through time to the moment of the initial creation, often fantasized today as the theory of the Big Bang when the universe virtually exploded into being from what modern science calls an "initial singularity" or what the traditions call the "primordial point". The traditional point of view that Islam sets forth returns us once again to the source, at the moment of the initial creation of the universe. God's existence is eternal, but the

---

[9] Etymologically, linguistically, and historically, science in its root meaning was always considered knowledge and knowledge understood as science, expressing or implying possibly a difference in degree, but not in kind.

knowledge of God's existence begins with the act of the initial creation. What science envisions as a singularity is actually the first manifestation of multiplicity, a multiplicity that will virtually characterize a created universe that reflects unity through multiplicity, the absolute through the relative, and the infinite through the finite. The secret of the divine mystery, the universal unknown that modern science aspires to uncover and categorize, lies embedded with the very substance and manifestation of the creation as the One, the Absolute and the Infinite.

We have, of course, a serious difference of opinion between the theory of cosmic origins portrayed through modern science and the perennial explanation of the creation set forth in the Religion of Islam. The Qur'anic phrase *kun fa yakoon* (be and it becomes) encapsulates within the divine speech of revelation the initial impulse of the Divinity to commence the unfolding of His Self Disclosure at the dawn of creation and refers to the auditory sound *kun* that virtually initiated the divine act of creation. The scientific model of the universe leads us back to the horizon of time to the moment of initial singularly beyond which the theoretical model of the universe portrayed by modern science breaks down. Any further speculation concerning the nature of reality has no consequence because it lies outside the paradigm of modern science as we define it in today's world.

In its search for the knowledge of universal origins, modern science takes us back to the edge of the time/space continuum at the outer periphery of the known universe, and then comes to an abrupt halt. Seemingly, it is enough to know that the universe began "in the beginning",[10] but the questions of "how" it began and more philosophically "why" find no place in the scientific inquiry, perhaps for no other reason than the fact that the answers lie outside the parameters of its sources of knowledge, namely human reason and the five physical senses, supported by the consistent and verifiable laws of nature, and is therefore irrelevant. Yet the 'how' and 'why' of the origin of the universe are questions that don't give up their challenge to human curiosity easily and linger at the gate of human inquiry expecting ultimately an answer. They simply don't go away and continue to suggest a purpose to the universe that makes a mockery of the "random chance" referred to in the theory of evolution, the spontaneous appearance of life, or the explosion of an unexpected universe that provides the ground for the laws of nature.

The scientific theory of universal origins fails on fundamental levels, partly because there is no "source knowledge" to speak of, but rather a dead-end set of theories bereft of any true mystery, and partly because it simply does not make sense and is without reference to anything the average person can freely associate

---

[10] Not "in the beginning of time", for example, as opposed to the atemporal context within the envelope of eternity. In fact, it is only in the last 30 years of this century that the modern scientific establishment has come around to the Biblical and Qur'anic view. From the time of Aristotle 2,300 years ago, scientific theory held the universe to be eternal. Now we accept the theory of the Big Bang as popular wisdom.

with either mentally or spiritually. As a scientific theory, it remains incomplete because it cannot tell us "how" the universe began and its power of prediction is fundamentally negative: it tells us that all physical theories break down at the beginning of the universe. In fact, modern science says Big Bang is a singularity because the space-time continuum cannot be extended beyond that and survive.

According to the traditional perspective of Islam, it is by virtue of the command of God that the question of origins is resolved. The universe, indeed the very existence of the cosmos, points beyond itself to a universal principle and a first cause. When the Bible asserts the well-known phrase "in the beginning", are we to interpret the Biblical *in principio* as an initiation and principle of time in a timely sense or a timely principle in a metaphysical sense that can serve as a reference point and framework within which to understand the genesis of the creation and the act of the Creator. In this context, the knowledge of the true beginning finds its "source" in God Himself, Who lies outside the reference point of time and outside the framework of the cosmos as such. Time actually begins in eternity through a vertical descent as a macrocosmic manifestation of a metacosmic Principle. Therefore, neither time nor its source-point in eternity are within the reach of modern science and cannot suffer from its dispassionate and cold scrutiny.

Instead, the initial singularly presents itself, in the words of Wolfgang Smith,[11] as an "incurably transcendent" point from which, according to modern scientific theory, the entire universe has sprung and continues to expand. This point is actually the origin of the Metacosmic Center that initiates the true Beginning, when the universe was brought into existence. It is the result of the Creative Act whose point within the Center, and whose time at the Beginning, affirm the unity of the creation within the very fold of a Divine and Transcendent Being who, through an act of vertical causation that originates outside of time and space, actually creates the continuum in which the universe is made possible. In this way, the revealed sources of knowledge clarify the event–perhaps the non-event as the case may be, since nothing can "happen" outside of the framework of the initial creation and re-create, in the words of scripture, the knowledge of the True Beginning.

Three fundamental questions concerning origins have proven to be as enigmatic and mysterious as they are magnetic and inviting to the human mentality. They are: What is the universe? What is Life? What is Man? They are perennial mysteries that every living individual asks him or herself at some point in their lives in order to come to terms with mysteries that affect their approach to live and the way they live. The search for answers to these three recurring questions represents the unending search of humanity for the First Cause to which all knowledge and experience can be referred. The answers to these questions would solve for humanity all the perennial mystery of the universe, of life, of man. Perhaps that is why we have no definitive answers to these questions,

---

[11] *Cosmos and Transcendence*, Peru, Ill: Sherwood Sugden & Co., 1990, p. 110.

except what comes to us through the self-disclosure of the Divinity through Revelation, through Nature and through Mankind (*insan*).

The problem of the genesis of life commences with the life force itself. What is it and from where does it originate? Modern science studiously avoids unnecessary speculation concerning the emergence of the life force itself. That must remain the sacrosanct preserve of the traditions which speak both eloquently and definitively about the origin of the life force and its implicit meaning as a manifestation of the Spirit that animates all of the creation. Instead, modern science focuses on the physically observable as a matter of course, and dismisses the initial process of creation that something emerged from nothing as a purely spontaneous happening, arising out of favorable conditions on the planet at that time.

According to modern science, the origin of the life force commences from within the time/space matrix that existed at the origin of the physical cosmos without the intrusion of any transcendent cause. Within a purely material and temporal matrix, modern science suggests that the life force issued accidentally and randomly out of non-life, and that both life and intelligence came forth out of brute and inanimate matter. There is nothing to prove that inorganic matter could have induced the creation of living matter when the determining factor for this phenomenon remains unknown.

We need to remember in this context the great biological discovery of DNA double helix. The life force itself represents sheer intelligence, commencing with the intelligent life force of a single cell.[12] Intelligent biology is perhaps the most meaningful message of the new biology. The micro-biological order is alive with intelligence, order and purpose that constitute the elementary particles of our very flesh. Why, then, do so many people today still cling "blindly" to the essentially mindless theory of natural selection as the cornerstone of evolutionary life? Similarly, scientists refer to hot little pools, primordial soup and primal seas in their speculation of the origin of life itself, and this coincides with the Qur'anic injunctions that everything originates from water. "Do not the unbelievers see that the heavens and the earth were joined together, then We broke them apart and We got every living thing out of water? Will they not believe"? (21: 30)[13]

Scientists freely confess that they have no direct evidence of the replication event that instigated the origin and replication of life on earth. "We do not know exactly what the original critical event, the initiation of self-replication, looked like, but we can infer what kind of an event it must have been." Further on, the

---

[12] Unicellular life forms are amazingly complex, even though the cells are measured in units of 1/1,000 of a millimeter. Cells have a highly complex chemical structure and a nucleus that is composed of many parts, including chromosomes that contain genes. These control every aspect of the cell's functioning, namely its life.

[13] The reference concerning water can have a double meaning: that everything living thing was made of water as its essential component, or that every living thing originated in water. Another revealing verse adds: "God created every living thing from water". (24: 45)

same author concludes: "What we can do is guess at a general chronology of a life explosion on any planet, anywhere in the universe."[14] We are witnessing in action the interweaving of a fabric whose woof constitutes the available facts and whose warp is derived from the fiction of inferences and suppositions that are freely admitted by scientists. Whatever angle we approach the problem, whether it is from the traditional or the scientific perspective, the creation of life seems either a miracle or an anomaly.

The idea that evolution could be significantly shaped by hidden harmonies and an ordered design reflecting purpose and intelligence is scorned by many, but not all, biologists. "Certain thinkers, who until now have approached the problem from a strictly materialistic point of view, are beginning to realize that the question must henceforth be seen in a light that introduces – at the very least – certain metaphysical considerations."[15] While the physicist Wolfgang Smith writes from a slightly different perspective: "There are first origins, then, and indeed there must be. Every chain of secondary causes, traced backwards, must eventually lead to the brink of a mystery; even physical cosmology, it seems, has at last come to this recognition. Likewise, so far as biological chains of descent are concerned, there must always be a "missing link": the only question is whether there are many – one for each natural species – or whether the branches of the genealogical tree trace back to one common primordial ancestor, so that the mystery of creation appears to be concentrated, so to speak, at a single point."[16] Until now, biology and physics are worlds apart, not only substantively by virtue of what they study, but also philosophically through the manner in which they approach their subject. Many physicists, in their study of the minutiae of the sub-atomic world, are beginning to see through the window to the other side of reality, while most biologists seem to be intent on proving the traditions "wrong".

Because of the traditional perspective they believe in, modern Muslims are standing on a horizon with a panoramic view overlooking two compelling worldviews, the one horizontal with an earthly horizon, the other vertical with a celestial horizon. The world of science looms ahead on this side of the horizon with its precision, objectivity in the name of physicality, and exactitude, insisting on the pre-eminence of matter as the ultimate reality and the sanctity of life as a natural process of selection. The substantive world of religion lies beyond the other side of the horizon and extends vertically upward. The traditional world of the revealed religions is a world of unity that speaks of realities that transcend matter and human reason and that offer spiritual meaning to the life of humanity, a meaning that encompasses the physicality of this world and transcends it

---

[14] George Johnson, *Fire in the Mind* (New York: Vintage Books, 1996), p. 138.

[15] Dr. Maurice Bucaille, *What is the Origin of Man?* (New York: Islamic Book Service, 2005), p. 194.

[16] *Cosmos and Transcendence*, Peru, Ill: Sherwood Sugden & Company, 1990, p. 89-90.

through the reality of the Spirit of God, the "Breath of the Compassionate" (*al-nafas al-Rahman*) that the Qur'an speaks of as the forward-driving and motivating force of the universe.

These two worldviews are virtually separated by the seam of an earthly horizon; but they could be united by the principle of Unity that the religion of Islam preserves for humanity and will continue to do so into the future. The mystery of cosmic genesis and the knowledge of a true beginning lie hidden within the mystery of a transcendent consciousness that has proclaimed as an eternal remembrance: "I was a hidden treasure and wanted to be known; therefore, I created the world" (*hadith*).

1.4 The Sources of Knowledge

In the encounter of traditional and scientific knowledge, it is no longer good enough to say that we know something and be satisfied with that. The worldview that people adhere to must address and answer the vital question in the minds and on the lips of every reflective person: How do we know what we know? The Muslims themselves must be ready to give an accounting whenever the question is asked. After all, Muslims are ready enough to say what they believe in; the beliefs and doctrines of the religion have been drummed into their heads since childhood and they can proclaim what they know from the rooftops along with the *adhan* that unfailingly gives the call to prayer five times a day from minarets across the Islamic crescent.

Lifting the veil or scratching below the surface of knowledge for the sources of our inspiration, however, may prove to be a challenging task, much less internalizing and living what we believe to be true knowledge. We as Muslims need to look beyond the horizon of "this world" and back to the edge of time when the universal mysteries originated. We must attempt to uncover once again the crack in the universe, providing a secret glimpse to that knowledge, according to the mystic poet Wordsworth, of a presence that gives us the joy of elevated thoughts and a sense of something sublime. There is a divine presence that leads beyond the known horizon "whose dwelling is in the light of setting suns, and the round ocean and the living air, and the blue sky, and in the mind of man."[17]

Yes, the human mind apparently holds the key to a higher consciousness that we should always remember and hope never to forget. We need to ask ourselves a number of questions before we take comfort in the certitude of a universal knowledge that can provide the framework to the way we live our lives. What are the original sources of knowledge? Are they valid, authentic and objective beyond any reasonable human doubt? Is there a headwater of knowledge or a well-spring of truth that serves as the fundamental source of all knowing, or is knowledge relative and all truth conditioned by the impulses of human minds such as contemporary scientists would have us believe? Is there a

---

[17] "Tintern Abbey", William Wordsworth.

source so otherworldly and profound that it has the power to wipe away all uncertainty and doubt, a mega-power that is able to synthesize, into a single unifying web, the different elements that we witness within the existential reality of our lives? In short, is there a knowledge that can neutralize the split image of Heaven and Earth that we see on the horizon and bring the various elements of the phenomenal and natural world into a unified Whole that is comprehensible to all and everyone?

When it comes to the question of a knowledge that explains certain fundamental mysteries, a knowledge that transcends any "provable" medium such as the alleged objectivity of matter as the yardstick of modern science, and a knowledge that rises above the level of pure reasoning to the realm of essential (metaphysical) meaning and purpose, the subject of sources and their authenticity must inevitably arise and be seriously considered. It does not matter to what extent we as a civilization are able to uncover aspects of a knowledge that may lead to the explanation of certain fundamental mysteries. What must sustain a workable credibility in the minds and hearts of mass populations around the globe will be the original sources of a particular paradigm of knowledge and the authenticity of its related worldview. Ultimately, the only thing that truly matters to humanity is whether the knowledge of the absolute Reality is true and whether it lives in the mind as an enduring certainty. Are there headwaters for the laws and principles that flow through the cosmos into the mind of man? Is there a wellspring of knowledge that covers in a protective mystery the origin of man and the birth of the universe that seals with certainty the meaning and the ultimate fulfillment of humanity and the entire creation?

We endeavor to answer these questions by referring to the three clearly articulated sources of knowledge as they are identified within the religion of Islam, namely Revelation as the divine disclosure of the mind of God, Nature as the naturalized and formal body of God and Man as the human image of God. Stephen Hawking, the well-known and controversial physicist, concluded his intriguing book *A Brief History of Time* with two surprising statements amounting to key points on his "wish list", firstly to discover a complete theory of knowledge concerning the true nature of the reality whose broad principle could be understood by everyone, and secondly the wish to understand why we and the cosmos exist. "For then," he concludes, "we would know the mind of God." For a contemporary scientist, it is a bold and courageous thought. From the traditional Islamic point of view, however, the mind of God has already been made manifest through the verses of sacred Qur'anic scripture and the other traditionally accepted scriptural revelations down through the millennia.

The Qur'an itself, of course, is the primary source of knowledge within the Islamic tradition as the sacred communication *par excellence* from the Mind of God to the mind of humanity. It is the direct descent of the essential knowledge from the Divine Being to the human being through Sacred Speech. The Religion of Islam began as a spiritual force with the first descent of the revelation to the Prophet Muhammad (PBUH), and with the descent of the final verses came the completion and fulfillment of the religion as a spiritual force on earth. "This day have I perfected your religion for you, completed My favor upon you, and have chosen for you Islam as your religion." (5:3)

Two other sources of knowledge made available for the benefit of humanity are specifically mentioned in the Qur'an. "Soon We will show them our Signs on the distant horizon and within their own souls, until it becomes manifest to them that this is the absolute Truth." (41:53) These alternative sources of knowledge are respectively the manifested creation in the form of Nature, and man (*insan*) himself who is considered in Islam a living source of knowledge, as well as a human revelation. "Know thyself in order to know thy Lord" is a well-known Holy Tradition (*hadith*) of the Prophet. What may prove enigmatic to the modern mentality, steeped as it is in the secular and scientist ambiance of the modern world, is the meaning of the word "knowledge" itself, since distinctions need to be made between the sacred and essential knowledge contained within a revealed scripture with its holy metaphorical tales and symbolic imagery, and the speculative, empirical and scientific knowledge that serves as the backcloth and worldview for the modernist mentality.

Within the Islamic tradition, the Qur'an clearly states that the source of all true knowledge lies within the phenomenal world as symbolized in the image of the distant horizon and within man as symbolized in the image of the near horizon of the self. The near horizon of the inner self represents a kind of isthmus and passageway between the outer and inner worlds of the human being. The distant earthly horizon marks the terminus of the known world that marks the end of knowledge and the beginning of mystery. Both horizons imply the possibility of a knowledge that finds its origin in the Absolute Truth and traces its roots back to the Divine Source.

The image of the near horizon within humanity and the distant horizon on the edge of the known world identifies through the bold stroke of a single, horizontal line the separation that exists between two alien worlds, the one physical, visible, and apparently real, the other rarefied, invisible and apparently unreal. The horizon traces the distinct realities of Nature and Man with a celestial line that cuts across the face of the phenomenal world of nature and across the ground of the soul of humanity. On the one side lies the visibly convincing, physical reality of this world, tempting us into believing the world to be an independent reality that is absolute within itself. On the other side of this dividing line we find the elusive world of the spirit that overlays all of physical reality with its vivifying force and its definitive presence.

To look at the distant horizon with its split image of heaven and earth is to gaze at the duality of the world. To gaze at the near horizon that exists within humanity is to bear witness to the duality that exists within us as the existential reality of our being. Heaven and earth, matter and spirit, body and soul, light and darkness, good and evil: These are the existential polarities that highlight the separation of two alien worlds that exist within man as a near horizon and manifest symbolically on the periphery of the world as the distant horizon. The image of the horizon, as macrocosmic symbol *par excellence*, is the remembrance of the unity of separate worlds that in appearance are two but in truth are one, for as the Qur'an repeatedly asserts, there is but one Reality and only one God.

The split image of the world and the duality of man have never held such prominence as during the present era at the dawn of a new millennium. This duality vividly expresses itself during these times in the way we understand ourselves, the way we express our self-image, the way we perceive our world, and the way we approach the very portals of knowledge itself. As individuals, we are living out the complexities of a split image that is embedded within our beings and reflected within the very framework of the creation. Heaven and earth is there on the horizon, as though it were traced across the celestial divide of the heavens with the ink of the Divine Pen. Body, soul and spirit constitute the totality of the human entity, as though the thin line of the near horizon cuts across our being with the invisible blade of the Divinity, thereby creating a clean and unbreachable chasm between the known and unknown self within a person.

This split image of man and the world manifests itself during the present era as the relentless revolution of the scientific point of view over the minds and hearts of people everywhere. There are now two points of reference and two paradigms of knowledge that vie for the attention of mass populations around the globe. There is the vision of a metaphysical knowledge, of eternal and supernatural realities, that is rooted in first principles and that is conveyed to humanity through revelation, through nature and through man. It is a principial knowledge that begins with revelation, becomes internalized in man through a faith in God that gives color to every thought and action, and ultimately ends with certainty in the reality of the Supreme Being. Then there is the vision of a physical reality, of rational and natural realities rooted in physical matter and conveyed to humanity through human reason and the observations and calculations of an experimental and mathematical science. It is a knowledge that begins with hypothesis and ends with the certainty of physical proofs as the definitive source of an objective knowledge and the only reality worth believing in and studying.

The age we live in offers frightening challenges, but it also inspires bold thinking. There is a feeling of the "eleventh hour" about our time. Modern speculation concerning the eternal mysteries is fast approaching an edge of time and space whose drop-off point is as abrupt and final as the end of the earth was for 16th century seafarers. Yet, a compensation of our time may provide an unexpected insight into the dilemma that confronts us by believing in a scientific conception of knowledge that has become equated with the only way of knowing there is. Yet, does this attitude need to set the norm for everyone? People are becoming increasingly aware of how little our rational knowing pushes back the frontiers of our conscious unknowing. What we know no longer satisfies the aching mystery of what we do not know. No matter what wondrous scientific revelation stimulates contemporary thinking–from the theory of relativity to the mysteries of the quantum universe—the parade of demonstrable facts that result from the high fever pursuit of the scientific inquiry throws no more light on the dark mystery that clouds our knowing than a bright wood fire throws into the dark, moonless night.

Still, there is a way of knowing that transcends the rational world of the mind for a higher consciousness of knowing. Every search implies a journey and every journey requires a final destination. The search for the authentic sources of knowledge begins with the words of revealed scripture, manifests through the symbolic messages of every created thing within the phenomenal world of nature, and ends with the self-revelation of mankind. It marks an inner journey across frontier lands that lie beyond the horizon and off the map. No well-defined road leads there and no one can find the way on his or her own. It is a journey that will take us to the central *mihrab*[18] of the inner self as the focus and prelude for the experience of that Center and Source of the Metacosmic Universe that exists beyond the edge of space and time, but that manifests here and now as the Divine Disclosure and the Sacred Presence of God.

The Religion of Islam highlights for modern humanity once again the importance of the primordial truth that lies as a reoccurring theme within each of the traditional religions. Allah is the Source and Origin of all knowledge; He is the creator of the universe and all life within its realm; from His Throne flow the headwaters of the human narrative. "We come from God and to Him we will return." (2:152)

1.5 The Islamic Worldview

In the first four sections of Part I, we have outlined the basic elements of what constitutes in modern terminology a global worldview. Most people today are well familiar with the conceptual thinking behind the modern scientific worldview that dominates the mentality of contemporary societies around the world at the expense of the traditional and spiritual perspective. A worldview as such is not only a well-defined body of knowledge that people come to accept as the driving force of their perceptions; it is also a reflection of the society's fundamental attitudes and manner of approach to the great questions that underscore their lives with their ever-elusive and perennial mystery that follows us around like a shadow self. We have endeavored to put the concept of religion itself into a clear context and identified the specific and unique meaning of the term within the religious and spiritual context of Islam, not only as a prescriptive body of doctrines, but also as a complete way of life that is based on the revelation of the Qur'an and the Sunnah or life practices and sayings (*hadith*) of the Prophet.

We have clearly outlined the two kinds of knowledge (science) that have emerged down through history to the present moment, namely a traditional

---

[18] Every mosque contains a central prayer niche that faces Makkah and serves as the orientation point for the prayer.

knowledge that finds its origin and source within the great world religions and the scientific knowledge that has evolved since the Renaissance with its well specified reliance on human reason and an empirical method of investigation based on reasoning and the pinpoint observation of facts and data. We have raised the question that is on everyone's mind concerning the concept of origins of the universe, of life, and of mankind in an effort to identify the grand "first cause" of all that we now believe in. Finally, we have asked and answered the question how do we know what we know, in an attempt to come to terms with the identification of true and irrefutable sources of knowledge that provide the certitude we are seeking as the basis of our lives.

We are not concerned here with either the existence or the definition of traditional knowledge although it forms the texture and framework of which we write; rather we are concerned with clarifying why and how a given body of knowledge–its structure and its ensuing worldview–is traditional. The knowledge itself cannot be everything, or an end in itself. What makes knowledge the basis of a complete world order is the fact that far beyond its actuality lies its divine source that substantiates it and gives it meaning and substance. What makes traditional knowledge unique is the fact that, because of its source within the Divinity, everything within the body of the tradition must already be there from the very beginning in its essence. The latter developments of the tradition and its full articulation, the shades and colors of the traditional knowledge, and the diversity of its scope and application down through the ages only serve to make it more explicit, without adding new elements from another, arbitrary–perhaps we should say human–source. According to Islamic doctrine, there is only one first origin and source, namely the knowledge of Unity (*tawhid*) and the knowledge of the One (*al-Ahad*).

We wish to highlight that traditional knowledge generally is shaped by the nature of its origins and we wish to emphasize the importance of identifying the first principles that form the coloration and ambiance of its enduring truth. The recognition of truth, the pursuit of knowledge, and the wisdom of life find their impetus and source within a realm that transcends the temporal and the earthly. It is the sacred realm of universals, of first principles, of first knowledge and first origins that live now and forever as they exist in the timelessness of eternity. It is a realm, needless to say, that has been identified through the revelation with the names of God representing His qualities and attributes. He is the First (*al-Awwal*) and the Last (*al-Akhir*). All that we know and the entire basis of our lives comes from He who is the Knowing (*al-Alim*), the Living (*al-Hayy*) and the Eternal (*al-Samad*).

The question of the source and authenticity of knowledge that serves as a paradigm of self-knowledge and as a worldview to explain the true nature of the cosmic reality strikes at the heart of modern man's understanding of the word "knowledge" and the modern scientific approach to its acquisition. The question of source is fundamental to the entire endeavor in the search for knowledge and will ultimately define the contours, color and shape of any framework of knowledge that calls itself a worldview, whether it is metaphysical, traditional, rational or scientific knowledge. The question of the truth of a given framework of knowledge highlights, perhaps more than we may care to admit, the modern-day approach to the search for a unified theory of knowledge that serves as the purpose of the scientific enterprise. A comprehensive worldview will project into the consciousness of the world its objectivity, its persuasiveness, and its validity to the extent that it is accessible and believable to mass populations at its source, is convincing at simple levels of expression, and is profound in its truth in the way it shapes our lives for the betterment of ourselves and the society we live in.

While no one would deny that a comprehensive knowledge of the reality is of vital interest and importance to humanity and always has been, during these times the modern-day approach and understanding of existential and ultimate knowledge has been two-edged and the search for a complete knowledge runs forward on dual tracks. On the one hand, we have the traditional knowledge that has come down to us through the millennia and is followed instinctively by billions of people. Down through the ages, the traditional worldview has embodied a higher knowledge, spiritual knowledge, essential knowledge, traditional knowledge and metaphysical knowledge that ultimately reflects the instinctive and universal inclination of people in every time and place to resolve their doubts, have faith and believe in God. On the other hand, the defining worldview of the 20th–now 21st–century is a "scientific knowledge" that marks the parameters of the contemporary worldview. Alternatively, this knowledge has been referred to as speculative knowledge, rational knowledge, secular knowledge, empirical knowledge, and of course scientific knowledge, but it ultimately reflects a self-proclaimed knowledge in the objectivity of physical matter, rational thinking and mathematical formulation that dominates the intellectual horizon of our time.

What people yearn for, however, is definitive knowledge, principial knowledge, and first knowledge that has the power to resolve the perennial mystery that lies at the heart of existence, as well as within the heart of humanity. What we are faced with first and foremost is mystery rather than knowledge, and what we need to resolve before all else is to know the true origin of existence and have available the true sources of knowledge gathered together into the comprehensive form of a worldview that can be drawn from one's pocket at will and relied on to provide the guidance that the demands of life call upon us. At face value, we do not know "on our own" what constitutes the true nature of the human reality in terms of first origin and final end, nor do we know what empowers and governs the reality of phenomenal nature that extends within our depths and into the deep dark depths of the night sky. At the heart of existential knowledge on earth lies a divine mystery that declines to give up its secrets and refuses to resolve the enigmatic challenges of life during this or any other time.

In the Islamic worldview, God is the ultimate source of all existent things in their multi-faceted manifestations and forms. God, as "unseen mystery" (*al-ghaib*) as well as "hidden secret" (*as-sirr*), is the Originator and Source of all that exists.

He is, therefore, the Originator of time in the beginning; He is the Source of all that exists as created and manifested form. Out of the headwaters of the Source flow all primordial forms, all archetypes, all embryos, all seeds, germs, buds, eggs, rootlets, and sprigs. According to Ibn al-'Arabi, buds are possibilities that have not yet "smelled the perfume of existence". In the Source, all things are eternally present, just as in the bud lies the blooming of the flower and in the silence of the bell lies the promise of its ringing. Nothing can appear on the plane of physical manifestation without having its transcendent cause and the primary root of its being well placed in the soil of the Primordial Source. Similarly, all existent things both contain and preserve the integrity of the bud, sprig, embryo, seed and source that begot it.

The notion of origin refers to a Supreme Being that is before us, behind us, below us and above us, both now, in the past and in the future, in short in a time that is summarized by the eternal moment. "It is He who beginneth the process of creation, and He repeateth it." (10: 4) The Name of Allah identifies an eternal Presence and a living Reality that is certainly not subject to the conventional notions of time and space. He does not have a beginning in time; instead, He represents the ever-present Origin, Source, Center and Final End that we find on the spiritual compass. According to a Holy Tradition of the Prophet (*hadith*) in Islam, we learn that "there was a time when God existed, and nothing else existed alongside Him."

Do we know why the Divinity created the universe? As human beings, we might project anthropomorphic feelings of loneliness in the face of an eternal solitude, but God has revealed another reason. We have come to know why God created the universe because a well-known *hadith qudsi*[19] has conveyed this rarefied knowledge to humanity. "David (peace be upon him) said, 'Oh Lord, why did You cause creation to come into being?' God replied, 'I was a hidden treasure and I wanted to be known, therefore I created the universe.'" We have here in the words of God a direct statement of divine motivation and purpose that is conveyed to man as a divine disclosure through the prophets, so that humanity may know once and for all time the reason for our existence and the purpose for which we live, namely to know the Divinity, and through the realization of this knowledge, to worship and praise Him. The miraculous faculty of consciousness implicit in this revealed knowledge is the counterpart and reflection of the magnificent beauty of the creation.

To have faith in a body of traditional knowledge and to live a traditional life of spirituality is to live within sight of the Origin every day of our lives. It is because of the origin of existence and the sources of knowledge that every moment of life can be lived at all, giving life its spiritual and transcendent character, leading every human being toward a living awakening with the power to transform human destiny into a journey beyond the stars. To deny this

---

[19] One of the traditional Holy Sayings of the prophet Muhammad (PBUH) that is said to be the direct speech of Allah.

concept is to deny the living reality that exists within humanity. To live "as if Allah exists" is to live in the fullness of a living reality, for according to a well-know *hadith*, we are encouraged to "worship Allah as if He truly exists, for even if we do not see Him, nevertheless, He sees us."

If the Divinity is the Primal Origin and Original Source of all knowledge as embodied in the revelation, in nature and in man, then the revelation as a transcendent world, cosmic nature as a book of phenomenal existence and man as microcosm and world within a world represent the intermediary sources of knowledge in the form of a written book, as a theatre of nature reflecting through multiple mirrors the Face of the Beloved (*Wherever you turn, there is the Face of God* [2:115]), and as the human revelation in which humanity itself within the species *Homo sapiens* becomes a true mirror reflection of the Reality of the Divine Being. The correspondence between man, nature, and revelation is crucial in the religious understanding of Islam, partly because each element forms a contiguous part as the source material for the religion and partly because the written wisdom, the natural wisdom and the human wisdom contained in the scripture, nature and man all deliver the essential knowledge that bespeaks of the true nature of the one Reality.

As such, revelation, nature and man each exhibit signs that are direct reflections of the Divinity and these "signs" are intended to serve mankind as a means of lifting the veil that separates humanity from direct knowledge of the Divinity. The revealed words of the Qur'an descend from the Mind of Allah, pass through the mind of the Messenger of Islam and ultimately set down as a written book (*al-Qur'an al-tadwīnī*) with verses that in Arabic are called *ayat* which when translated means "signs" or "verses", linking the verses of the Book with the well-known Qur'anic verse "We will show them Our signs on the horizon and within themselves." (41:53) The cosmos itself, referred to in Arabic as the cosmic Qur'an (*al-Qur'an al-Takwīnī*) or the book of existence,[20] represents a vast book in complement to the Islamic book of revelation, and like the revealed scripture, it also contains signs and symbols, verses if you will, that have the power to reveal as much as they conceal and possess levels of meaning that can serve the needs of every mentality and that ultimately lead toward a complete understanding of the true nature of reality. Finally, man himself is a book of self-revelation whose story becomes a conscious human life and whose thoughts and actions become the signs and symbols of a tale well lived.

---

[20] The 8th/14th century Sufi 'Aziz al-Din Nasafi has written the following concerning the book of nature: "Each day destiny and the passage of time set this book before you, *surah* for *surah*, verse for verse, letter for letter, and read it to you ... like one who sets a real book before you and reads it to you line for line, letter for letter, that you may learn the content of these lines and their letters." Quoted in *Islamic Spirituality: Foundations*, Seyyed Hossein Nasr (ed.), New York: Crossroad, 1987, p. 355.

Therefore, the *ayat* manifest themselves within the Holy Book, within the macrocosmic universe, and within the soul of man, in other words *on the distant horizon and within their own selves*. "The Qur'an and the great phenomena of nature are twin manifestations of the divine act of Self-revelation. For Islam, the natural world in its totality is a vast fabric into which the 'signs' of the Creator are woven."[21] The Muslims understand themselves as a sign of God, the cosmos as a grand theophany and mirror of the Divine Qualities and Attributes, and the revealed book that contains all the verses and thus all the knowledge that a human being needs to know in order to come to terms with him/herself and the universe as the *vestigia Dei*, according to Christian terminology. Each element has its own form of metaphysics and its own mode of prayer, man through living the tale, the cosmos through being the sanctuary and theatre wherein the Divinity can become known, and revelation by recreating for humanity knowledge from the mind of God through words.

To understand the vision of the world of man and the world of nature as being closely related to the world of revelation is to live and experience ourselves and the world we live in as the sacred realities that they are. Without a sense of the sacred and without a feeling for the sublime articulation of the Whole—of man and nature and the cosmos that envelopes them both—we would simply remain the three-dimensional figures we now envision ourselves to be, on the road to self-destruction and ultimate oblivion. We need to abandon a paradigm of thought that relies solely on facts and figures to determine our self-image and worldview. We need to see through the one-sided and narrow perspective of modern science whose vision does not extend beyond human perception of self and that uses reason alone to interact with the "stuff" of matter that constitutes the physical world.

When we think of the universe, how do we picture it and therefore what does it mean to us? Do we recreate in our mind's eye, for example, the dark matter and black holes, the red hot suns and white dwarfs, the vast distances that preclude any thought of deep space travel and the tremendous aeons of time required to allow the universe "to happen"? Or do we recreate in our mind's eye the vision of a sublime totality that lives eternally as a Transcendent Center; but that has created the primordial point that expanded into the grand manifestation of a living and organic universe, because this transcendent and eternal Center wanted "to be known" and therefore executed the miracle of cosmic and human consciousness? Do the laws that govern what we witness to be an ordered cosmos exist as the expression of an inevitable reality and a blind expression of random fact, or are they the evidence of a divine self-disclosure and the reflection of intelligence, the Supreme Intelligence if you will, that has created, governs and sustains the universe? When the spiritual traditions say that *Homo sapiens* is the microcosm and the universe is the macrocosm, implying that the universe exists

---

[21] Charles Le Gai Eaton, *Islam and the Destiny of Man*, Albany, NY: SUNY Press, 1985, p. 87.

within human beings just as humans exist within the universe, what does that mean and does anyone really know? Whatever may be the true answer, one thing is clear: In whatever sense or in whatever way the universe can be reflected in what the Muslims call *insan*, can I claim to be that true man? Is order and purpose reflected within nature a motivating force in my awareness and behavior? Is the universe a conscious and living reality, just as I know myself to be?

The modern, scientific scale of the universe is staggering, benumbing the mind with its vast time frames and incredible distances because it is outside of us and we are not a part of it in some qualitative manner. The ancient and traditional scale of the universe is equally awesome, but in an entirely different way. The modern scale of the universe exceeds all of our expectations of quantity by dwarfing us in size in relation to the vast physical perspective, and leaving us bereft of purpose and meaning that can be integrated into the Whole, thereby disassociating people today from the world of nature and the universe in which they must inevitably takes part. In addition, the modern speculative discoveries of such things as dark matter, black holes and parallel universes have no symbolic value. Their theoretical existence may intrigue the mind with technical virtuosity and imaginative flare, but in terms of how they might possibly relate to people in this world here on earth, they mean nothing.

Once upon a time until time is no more, the sources of traditional knowledge will continue to inspire the minds and hearts of humanity. The night sky will always be the "city of God" and the vast cosmic universe will always be a magnificent universal book and a mirror reflection of the Divinity. The traditional scale of the universe fully establishes the value of the qualitative experience behind the cold face of quantity. It weaves an intricate web of purpose and a hierarchy of meaning that permits humanity to find their place in the universe precisely because the essential elements of the universe exist within the human being, namely knowledge, intelligence, existence, life, and consciousness. The mystery of cosmic genesis and the knowledge of a true beginning lie hidden within the mystery of a transcendent consciousness that has proclaimed as an eternal remembrance: "I was a hidden treasure and wanted to be known. Therefore, I created the world."

PART TWO

The World Religions

2.1 Individual Religions in Context

We wrote in the preceding part that every religious form builds its supporting tradition–social, cultural or otherwise–from the bedrock of a direct revelation that lays out in detail the essential knowledge of God and all that relates to the human response to that knowledge. This revelatory knowledge speaks directly to the human faculties and senses that in turn process this knowledge and set the scene within the mind and heart for the development of human excellence (*ihsan*) over the course of life. As knowledge from the Divine Realm, universal revelation substantiates each of the individual religious forms with its knowledge of universal existence and the metaphysical principles that underlie all of existence. As such, the main significance of revelation lies in the fact of its "word of God" quality, partaking as it does in the character of absoluteness, from sacred laws, to rites and rituals, to the importance of sacred symbols and myths and to the efficacy of the spiritual disciplines, all of which contain blessing (*barakah*) for Muslims as well as knowledge that is absolute and beyond the scope of human argument.

    The question is how can these fundamental insights that are self-evident to all be realized, not only in this life, but within the context of a greater, inner journey of the human soul adrift within a vast universe? The great world religions provide a historical context and a foundation of knowledge that places the very meaning of religion into a clear context. It is important for young people of all religions and denominations in today's world to both know and fully understand the birth, development, and evolution of the world's great religions within the concept and context of "religion as such" both in principle and in their manifestation as individual forms. These religions have played a great historical role down through the ages; it is not appropriate to enhance the sentiments about one's own religion at the expense of the religious experience of people from other traditional cultures down through history.

We mentioned earlier that the idea of religion is like a house of many rooms. Perhaps it would have been more appropriate to suggest that the idea of religion is like the idea of home, not a place as such with four walls and a roof, but a place of eternal peace and fulfillment, a base from which to take courage and journey forth into the true meaning of religion that comes from the life experience and the way people meet their own destiny, but that actually lives and takes root within the heart and soul of the individual. The idea of religion as the universal home of humanity serves us also as a promise and a destination as well as an inner base of security and source of contentment. After all, the phenomenon of homesickness is a deep-seated emotion that expresses a desire to return to the hearth of security and love as it is a remembrance of that deep well within us that defines who we are and what the true nature of our vocation and destiny are. In other words, it is possible to be homesick for not only the deepest meaning that lies within ourselves, but also for those revelations that come to us from places we have never been and may never visit in person.

The rest of this chapter endeavors to portray as principles of existence that are both universal in their wisdom and practical in their application. The formal religions came down to humanity at various stages of history that actually represent stages of development of humanity down through the ages. As in some pictogram, you will have fleeting images of the Biblical lands of the prophets, follow in the footsteps of the Christ, a simple carpenter who walked the dusty roads of Nazareth and Jerusalem only to walk into the history of religion as a man who shaped an entire civilization as well as creating a great world religion, and revisit the fundamental principles of Islam as a body of knowledge and a way of life that define the heart of the Islamic experience. The Jews may claim that they are the "chosen people"; the Christians may claim that Christ was the only begotten "son of God"; the Muslims may claim that Muhammad (PBUH), is the "seal of the prophets"; but these designations are but the watermarks of a larger parchment that records the progress of the religions down through the ages in the name of Religion itself as a universal concept of unity that transcends the individual forms.

Religion has taught us that it is important to find similarities that bind the religions together rather than differences that separate them. If nothing else, the modern world has taught us that there is wonder in diversity and small miracles that give life to the many cultures and traditions of the world. The planet grows smaller every day; the challenge of people living in the modern world is to find certitude and peace, not by insisting on their truth as the only truth, but rather that peace among nations will come only from a deeper understanding that the truth finds its strength in unity, a universal principle that Islam has come to proclaim once again and for the last time to the family of humanity.

up of the five books of Moses, including Genesis, Exodus, Leviticus, Numbers, and Deuteronomy. The Jews have revered the *Torah* down through the ages as the very word of God as have the Christians. Christian Bibles incorporate the Hebrew Bible into its Old Testament, while the gospels of the four apostles of Christ make up the bulk of what is called the New Testament. The traditional practice of the religion of Judaism draws its inspiration from the study and observance of the laws and practices taken from the *Torah* and explained in the *Talmud* which is the record of the discussions of the Rabbis regarding Jewish law, customs, ethics and history. There is much speculation when the Torah was actually compiled as a text for posterity. One quickly gleans from reading the Torah and Talmud that the sense of time within sacred history had a different quality than time holds for us today in our fast-moving world. General consensus suggests that the time period between 900 and 500 BC witnessed the compilation of the five books of the Torah, passing through four distinct texts that began during the time of Solomon and reaching its final form around 450 BC. A sixth book, the Book of Joshua, actually completes the story of the conquest of the promise land, Moses having been denied right of entry to this land by God.

A crucial component of the sacred history of the Jews lies in their deliverance from slavery to the Pharaohs of Egypt, as portrayed in the Book of Exodus in the *Torah*. It describes how Moses led the Israelites out of Egypt and through the wilderness to the Mountain of God (Mt. Sinai) where He promised them entry into the land of Canaan, an ancient term for the land of present-day Israel, Palestine, Lebanon and Jordan, in return for their faithfulness. There the God of the Jews, Yahweh, gave Moses and his people their laws and commandments and entered once again into a covenant with them, in remembrance of the sacred trust that Abraham established with God and recalling as well the sacred trust that was offered by God to the human soul in the pre-dawn of creation when the Divinity ask: "Am I not your Lord?" and the human soul responded: "Yes, we witness You" that is referred to in the Qur'an. (2:115) The theme of trust between the Divine and the human runs like a golden thread through the sacred human narrative as a critical key in understanding the intimate relationship that exists through sacred time between God and humanity.

The image of *Homo sapiens* in the Jewish tradition is both realistic and unflattering, an image that is echoed in the Qur'anic depiction of *insan*.[23] Of human limitations, the Jews were very much aware. Compared with the Paradise, he is "as dust" (Ps. 103:14) and compared with the forces of nature that surround him, he is frail when we read in the Book of Job that he is as weak as those "crushed before the moth!" (Job 4:19) His time of earth is quickly spent. In the morning, he grows and at noon he flourishes, but "in the evening he is cut down

---

[23] The Arabic word *insan* is a broad and fully comprehensive Qur'anic term that is roughly translated as humanity and that fortunately does not bring with it the modern-day baggage of politics and gender-referencing that the use of the term "man" stirs up in today's ultra-sensitive world.

and withereth." (Ps. 90:7) To make matters worse, there is much pain and suffering brought on by human limitations that cause humanity to "spend our years as a sigh." (Ps. 90:9) For the Muslims, there is a ring of familiarity about these biblical quotations because they echo amid the verses of the Qur'an with an air of truth when identifying, for example, human nature as a primordial, pure and pristine nature (*fitrah*). But then, upon close scrutiny, we learn the truth about the creation of *insan*, namely that he has been created "weak", that he can be characterized as "in a hurry" and that he "was created in the best of forms, and then cast down to be the lowest of the low." (Qur'an 95:4) The idea that humans take part in the great chain of being, above the animals but below the angels, except insofar as they can transcend the limitations of their human nature, took shape with Judaism and comes to fruition as a clear doctrine with the coming of Islam.

Another component of the Jewish experience lies in their perception of the importance of history as coming from God who was the ruler of the history of humanity and provided the forces of destiny that would shape their early experience and future life. The historical integrity of the nation is emphasized over any official creed or belief system that one must accept when a person claims to be Jewish. The Bible and the Qur'an are full of the tales of sacred history, including the Garden of Eden, Noah's flood, the Tower of Babel, sacred tales that amount to history lessons on the life and pursuits of humanity. Perhaps the most defining moment in Jewish history was their *exodus* from the slavery of Egypt, their wandering for years through the wilderness, and ultimately their entry into the land of milk and honey in the promised land of Canaan. At one point in the narrative, Moses hears the voice of God–but does not see the Face of God as we learn in the Qur'an–and is commanded to lead his people, his nation, out of the bondage of slavery in Egypt. 600,000 men and women, together with their animals, gathered and fled to the Red Sea with the Pharaoh and his armies in hot pursuit. There was a miraculous parting of the waters for the Jews to cross into Sinai; Pharaoh and his armies were drowned in the sea, according to both the Biblical and Qur'anic accounts.

With the arrival of the Ten Commandments and the entry of Moses' followers into the Promise Land, the Jews finally became a nation with a well-defined history and a clear covenant. They had not accidentally stumbled over the Divinity while wandering through the desert. God had disclosed Himself and revealed His true nature to them as a chosen people, directly and inescapably. He was the God of strength and power, capable of overthrowing the mightiest nation on earth and He had chosen the oppressed Jews of Egypt as His beloved nation. It is certainly a notion that has come down through history as distinctive to the nation of the Jews, in which they cast themselves into a mold of special dispensation and divine favor, who have separated themselves on intellectual and psychological levels from the rest of the family of humanity. While it may be an awkward concept in the present era of modern time with its elitist overtones, in the far distant events of these early moments of recorded history, when you consider this concept of a chosen elite within the timeframe of early history, it makes sense that they would feel chosen and would choose to attempt to live up to the special status this doctrine implied. Moses is quoted as having told his nation: "The Lord God has chosen you to be a people for His own possession, but above all the peoples that are on the face of the earth." (Deut. 7:6)

This doctrine of exclusivity is one that many early religions upheld and has continued to be a part of an indrawn perception that, on some psychological level, makes the followers of a given tradition feel as part of a unique community of worshippers within a clear context that has no equals. Interestingly enough, the concept of the "seal of the prophets" that Islam has come to proclaim actually opens the door to understanding and accepting the arrival and presence of earlier religions that have their own validity within their own timely context and preceded Islam within the grand procession of awakening that marks the coming of the various religious forms that uniformly highlight the perennial philosophy that underpins these great traditions. The Prophet Muhammad's (PBUH) seal of hot wax lies across the envelope of religion itself, confirming what has come before its time, and affirming the process of the descent of knowledge through revelation from God that finds its fullest realization and fulfillment in the ascent of human hearts in worship of the Divinity.

2.3 Christianity: The Way of Love

Judaism could be summarized as "the way of the law"; given the fact that the revelation of the Ten Commandments to Moses on Mount Sinai has turned Hebraic morality into a force that has made a tremendous impact on the rest of the world. Taken over by Christianity and having also had an impact on Islam with its singular insistence on the one God,[24] the Ten Commandments virtually form the moral foundation for the majority of people now living on earth. Life is nothing if not dynamic, however, and nothing stays the same for long, rather it continues to undergo a process of evolution and development in the service of humanity. God demands righteousness from the faithful, otherwise there will be consequences to be experienced and suffered. From the 8th to the 6th centuries BC, the Jewish nation was tottering before the aggressive power of Syria, Assyria, Egypt and Babylon. Because the Jews had forsaken righteousness, Jeremiah writes" "Thus saith the Lord: . . . Surely I will make you a desert, an uninhabited city. I will prepare destroyers against you." (Jer. 22:6, 7) Having gained the promise land in an earlier era, they would eventually return to a state of exile down through much of recorded history.

By the time Christ appeared on earth at his birth in Palestine in 4 BC during the reign of Herod, Rome has already conquered much of the known world and had established itself as a force to be reckoned with on the global scale of that time. In religious terms, however, the Romans were awash in polytheism and the

---

[24] "I am the Lord thy God. Thou shalt have no strange gods before Me."

worship of many gods, an inheritance they had taken over from the Greeks who had a pantheon of 13 major gods including the well known Zeus, Apollo, Aphrodite and Dionysius. Based heavily on Greek mythology, the Roman religion at the time of Christ drew influences from many other belief systems and developed a complex mythology that even included an imperial cult in which some of the emperors, such as Julius Caesar, were actually considered gods. It is small wonder, perhaps, that the coming of Christ had such a sweeping effect across the mentality of the time, when people were willing to accept, if not fully believe, that a human being could actually be a god. After the death of Jesus, the early Christians were persecuted and oftentimes put to death for their beliefs. In 313 AD, the Church, which was what the growing establishment of Christianity was called, became legally recognized and enjoyed equal rights with other religions of the Roman Empire. Before the century was finished, in 380 AD, Christianity became the official religion of the Roman Empire.

In the first thousand years of its development, Christianity remained substantially one institution, following the succession of popes that began with Peter when Jesus said to him, according to the gospel account: "I tell you, you are Peter, and on this rock I will build my church. . . . I will give you the keys of the Kingdom of Heaven, and whatever you bind on earth shall be bound in heaven, and whatever you loose on earth shall be loosed in heaven." (Matt. 16:18-19) The first break in the unity of the Church occurred in 1054 when the first great division in Christianity occurred, between what came to be known as the Eastern Orthodox Church in the East and the Roman Catholic Church in the West. There were a number of complex reasons for this separation that would require a special study to more fully explore; it is enough in the context of this summary to suggest that they were geographical, cultural, linguistic and ultimately political. The Eastern Orthodox Church today has roughly 200 million worshippers. When the Orthodox Church broke away from Rome and the Pope in 1054 AD, each blamed the other as the cause of the break. The Orthodox Church can now be found in places such as Albania, Bulgaria, Georgia, Greece, Poland, Rumania, Russia, Serbia, and Sinai. In many ways, these two Churches are still very close in principle and only differ in the formal expression of some of the rites and rituals. They both have the seven sacraments and interpret them in fundamentally the same ways. There are only differences of degree, and interpretation, and not necessarily of substance.

The next great division occurred in the 16th century with the rise of Protestantism within which there developed four main sects, including Baptist, Lutheran, Calvinistic and Anglican. Perhaps the most highly publicized of these sects is the Anglican Church, which arose in England when King Henry VIII broke away from the authority of the pope in Rome, because the pope would not allow him to divorce his first wife and enter into another marriage. Protestantism is quite distinctive when set up against the Catholic Church with its allegiance to the Pope in Rome. In Protestantism, faith takes on a larger role than just belief in a body of doctrine. Faith becomes something much more personal and intense, involving the whole person who must express his/her faith as a unique aspect of the personality and the life. This comes clear in a statement of Luther, the founder of Protestant Lutheranism when he wrote that "Everyone must do his own believing as he will have to do his own dying."[25] Doctrines serve their purpose in Protestantism, but unless they help to transform the believer's heart, they are considered inadequate.

The heart and soul of Christianity unfolds on the global stage as a historical drama following the life and embodied in the person of a unassuming son of the carpenter Joseph, born in a stable where animals slept, who lived an unpretentious life until he was about thirty years old and had an active ministry for only three years before he was put to death according to the traditional chronicles. Nevertheless, his birth continues to be celebrated around the world as the highpoint of the seasonal Western calendar and his death is enshrined as a sacred universal symbol of suffering and redemption for the entire Christian community of worshippers down through history until the present time. His words and actions are reported by the four evangelists in the Gospels of the New Testament and are perhaps the most oft-repeated words in the world. "Love thy neighbor as yourself." "Whatsoever ye would like men do unto you, so also do unto them." "You shall know the truth and the truth shall set you free." Christ was famous for telling stories and parables with a spiritual message embedded within the narrative, and these stories have been repeated down through the ages to inspire men and women of all times to rise above themselves and transcend their limitations within "this world" for the sake of the "next world".

There was an overwhelming theme, however, behind the stories, parables and words of wisdom found in the New Testament, a theme that could only be summarized in one word: Love. It begins with God's overwhelming love for humanity, then highlights the need for people to both recognize this love and express it back out into the world in the form of love of one's neighbor through words and actions. What echoes down through the ages since the coming of Christ is not the fact that Jesus spoke these words, but that he actually lived what he proclaimed to be true. His entire life was one of complete humility; giving of oneself and love within the community extended to all that he came in contact with. He comes across in the Gospels as extremely self-effacing and charming beyond measure. He liked people and they liked him in return. They loved him intensely in fact, and many people were immediately drawn to him, flocked around him, wanted to follow in his footsteps and bask in the good will and peace that he symbolized. He hated injustice; he loved children; nothing stood in his way to communicate his message of love to others, not even Mary Magdalene, a known prostitute of the time whom he forgave and brought into the fold. Here was a man who loved a woman for herself and the potential of her soul and spirit. While he is identified in Christianity as the Son of God, in Islam

---

[25] Huston Smith, *the Religions of Man* (New York: Harper & Row, Publishers, 1958), p. 343.

he is referred to as a prophet: "He said: 'I am indeed a servant of Allah. He hath given me revelation and made me a prophet'" (19:30) and as a sign to future humanity down through the ages: "And We made the son of Mary and his mother as a sign." (23:50)

The three most distinctive beliefs within Christianity are the Incarnation, the Atonement, and the Trinity. The incarnation is the belief that God allowed part of His essence to assume the form of a man as a kind of God-man or incarnation on earth of the Divine Being. It is of course paradoxical even to most Christians, but in loving Jesus Christ the believer also loves God. It is within this context that Jesus is often referred to as the "Son of God", a paradox that finds its resolution as a symbol in which the divine qualities are reflected in the image of a man. The doctrine of atonement refers to the coming of Jesus in order to symbolically atone for the sins of Adam and his offspring. The fall of humanity through the image of Adam could only be reconciled by Christ taking upon himself the guilt of humanity and dying for their sake. Finally, the third most distinctive belief of the Christians is in the concept of the Trinity. This is, of course, a complicated concept that cannot be reduced to a few explanatory words. Basically, the idea of the Trinity is a fundamental mystery that most Christians accept as a matter of doctrine without fully understanding the complicated implications of the concept. Whether the idea of the Trinity means the idea of a Godhead that has three aspects, or that the starting point is the concept of a Trinity that finds its unity in the One God, the doctrine of the Trinity has been an important aspect of the Christian mystique, invoking the image of God the Father, the Son and the Holy Spirit that represent different aspects of the one Supreme Being. The oneness of God may come to and appear to mankind through different aspects, but the unity of the Supreme Principle cannot be compromised.

Regarding the practices of the Christians, since the 12th century, there are a number of formal sacraments–spiritual rituals or disciplines–that shape the Christian experience. At birth, when the child enters the natural world on earth, the infant undergoes *baptism*, a ritual of purification in which God places His special grace within the soul and raises the infant being onto the supernatural plane of existence by virtue of its participation in the sacred ritual. When the child reaches the age of reason, he/she undergoes a ritual of *confirmation*. This marks the stage of development when in body, mind, and heart; the young person is strengthened for the life challenges that lie ahead. The solemn moment of holy *matrimony* marks the next stage when a person links together in respect and love with a life partner "until death do us part." Also, a person may dedicate his or her entire life to God through priesthood or sisterhood within the Christian tradition. At the end of a Christian life, the sacrament of *extreme unction* takes place, a ritual offer of prayer for the dying to ensure a smooth passage to the "other side" of reality.

Two other sacraments are repeated more often throughout the course of life. One ritual is called confession or absolution and the other is the celebration of the Mass. Confession is a practice that Christians undergo on a regular basis in which they confess their sins and weakness to the priest in the solitude of the confessional box. Through the verbalization of one's sins in this active, participatory manner, a form of purification takes place that is complemented by the ritual prayers and absolution of the priest who is acting in the name of Jesus in absolving the penitent of his or her sins. Repentance forms the foundation of the confessional experience and fuels the overwhelming sense of purification for the mind and heart that the ritual produces.

The celebration of the Mass is the central participatory sacrament of the Christian tradition. Also known as the Holy Eucharist, Holy Communion, or the Lord's Supper, the Mass is the re-enactment of the Last Supper of Christ when Jesus gathered together with his disciples, broke bread and wine with them, and said: "This is my body that was broken for you. . . . This is my blood that was shed for you." (Mark 14:22 ff) The Mass is a celebrated ritual between the priest and the faithful congregation that is fused with spiritual energy and has deep symbolic meaning for the congregation. According to the Christian belief, the spiritual presence of God comes down into the ceremony as a vital spiritualizing force. In partaking of the bread and wine, the celebrant is actually united on symbolic and experiential levels with the very presence of God. It is a mystery that comes alive through ritual practice and has sustained the devotion and spiritual energy of Christians down through the ages.

2.4 Islam: The Way of Return

In our survey of the monotheistic religions, we have suggested that Judaism came within an era that represented the young soul of humanity, a collective soul that needed to be reminded of the universal principle of the one God and the unity that lies at the heart of the cosmic reality. It was a religion of strict laws and professed obedience to the Grand Patriarch of the Lord God, a religion that created the Jewish nation within the framework of a sacred history that saw these people led out of the bondage they experienced in Egypt, a way of exile that eventually brought them to the Promise Land. Christianity, on the other hand, was born out of the historical life of Jesus of Nazareth who became the living revelation that embodied within the incarnation of a man the knowledge and spirit of the Divinity. Christianity came to be known as the religion of love precisely because it was the love that Jesus expressed to others that formed the ground and overarching spirit of the religion. We come now to Islam, the most recent revelation bestowed upon humanity as a living document of the Word of God. Islam distinguishes itself as a way of life that remembers the primordial religion of the Golden Era of Eden, the *din al-hanif* in Arabic terminology, when the Adam and Eve walked and talked with God, a religion that also puts the "seal of the prophets" upon the entire process of revelation, and brings the concept of religion to completion and perfection as the last of the revelations from the Divine to the human.

The term Arab rose to greatness with the coming of Islam. Within a century after the coming of Islam through the Prophet (PBUH), the Islamic nation became the masters of an empire extending from the shores of the Atlantic in the so-called Maghreb (the land of the setting sun) to the Great Wall of China, surpassing Rome even in its extent at the height of its conquests. The world into which the Prophet Muhammad (PBUH) was born has been described quite simply as "barbaric" during the pre-Islamic era. The people then seemed to be inspired with a form of animistic polytheism, a far cry from the strict monotheism of either Judaism or Christianity that were religions firmly established before the coming of the Religion of Islam. Muhammad (PBUH), whose name means "the one praised", grew up with his uncle as a gentle soul, sensitive to human suffering in every form. He came to be known by other names among his community, such as "the True", "the Upright", and "the Trustworthy One".

During the last days of the holy month of Ramadhān[26], which was the traditional month of retreat even in pre-Islamic times, the Prophet saw something strange and unexpected in a seemingly miraculous vision during his meditations. At first, he did not know what was happening, the shock of the experience was so raw and powerful. A Qur'anic verse has later documented and fully confirmed what occurred to the messenger at that time: "He was taught by one mighty in power, endued with wisdom, for he appeared (in stately form) while he was in the highest part of the horizon, then he approached and came closer and was at a distance of but two bow-lengths or (even) nearer. So did (Allah) convey the inspiration to His Servant what He (meant) to convey." (53: 5-10)

The abrupt and unexpected visitant that he beheld was none other than an archangel in the form of a man. He was carrying what appeared to be a written document, enfolded upon a "magical brocade". The archangel said: "I am Gabriel. God has sent me to communicate to you His message." He then intoned with sonorous majesty: "Recite (or read) this", and the Prophet immediately replied: "I am not a reciter (I do not know how to read)."[27] In fact, the Prophet was *ummī*, meaning unlettered and unable to read; he was the pure, uncorrupted vessel called upon to receive the sacred words and thus the perfect receptacle to receive the divine revelation. Three times the archangel exhorted him to "Recite", and three times the Prophet replied that he was not able to recite. Finally, the first revelation passed through his heart and soul and out into the world: "Recite (*iqra*) in the name of thy Lord who created, created man out of a blood clot. Read and thy Lord is most bountiful." (96:1-3)

---

[26] According to the traditions, the Qur'an began to descend during the holy month of Ramadhān on a night identified as the *Laylat al-qadr*, the Night of Power, a night that is "better than a thousand months." (97:3)

[27] Perhaps there lies providential ambiguity in the fact that the first word of revelation was alternatively understood as both "recite!" and "read!" – recalling the cry of the Prophet Isaiah (xl:6) when he heard a being say: "Recite!" and he said the very words: "What shall I recite?"

It was a brief and stunning moment for the unsuspecting merchant from Makkah when the invisible had suddenly become visible and the inaudible Word of God had momentarily become audible to receptive human ears. The Prophet had experienced a moment in which he was able to witness the monumental unveiling of one of the unseen mysteries (*al-ghaib*) that perennially protects, as from behind a veil, all direct knowledge of the Divinity. However, this was no ordinary human being; he was the Prophet (*nabi*) of God and Messenger (*rasul*) to the world. Indeed, at that moment, in the deserts of western Arabia, the unseen mystery had commenced to become a living knowledge for all of humanity, both at that time and for future generations around the world until the end of time as we know it.

The descent of the first verses of the Qur'anic revelation through an archangelic messenger marked the formal descent of a divine knowledge to be preserved and acted upon by people within the earthly environment. As Divine Speech, it was an absolute and final[28] communication of the Divine Being to present humanity. After an initial interlude of silence that lasted for three years, the descent of the verses of the revelation continued to pass through the heart, soul, and mind of the messenger for twenty-three years until just before the end of his life. During the moments of revelation, the Prophet had become a kind of human horizon over which the miraculous and blessed communication from the Divinity continued to emerge until all 6346 verses of the Qur'an had fully arrived within the human frame of reference and the revelation was complete.

The messenger witnessed the initial descent of the Qur'anic revelation through the archangel Gabriel, a luminous and virtually invisible 'being' made momentarily visible to the human eye. He heard the first sacred sound, the first word and the first verse that would come to be known the world over as the sacred Speech of Allah. Throughout the course of the Prophet's ministry, the verses of the Qur'an entered upon his mind, his heart, his consciousness and in fact the whole of his being, and then passed through his heart and out into the collective consciousness of humanity both then and for all future generations. The love of the Prophet Muhammad (PBUH) continues to be a strong spiritual emotion among Muslims, and one of the main reasons is the fact that through him the descent of the luminous in the form of the Noble Qur'an was made possible.

The meaning of religion in the Islamic context goes beyond the concept of revelation as the descent of knowledge from the Divine to the human as point of departure and source of the religion. The Arabic word *din*, usually translated into English as "religion", does little justice to the full significance of the word's meaning in Arabic, because the concept of *din* in Islam is less formal and more practical than one can find within the context of English. It consists in being a

---

[28] Muhammad (PBUH) is identified in the Qur'an as "the seal of the prophets," which effectively closes the book on the plenary descent of knowledge in revelatory form.

way of life that adheres to a sacred norm in which the entire life is molded to become a way of being, in addition to being a way of knowledge that commences with the descent of the Book and the inscription of the pen on the heart of the Muslims, echoing the very first verse, in the form of a direct command, to descend into the mind and heart of the Prophet in the cave of Mt. Hira: "Read (recite) in the name of thy Lord Who created." (96:1) To that end, what the Muslims call the Sunnah comprises not only the verses, laws, and entreaties of the Holy Qur'an; but also the sayings of the Prophet, compiled by scholars a century or more after his death, that perpetuate his attitudes, his behavior and virtually his way of life for future generations. The Prophet himself represents the supreme example of a human being who was the receptacle and instrument of the sacred verses, the very words and vibration of the Holy Spirit.

The question is how can these fundamental insights that are self-evident to all be accomplished not only in this life but within the context of a greater, inner journey into the soul and spirit of humanity? We cannot just run through fields with our shoes off or desire to float upon clouds and expect to arrive at the true destination that is built into the human condition. The great gift of Islam is that it provides the Muslims with the means to achieve transcendence within the human condition. This transcendence means an escape from their own weaknesses and limitations through the inner *jihad al-nafs*, or battle of the mind, heart, and soul, and the ability to rise above themselves to higher level of consciousness through the remembrance of God every moment of their lives and to achieve a high level of virtue through application of the principles of the religion in their actions and in their lives. The *shahadah*, or testament of faith in Islam, is not just a one-time recitation, but an inner truth that shapes and colors every moment of a Muslim life.

It is not so much what we believe as Muslims, but rather how we can give meaning to the form of the religion through our actions and lives. It is not the ritual acts of prayer and fasting and the other duties that make Muslims what they are. These are just the artifacts of a ritual foundation to the religion that attempts to remember and uphold the truths of the religion through a scaffolding of rites and rituals. We should not say that I am Muslim because I pray and fast and have made the *hajj*. These things are between you and God whose effectiveness depends on their level of sincerity and commitment, especially the fast, for who knows but God whether a person has truly abstained from food and drink during the daylight hours. If being a Muslim means being a member of a club whose clubhouse contains all the tomes of literature that describe the knowledge of God, then we can close the door of this house and confine ourselves within some small box and remain content with what we have. But that is not what the great sheikhs and walis and spiritual poets of the past have left behind as a legacy of the spiritual life. What they have left behind to emulate is the manner of being Muslim, the "how" and not the "what" of a Muslim life, through actions that contain their own truth, through intentions that have the backing of the divine will, through surrender that meets the moment of the divine command and through virtue that contains its own light and that shines from the human face to light the way.

This is the true meaning of the Islamic *din*. As one of the family of the great and revealed world religious, Islam adds its own particular perspective to the history of formal religious unfolding by highlighting once again the supreme principle of unity (*tawhid*) expressed in the first of the two statements of the *shahadah* that there is "no god but God". Secondly, Islam emphasizes the importance of commitment to the singular Islamic path in the second of the two statement of the *shahadah*, namely that "Muhammad (PBUH), is His Messenger". As such, Islam's unique angle of vision rests with the polarity "knowledge and action", or alternatively "faith and surrender", or yet again "law and path".

As Muslims, young people need to understand the unique position that Islam now plays as a religion both worthy of the world's attention and capable of leading people into the future of themselves and the world. It identifies itself with the primordial religion that always was since the symbolic time of Adam and the Golden Era, and as the final religion and "seal" of all religion-hood, it recognizes and accepts the chain of prophets and religions that have preceded it. It could be called the "natural religion" insofar as it is the religion of proto-nature (*al-din al-fitrah*), that is to say that this religion is in the nature of things and identifies the true nature of both man and the natural order. The Oneness of the Absolute is revealed in the natural order and in the heart of humanity as the "primordial message" that lies within the very heart of the universe. This is the true meaning and significance of Islam as a religion within the broader concept of religion "as such", as a principle of unfolding spiritual life in the knowledge of God that is expressed and realized within the *Ummah* (community) of Islam as a living tradition.

Any betrayal in preserving a way of life that reflects the very spirit of *din* as understood in the Islamic worldview as an elaborate and well specified way of life of precepts, dogmas, and modes of action runs the risk of a self-betrayal in the way Muslims understand themselves and their place in the world. As bearers of the banner of Islam, they set the example that needs to be upheld like a flag in the wind of a way of living and of being that reflects the traditional knowledge and the universal truth, the individual religion and the universal prototype of religion coming together in the silhouette of man against the distant horizon. Islam has bestowed a powerful gift upon the Muslims; a gift that they themselves can become in their encounter with the Spirit of God within this world.

2.5 The Eastern Religions

No survey of the concept of religion as such, and examples of the religious forms that have come to humanity throughout historical time, would be complete without mentioning the great Eastern religions that have had a profound effect on a broad range of humanity, both in the early stages of recorded history and even now down into the present era. When we evoke the names of Hinduism,

Buddhism and Taoism, we are calling to mind majestic spiritual traditions of the highest order that have sprung from the source of the Ganges, from the shadow of the Bo Tree in India, and from the snow-capped mountain peaks of ancient China. The spirit of Hinduism lingers within the modern world as a source of universal knowledge of metaphysical principles; the serene image of the Buddha leaves the faint smile of ultimate enlightenment among faithful Buddhists of the modern era with its suggestion of inner peace and fulfillment; the way of the Tao leads us into the future of ourselves by taking its practitioners by the hand and leading them down a pathway that disappears into the mists of an ancient mystery that will live forever in the heart of humanity as the question answered and the secret revealed.

Hinduism

Hinduism is the world's oldest religion that is still practiced today in the sub-continent of India. Referred to as *Sanatana Dharma*, a Sanskrit word meaning "eternal path", the religion emerges from the mist of time during the ancient Vedic civilization that existed in the northern part of the Indian subcontinent from the second millennium BC and flourished in the first millennium BC during the golden era of classical Sanskrit literature. No one single person emerges as the founder of the religion, but it was during this time frame that the ancient Vedic texts were being composed that make up the source material for the basic Hindu scriptures. The most famous of these inspired documents is no doubt the Bhavagad Gita or Song of God, a Sanskrit text from the Mahabharata epic that has the status of a revealed text. It is often referred to as a concise guide to Hindu philosophy as well as a practical, self-contained guide to spiritual life.

Hinduism contains an elaborate system setting forth a philosophy of life that can be summarized in three simple words: Being // knowledge // joy. Firstly, human life is centered within the concept of the self or *atman* and this is none other than the reflection of Brahman, the Godhead or Supreme Principle of Being. Secondly, knowledge is important because we need to know the essential knowledge of truth and reality and this is contained traditionally within revelation. There is a consciousness within the human being that is not only self-reflective, but also needs answers to the mysterious questions that arise within a life that does not fully explain itself. Thirdly, joy is crucial because it is the direct result of the knowledge that we have come to know as an essential part of our being. The three components of "being", "knowledge", and "joy" interact with each other in a harmonious interplay of forces that make up the totality of the life experience that can be summarized in these three simple words.

Every religion has its concept of God and a corresponding name. In Hinduism, the name the Hindus give to the Supreme Reality is *Brahman*, from the root *brih* meaning "to be great". The chief attributes associated with this name are *sat, chit* and *amanda*; God is none other than Being, Awareness (knowledge) and Bliss (joy). Unlike the Jewish and Islamic perception of the Supreme Being, with their well defined divine qualities and attributes that are reflected within the human soul, the Hindu *Brahman* God cannot be described with words, except in the most universal terms, imagining for example what "pure being" would be like. His knowledge lies far beyond anything our imagination can come up with on its own. As for pure bliss, only our wildest dreams might approximate the remotest fantasy that could even begin to walk down the road of bliss. It is making one's way through the world that the Hindu believer has to be concerned with, meeting destiny with fortitude and dignity according to his or her station in life.

Hindus believe in a number of fundamental laws that pertain to the evolution and progression of the soul from one state to another. Firstly, they believe that the individual soul passes through a number of bodies in a process known as reincarnation or transmigration of the soul, in Sanskrit called *samsara*, a word which literally means "passing through intensely". Secondly, the mechanism that binds these experiences together is the *law of karma*. As a doctrine, the meaning of *karma* is the psychological and spiritual equivalent of the law of cause and effect on the physical plane of existence, similar to the Christian saying of Christ: "What you sow, so also shall you reap." In other words, actions have consequences and everything that we say and do goes out into the world and has a subsequent effect. It is a law that actually transcends visible and invisible worlds, but that also moves across all the religions as a recurring and perennial theme. The law of *karma* forces people to take upon themselves personal responsibility, not only for what happens in their lives, but also for their own present life condition. Hinduism emphasizes the karmic law of responsibility, just as Islam emphasizes the accounting of one's thoughts and actions on the Day of Judgment, alternatively called the Day of Accounting (*yawm al-hisab*).

Finally, Hinduism reminds humanity that they are never alone on their pilgrimage back to Brahman or God. The soul or *atman*, with all of its conflicting thoughts and illusions and emotions, is never fully alone, but rather is uplifted and supported, like birds in flight or clouds in the heavens, by the self-luminous and forever eternal Spirit of God. Although *Brahman* lies buried deep and invisible within the human being, He is the sole ground of humanity's Being, Awareness and Bliss. "The immutable . . . is never seen but is the Witness; It is never heard but is the Hearer: It is never thought, but is the Thinker, is never known, but is the Knower. There is no other witness but This, no other hearer but This, no other thinking but This, no other knower but This."[29]

Buddhism

Like Christianity with its focus on the person of Jesus Christ as a kind of human revelation, Buddhism also begins as a religious form and takes its inspiration from the image and living persona of a man. This image is none other than the serene symbol of the Buddha, immortalized down through the ages as

---

[29] *Brihadaranyaka Upanishad.*

the image of serenity, contemplation and contentment of the highest order. The very sight of the image of the Buddha inspires higher feelings of righteousness and reflective living in the Buddhist soul both in history and down through the modern era. Buddhism is still a living force in the Far East where people take very seriously the message that the Buddha conveyed several millennia ago.

Who precisely is the Buddha? Is he a God, an angel, an incarnation as a being come down from heaven? We are told through Buddhist traditions that the people asked him "Are you a god?"

"No," he replied.

"An angel?"

"No," he again replied.

"A saint?"

"No," came the answer once again.

"Then what are you?" the people asked finally in frustration.

The Buddha answered simply: "I am awake."

This answer actually became his signature title, for this is what the word "Buddha" means. The Sanskrit word *budh* means to wake up and to know. Buddha, then, means the "Enlightened One" or the "Awakened One."

The story of his enlightenment is legendary and can be read in any number of books on the subject. Briefly, he was born into the privileged class and lived a life of luxury as a young prince coming of age. He is quoted as saying: "I wore garments of silk and my attendants held a white umbrella over me." Despite having in reality what most people only dream about, he became disillusioned with life as he experienced it in his twenties and that lead to a complete break with the worldly life he was born into. He changed out of the clothes he was wearing and went into the forest in search of enlightenment. After a number of years of poverty and asceticism, he sat beneath a fig tree which has since come to be known popularly as the Bo tree, short for *bodhi* or enlightenment. The great awakening had finally taken place, the man known as the Buddha had become transformed and he emerged into history as the Buddha.

In his very first sermon, which the Buddha preached when he returned to Benares after becoming enlightened, he took up his theme and identified the Four Noble Truths, a declaration of his discovery after six years of seclusion and meditation. The first noble truth is that life is *dukkha*, or suffering. It was the belief of the Buddha that existence meant suffering and that it was the duty of humanity to try to escape the round of suffering that the earthly life offered humanity, including pain, sickness, old age and ultimately death. The second noble truth is *tanha*, meaning desire. In this sense, human desire is actually the cause of life's problems, especially when human beings want the wrong thing and seek that which will lead them away from their true vocation in this world. This is the desire that is routed, not in the soul, but rather in the ego as we understand the word in modern times, a desire that has no universal application and can only lead away from humanity's true universal desires for peace and fulfilment. The third noble truth is that there is a cure from life selfish desires so that humanity can escape from the narrow limits of self-interest and find the way into a more universal experience of truth. The fourth noble truth seeks to give advice concerning how this cure from the ills of the world can be accomplished.

The question the Buddha had to answer for his faithful followers was how this cure could be brought about as a reality. What was the path to awareness, and then enlightenment? To that end, he spoke about the Eightfold Path as the course of treatment. Briefly, this path consisted of the following points:

1. Right knowledge: a person must believe in something and have access to the essential knowledge that will lead in the right direction.
2. Right aspiration: right knowledge tells the mind what it should believe in, whereas right aspiration makes that knowledge into heart knowledge that knows what it should want.
3. Right speech: What we say must speak the truth; forms of communication must express a charity in what we say; we must speak about others as we would have others speak about ourselves.
4. Right behavior: How we behave recalls the Ten Commandments of Judaism and the importance of good works in Islam. It is our behavior that can shine forth like a torch light or cast shadows wherever we walk. The Buddha stressed the importance of good behavior in everything we do.
5. Right livelihood: the Buddha laid great importance of the benefit of work and the fulfillment of one's vocation in life. "The hand of the dyer is subdued by the dye in which it works." It is interesting that an injunction such as this was of primary importance in Christianity and also Islam, which places special emphasis on good works, in addition to the work that the hand has wrought.
6. Right effort: Effort, of course, means the exercise of the human will to accomplish a whole host of things, and the Buddha laid great emphasis on the exercise of the will. "Those that follow the way," said Buddha, "might well follow the example of an ox that marches through the deep mire carrying a heavy load. He is tired, but his steady gaze, looking forward, will never relax until he comes out of the mire, and it is only then that he takes a respite. Oh monks, remember that passion and sin are filthier than the mire, and that you can escape misery only by earnestly and steadily thinking of the Way."[30]
7. Right mindfulness: The Buddha laid great emphasis on the mind and human consciousness as instruments of higher perception in coming to terms with our self-identity. The great Buddhist text, the *Dhammapada*, opens with the following comment: "All that we are is the result of what we have thought in the mind." He laid great emphasis on seeing things

---

[30] J. B. Pratt, *The Pilgrimage of Buddhism and a Buddhist Pilgrimage* (New York: The Macmillan Co., 1928), p. 40.

"as they really are", recalling the saying of the Prophet Muhammad (PBUH), "Oh Lord, show me things are they really are."
8. Right absorption: As final step on the eightfold path, absorption represents the taking in and full realization of all the benefits of the preceding seven rules. All human effort would be useless without the internalization and full absorption of the benefits that lie in wait behind the other seven rules of conduct leading to enlightenment.

A final word should be said about the Buddhist concept of *nirvana*. The word literally means "to bow out" or "to extinguish" as in a fire. Some people believe that *nirvana* means absolute nothingness or non-existence. On the contrary, Buddhist scholarship clearly suggests that *nirvana* is, on the contrary, the highest destiny of the human spirit. There is the sense of extinction, not of existence itself, but rather extinction of the boundaries of the human ego and the fragments of personal desire are extinguished for the consciousness of a higher reality, leading to the perception that life itself is transitory and will lead to extinction, "a phantom, dew, a bubble, a dream, a flash of lightning, and a cloud: Thus we should look upon all that was made."[31] According to the Buddhist concept, the ultimate destiny of the human soul is an awakening to an enlightenment of a higher order of experience far beyond the finite self. As the dream vanishes upon awakening, as the sun eclipses the moon and stars, so also the dew drop slips quietly into the shining sea and in loosing itself there finds itself in the oneness of the natural, universe order. Some say that the dewdrop slips into the shining sea; others suggest the other way around, that the shining sea disappears into the primordial dew drop in the oneness of God.

Taoism

According to the ancient traditions, Taoism originated with a man named Lao Tzu, said to have been born about 604 BC. In truth, we know next to nothing about him with any certainty. Even his name, when translated into English, actually means "Old Boy" or "Old Fellow" or perhaps more appropriately "Old Master", none of which suggests the founder of a great world religion. Yet, there is a mosaic of legends that have survived down through the ages about this mysterious man who literally walked off into the sunset and was never heard from again as a living person. He left behind, however, a powerful legacy that continues to poke holes in the sophisticated self-assurance of the modern scientific worldview that the vast majority of the global population have now willingly embraced.

Lao Tzu is said to have climbed upon a water buffalo and began a journey toward the mountains of Tibet. At the Hankao Pass, the gatekeeper asked the "Old Boy" to turn back and not venture forth into the dangerous conditions of

---

[31] Quoted in Huston Smith, *The Religions of Man* (New York: Harper & Row, Publishers, 1958), p. 129.

the rugged mountains. When it appeared that he wasn't going to stop, he was asked to write down a record of his beliefs for future generations and as a guide for the civilization he was leaving behind. He retired for three days and returned with a small volume of sayings entitled *Tao Te Ching*, or "the Way and its Power". To this day, it remains the basic text of all Taoist thought.[32]

The entire religion revolves around the pivotal concept of the *Tao* itself. To that end, there are three meanings generally understood for this conceptual word that is not easy to translate. The first meaning of Tao is "the way of ultimate reality". Perhaps this is not surprising because it is a perennial theme that all the religions have taken up as fundamental to their philosophy of beliefs. Everyone wants to know what the "ultimate reality" is in order to know how to behave and to how to achieve that reality. Words cannot define what the Tao actually means according to the text. "The Tao which can be conceived is not the real Tao." Although this ultimate reality is a fundamental mystery, the texts exclaims: "How clear and quiet it is! It must be something eternally existing."

Although the Tao is something far from our immediate experience by virtue of its "ultimate reality", it is also something near and comprehensible to us. It is "the way of the universe". This means that the Tao is reflected in all of nature, through its beauty, its harmony, its incomparable quality, the driving principle of all existence. It may be called "the Mother of the World" because of its generosity of spirit. When autumn comes "no leaf is spared because of its beauty, no flower because of its fragrance." The third meaning of the Tao is the manner in which a person "should order his life". As in the grand universe, so also is the Tao evident within man as a miniature universe. The harmony that prevails is always a reflection of the Tao.

One of the basic concepts that the Tao stresses as a fundamental doctrine is the concept of *wu wei*. This concept suffers a similar fate to the concept of *nirvana* in Buddhism. The word itself is often translated as "doing nothing" or a kind of "non-action", suggesting a passive attitude of non-attention. A better explanation would be that *wu wei* suggests an "active quietude". Wouldn't it be ideal if we could perform at a consciously active pace, while at the same time remaining innerly calm and relaxed, without worry or concern about present or future outcomes? In the Tao, *wu wei* represents supreme action, while at the same time maintaining an attitude of simplicity and freedom that flows naturally from the harmonious soul. In this way, a person's behavior is the natural result of who they are inside themselves. "The way to do is to be," According to the Tao. And again: "One may move so well that a foot-print never shows, speak so well that the tongue never slips, reckon so well that no counter is needed." (ch. 27)

The Tao always refers to the symbolism of nature in coming to an understanding of the meaning of the Tao in real life. The natural phenomenon

---

[32] There is no true consensus about the truth of this legend and/or the beginning of the Tao religion; what remains is the reality of its legacy as a philosophical guide of great stature for subsequent generations.

which has the closest resemblance to *Tao* itself is water. Water supports objects and carries them effortlessly on its current, bringing them to their true destination by making its way in, around and through every obstacle.

> Those who flow as life flows know
> They need no other force:
> They feel no wear, they feel no tear,
> They need no mending, no repair. (Ch. 15)

Even the human being can be compared to the actions of water, in the way it adapts itself to its surroundings and seeks out the lowest places.

> Man at his best, like water,
> Serves as he goes along:
> Like water he seeks his own level,
> The common level of life. (Ch. 8)

Infinitely flexible while at the same time incomparably strong, the virtues of water are virtually the same as the wisdom of *wu wei*. It is a condition or doing work "without working" or singing a song "without singing." Actions are performed without effort or strain, but rather flow from the person as a natural grace, the inner soul in complete harmony with the outward soul of nature.

One final concept bears mentioning in this context and that is the well known Chinese symbol of *yin* and *yang* which is considered a principle of relativity and a principle of complementary opposites. Life is full of basic oppositions or relativities that we all know and experience, including active-passive, male-female, light-dark, summer-winter. In the end, all opposites are resolved in the unity of the *Tao*. What is referred to in one tradition as Brahman is referred to in another tradition as the *Tao*. As Lao Tzu wrote: "I do not know its name, and so I call it Tao, the Way, and I rejoice in its power." (Ch. 25) No doubt, the Tao took him to his rightful destination, even if we will never know what that destination was and never heard from him again to further enlighten future generations.

PART THREE

Historical Context

3.1 Pre-Islamic Arabic

A glimpse of pre-Islamic history, and the Arabs who lived at that time in Central Arabia, is more than a snapshot of what went on before the time of the Prophet, and more than just a brief footnote to the rise of a new religion that would not only sweep across Arabia, but across the broad expanse of the earth, as though the Hand of God had cast the brush stroke of a lunar crescent across the equator of the earth from North Africa to the Far East, creating a handprint of the Divinity on the earth that is reflected in the heavens.

The facts of linear history are interesting to know about, like a photo that gives insights into the customs and fashions of another era. They sit on the pages of history books like gazelles grazing on the African savannah that with close scrutiny become subject to flight. The facts may enter the mind and roam around the various faculties such as reason and imagination like animals in search of water; but they end up leaving behind their bleached bones, giving rise to an appreciation that comes from an understanding of the tendencies, moods and colorations of a civilization on the brink of an impending disaster, a civilization whose value and belief system no longer represented their own self interest much less the truth that should be its foundation, a civilization ripe for overturning and rejuvenation, like tired soil in need of sun and water after the relentless sun and the upheaval of the plow.

It is not surprising, when we scrutinize the cultural life in pre-Islamic Arabia, that the worldview serving the people of that time was quickly abandoned by those who instinctively responded to the new wave of knowledge that was descending upon them in the form of an alien, yet strangely attractive and compelling wisdom. The new Muslim converts responded with such an inner burning of the mind and heart that nothing and no one could turn them away from their new-found beliefs. They were quite simply on fire with the revelation of the one God and the principle of unity that tied their universe up into a unified whole and made perfect sense in an otherwise mysterious world full of questions and contradictions. A secret had come down "from the heavens above", a wonderful secret, revealed to their townsman and companion Muhammad (PBUH), known as the Trustworthy (*al-amīn*), truths that all the wise men of the world were not able to discover. The newly converted companions of the Prophet could see with the vision of a clear day that the ancient beliefs were as worthless as the rolling sagebrush of the desert they inhabited. It was not just the tired old pagan rituals and useless clay idols that suddenly seemed shameful, if not downright silly, a kind of insult to a person's native intelligence; but paying tribute to these vestiges of a pagan mentality represented a way of life and a state of being that was in stark contrast to the new wave of the religion of surrender and return that was about to overturn and wash away the residue of an old and tired way of thinking that no longer served the needs of the people.

In pre-Islamic Arabia, the nomadic and marauding desert Bedouin worshipped things and images with shameless abandon; but in truth they believed in nothing but their own desires and needs; they lived for the moment in this world. Nothing existed beyond the horizon of their minds but their immediate satisfactions and their fleeting whims. With no grounding in the bedrock of a higher vision, they ended up living for the moment, for this world, for their own desires and whims. They lived for the life of this world and brought the life of pre-Islamic Arabia into being with its characteristic profanities, ignorance and vulgarity, destined to lie stagnant on the pages of history as the footnote they deserve to be. This was an era of stagnant and lifeless history that provided the stuff out of which visions and enlightenment would be born. The era of pre-Islamic history lies in shame before the great portal of the Islamic awakening in the dim corridors of time, with no future and no past, only a signpost of destiny and as a remembrance of what needed to be overturned within the world at that time and with the people who lived in the shimmering shadow of their personal desires.

It's worth reviewing once again the true nature of the pre-Islamic times because the pitfalls that people fell victim to during that era are not that far removed from our own weaknesses and inclinations during our own modern era and its idol-worship of money, success, fame, not to mention the love of materialism that drives the world economy. We blame them for worshipping little idols and we laugh at the silliness of their mentalities that they could invest meaning into something as ridiculous as clay images with crude faces. These images and idols were not just play things to soothe weary minds or a psychological crutch to soothe weary souls. They took up residence in the very Ka'aba in Makkah, a traditional pilgrimage point down through the ages from the time of Abraham, who according to the traditions and the Qur'an, built this house of God on earth.

The themes of ignorance and false idols are shockingly familiar. In fact, we are not that far removed from such attitudes, primitive though they may seem to our supposedly sophisticated and enlightened 21st century minds. What about our own idols during this era? Admittedly, they aren't clay dolls stacked in rows on a shelf with enlarged eyes and bushy eyebrows, but they seize our minds and worse our imagination with the same pagan vengeance that they seized these more primitive peoples of the desert. Why aren't we laughing at ourselves; perhaps if we did we would realize how ridiculous we can be sometimes in our pursuit of objects and power, money and possessions that ultimately will have no true hold over us as we leave them behind. They are not clay dolls; but they are every bit a form of idol worship as the primitive gods of those pre-Islamic times. At least those people didn't know any better, until the commencement of the mission of the Prophet and the beginning of the descent of the Qur'an. What exactly was the true nature of that era that in curious ways resembles tendencies in our own time? Let us open once again the archives of history to glimpse for a few moments the flickering lights of another era, before they return to the night out of which they have been lifted.

The pre-Islamic era has been characterized by later Muslims as an era of idolatry and a time of ignorance known as the *jahiliyyah*. It was an age of moral depravity and religious discord with its worship of idols, the plurality of gods, the killing of daughters, and the low status of women among other evils, obscuring the belief in the one true God and plunging 6th century Arabia into the confusing turmoil of a polytheistic religious environment. The nomadic desert Arabs of that era had fallen into a kind of pagan, although complex, belief system[33] whose religious perspective embodied a pantheon of gods and idols in which each tribe had its own special favorites, such as Lāt and 'Uzzah for the Quraysh Tribe. The intercession of these gods was sought for any number of reasons; but the ancient memory of one great God still lingered, by name *Allah*, which was not a proper name as such, but a contraction of the word *al-ilah* which literally means "the god". While Allah was considered a god above the others, the pre-Islamic Arabs still turned for the sake of expediency to the lesser, more accessible gods who acted as Allah's intercessors. There were over 360 idols housed in and around the Ka'aba, representing every god recognized in the Arabian Peninsula. No doubt these were troubled times; but there were also signs seen in the heavens and on earth that portended the coming of a great man, a prophet and messenger to the world.

In Makkah, the Quraysh tribe was a powerful and wealthy clan that had settled there centuries earlier and whose members were known throughout the

---

[33] The Latin root word *paganus* actually means "a rustic bore" and was used by Christians to refer to a person who followed any religion but Christianity, rather than the derogatory suggestion it now conveys to mean a person totally outside any formally recognized tradition with ritual practices based on the most primitive impulses.

mountainous Hijāz region of present-day Saudi Arabia as *ahl Allah*, people of God and wardens of the sanctuary. They presided over a city nestled in the rugged and barren hills just off the coast of the Red Sea, a prime location on the main international trade route from Yemen in the south to Syria and Palestine in the north. To the south-east of Makkah lies the ancient city of Taif, known as the "garden of the Hejaz" because of its location atop an antediluvian escarpment that leads into the Hejaz mountain range and overlooks the Makkan plain below from the dramatic height of over 2,000 meters. To the north-west lies the city of Madinah, called Yathrib during the pre-Islamic era until the Prophet migrated to the city, whereupon it was renamed *Madinah al-Munawwarah* (the radiant city). Ancient caravans making their way due north and north-west ultimately arrived at the sacred crossroads of Jerusalem, the holiest city of Judaism and venerated as the site of Golgotha, the Hill of Calvary in Christianity, which the New Testament describes as the place where Christ was crucified. In Islam, Jerusalem marks the site of the Dome of the Rock visited by the Prophet before his ascent on a night journey through the seven heavens unto the Throne (*al-arsh*) of God. A virtual sacred geography entwines the three great monotheistic religions together with Jerusalem and Makkah as the *terra firma* and provenance of a universal sacred history.

The city of Makkah itself was endowed with a special aura by virtue of the Ka'aba, considered an ancient sanctuary and place of pilgrimage even in pre-Islamic times. This in turn enhanced the prestige of the Quraysh and made the city of Makkah a mandatory stopping off point at that time for reasons other than trade. As such, the entire surrounding area was transformed into sacred ground and created a neutral zone in which fighting was not permitted and weapons were not allowed. Traders passing through on their way to Jizan and Yemen to the south, or Palestine and Syria to the north, would stop for a perfunctory circumambulation around the Ka'aba, a universal shrine that housed the complete pantheon of all of the idols and gods of Arabia within a single sanctuary.

In the modern era throughout the entire year, pilgrims flock from all parts of the globe to make their way to Makkah, not in perfunctory tribute to an ancient ritual as did the Hejaz traders of pre-Islamic Arabia, but rather in fulfillment of a lifetime aspiration to perform the final earthly duty of Islam, the *hajj* (pilgrimage) before they die. According to the Qur'an (2:127), the Ka'aba itself was built by Abraham and his son Isma'il (Ishmael), asking God to make this place a "city of peace" (*balad amanah*). Abraham originally came from Ur in Babylonia; but eventually migrated westward to escape the atmosphere of idolatry that prevailed there at that time as well. He lies buried in the Cave of the Patriarchs in Hebron on the West Bank, a place revered by the followers of all three religions. As one of the key rituals of the *hajj*, modern-day Muslims recreate the plight of Abraham's wife Hajar who ran between the hills of Safa and Marwah with her son Isma'il in a desperate search for water to quench his thirst. In entering the sacred territory of Makkah and Madinah, Muslims return both physically and symbolically to an ancient and primeval landscape of undulating sands and rugged black hills that provided the backdrop to the coming of a new world religion. The stark frontier is as ancient and primordial now as it was at the time of the Prophet, a sacred geography whose dry, pristine wilderness still mirrors today the austere, pure spirituality that forms the basis of the Islamic spiritual experience.

Beyond the geographic location that marks the setting for the descent of the revelation, and in order to appreciate more fully the origins and initial development of the religious experience of Islam, it is important to understand the social and cultural milieu of the pre-Islamic Arabs. While the society of that time could be characterized as being steeped in idolatry and tribal rivalries, it was also a time of poetry, nobility and valor. The Arabic language is noted for both its poetic and rhetorical flourishes and the Arabs of that time had cultivated an appreciation for both poetry and the rhetorical style compatible with an oral society. Poets already had an important role in pre-Islamic society as bards, tribal historians, social commentators, foretellers of the future, dispensers of moral philosophy, and on occasion, administrators of justice.

Similarly, the nomadic Arabs called Bedouin, who move from place to place seeking their livelihood in the arid desert and have a legendary affinity with the harsh rhythms of nature, are well-known for their character traits of fidelity in keeping one's word, neighborliness in defending one's neighbour as one would defend oneself, hospitality elevated to an exclusive virtue, and finally chivalry that included both courage and courtesy. It has been said that a Bedouin would sacrifice his life to the utterance of a single word, or to escape hearing one. As such, it does not stretch the imagination to link Bedouin pride and Arab chivalry with the religious fervor required to become a part of a new and growing community of believers and to adopt the alternative spiritual worldview of a single, all-inclusive Reality that was the heart of the Islamic message. It appealed to the innermost sympathies of the Arab soul. "Muslims are brothers," the Prophet was fond of reminding his Companions, adding that "all men were of Adam, and Adam himself of the dust."

Finally, it should be noted by way of geo-historical background that the Byzantine, Assyrian and Sassanid empires were in proximity to the country of the Quraysh and other Arabian tribes. Islam was born in an era of grand empires and global conquests as much as it was a part of the continuous raids and repercussions that are endemic to tribal life, an era in which the Byzantines and Sassanids were locked in a permanent state of religious war for territorial expansion.[34] Zoroastrianism, Christianity, and Judaism intermingled in the region of the Near East, creating a pluralistic environment that was soon to become a breeding ground for bold new ideas and an unexpected religious fervor. It is precisely a moment such as this, when sacred and linear history collide to create a new spiritual dispensation where the elements of a primordial tradition would

---

[34] The Persian Empire fell to the Arabs in 640 CE. The last Sassanid King died a fugitive in 651.

come to life once again precisely at the place where the age-old mystery of the Abrahamic tradition embodied in the Ka'aba flourished. The Islamic message was an attempt to reform the existing religious beliefs and cultural practices of pre-Islamic Arabia in order to bring the one God of the Jews and Christians to the Arabs and ultimately the rest of the world. "[God] has established for you [the Arabs] the same religion enjoined on Noah, on Abraham, on Moses, and on Jesus." (42:13)

3.2 The Descent of the Qur'an

The earliest sources of the Islamic tradition will help us examine the extraordinary circumstances in which the Qur'an made its descent into the world of 7th century Arabia, a vertical descent that cut through the fabric of "this world" with the knife-blade of a transcendent reality, illuminating the dark mind of humanity with an insight comparable to a flash of lightning that was destined to illuminate the entire world until the last believing Muslim takes leave of the earth. This miraculous occurrence pierced forever the world of appearances and left behind a religion and a way of life, the Islamic *din*, that made possible a new world of spiritual experience to resolve the uncertainties and contingencies of this world. In Islam, the Qur'an forms the absolute basis of the religion, including its knowledge, its doctrine, its spiritual practices, its rich symbolism and art, its sacred sentiments and holy ambiance. When the verses of the Qur'an began to descend from the Divine Mind into the human sensibility of the Messenger Muhammad (PBUH), the religion began to manifest itself and take form since the religion is first and foremost the Qur'an from the point of view of its origin and source.

Every Muslim both knows and holds in holy remembrance the story of the descent of the Qur'an from the Divine to the human, a descent of the luminous into this world of shadow and contingency. The story brings to light the descent of a criterion in the form of a book and a recitation—"the mother of all books" according to the Qur'an itself (43:3)—that allows existing and future generations the ability to discern right from wrong, truth from falsehood, and the real from the illusory. It is a story that bears repeating, because of its miraculous quality and its ability to fill the heart with a spiritual emotion that we seldom have access to in today's modern, secular world and that is hard to recreate in our daily lives.

A brief glimpse at what occurred in Central Arabia during the early 7th century AD, at a time when Europe was still engulfed in the Dark Ages, will highlight certain extraordinary events and may reveal to the modern mentality an unexpected insight. The Noble Qur'an and the Traditions of the Prophet of Islam, commonly referred to in English as *hadith*, both recall the miraculous event that occurred when the Archangel Gabriel first appeared in a vision to a simple Arab trader of pure character from Makkah with the initial verses of what were to become, over a twenty-three year span, the full revelation of a Divine Being who identified Himself with the Supreme Name of Allah. At the time, this future messenger of Islam was unsuspecting of the great role that was being placed upon his shoulders and was initially unacquainted with the full significance of both revelation and faith. "And thus have We, by our command, sent inspiration to thee: Thou knewest not (before) what was Revelation and what was Faith, but We have made (Qur'an) a Light, through which We guide such of our servants as We will; and indeed thou do guide (mankind) to the straight path." (42:52)

Early biographical sources have recorded that the Prophet was about thirty-five years old, approximately five years before the first descent of the initial verses of the Qur'anic revelation, when he began to retire into a cave near Makkah, called the Hira' cave, located within the *Jabal al-Nur*, the Mountain of Light. Traditionally, the cave[35] has been considered as a symbol of sacred space down through the ages, and thus was the perfect environment for the inward practices of contemplation and inner inquiry for a contemplative mind such as that of the Prophet. People have been fascinated with caves for millennia and mystics and saints have traditionally retired to the isolation and safety of a natural cave because such places offered perfect seclusion and were often inaccessible to both men and animals. The Prophet was merely following the example of earlier descendants of Isma'il who would periodically make retreats in mountain caves for the purposes of purification and enlightenment. The early traditional sources[36] of the life of the Prophet record that he spoke of "true visions" during these moments of retreat, visions that came to him clearly while he was at rest or asleep in the cave of Hira', visions that were "like the breaking of the light of dawn."

During the last days of the holy month of Ramadhan[37], which was the traditional month of retreat even in pre-Islamic times, the Prophet saw something strange and unexpected in a seemingly miraculous vision during his meditations, a vision that ranged far beyond anything he had ever experienced before in his life. At first, he did not know what was happening, the shock of the experience was so raw and powerful. A Qur'anic verse has later documented and fully confirmed what occurred to the messenger at that time: "He was taught by one mighty in power, filled with wisdom, for he appeared (in stately form) while he was in the highest part of the horizon, then he approached and came closer and was at a distance of but two bow-lengths or (even) nearer. So did (Allah) convey

---

[35] The Prophet was later to rely once again on a cave to evade with his companion Abū Bakr the pursuing Makkans during the *hijrah* or migration to Madinah, well-known in the prophetic traditions because of the spider that sealed the cave with his web in order to deceive the Makkans into thinking that no one had entered the cave.

[36] Ibn Hisham, an Egyptian renown as a grammarian and student of language and history (d. 834), edited the biography of the Prophet written by Ibn Isḥāq whose original work has been lost and is now only known in the recension of Ibn Hishām.

[37] According to the traditions, the Qur'an began to descend during the holy month of Ramadhān on a night identified as the *laylat al-qadr*, the Night of Power, a night that is "better than a thousand months." (97:3)

the inspiration to His Servant what He (meant) to convey." (53: 5-10) Of course, God does not speak directly to human beings; but He does speak through His Word and archangelic agencies to His prophets as He did to the Prophet of Islam, through whom the Divine Word was revealed to the world in the form of the Qur'an. "It is not fitting for a man that God should speak to him except by inspiration, or from behind a veil, or by the sending of a messenger to reveal, by God's permission, what God wills; for He is most High, Most Wise." (42:51)

The abrupt and unexpected visitant that he beheld was none other than an archangel in the form of a man. He was carrying what appeared to be a written document, enfolded upon a "magical brocade" according to Ibn Hisham. The archangel said: "I am Gabriel. God has sent me to communicate to you His message." He then intoned with majesty: "Recite (or read) this", and the Prophet immediately replied: "I am not a reciter (I do not know how to read)." In fact, the Prophet was *ummi*, meaning unlettered and unable to read; he was the pure, uncorrupted vessel called upon to receive the sacred words and thus the perfect receptacle to receive the divine revelation. Three times the archangel exhorted him to "Recite" and three times the Prophet replied that he was not able to recite. Finally, the first revelation passed through his heart and soul and out into the world: "Recite (*iqra*) in the name of thy Lord who created, created man out of a blood clot. Read and thy Lord is most bountiful, who has taught by the Pen, taught man what he knew not." (96:1-5)

The Prophet came back to his ordinary consciousness, terrified by what he had experienced. Was this a devil, a spell, an angelic inspiration, a divine revelation? The simple Makkan merchant–known as 'the trustworthy' among the people of his tribe–did not know exactly what he had encountered. Yet the words he heard rang out like a bell and later he was to say: "It was as though the words were written on my heart." He fled the cave and proceeded down the side of the mountain, in a state of confusion and doubt. But as he stumbled down the slope, he heard a voice saying "O, Muhammad (PBUH), thou art the messenger of God and I am Gabriel!" The Qur'an itself records that the Prophet raised his eyes and saw the vision of Gabriel now as an archangel, an image that filled the breadth of the horizon. "Without a doubt he saw him in the clear horizon, neither doth he withhold grudgingly knowledge of the Unseen." (81:23, 24) Again, the archangel said: "Oh Muhammad (PBUH), thou are the messenger of God and I am Gabriel!" Muhammad (PBUH) turned to descend down the slope once again. But in whatever direction he turned, whether to the north, south, east or west, he saw the magnificent archangel standing astride "the highest part of the horizon." The only thing equal to this angelic vision was the prophetic mission of this messenger of God soon to spread forth across the world.

After the archangel turned away and disappeared, the Prophet of Islam descended the slope and went to his house trembling from this unexpected and intense experience in the cave. His wife Khadijah consoled him by saying: "Be of good cheer and comfort thyself! I swear by Him in whose hand the life of Khadijah is, that I hope thou wilt be the prophet of this nation." His wife

Khadijah instinctively believed in him and completely accepted was true what God had revealed to him. "By her God lightened the burden of his prophethood. She strengthened him, lightened his burden, proclaimed his truth, and belittled men's opposition."[38] With the coming of the second verse of the revelation, God relieved the Prophet of any lingering anxiety about his sanity. "By the grace of your Lord, you are not a madman. Yours will be an unending reward; for you are a man of noble character. Soon, you shall see, and they shall see, who the madman is." (68:1-5)

It was a brief and stunning moment for the unsuspecting merchant from Makkah when the Invisible had suddenly become visible and the inaudible Word of God had momentarily become audible to receptive human ears. The Prophet had experienced a moment in which he was able to witness the monumental unveiling of one of the unseen mysteries (*al-ghaib*) that perennially protects, as from behind a veil, all direct knowledge of the Divinity. However, this was no ordinary human being; he was the Prophet (*nabi*) of God and Messenger (*rasul*) to the world. Indeed, at that moment, in the deserts of western Arabia, the unseen mystery had commenced to become a living knowledge for all of humanity, both at that time and for future generations until the end of time as we know it.

The descent of the first verses of the Qur'anic revelation through an archangelic messenger marked the formal descent of a divine knowledge to be preserved and acted upon by people within the earthly environment. As Divine Speech, it was an absolute and final[39] communication of the Divine Being to present humanity. After an initial interlude of silence that lasted for three years, the descent of the verses of the revelation continued to pass through the heart, soul, and mind of the messenger for twenty-three years until just before the end of his life. During the moments of revelation, the Prophet had become a kind of human horizon over which the miraculous and blessed communication from the Divinity continued to emerge until all 6346 verses of the Qur'an had fully arrived within the human frame of reference and the revelation was complete.

The messenger witnessed the initial descent of the Qur'anic revelation through the archangel Gabriel, a luminous and virtually invisible being made momentarily visible to the human eye. He heard the first sacred sound, the first word and the first verse that would come to be known the world over as the sacred Speech of Allah. Throughout the course of the Prophet's ministry, the verses of the Qur'an entered upon his mind, his heart, his consciousness and in fact the whole of his being, and then passed through his heart and out into the collective consciousness of humanity both then and for all future generations. The love of the Prophet Muhammad (PBUH) continues to be a strong, living

---

[38] Ibn Ishaq, *The Life of Muhammad*, A. Guillaume (trans.) (Lahore, Pakistan: New Impression Edition, 1989), p. 106.

[39] Muḥammad is identified in the Qur'an as "the seal of the prophets," which effectively closes the book on the plenary descent of knowledge in revelatory form.

spiritual emotion among the faithful of Islam, and one of the main reasons is the fact that through him the descent of the luminous in the form of the Noble Qur'an was made possible.

3.3 The Compilation of the Book

The first verses of the Qur'an may have originally been shown to the Prophet on velvet brocade, but the text itself as a written document was not compiled in book form during his lifetime. It was inscribed on his mind and engraved upon his heart, but the words that poured forth from his mouth were memorized at first by a small group of close companions, including Zayd bin Thabit, Abu Bakr and 'Ali. Without doubt, verses of the Qur'an were also written down on such things as skins, camel bones and parchment leaves by Zayd and 'Ali and perhaps others during the life of the Prophet, and the order of *surah and ayah* were made by him on Divine Command. Later, as the multitude of verses increased, a new class of scholars emerged, called *qurrah* or readers, whom the Prophet personally instructed in the correct and accurate recitation of the sacred text. Eventually, large numbers of new Muslims committed the verses to memory because the Prophet said that there was implicit blessing in doing so. Those who could recite the Qur'an during the lifetime of the Prophet numbered in the thousands, while the number of Muslims at the time of his death exceeded 100,000. There can be no doubt that most of them had committed some, if not all, of the Qur'an to memory. These early believers were living torches of faith, on fire and fully committed in their surrender to God.

In the beginning, the verses came in intervals of months and in small segments. During the entire 23 year span that followed the initial descent in the cave of Hira'; they swelled into a continuous stream of revelatory knowledge, revealing the doctrines of the religion often through the many particular circumstances that occurred during the life of the Prophet, although all the Qur'anic verses have a significance that extends far beyond these specific circumstances. The early verses came when the Prophet was still in Makkah, while the later verses came after the *hijrah* to Madinah. Therefore, the Qur'an is divided into Makkah and Madinah verses and chapters. The arrangement of the verses was ultimately systematized in an order of descending length according to the instructions of the Prophet himself, with the longer *surah* coming first. The traditions say that once a year he collated the verses that had thus far been revealed with the archangel Gabriel.

The first official recension was made during the caliphate of Abu Bakr between 11 and 15 CE at the bidding of Umar. During the Battle of Yamamah about ten years after the death of the Prophet, some 500 of the *qurrah* or readers who knew the Qur'an by heart were killed, giving Umar, the second Caliph, the idea that the Qur'an should be formally collected in a book lest any of its parts be lost. He suggested this to Abu Bakr who appointed Zayd bin Thabit, the former secretary to the Prophet who was already known for his prodigious memory of the verses and who along with Ali had also written down the received verses during the lifetime of the Prophet. At first, Zayd refused to undertake the compilation of the Qur'an into book form on the grounds that the Prophet himself had never done so. "What right have I," said Zayd to Abu Bakr, "to gather in the form of a book what the Prophet has never intended to transmit to posterity by this channel? And since the Prophet never designed to give his message in this way, is it a lawful work that I am commanded to do?" Eventually, Abu Bakr convinced him to undertake the daunting task of collecting the text of the Qur'an in one volume and have it certified to be correct by others who knew it by heart as a heritage for future humanity. Then, in addition to his own collection, Zayd gathered fragments of the Qur'an from every quarter, including the ribs of palm branches, bits of leather, stone tablets and "from the hearts of men". He copied out what he had collected on sheets or leaves (*huhuf* in Arabic).[40] After the death of the Prophet, the *qurrah* spread through the fast-growing community of Muslims as the authorized teachers of the Qur'an. A copy of the holy book was given to Umar who bequeathed it to his daughter, one of the widows of the Prophet.

Ultimately, it was Uthman, the third Caliph, who authorized the legendary prototype Qur'an as the universally definitive text about 65 CE. During his governance, Hudayfah ibn al-Yamani the commander-in-chief of the Muslim army in Central Asia, discovered that Muslims from other parts of the world recited the Qur'an in different ways. In addition, dialectical peculiarities had crept into the recitation because of the wide variety of Arab dialects existing at that time among the Arab tribes of the Arabian Peninsula. He turned once again to Zayd bin Thabit and entrusted the matter of the new compilation to him and three other leading Quraysh. They borrowed from Hafsah the copy commissioned by Abu Bakr and brought together as many copies as they could lay their hands on, to prepare an edition which was to be considered the canonical codex for all Muslims. To prevent any further disputes, they burned all the other codices except that of Hafsah, who had the original compilation developed years earlier that formed the basis for the new and final version of the Qur'an. Three copies were sent to the capitals of Damascus, Basrah, and Kufah, where they became metropolitan codices, while a fourth copy was retained at Madinah. All later manuscripts are derived from these four originals. Many early sources, especially but not only Shi'ite, believe that there was also a text of the Qur'an compiled by Ali, but later lost.

In this way and over time, the Qur'an finally became documented and fixed as a physical book that is readily available for the Muslims, faithfully preserved word for word for future generations as it was originally delivered to the Prophet by the Archangel Gabriel.

---

[40] To this day, the Qur'an is still referred to as the *mushaf*, whose root meaning refers to the *huhuf* or leaves of the original hand-inscripted Qur'an.

3.4 The Impact of the Qur'an

To this day, the Qur'an continues to be memorized in full by many devout Muslims, called *hafiz al-Qur'an* in Arabic. Every Muslim gives special attention to even the simplest reading to ensure that the sacred words are pronounced accurately and meticulously follow the science of *tajwīd* (pronunciation) with its strict rules of recitation and pacing. Western scholars have questioned the accuracy of the Qur'anic verses, citing the fact that the text itself was only compiled some years after the death of the Prophet. However, what they do not realize or accept is the true spirit of the verses as the absolute Word of God and how deeply the decisive words were etched on the memories of the first believers, who like other Arab and nomadic people had prodigious memories. As such, the verses have always been held in awe until the present era and their accuracy as words of a true revelation never comes into question in the minds of the Muslims who in questioning the veracity of the Qur'an would be overturning the very ground upon which the religion is built, the very ground into which the Muslim soul has cast its roots for nurturing and development.

Imagine then the intensity and fervor with which the immediate companions of the Prophet must have regarded the words of the Divine Speech coming from the lips of the Prophet. What touched his heart with fire and light must have seared the hearts of his Companions with a burning within the heart that is hard for us to imagine. The spoken words of the revelation rose up from the flames of a burning heart like smoke rising into the firmament, the Arabic letters representing a calligraphic script of devotion and worship seemingly endless in its possibilities. In meeting the needs of future humanity, however, the sacred words of revelation had to find a place to reside, thus preserving the letter as well as the spirit of the Divine Speech. It would be enough if they found permanent repose in the cavern of the heart of all peoples; but since that would not be the case for every Muslim in the future, these holy seed-words of the Divinity found themselves inscribed on leaves and bone and parchment, as well as within the breasts of men and women, to lend of their blessing, power and knowledge.

In this manner during the early history of Islam, the Qur'an came to be preserved for present and future generations of Muslims. To this day, most Muslims experience the Qur'an orally rather than through the written word, and by following the precepts and doctrines of the religion, they are able to internalize the very meaning of the revelation as it was intended to be. The sacred verses have been copied in meticulous splendor down through the ages in a variety of classical calligraphic styles. However, what decorates the manuscript of an individual life are not the *marginalia* or *illuminata* of an earthly scribe; what qualifies the narrative of a Muslim life with its own calligraphic splendor are the letters and words of a life story steeped in the mystery of the revelatory words of God, creating within one's life the simplicity and grandeur that characterize the revelation, and invoking a life of love and action through the words of the Book.

Another rarefied aspect of the Qur'an for the Muslim community lies in the "presence"—for want of a better term—that accompanies the physical appearance of the book in a mosque or home. The true presence of the Qur'an lies not in the pages and binding as with other books, but rather in its resonant brilliance and its calligraphic majesty. Muslims read the Qur'an for the knowledge, guidance and truth implicit in the words and verses; but they also read the verses because they contain a "spiritual presence" through the recitation and intonation of the divine speech that remembers the beloved personality of the Prophet of Islam (PBUH) before literally bringing them into the Presence of God. The recitation resonates as sacred vibrations of sounds and rhythms that echo first in the mind as real intonations before blowing through the caverns of the heart as a wild wind that moves as a spirit of awakening to the weary soul.

As sacred sound, the letters, syllables, words, and verses of the revelation call forth the inner voice of the self, the voice of the prophet, the voice of the archangel, and the Voice of the Supreme Being[41] who has chosen to reveal knowledge of Himself and speak in words of the knowledge of creation and origins, thus recalling the primordial person of Adam within each of us, male and female, through the power of sound. When the Muslims recite the verses orally, they hear their own voice reciting the words first of all in the here and now. Then, as a kind of echo beyond the voice of the individual, there reverberates the voice of the Prophet Muhammad (PBUH). Through the voice of the Prophet passed the divine revelation of God to humanity, whereby he became the instrument and intermediary through whom the world of the Spirit was able to enter and influence the spirit of the world. Beyond the voice of the individual self and the voice of the Prophet lies the voice of the Archangel Gabriel who, as intermediary of the Divinity, delivered the verses directly to the Prophet, standing in full glory on the horizon.

Finally, all these voices are earthly echoes of the Voice of God Who communicates through these revelatory words to the soul of every human being a profound sense of wonderment for the numinous and the other-worldly. Through words, the Divine Being is able to pluck the violin strings of a person's inner being to sound a cord of the timeless Reality whose echo reverberates throughout the human entity in all its physical, mental, psychic and spiritual aspects. In chanting the verses, the individual reciter becomes a bow string of God, reverberating the sacred vibrations of the holy Spirit throughout his or her entire being in remembrance of the sublime power that lies behind these sacred words.

Needless to say, these primordial, revelatory words of God create a feeling of proximity to the Divine Presence that emanates from within the sounds themselves, and once spoken aloud or whispered within the mind in faith and

---

[41] A *hadith qudsi*, which is a saying of the Prophet that quotes the direct speech of the Divine Being, has this to say of those who regularly recite the Qur'an: "Someone who reads the Qur'an is as if he were talking to Me and I were talking to Him."

with sincerity, they reverberate deeply within the cave of the heart and take root in the ground of the soul. The Muslims who read the sacred verses over and over on a daily basis can create within their mind and heart a pulsating wave of energy that is based on sacred auditory rhythms embedded within the letters and words of the text itself. In turn, the Qur'an creates an inner harmony that in the eloquent words of Seyyed Hossein Nasr produce "an echo in the minds and world of the men who read it, and returns them to a state in which they participate in its paradisal joy and beauty. Herein lies its alchemical effect."[42]

The Qur'an contains a majesty, rhythm, and cadence that characterize the sacred text that cannot be translated without seriously altering the nature of the profound blessing that emanates from the spiritual presence contained within the letters and sounds. There is a majestic projection of sound that is primordial, central and eternal; primordial in that the sound and meaning evoke within the heart of the reciter feelings for the mythic dimension of primal origins; central because it brings the Muslim immediately back from the periphery of earthly existence to the very center of one's being; eternal because it lifts the reciter out of the march of a lateral, advancing time to the eternal now, the sacred present, that transcends and extinguishes the temporal march of time with its window into eternity.

Revelation embodies doctrines that convey meaning that clarifies human responsibility, morality that establishes a purpose, and spiritual sensibilities that lead to a virtuous life, culminating in the perfection of the soul and a consciousness fully united with the knowledge of God. The depth and profundity of the knowledge of the Origin, the Real, the Truth, the Supreme Intelligence, and the One Reality, given the abundant luminescence and spiritual consequences for humanity, cannot be known and realized without the descent of a supernatural communication, whose divinely inspired text neutralizes all mystery and whose supernatural radiation suffuses the mind, heart and soul with its radiance (*al-nur*) and blessing (*al-baraka*). Muslims would feel abandoned and virtually lost without the comforting presence of the book within their households and all of the knowledge and blessing the book contains within its sacred sympathies.

The Qur'an has alternatively been described as a recitation (*al-qur'an*), a discernment (*al-furqan*), the mother of all books (*umm al-kitab*), the essential guidance (*al-huda*), perennial wisdom (*hikmah*), and ultimate remembrance (*dhikr*). The very name recitation (*al-qur'an*) recalls the manner in which it was delivered, the way it was received and remembered, and the means with which it is treasured and preserved, for the Qur'an is a reading and a recitation first and foremost, a compilation of verses and the word of God on the tongues of the faithful. As a criterion and discernment, it establishes once and for all time the true nature of the Real as opposed to the unreal, the light of truth overshadowing the darkness of falsehood and ignorance. The Qur'anic guidance shapes all

---

[42] *Ibid.*, p. 77.

personal and ethical conduct, giving definition and color to the actions of the believers, who may not always know how to behave in the light of their true desires; while its wisdom becomes an internalized knowledge within the heart and ultimately manifests itself back out into the world community as virtuous behavior.

As Divine Remembrance, however, the Qur'an is the ultimate sacred psychology, leading the human soul back from the periphery to the Center and establishing the doctrinal knowledge and the sacred sentiments necessary for the soul's journey of return to God. The Qur'an is identified as the *dhikr Allah* which is also one of the names of the Prophet and remembers the Qur'anic verse: "Nothing is greater than the remembrance of God." (29: 45) Its living presence, as a kind of spiritual perfume within the mind, focuses the human consciousness on "the one thing needful" and recreates the ambiance of primordial beatitude found in the pure consciousness of Adam before the monumental fall from the Paradise.

The interaction of human consciousness and Divine Remembrance is subtle and intricate. The very *raison d'etre* of the human consciousness is to realize within the individual self the knowledge of the Universal Self. Remembrance, then, whether it is through the Profession of Faith in the Islamic *shahadah*, in the repetition (*dhikr*) of the Name of God, or any one of the best of names (*al-asma' al-husna*) through the ceremony of prayer, or the remembrance of God through Qur'anic recitation, activates the human consciousness with the living presence of the Divinity. To enjoy a consciousness of the individual self without the possibility of connecting to the Supreme Self actually constitutes a desire to roam on the periphery rather than be at the center, to live in an evanescent rather than a transcending world, and to recognize a fundamental mystery at the heart of existence, while denying its true origin and source.

The Qur'an, as Divine Discourse and Revelatory Word, remains the ultimate source of all essential knowledge, the well-spring of all morality and ethics, and the means of spiritual worship that permits the faithful to transcend their limitations and approach the true knowledge of the Reality as Truth and as Presence. Like the topographical features of the earth with its arctic and tropic regions, its seacoasts and plains, its mountain ranges and valleys, its deserts and savannas, its forests and woodlands, the Qur'an has a broad range of topical representation, including poetic heights and legalistic depths, dogmatic theology and mystic aphorisms, litanies and prayers of entreaty. Every letter, word, and verse is packed with layers of symbolic meaning that reach the human mind according to the receptiveness of the recipient. There is fresh meaning with every reading and the verses of the book are never stale or outdated.

Whether recited from memory or read from the leaves of a palm tree, the words hover in the mind like dragonflies floating above the surface of a pond, with the force of a spirit whose fluttering wings create waves of inspiration across the surface of the human heart to its very center and core. From the man who initially protested that he could not read or recite flowed the words of a luminous knowledge to be recited and revered by generations of devout Muslims until the end of time or until God Almighty brings their sounding to a silence that will be deafening. In reading or reciting the sacred text, the verses become God's voice on earth for those whose hearts burn with a Godly flame, just as the Prophet himself, in becoming the human receptacle and transmitter of the sacred knowledge, became God's passageway of return of His creation to the primordial truths embedded in the ancient wisdom of the universe.

As living legacy of a distant land from a remote era of the past, the Qur'an as Remembrance (*Dhikr*) and Guidance (*Huda*) is the living embodiment of a voice that will never fade so long as human beings have faith in supernatural realities, have contact with the invisible, and preserve their ability to know things, not just as they are in their physical appearance, but to unveil their true nature through the language of a divine revelation. Every reading becomes a luminous echo of the Voice of God that hovers over the waters of creation with its abiding spirit. Every intonation becomes an evocative memory of the voice of the archangel, majestically standing on the horizon with wings outstretched in glory, robed in a mantle of light. Every utterance becomes once again the voice of an unlettered trader, in a secluded cave within the Mountain of Light, who listened and repeated in clear, resounding Arabic what no man had heard before, "Recite in the Name of thy Lord who created."

3.5 The Love of the Prophet

Muslims love the Prophet for any number of reasons, not the least being that their love is a reflection of the love of Allah bestowed on His beloved Messenger who existed, according to an Islamic tradition, before Adam was even born. There are of course mysteries that cannot be explored too deeply without shattering the quality of the mystique that surrounds them. The true nature of the human soul is one of them which, according to a specific verse of the Qur'an, lies at the discretion of the "command of thy Lord". Another one is the place the Prophet holds within the grand scheme of prophethood, preceding Adam even in the procession of the Prophets that have come to nations with a revelation from the Divinity. As complement, the Prophet is also clearly identified in the Qur'an as the "seal of the prophets" and thus of all prophethood, implying that not only has the descent of knowledge in the form of prophecy come to completion, but that in a temporal sense, there will never be another prophet within this cycle of time. The indelible seal not only closed the cycle of prophethood, but also of prophecy as such, by a process in which a direct revelation containing the essential knowledge of the Divinity has come down to many different nations during the lifetime of humanity. The seal of prophecy closes the progression of knowledge through the ages; but resurrects again the primordial knowledge of unity (*tawhid*) that initiated the universe to begin with.

In another piece of writing, I have attempted to describe the unique phenomenon that the Muslims refer to as the love of the Prophet. Of course, love under any manifestation or guise is a difficult thing to explain, and perhaps rightly so it remains the exclusive prevue of experience within the human framework, but if the following experience sheds any light on the spiritual emotion of love being described, then it may be worth retelling. Like the facts of pre-Islamic Arabia, the details that outline the progression of the Prophet's life are well documented and have been studied and memorized by Muslims down through the ages until the present time. These facts also sit on the pages of the history books like clouds in the blue sky floating over the desert landscape, but what is the meaning of the shadows they cast down into the cave of our hearts, waiting for an explanation of their true import and significance in our lives and in the life of spirituality that we are attempting to pursue as true Muslims?

I found myself one blessed day making my way to the back of the great mosque of Madinah deep into the inner sanctum of the original mosque, which became the extension of the family quarters of the Prophet. It is here along the original southeasterly section of the mosque that the Prophet lies buried, together with his Companions and first Caliphs Abu Bakr al-Saddiq and Umar bin al-Khattab. It is customary to visit the tomb of the Prophet and greet him with salaams upon first entering the sacred enclosure of the mosque. I make my way slowly amid the multitude and savor every moment. The mosque is still jam packed with people of every race and nationality. Old and young intermingle; many are lying supine, others are gathered in groups or sitting in circles sharing their impressions. People are moving about as I am, deferring to the space of others, careful to step over those who are resting supine on the floor without a care in the world.

As I move deeper into the mosque, I notice that the upper walls and ceiling are embellished with geometric forms, arabesques, Qur'anic calligraphy and mini domes hand-carved from wood in remembrance of the traditional era when the handcrafts represented a form of sacred art. Given the size and dimensions of the mosque, it is quite a trek from front to back. Deep within the well of the enclosure, I come upon an inner open courtyard that gives rise to the heavens. It comes upon you unexpectedly and already the dawn light is bathing the inner courtyard in beams of early morning daylight. I take note, however, of a group of huge, light-colored sunshades that have been cleverly designed to open at the push of a remote controlled button and fan out overhead in perfect symmetry to protect the worshippers from the onslaught of the mid-day desert sun that promises to fill the courtyard open to the elements. I am told that the opening of these gigantic mechanical umbrellas is a sight to behold.

I know I am nearing the tomb of the Prophet through two pieces of evidence. Firstly, the architectural change of the building which has a smaller, more crowded, and less grandiose aspect and dates back many centuries to the time of the Prophet and the early Caliphate era, and secondly by the density of the crowds of people all vying for proximity to the resting place of the Prophet. There is a section of the mosque cordoned off and positioned adjacent to the wall of the Prophet's tomb that is referred to and revered as the *al-riyadh al-jannah*, which roughly translates as a "garden" of the Paradise. The Prophet has referred to this part of the mosque by saying: "What is between my house and my *minbar* is a garden from the gardens of Paradise." It is an area that according to the traditions of the Prophet is actually a part of the Paradise that will rise upward and return to its original home on the Day of Judgment, which in Islam is alternatively referred to as the Day of Accounting and the Day of Religion. Whatever the truth may be, this *riyadh* is certainly a place to sojourn and rest.

    I quietly enter this section of the mosque and sit myself on the light blue carpet, distinguished from the red oriental carpets spread through the rest of the mosque. There was indeed not only a special quality of serenity and calm there that one would come to expect in the paradise, but I felt as I sat cross-legged on the carpet as if I had come home at last and that there was nowhere else I needed to go. An otherworldly fragrance seemed to unexpectedly permeate the air and I remember considering what that scent reminded me of until I had to confess that it reminded me of nothing related to this world, that it had an otherworldly quality that seemed exquisite and heavenly.

    As I sat in this "garden of Paradise", my mind took on wings and I began to fly. Call it auto suggestion of the tradition if you like, but a dream quality seemed to emerge like dawn mist over the waters of a lake. The strange, otherworldly scent began to raise my level of consciousness from the mundane to the sublime in some unconscious manner, and I felt I was entering another dimension virtually impossible to describe. Then without warning, I felt a surge of emotion well up inside me from depths I didn't know existed, an emotive feeling so strong and satiating that I could do nothing but surrender to the power of these sacred emotions and I began to sob a storm of hot tears that came from some deep emotion. At first, I did not know why I was crying, except that I realized that the place, the moment, and the overall ambiance were powerful enough to evoke such an unexpected, powerful reaction. The outburst was not convulsive or hectic; it was sheer weeping without an obvious catalyst. It was not the kind of grief cause by the death of a loved one or the loss of a valued treasure; instead it was an emotive collapse without hill or valley, a release from the rigidity that holds us together in life, vast and inconsolable at first as a child's first confrontation with the unknown. The hot tears came as a soothing balm for the trials and tribulations of my life, the frustrations and the shattered hopes, the dreams, the remorse, the failures and perhaps even the successes. I sobbed for the person I had been and the person I might well become. The sobbing slowly died within me throb by throb until a wave as cool as spring water flowed across the shore of my being and an abiding peace streamed through my mind and body. I had received the gift of tears sometimes spoken of in the traditions in which the soul uses the mind and body to free itself of certain unwanted complexes of the psyche and psychological knots of the spirit as a form of liberation from the lower self and as a form of purification.

    I left this blessed area packed with worshippers wrapped in meditation and joined the more sober, turgid throng making its way down the aisle that passes in front of the three tombs of the Prophet and his beloved companions, Abu Bakr and Umar. The energy of the place was intense and the atmosphere was electric. It was slow going indeed, and except for the occasional shove or elbow in the ribs, perhaps it was a good thing, because as you approach the front door of the tombs, with their silver-encrusted plating covered with Qur'anic verses, the realization suddenly dawns with an expectation brimming beyond belief that one is approaching the very presence of the Prophet. Here is where he lived, where he prayed and where he died. Here lies the man that Allah chose to receive His revelation and to deliver it as the Holy Qur'an to future generations of humanity. Through his mind passed the very words of God and from him, they passed out into the world of humanity down to the present time. Muslims spend a lifetime attempting to find ways to express their love of God, but their love of the Prophet comes naturally and spontaneously because he is the vehicle and the path through which the love of God is possible.

As I turn a corner and approach the aisle that passes in front of the enclosed rooms containing the various tombs, the dense but still orderly crowd thickens considerably. People with cupped hands in an attitude of prayerful supplication are moving slowly forward at the pace of molasses and everyone proceeds deferentially, concerned for the comfort of their Muslim brothers and not wishing to create an undue stir. Then I am there in front of the tomb, and I send forth my salaams to the beloved Prophet Muhammad (PBUH). Neither the hectic throng, nor the imposing and unexpected presence of military guards at the doors of the tombs, can disturb the surging feeling of humility and onrushing awe that begins in the pit of my stomach and rises to the tip of my cognitive consciousness, lifting me off my feet and beyond the gravity limits of this world.

As I shuffle along with baby steps as one of a surging crowd of worshippers, I feel lost in the wave of a deep and abiding emotion and I think: We remember the Prophet Muhammad (PBUH), every day in our prayers and we invoke his name and sayings as a matter of course, but now I am here at his tomb, visiting his ancient home and place of earthly investiture. I have presented myself here in person to make my holy salaams to the memory of his sacred person and his exemplary life.I feel a deep and overwhelming love for the Prophet to the extent that the evocation of his memory creates a melting in the heart and brings tears to the eyes. It is a powerful, indeed an overwhelming moment. In the presence of greatness, I utter my humble prayer as intercession to God through the Prophet, as I remember all those in need within the circle of my life, a dying brother on life support, my diabetic friend and all those who asked me to intercede on their behalf. There is an unearthly quality to the moment, as thought a shaft of light were shining down upon my heart, filling me with a sacred and miraculous sense of wonder. I feel held aloft momentarily by angel wings before being lowered down back to reality by the movement of the crowd of worshippers.

A moment whose quality will be remembered for years to come has passed me by, just as the slow-moving sea of humanity I am part of has passed by the tomb enclosure. Before I fully realize what has happened, the crowd has deposited me outside the mosque again like a piece of driftwood thrown ashore by the sea. I gaze distractedly and a little disoriented at the luminous glow on the eastern horizon as the sun announces its arrival and bathes the eastern face of the mosque with its harsh desert light, without any thought or mercy for the faithful.

For the Muslims, the Prophet Muhammad (PBUH) touches the heart to the point that you feel the pull of heart strings as pain while tears fill the eyes as pools of emotion. In addition to all the things we know the Prophet to be, including the elements of his humanity, his leadership, his role as general of the armies, his family life and companionship of others, he is also identified as 'Abd or Servant, Nabi or Prophet, Rasul or Messenger and Habibi or Friend. Each name highlights a unique human quality, the servant representing the ultimate surrender of creature to Creator, the Prophet as the human receptacle of a heavenly gift and beatitude, the Messenger as the instrument to announce once again the true nature of the Reality, and finally the Friend as the beauty and love of the individual in intimacy with the Divine and that is expressed here on earth as love of one's family and friends. The Prophet is the representation of these things to the Muslims and much more that cannot be articulated in words, but that are felt within the deep recesses of one's being.

In that sweet and innocent inability to truly understand the power of the emotion that drives the Muslim relationship with the Prophet there lies perhaps the ultimate mystery the Muslims feel in the love of the Prophet. Not only is the Prophet the true Friend of Allah to the extent that the Supreme Being bestowed upon him the ultimate blessing of being the human instrument in the transmission of the essential knowledge of God; the Prophet is also our Friend. We need only to be his true friend in return. Like the experience of friendship that we all know and yearn for in this world, the experience of being the friend of the Prophet, who is none other than the friend of Allah, is both unique and sublime to which nothing can compare. When the ministry of the Prophet began with the descent of the initial verses of the revelation, followed by many subsequent verses until both the Book and the Religion itself was brought to completion with the hot wax seal of prophecy through the Divine Command, something dramatic had occurred that literally changed the parameters of the world. It was as though time had stopped for a moment and a piece of eternity had entered the heart of the Prophet, as prelude to entering the heart of the world, stirring memories of beauty and truth that would change the future destiny of mankind.

This is what happens to us, every time we follow in the footsteps of the Prophet and surrender to the command and will of God. Time stops for the expression of an eternal moment that lodges itself in the heart as the emotive experience of a love that has no limits. The love of the Prophet by every devoted Muslim represents the recreation of that initial stirring of wonder and awe, when the Prophet heard the first verses of the Divine Revelation, the very words of God, entering not only his mind, but the very portals of his heart, with all the wisdom and love that the universe could contain. It is a love that recreates in time this moment of eternity, let in through a crack in the universe by the divine Compassion for a wayward humanity in love only with themselves. It is a love that stirs instinctive memories of fresh air and sunlight, peace of mind and clarity of thought. It is a love that forgets all ignorance and misery, and fills the soul like a cup brimming with the love of the Prophet as a way station to a genuine love of God. The facts of the Prophet's life have been written down as a legacy of information for future humanity; but the love of the Prophet fills the heart with the love of God and places the experience of eternity firmly within the human soul as an experience of true spirituality here on earth.

PART FOUR

Islam and Science

4.1 Islamic Science as Sacred Science

Before investigating, in summary fashion, the Islamic contribution to the enrichment of scientific knowledge down through history, a brief introductory clarification needs to be made regarding words and their meaning as they have evolved over time and within certain social and cultural contexts. When we write "Islamic sciences", what exactly does the word "Islamic" mean and what are the implications in today's world for the word "science"?

When we think of "science" today or even hear the word, visions come to mind of black holes and event horizons, parallel universes and the theory of relativity (the famous and deceptively simple theorem $e = mc^2$), the Big Bang and the expanding universe. These modern-day mental constructions are not only examples of what modern science is capable of, they are also indicative of the kind of success and achievement that modern science symbolizes, casting a glow of wonder across the mind of modern humanity. We think to ourselves: this is what we humans are capable of, tracing our origins back to the edge of time and down into the center of the nucleus of matter. If we can put a number to the birth and age of the universe and capture the singularity of the Big Bang on giant telescopes that float through the heavens with imperiousness, it leads to the notion that we are smokin', as the saying goes, and that nothing can stop us; we can do it on our own and without the aid of Heaven. The price we have to pay for this extravagant illusion, however, lies in the loss of our own souls and our inability to lift the veil that becomes increasingly heavy as it continues to separate us from the other side, the unseen side (*al-ghaib*), of Reality.

Yet, the question remains to haunt us: What is the good of standing on the edge of time, if we have to give up the promise of eternity in return?

In the more traditional worlds, whether it be Hinduism, Buddhism or Christianity, the word "science" used in its Sanskrit and Latinate contexts had a far different meaning than it does in today's world of modern scientific achievements. This is no more apparent than the meaning of the word "science" within the Islamic context in which the pursuit of knowledge, whether it be earthly or otherworldly, was brought to a height never before seen in the history of the world during the so-called Golden Age that lasted roughly 8 centuries from the first century after the death of the Prophet in the latter part of the 8th century to the end of the Medieval Era, or the beginning of the Renaissance in roughly the 16th century. First of all, there was no distinctive word representing a unique and well defined concept of science as we have today with its aura of precision and technology, based on laws of mathematics and verified through reason and the scientific method.

The Arabic word for knowledge, *al-'ilm*, embraced a far broader concept that was based on the metaphysical and universal principles laid down within the verses of the Qur'an. The starting point of this knowledge, its primordial point as it were, has been clearly identified in Islam as *tawhid*, the principle of unity, that forms not only the pinnacle of all knowledge, but also the golden thread that sews together all the various elements of the creation and of life into the fabric of a singular totality. From the pinnacle of this starting point flows a structured hierarchy of knowledge–science if you will–that forms a grand procession of knowledge that leads into deeper and more formalized classifications of knowledge, together with the classification of the sciences, the levels of knowledge embedded within the verses of the Qur'an, the great chain of being that begins with God and passes through interconnecting links through angels, jinn, humans and lower forms of animals, and finally the varieties and levels of experience that represent the kind of knowledge we experience within life as truly human experience.

When the term science is invoked within the Islamic context, it is above all a traditional science or what can be called *sciencia sacra* (sacred science). It is traditional, and by correspondence sacred and universal, because it is based on principles that are unchanging and metaphysical, beyond the horizon of the physical world and reaching into the world of the Unseen (*'alam al-ghaib*) for their source and nourishment. The true origin of all knowledge, no matter what its level of manifestation, is both sacred and original, sacred because it reflects something infinitely more than itself that it only gradually discloses and manifests through a veil as it were, and original, not because it is first or new, but rather because it is a faithful image of the Origin and originates in the One Reality. "To Him is due the primal origin of the heavens and the earth." (6: 101) The point of departure of the traditional approach to understanding the true nature of the reality and the pursuit of knowledge is the same in all religious traditions, despite the wide diversity of the religious experience and the historical development of a variety of traditional civilizations. Knowledge, including scientific knowledge, is understood in the traditional context as proceeding from a prime cause or first origin. This first cause is identified as the Transcendent with regard to the unveiling of the creation and the Center with regard to its presence within existence.

Modern science, on the other hand, has its starting point in what amounts to a revolution in human consciousness, a revolution that is an abrupt turning away from the traditional perception of a transcending knowledge that finds its origin and source in the Divine Principle. This revolution of consciousness marks the revolt against Heaven and a turning inward toward man himself, not through the intelligence of his heart and the emotions of his higher sensibility, but through the purely human faculty of reason, together with a rigid, earth-bound logic, that combined with the input of the senses forms the *modus operandi* of the scientific method. This approach limits rather than transcends the human perspective by denying *a priori* the authentic sources of knowledge and rejecting the powers of the higher faculties such as intuition, and the spiritual instincts such as faith and spiritual sentiment. As a consequence, the conceptions of modern science, relying as they do on the external world of sense-data and sense-impression to establish what constitutes knowledge of the self and of reality, refers only to what is temporal and finite in the world, and reflects only the logical, mechanical, and "reasonable" criteria that conform to the five external senses and to human reason.

It is important that young Muslims understand the differences in meaning for these basic concepts such as "knowledge" and "science" that exist in counterpoint between the Islamic and modern scientific worldview. Modern Western science understands the world to be an independent reality unto itself in addition to being the only reality. That is why the scientific method of investigation relies so heavily, and indeed exclusively, on human reason and empirical sense experience as the sole verifying evidence of the true nature of reality. The parameters of the physical world, including space, time, matter, motion and energy, are all realities that are independent of all higher levels of being or knowledge and have nothing to do with the over-riding and omniscient power of a Supreme Being. As such, modern science is based on a number of assumptions about the nature of physical reality that are observable and verifiable. It is on the basis of these assumptions and the pursuit of the scientific method of observation that an understanding is finally arrived at regarding the true nature of reality.

The traditional sciences, on the other hand, operated within the framework of a traditional or sacred science that shaped not only the assumptions of Islamic scientists, but also provided the source material and principles that led to a complete understanding and philosophy of life. For example, through the pursuit of knowledge of the traditional sciences, the goal was never science in itself, nor was it the pursuit of a utilitarian knowledge that humanity could use only for its own benefit and control for its own questionable ends, without the guidance of

God and His metaphysical principles. The lower domains that traditional science investigated were significant precisely because they were able to relate knowledge of the lower domain of reality to the higher plane of existence. In this way, the knowledge of physics, chemistry, and astronomy was placed within a context that led far beyond the individual facts of those individual sciences. The knowledge of these individual sciences was actually formal and mathematical expressions of a linear, physical reality that belongs to a higher metaphysical order. The physical manifestations here on earth revealed through the various sciences were not physical veils that blocked out all knowledge of higher levels of experience, rather they were symbolic expressions here on earth for a higher reality that is revealed when we lift the veil that separates the human mind from the higher, unseen realities (*al-ghaib*).

Increasingly, it seems that we find ourselves in the uncharted territory of an exploratory and descriptive science, rather than the revealed and illuminating knowledge of the holy traditions, a knowledge that was the embodiment of a sacred science and a repository of meaning for the enigmatic mysteries of life. We roam today through the unknown territory of a frontier wilderness as wild and uncomprehending as anything encountered beyond the spiritual horizon of our time. Moreso now than ever before, there is a profound need for a comprehensive world-view concerning the nature of reality, such as Islam offers to the Muslim community, and there is a need for a perceptive approach to human origins and ends that can contextualize the identity of humanity within a framework of comprehensibility and true significance.

We have lost the knowledge of the Absolute, the Eternal and the Infinite. We have lost the traditional message that was implicit in the symbolic image of the horizon, a message that spoke of the duality of man and the world, in which reality itself was shattered into two parts, the one above, the other below, with the horizon as the seam of the world that symbolically united once again the reality of this world into the seamless whole that mirrored the Transcendent Reality. We have lost the symbolic messages of Nature in which every divinely-created thing within the natural order expressed the unity of the Transcendent Reality. We have lost the ability to express the sacred sentiments of an inner spirituality that was once the human expression of higher emotions that reflected the knowledge and presence of the Divine Being. As a consequence, we have lost the *barakah* or channels of blessing and grace that flow through the arteries of the universe as a perennial dispensation from the Divinity to humanity to preserve the image of the Way.

Modern science risks developing a crisis of identity that is as objective and real as the findings that scientists have genuinely uncovered and have value in their own right. Modern science and her faithful scientists proclaim as a matter of pride to be objective, rationalistic, secularist, and empirical to a measure; yet in order to fill the incredible chasm that exists between traditional and perennial wisdom with speculative theory and hypothesis, scientists are trying to assess the metaphysical and/or human significance of their findings without the blessing (*barakah*) and benefit of true metaphysics and its corresponding spirituality that can be found within the pages of universal revelation.

We have the legitimate right to ask, therefore, what we are dealing with: science, philosophy, or a philosophy of science when it comes to the pursuit of scientific knowledge. Can science live with the prospect of routinely denying the existence of a "sacred science" while attempting to draw conclusions that are solely within the domain of the sacred? Can science pursue the discovery of facts and mathematical formulas without permitting itself the luxury of interpreting this knowledge within a cosmic framework of sacred philosophy and metaphysics, the very realm of which modern science fundamental denies? What does modern science want to achieve? What is its purpose and goal within its self-proclaimed random, purposeless and chance environment, a point of principle that scientists so meticulously hold fast to like some kind of lifeline? Indeed, how does modern science identify itself, what does it stand for, and what is its mandate for a civilization that will share its fate?

The traditional sciences were never considered purely utilitarian in the modern sense, and "sacred science" was never a science purely for the sake of science. Traditional science always maintained a window to eternity. Through the use of his faculty of reason alone and without the aid of his spiritual intelligence and his sacred intuition of things, which in the traditional perspective are actually faculties of objectification of the reality, modern man relies solely on the domain of his senses and his mind, thus declaring the primacy of discursive thought and sheer intellectual prowess over spiritual intuition. Through a science of his own creation, modern man attempts to face nature directly, without any intermediaries or veils such as symbols or revelation, that were the traditional go-betweens of man and the super-natural.

When you withdraw the knowledge and the illumination of the Divine Principles from the intellect, the intelligence, and the faculty of reason, what remains is a human reason that must turn for information to the phenomenal world in which it will be preconditioned by its own accepted suppositions and assumptions. In its analysis and classification, it will take account only of those aspects that can be verified through some kind of measurable frame of reference. Thus, a purely scientific reason cannot avoid imposing its own limitations on the analysis and conclusions it arrives at. It is small wonder that the word knowledge, as it is now understood, consists mainly of human characteristics and is limited by the secular assumptions it has adopted. It is but a pale reflection of the "sacred science" and "illuminative knowledge" found within the traditional literature and the universal knowledge found within revelation. Without the benefit of this sacred and illuminative knowledge, we find ourselves back once again at our starting point in rationalism and empiricism, in the circulatory and peripatetic world of mind and matter without the vision of an alternative reality to substantiate the physical world within its mystic embrace.

In the pursuit of a scientific knowledge in the warp and weft of the fabric of a physical knowledge, modern science has settled for the external appearance of things and for their surface qualities. It has limited its scope to the rationally observable and purely quantitative aspects of what is actually a dynamic and living reality. It has adopted an exclusive view of the world that takes into account merely natural causes and ignores all supra-formal and spiritual causes that actually form the essence of all natural manifestations and provide their qualitative aspect. What things are in themselves, in their living reality, and what they reflect on a higher level of reality, is not the purview of the scientific inquiry.

In the pursuit of a purely human and terrestrial knowledge, without the aid of Heaven and without the guiding influence of the Supreme Intelligence, those who embrace the scientific endeavor and uphold its limited worldview have lost the human ability to recognize the truth when it presents itself. They have forfeited the right to perceive a knowledge that can be understood as a truth, and they have lost the ability to incorporate that knowledge into their lives as wisdom. Let us now turn to the Qur'an to investigate and briefly summarize what it offers in terms of a scientific knowledge that transcends the limitations of "this world".

4.2 The Qur'an and Science

The Qur'an not only reminds us of the knowledge of first principles and thus represents a knowledge of a sacred science, it also reminds us again and again that we are living in a sacred universe and that we ourselves are sacred individuals with human faculties such as intuition, intelligence and reason that open us to the sacred quality in life and offers us a sense of the sacred inspired by the holy presence of every created thing. One of the truths that shines clearly through the verses of the Qur'an is that both the world we live in and the universe that surrounds us are not just facts and objects to be discovered by modern scientific inquiry; but rather are symbols and mirrors of a greater and more universal truth that the Qur'an repeatedly identifies as the principle of unity (*al-tawhid*) and the oneness of Allah's omni-presence. Everything in the universe reflects and points toward this principle of unity to the extent that "Wherever you turn, there is the Face of God." It is in every aspect of the creation that you will find the Face of God who originated every created thing "and to Him will you return."

Because of the unique status of the Qur'an as a revelation and the spoken words of God that are still preserved, as delivered, down into the modern era, the very words and sounds of the Qur'an have inspired an elaborate system of esoteric sciences connected with the Arabic language and alphabet. As such, Arabic is considered a sacred language and every letter of the alphabet has symbolic value. According to Islam, there is an archetypal Qur'an that is unwritten and uncreated, called the 'cosmic Qur'an', in Arabic *al-Qurān al-Takwīnī*, and the Holy Book that was delivered to the Prophet Muhammad (PBUH), by the Archangel Gabriel, called in Arabic *al-Qurān al-Tadwīnī*. The cosmos itself is referred to in Arabic as the cosmic Qur'an or the book of existence,[43] representing a vast book in complement to the Islamic book of revelation, and like the revealed scripture, it also contains signs and symbols, verses (*ayat*) if you will, that have the power to reveal as much as they conceal and possess levels of meaning that can serve the needs of every mentality and that ultimately lead toward a complete understanding of the true nature of reality. The traditional sciences that developed over time were concerned with both the sounds and the alphabet of Arabic because they were virtually the keys, not only for understanding the verses of the Holy Book, but also the meaning and significance of the cosmos itself.

Therefore, the *ayat* manifest themselves within the Holy Book, within the macrocosmic universe, and within the soul of man, in other words "on the distant horizon and within their own selves." (41:53) "The Qur'an and the great phenomena of nature are twin manifestations of the divine act of Self-revelation. For Islam, the natural world in its totality is a vast fabric into which the 'signs' of the Creator are woven."[44] Man can realize his own being as a sign of God, the cosmos as a grand theophany and mirror of the Divine Qualities and Attributes, and the revealed book that contains all the verses and thus all the knowledge that a human being needs to know in order to come to terms with him/herself and the universe as the *vestigia Dei*, according to Christian terminology or *ayat Allah*, according to Islamic terminology. Each element has its own form of metaphysics and its own mode of prayer, humanity for living the human narrative, the cosmos by being the sanctuary and theater wherein the Divinity can become manifest, and revelation by recreating for humanity aspects of the mind of God through words.

The traditional world of religion, and the genuine expression of a human spirituality always associated with that world, lays a foundation of faith on the principles of knowledge whose origin and source take root in a divine revelation that originates within the all-encompassing knowledge of a Supreme Being Who is the First Cause, the Final End, the Absolute and the One.[45] This knowledge forms the parameters, the substance, and the essence of a knowledge that is

---

[43] The 8th/14th century Sufi 'Aziz al-Din Nasafi has written the following concerning the book of nature: "Each day destiny and the passage of time set this book before you, *sura* for *sura*, verse for verse, letter for letter, and read it to you . . . like one who sets a real book before you and reads it to you line for line, letter for letter, that you may learn the content of these lines and their letters." Quoted in *Islamic Spirituality: Foundations*, Seyyed Hossein Nasr (ed.), New York: Crossroad, 1987, p. 355.

[44] Charles Le Gai Eaton, *Islam and the Destiny of Man*, Albany, NY: SUNY Press, 1985, p. 87.

[45] The Qur'an officially identifies 99 qualifying Names of God in addition to the reference of other attributes that are implicit in the Qur'anic text. Needless to say, these "Names" aid considerably the human mentality in coming to terms with the great unknown and unknowable quality – the factor of mystery – that hovers perennially around the idea of God.

identified as the Truth and that represents the true nature of the Reality. It is the vision of the Absolute from the perspective of the Absolute; a Self-Disclosure from God to man that recalls the primordial revelation[46] and recreates knowledge from the ultimate source. Revelation views the physical world as the consequence of actions initiated by the Creator and it offers the study of Nature as a virtual science of signs and symbols that reflect the order, pattern and levels of higher reality that ultimately arrive at *the Throne* (*al-arsh*) of the Supreme Being. It understands human beings to be thinking beings made in the image of the Divine Being, with a consciousness that both reflects the supreme consciousness and connects with this higher order of Reality. Thus, the Truth has been made manifest to the human mentality in an absolute and unequivocal manner. Because of free will, we are at liberty to accept, turn to and surrender our minds and hearts to this Supreme Intelligence and this Absolute Being. Human intelligence, supported by both intellect and reason, forms its own conclusion and the expression of one's life becomes sufficient evidence of the validity of any choice.

Today's emphasis on human reason has overshadowed the fact that humanity enjoys another faculty that makes possible the reception of a knowledge "from above", namely the faculty of the intellect, which according to the traditional perspective is the faculty of direct perception and the human repository of the divine knowledge. Needless to say, modern science refuses to recognize the intellect of man as the receiving faculty of the essential knowledge of God and the filter through which people can perceive the higher truths directly as it were, without any intermediary or veil. The human intellect knows in a direct manner, in principle and with an irrefutable certainty, the reality of God and the truths that govern the universe. It is a faculty of perception capable of receiving and reflecting the objective and raw knowledge of the Intellect. The uncreated Qur'an–the Logos–is the Divine Intellect and this is what the religion means when it refers to the Mind of God being made manifest in the form of revelation, since the Divine Mind or Intellect has become crystalized in the form of an earthly revelation and provides to the subjective, human intellect the objective knowledge it instinctively yearns for.

According to a Holy Tradition,[47] God wrote with a Mystic Pen that symbolizes the Universal Intellect, the inner reality of all things preserved on the Guarded Tablet before the creation of the world. "The first of the things Allah created is the Pen (*Qalam*) which He created of Light (*Nur*), and which is made of white pearl; its length is equal to the distance between the sky and the earth.

---

[46] The typical point of origin of any well-developed traditional culture was an external revelation, such as Moses for Judaism, Lao-Tzu for Taoism, the Buddha for Buddhism, Jesus for Christianity. Each of these revelations, which contained multivalent meanings *ab initio*, both remembered the Primordial Tradition in its essential form and resulted in creating an established "religion".

[47] Another tradition, reported by Ibn Abbas, says that "Allah created the Pen before He created the Creation." Also, "the Pen burst open and the Ink flows from it until the Day of the Resurrection."

Then He created the Tablet (*Lawh*, or *Lawh al-mahfuz*, the 'guarded tablet'), and it is made of white pearl and its surfaces are of red rubies; its length is equal to the distance between the sky and the earth and its width stretches from the East to the West." The Supreme Pen (*al-Qalam al-a'la*) has traditionally been identified with the Universal Intellect, while the ink is the reflection of All-Possibility and results in the possibility of the manifestation of the creation, recalling the Qur'anic verse: And "if all the trees on earth were pens and the sea–with seven seas added–[were ink] yet the words of Allah could not be exhausted." (31: 27) The Pen also symbolizes the Word, the Logos, in addition to the Universal Intellect, while the Tablet recalls the Universal Substance, so that it can be said that all things are created by the Word. These are the two instruments– symbolically speaking–that bring about and perpetuate the miracle of universal manifestation.

Under the circumstances of the descent of the revelation and the entire context in which the Holy Book of Islam is enwrapped, it is understandable that the validity and veracity of the Qur'an is never questioned by the Muslim Ummah. With the descent of the Qur'an, the religion of Islam came into being and with the descent of the final verse of the revelation, the religion itself was brought to completion and perfection as the Word of God on earth for the benefit and guidance of humanity. As such, it is taken for granted that the knowledge and more specifically the well specified facts and data contained with the Noble Book is accurate in every sense and does not come into conflict with emerging scientific data. While much of the Qur'an deals with the broader, more universal themes relating to the cosmos and the sacred histories and ethical questions relating to the human soul, there are many subjects in the Qur'an of a scientific nature–the word scientific in this context referring to the modern understanding as a literal and evidenced fact of nature–that are of great interest to modern science.[48] In fact, none of the scientific facts referred to in the Qur'an can be contested within the modern scientific framework.

In addition to the grand cosmic questions that affect the soul of man, the Qur'an also makes repeated reference to natural phenomena on earth and within the universe. It will not be possible to give an extensive study of the verses that make reference to the phenomena of Nature regarding the origin of the universe, of life, or man, etc. For our limited purposes here, it will be enough to make the point that references to specific scientific data in the Qur'an do not contradict existing, known scientific facts that have been clearly proven beyond a shadow of a doubt. Let's look at a case in point. The Qur'an, like the Bible, says that "Your Lord is God Who created the heavens and the earth in six days." (54:7) Now the

---

[48] It needs to be clearly footnoted that we are referring here to absolute, fully verified facts that cannot be questioned. This rules out any number of explanatory working theories that may conflict with the Qur'anic account, such as the (in)famous theory of evolution, that are indeed in direct conflict with both the letter and the spirit of the Qur'anic verses.

question is less about the meaning of day and more about the meaning of the word in the original Arabic. The Arabic *yawm* and the plural *ayam* have the broader symbolic meaning of a (long) period of time in addition to the literal 24-hour concept that we swear by in today's world. To further shed light on the subject of time, there are a number of verses in the Qur'an that actually emphasize the transient and relative nature of time. First: "in a period of time (*yawm*) whereof the measure is a thousand years of your reckoning (32:5)," and second: "in a period of time whereof the measure is 50,000 years." (74:4) The clear message here is that time is relative, and not just a matter of "your reckoning". To further complicate the matter, the word day in Arabic could also be understood to mean "events". Indeed, the concept that Allah created the universe "in six days" is simply not understood on its literal level by anyone, except perhaps Western scientists who take the verse literally to mean "six days" as a means of ridiculing the true symbolic significance of the Biblical and Qur'anic verses.

In addition to multiple verses that qualify the nature of the creation and how it was created, verses on astronomy also feature highly in the Qur'an; the Qur'an is full of reflections on the Heavens. There are over 50 verses of the Qur'an that provide information of one sort or another on astronomy. Some examples are as follows:

Seven Heavens

"Say: Who is Lord of the seven heavens and Lord of the tremendous throne?" (23:86)

The Heavens Subjected to Divine Order

"The Sun and moon (are subjected) to calculations." (55:5)

"(God) appointed the night for rest and the sun and the moon for reckoning." (6:96)

For you (God) subjected the sun and the moon, both diligently pursuing their courses." (14:33)

"And for the moon We have appointed mansions till she returns like an old shriveled palm branch." (36:39)

The Nature of the Heavenly Bodies

"Blessed is He One Who placed the constellations in heaven and placed therein a lamp and a moon giving light." (26:61)

"Did you see how God created seven heavens one above another and made the moon a light therein and made the sun a lamp?" (71:15-16)

"We have built above you seven strong (heavens) and placed a blazing lamp."[49] (78:12)

---

[49] The moon is defined as a body that gives light (*munir* from the same root as *nur* or light). The sun, however, is compared to a torch (*siraj*) and a blazing lamp (*wahhāj*).

The Planets
"We have indeed adorned the lowest heaven with an ornament, the planets." (37:6)

The Orbits of the Sun and Moon
"(God is) the One Who created the night, the day, the sun and the moon. Each one is traveling in an orbit with its own motion." (21:33)
"The sun must not catch up the moon,[50] nor does the night outstrip the day. Each one is traveling in an orbit with its own motion." (36:40)

The Evolution of the Heavens
A number of Qur'anic verses (13:2; 31:29; 35:13; 39:5) state that: "God subjected the sun and the moon: each one runs its course to an appointed term."
"The Sun runs its course to a settled place. This is the decree of the All Mighty, Full of Knowledge." (36:38)[51]

The Expanding Universe
"The heavens, We have built it with power. Verily, We are expanding it." (41:47)[52]

Once again, it is not possible within this context to provide a comprehensive overview to the number of subjects and verses that contain interesting scientific information that was not only well ahead of its time, but also has later been given evidence and affirmed by modern science. For our limited purposes here within this context, and to make the point that there is a close correlation between certain scientific facts laid out in the Qur'an that do not contradict the facts and discoveries of modern science, we will provide samples of verses in the Qur'an with interesting scientific data concerning the earth, the origin of life and the reproduction of the human being.

The Earth
Verses containing general statements

---

[50] Modern science has finally worked out the details of the sun's orbit around the center of its own galaxy. To complete the revolution on its own axis, the galaxy and the Sun take roughly 250 million years. The Sun travels at roughly 150 miles per second in the completion of this orbit. As with many other issues relating religion and science, the devil is in the details; but God lies within the first principles!

[51] Modern science verifies that the sun has "an appointed time" and will arrive at a final destination, called the Solar Apex. The solar system is evolving in space towards a point situated in the Constellation of Hercules (*alpha lyrae*) whose exact location is firmly established. The sun is moving at a speed in the region of 12 miles per second.

[52] Needless to say, the expanding universe is the most imposing discovery of modern science.

"Behold, In the creation of the heavens and the earth, in the disparity of night and day, in the ship which runs upon the sea for the profit of mankind, in the water which God sent down from the sky thereby reviving the earth after its death, in the beasts of all kinds He scatters therein, in the change of the winds and the subjected clouds between the sky and earth, Here are Signs for people who are wise." (2:164)

"The earth, We spread it out and set thereon mountains standing firm. We caused all kinds of things to grow therein in due balance. Therein We have provided you and those you do not supply with means of subsistence and there is not a thing but its stores are with Us. We do not send it down save in appointed measure." (15:19-21)

The water cycle and the seas

"We sent down water from the sky in measure and lodged it in the ground." (23:18)

"We sent forth the winds that fecundate. We caused the water to descend from the sky. We provided you with the water; you could not be the guardians of its reserves." (15:22)

"God is the One Who sends forth the winds which raised up the clouds. We drive them to a dead land. Therewith We revive the ground after its death. So will be the Resurrection." 35:9)

The seas

"(God) is the One Who subjected the sea, so that you eat fresh meat from it and you extract from it ornaments which you wear. Thou seest the ships plowing the waves, so that you seek of His Bounty." (16:14)

His are the ships erected upon the sea like tokens." (55:24)

"(God) is the One Who has let free the two seas, one is agreeable and sweet, the other salty and bitter. He placed a barrier between them, a partition that it is forbidden to pass." (25:53)[53]

The formation of the Earth's relief

"For you God made the earth a carpet so that you travel along its roads and the paths of valleys." (71:19-20)

"The mountains, how they have been pitched (like a tent). The Earth how it was made even." (88:19-20)

"Have We not made the earth an expanse and the mountains stakes." (78:6-7)

The earth's atmosphere

"Those whom God wills to guide, He opens their breast to Islam. Those

---

[53] This phenomenon is well known and often seen whereby the immediate mixing of salty seawater and fresh river water does not occur.

whom He wills lose their way. He makes their breast narrow and constricted, as if they were climbing in the sky." (125:6)[54]

Electricity in the atmosphere
"Hast thou not seen that God makes the clouds move gently, then joins them together, then makes them a heap. And thou seest raindrops issuing from within it. He sends down from the sky mountains of hail, He strikes therewith whom He wills and He turns it away from whom He wills. The flashing of its lightning almost snatches away the sight." (24:43)[55]

The Origin of Life
"Do not the Unbelievers see that the heavens and the earth were joined together, then We clove them sunder and We got every living thing out of the water. They then do not believe?" (21:30)[56]
"God created every animal from water." (24:46)
"There is no animal on earth, no bird which flies on wings, that (does not belong to) communities like you. We have not neglected anything in the Book." (6:38)[57]
"Have they not looked at the girds above them spreading their wings out and folding them? None can hold them up (in his power) except the Beneficent." (67:19)[58]

Human Reproduction
Fertilization is performed by a small volume of liquid[59]
"Was (man) not a small quantity of sperm which has been poured out?" (73:37)
"Then We placed (man) as a small quantity (of sperm) in a safe lodging

---

[54] Reference here is made to the levels of altitude and oxygen in the earth's atmosphere.

[55] Here we have the correlation between the formation of heavy rain clouds or clouds containing hail and the occurrence of lightning. The connection between the two phenomena is verified by present-day knowledge of electricity in the atmosphere.

[56] Scientific data tell us that life in fact is of aquatic origin and water is the major component of all living cells. Without water, life is not possible.

[57] Animal behavior has been closely investigated in recent times, with the result that genuine animal communities have been shown to exist. The most studied and best known cases are of bees and ants.

[58] Modern data shows the degree of perfection in the migratory movement of certain species. Only a migratory program in the genetic code of these birds could account for the extremely long and complicated journeys which very young birds make, without any prior experience or guide, to accomplish this feat. There is the well-known case of the "mutton-bird" that lives in the Pacific, with its journey of over 15,500 miles in the shape of a figure 8. They are most definitely programmed, but who is the Programmer?

[59] Repeated 11 times throughout the Qur'an.

firmly established." 23:13)

The implementation of the egg
"We cause whom We will to rest in the womb for an appointed term." (22:5)
"We have fashioned the small quantity (of sperm) into something that clings." 23:14)

Evolution of the Embryo inside the Uterus
"We fashioned the thing which clings into a chewed lump of flesh and We fashioned the chewed flesh into bones and We clothed the bones with intact flesh." 23:14)
"And (God) made of him a pair, the male and female." (75:39)
"God created you from dust, then from a sperm-drop, then He made you pairs (male and female)." (35:11)

These examples form only a very brief selected summary of the many points of interest that were embedded within the Qur'an in the 8th century of this era, data that were later to become genuine scientific facts verified during the era of modern science. From the creation of the universe, the constitution of the universe, the nature of the earth and its atmosphere, the habits and communities of animals and finally the miracle of the inception and birth of the human being, all of these examples show the modern world that the verses of the Qur'an contain data and points of interest that are not only scientific in nature according to the modern use of the term, but that actually pre-dated their discovery in time through the development of the individual sciences. More than a thousand years before the current era of science and technology, the early Muslims had a knowledge contained within the Qur'an that provided statements that express simple truths of an essential importance to a fuller understanding of humans and the universe they inhabit, information that it took many centuries to discover.

4.3 Classification of Knowledge in Islam

The point of view of the Islamic sciences must always be understood as being independent and clearly distinctive from the framework of Western science that maintains essentially secular philosophic approaches to an understanding of the idea of science and its broader questions. Granted, Islamic science was influenced initially by its predecessors of the sciences of antiquity, such as were found in Mesopotamia, Greece, Egypt, India, and China. In some ways, the Islamic sciences are a continuation of the groundwork of those sciences together with its own special Islamic flavor and coloration, aided as it was by the knowledge that came with the Qur'anic revelation. The Islamic sciences are a completely independent way of studying the phenomena of nature, the relationships between minerals and plants and animals, the meaning of the changes and developments that we observe within nature, and finally nature's true significance and final goal as a sacred sign of a higher Reality. As such, it is important to understand the Islamic sciences, not just from the point of view of their historical development in time, but as they are set within the totality of the Islamic spiritual, intellectual and cultural setting.

As bridge between the ancient scientific approaches of the Athens and Alexandria schools of thought and the modern scientific approaches to the investigation of natural phenomena, the Islamic sciences distinguished themselves in two incredible ways. Firstly, they paved the way for the new methods of investigation, that of experiment, observation, measurement and the reliance on and development of mathematics. The ancient world was essentially pre-scientific as we know it. The astronomy and mathematics of the Greeks were more general and theoretical, but the patient ways of investigation, the accumulation of positive knowledge, the minute methods of science, with its detailed observation and experimental inquiry, were actually alien to the Greek mentality. What we now call science arose in Europe in the 1600s as a result of a new spirit of inquiry and new methods of investigation that were actually introduced into the European world by the Arabs.

Secondly, what genuinely distinguishes the Islamic sciences from the rest of either ancient or modern science is its reliance on the concept of the hierarchy of knowledge that one finds clearly within the traditional Islamic framework. Within the Islamic intellectual and spiritual tradition, there were hierarchies or levels of knowledge and experience not only within the domain of religious faith and spirituality, but also within the domain of knowledge and all that it contains. Just as there is clearly identified levels of faith expressed within the Qur'an, so also there are levels of knowledge that are reflected within the natural world of phenomena, from the astronomical world of the cosmic universe to the quantum world of quarks and quasars, levels and planes of existence that are brought together within the Islamic framework by the spirit of *tawhid* or unity that lies at the heart of the Islamic universe. The search and discovery of the key relationships between the various disciplines within the fields of the individual sciences was the goal of the leading Islamic intellectual and scientific figures of their time, from philosophers and historians to Sufi mystics. The principle of unity always lies at the heart of the Islamic scientific endeavor and this is what distinguishes the Islamic scientific and intellectual tradition.

The great chain or hierarchy of being begins first and foremost, of course, with Allah as the Supreme Being. He is the First (*al-Awal*) and the Last (*al-Akhir*) and "nothing compares to Him" as the Absolute Reality. Then there are the angelic orders, the intermediate imaginal world (the *ālam al-khayāl*), then the world of the *jinn*, the world of humanity and finally the world of the natural order of nature. The Qur'an continually refers to these levels of realities, and every Muslim takes this knowledge of levels of being and experience for granted as "second nature" to them as manifestations of the essential and absolute Reality of the Supreme Principle of Unity at the summit and pinnacle of all knowledge.

The universe itself is comprised of "seven heavens" and the revelation continually refers to the "heavens and the earth and what lies between".

In addition, there is a hierarchy within the human being representing levels of knowing and perception. The human being is not just the mind that processes knowledge and information as it comes to it; but rather humans enjoy a number of faculties that allow them to process a wide variety of knowledge in various ways, through the senses of course, but also through the faculty of the intellect that perceives God directly and unconditionally, through human reason that can be an instrument of the principle of unity as well as a reflection of the intellect, through the imagination and the higher emotions and through the heart which in Islam is actually the "seat" of the intelligence and what is often referred to in the Qur'an as the "eye of the heart" or the *ayn al-kalb*. In this way, the objective knowledge contained within the Qur'an and the subjective processes of knowing and perception with humanity come together into a unique harmony that once again reflects the principle of unity at work within the universe in which the modes of knowledge effectively interact with the modes of knowing.

Needless to say, this concept of the hierarchy of knowledge and levels of knowing and perception within humanity represents a unique philosophical approach to the classification of knowledge within the sciences, whether they be modern, traditional or ancient, to reach an understanding of the true nature of reality. It creates a unique and distinctively Islamic approach to the philosophy of science and clearly identifies the background and filter through which the natural sciences should be studied, a background that puts the natural and physical world within a greater context beyond the purely horizontal level of existence and a filter that fuses the physical creation with the Spirit of God. The philosophical approach of the modern sciences does not take into account either the great chain of being or the classification of knowledge, according to hierarchical manifestations of existence or levels of the creation. The Islamic perspective views as incredible the inability of modern science to put into perspective the knowledge of God, the angels, devils, and multiple forms of the animal kingdom, not to mention the kingdom of humankind, or even more incredibly, the knowledge that is based on the five senses and the faculty of reason in comparison with the knowledge directly derived from the faculty of the intellect and the "eye" of heart-knowledge.

Now, with regard to the classification of knowledge within the individual sciences, the natural sciences in the Islamic perspective are closely bound to the metaphysical, religious, and philosophical ideas that govern the entire Islamic civilization based as such on the revelations within the Holy Qur'an. What is at stake here is less the facts themselves that are uncovered through investigation and experiment, facts that may be based on certain natural laws together with the formulations of mathematics that are irrefutable, and more about how these facts are interpreted and into what philosophical context they are placed and understood. It is one thing to know that something is true and quite another to give meaning and significance to those facts and their truth that go beyond their surface meaning. Consequently, the knowledge uncovered within the fully comprehensive Islamic vision of the universe, indeed the cosmos itself, provides not only a key to a true understanding of the individual sciences, but also the foundation and background to the study of all natural phenomena. To this extent, there is nothing stopping the Muslims from taking the discoveries and irrefutable facts of modern science and placing them within the context of the traditional Islamic vision of the world with its hierarchical approach to the classification of knowledge, so long as it conforms to the spirit of the revelation and the traditional Islamic worldview based on that revelation.

Muslims living in earlier centuries used to live in their traditional culture and civilization without being overly concerned with the implications and significance of the cosmological sciences; in other words, they could get to Heaven without knowledge of mathematics, astronomy and the other individual sciences. In today's highly-strung world, however, young people and students of Islam are confronted with the effervescent revelations of modern science and its dogmatic approaches to the understanding of the natural order of reality, which set forth a secular worldview and, in effect, represent a totally different perception of the world than what people in the traditional world understood. As such, young Muslims today need to have a better grounding into the true nature of the Islamic sciences, what makes them Islamic as such, and what forms the basis of the philosophy of approach to the study of these sciences. They need to be aware of the implicit classifications within the framework of the grand scheme of knowledge that embraces the entire cosmos and not just the physical level of the creation as they are led to believe from the implications of the modern scientific worldview. Modern Muslims today must come to terms with the knowledge that they are confronted with from the modern natural sciences and they must place that knowledge within a credible frame of reference within their belief system and worldview that makes sense to them and does not go against the fundamental principles of Islam; otherwise they run the risk of having the very foundation of their way of life (*din*) irrevocably compromised.

After the descent of the revelation in the form of the Qur'an and the completion of the ministry of the Prophet with his death, the first several centuries of the development of Islam as a growing religious phenomenon were marked by the intensity of the religious and spiritual forces of the religion itself as a framework of a higher order of experience, with special focus on the solidification of the *hadith*, on Arabic and Qur'anic grammar, and on sacred history. The second century then witnessed the sorting out of political conflicts together with the development of the schools of law and theology. During the 3rd century, the Islamic spirit began to crystallize into its permanent form, through the formation of the schools of law and the Sufi brotherhoods. The 4th and 5th (10th and 11th centuries AD) centuries witnessed the formation of the Islamic arts and sciences, and the beginning of the period in which the basis of the Islamic sciences was laid down as foundation to the Islamic understanding of knowledge. The fourth and fifth centuries are often referred to as the "Golden Age" of Islamic culture, when literature and the sciences expanded in many different directions, and there was a corresponding economic prosperity. In the sixth century, the political climate shifted away from this kind of intellectual development, and with the Mongol invasions of the seventh century, there began a general intellectual and religious decline. The Golden Age of the Islamic intellectual and scientific tradition became a part of the firmament within the progress of Islamic history, an age that was never to return.

What makes the Islamic sciences Islamic is not the fact that they were pursued and cultivated by Muslim scientists; they are Islamic because the pursuit of these sciences is based on the principles of Islam and the entire spiritual, cosmological and metaphysical framework revealed by God and set forth in the Qur'anic revelation. The original frame of reference is always God and His handiwork and not humanity and the desire of people to control the forces of the natural order. Within the Islamic sciences, the end of a particular science lies outside the immediate area of that science; in other words, the individual sciences are a means to an end, but do not define the end in and of itself, which within the Islamic perspective is the understanding of the true nature of reality as created and defined (and sustained) by God Almighty. The goal of the Islamic sciences, and its defining quality, is always the interrelatedness of all things that lie at the heart of Islam, namely the doctrine of unity (*tawhid*).

Islamic science lays its roots in the concept of a Supreme Being who has created the natural universe, a science that reflects a systematic knowledge of nature in light of the principle of the Supreme Being, a science that classifies knowledge according to a grand plan of hierarchies and levels that reflect the levels of experience that extend beyond the physical world, and finally a science that understands all phenomena found within nature to be a sign and symbol of a higher reality that actually sing the praises of the one God and the principle of unity that He represents. Muslim scientists had the most rigorous standards of critical thought, while at the same time, they adhered closely to the principles they firmly believed in, thus maintaining their integrity as well as their vision of purpose. Let us now turn to a brief summative selection as a representative sample of those Islamic scientists who distinguished themselves during the Golden Age of Islam.

4.4 Islamic Scholars in History

From a very early period of the Islamic era, starting in the 8th century AD, successive Islamic scholars and intellectuals representing the Islamic intellectual tradition have devoted a considerable deal of their intellectual talents and particular genius to the classification of knowledge within the Islamic framework, together with an extensive description and development of the individual sciences. Many of these efforts have proved to be as influential as they were original at the time of their inception. The fundamental objective of all their efforts was to preserve the hierarchy of the sciences, together with the description of the scope of each of the sciences, within the grand scheme of knowledge based on the Islamic worldview as set forth in the Qur'an. They understood that this goal could be achieved through the classification of knowledge within the sciences.

What follows is a focused summary of the efforts and achievements of the Islamic scholars and thinkers who emerged out of the development of the Islamic sciences during the so-called Golden Age of Islamic science. For our limited purposes here, we present merely a selection–a taste if you will–of their achievement and not in any way an exhaustive study. The identification and summative understanding of their works and achievements will help put into perspective the true nature of the accomplishments these people achieved in furthering the pursuit of knowledge through both the theoretical and applied sciences. Their order of appearance is a chronological sequence as they appeared down through history.

Jabir ibn Hayyan (c. 103/721–c. 200/815)

Jabir is credited with being the founder of Islamic alchemy. He became known as an alchemist at the court of the well-known historical figure Hārūn al-Rashīd, and was especially associated with the viziers of the Abbasid Empire. He is credited with having written up to 3,000 short treatises on a broad variety of subjects. His important works include *The Hundred and Twelve Books, The Seventy Books*, and *The Books of the Balance* which outline the famous theory of the balance underlying the whole of his exposition of alchemy. He also wrote on logic, philosophy, medicine, the occult sciences, physics, and nearly every other domain of knowledge. There seems to have been no subject that escaped his profound interest and he wrote with fluency on a number of topics under the scrutiny of his investigative and inquiring mind.

Abu Yusuf Ya'qub ibn Ishaq al-Kindi (c. 185/801–c. 260/873)

Al-Kindi was the first of the Muslim philosopher-scientists. With an encyclopedic interest in the pursuit of knowledge, he wrote about 270 treatises in logic, philosophy, physics, and all branches of mathematics, as well as music, medicine and natural history. He was the founder of the Islamic peripatetic school of philosophy and was highly respected in the medieval and renaissance West. His philosophic influence was later to be seen directly in the writing of al-Farabi In the field of mathematics, al-Kindi played an important role in introducing Indian numerals to the Islamic and Christian world. He was a pioneer in cryptology, and devised several new methods of breaking ciphers. Using his mathematical and medical expertise, he was able to develop a scale that would allow doctors to quantify the potency of their medications. He also first experimented with music therapy. The central theme underpinning al-Kindi's philosophical writings is the compatibility between philosophy and other "orthodox" Islamic sciences, particularly theology. Many of his works deal with subjects that theology could have a profound influence upon. These include the nature of God, the soul, and prophetic knowledge that descend to earth through revelation. Despite the important role he played in making philosophy accessible to Muslim intellectuals, his own philosophical output was largely overshadowed by that of al-Farabi and very few of his texts are available for modern scholars to examine. Despite this, he is still considered to be one of the greatest philosophers of Arab descent, and for this reason is known simply as "The Arab Philosopher".

Abu Nasr al-Farabi (c. 258/870–c. 339/950)

Al-Farabi was one of the greatest scientists and philosophers of Persia and the Islamic world of his time. He was noted as a cosmologist, logician, musician, psychologist, and sociologist. He was the first person in Islam to completely classify the sciences and to firmly establish each branch of learning. He was often called the "Second Teacher," the first having been Aristotle who accomplished the same task in earlier times and set the precedent for the Muslim philosophers that followed him. He wrote over 70 works, half of them were devoted to logic and much of what he wrote was a rich commentary on Aristotle. One of his most notable works is *al-Madinah al-Fadila* where he wrote about an ideal state, the classic theme also found in Plato's *Republic*. He wrote works on physics, mathematics, ethics and political philosophy. He was a practicing Sufi and the spirit of Sufism runs through all of his works. Interestingly enough, he was also one of the foremost medieval theoreticians of music and some of his musical works have survived in the Sufi brotherhoods in Turkey until modern times. In physics, he was known for his investigations into the nature of the existence of the void. In psychology, al-Farabi's *Social Psychology* and *Model City* were the first treatises to deal with social psychology. He stated that "an isolated individual could not achieve all the perfections by himself, without the aid of other individuals." He wrote that it is the "innate disposition of every man to join another human being or other men in the labor he ought to perform." He concluded that in order to "achieve what he can of that perfection, every man needs to stay in the neighborhood of others and associate with them." We see here the seeds of an Islamic sociology as a precursor of what would later follow in terms of the understanding of the Islamic *ummah* as a collective, unifying force among the faithful.

Abu 'Ali al-Husain ibn Sina (c. 370/980–c. 428/1037)

Ibn Sina was also an astronomer, chemist, *hafiz* of the Qur'an (reciter from memory), logician, mathematician, poet, psychologist, physicist, scientist, soldier, statesman, and theologian. He wrote almost 450 treatises on a wide range of subjects, of which around 240 have survived. In particular, 150 of his surviving treatises concentrate on philosophy and 40 of them concentrate on medicine. His most famous works are *The Book of Healing*, a vast philosophical and scientific encyclopedia, and *The Canon of Medicine*, which was a standard medical text at many Islamic and European universities until the early 19th century. Ibn Sīnā developed a medical system that combined his own personal experience with that of Islamic medicine, the medical system of the Greek physician Galen, Aristotelian metaphysics, and ancient Persian, Mesopotamian and Indian medicine.

Ibn Sina is regarded as a father of early modern medicine, particularly for his introduction of systematic experimentation and quantification into the study of physiology, his discovery of the contagious nature of infectious diseases, the introduction of quarantine to limit the spread of contagious diseases, the introduction of experimental medicine, clinical trials, and the importance of dietetics and the influence of climate and environment on health. He is also considered the father of the fundamental concept of momentum in physics, and regarded as a pioneer of aromatherapy. George Sarton, referred to as the "father of the history of science", wrote in his *Introduction to the History of Science*: "One of the most famous exponents of Muslim universalism and an eminent figure in Islamic learning was Ibn Sina, known in the West as Avicenna. For a thousand years, he has retained his original renown as one of the greatest thinkers and medical scholars in history. His most important medical works are the *Canon* and a treatise on cardiac drugs. The *Qanun fi-l-Tibb* is an immense encyclopedia of medicine. It contains some of the most enlightening thoughts on a broad range of subjects, including mention of diseases of a contagious nature, a careful description of skin troubles and an account of nervous ailments.

Abu Raihan al-Biruni (c. 362/973–c. 442/1051)

Some commentators have suggested that al-Biruni was the greatest Muslim scientist and no doubt he was one of the leading intellectual figures of Islamic science in its early history. He is known to have written about 180 scholarly writings. His book *India* is the best account of the Hindu religion and of the sciences and customs of India in medieval times. His *Chronology of Ancient Nations*, dealing with the calendar and festivities of different nations, is unique. His *Canon of al-Mas'udi* was highly valued and his *Elements of Astrology* was the standard text for astronomy for centuries. He also wrote highly valued works on physics, mathematical geography, mineralogy and nearly every branch of mathematics, astronomy and astrology. Of all his works, only 22 have survived down through history and of those only 16 have been published in modern times. Will Durant wrote the following on al-Biruni's contributions to Islamic astronomy: "He wrote treatises on the astrolabe, and formulated astronomical tables for Sultan Masud." He took it for granted that the earth is round, noted "the attraction of all things towards the center of the earth," and remarked that astronomic data can be explained as well by supposing that "the earth turns daily on its axis and annually around the sun, as by the reverse hypothesis."[60]

Abu Hamid Muhammad, al-Ghazzali (c. 450/1058–c. 505/1111)

Al-Ghazzali, not a scientist or philosopher in the usual sense, left a profound

---

[60] Will Durant, *The Age of Faith*, (New York: Simon & Schuster, 1980) p. 249.

mark upon the intellectual life of Islam. He was introduced to the teachings of Sufism and eventually became famous as a theologian and scholar of religious sciences. His most important religious work is *The Revivification of the Religious Sciences*, which is an important Muslim work on spiritual ethics and morality. He also wrote on logic and philosophy. In *The Purposes of the Philosophers*, he summarized Peripatetic philosophy so well that when this work was translated into Latin, he became known in the West as an authority of Peripatetic philosophy. He also wrote *The Incoherence of the Philosophers* where he attacked the rationalistic tendencies in Aristotelian philosophy and criticized some of the views of Ibn Sina and al-Farabi. He helped more than any other single individual to bring about the intellectual transformation that took place in the Islamic world during the sixth/twelfth century. He is in every way one of the most notable religious and intellectual figures of Islam.

Abu'l-Fath Umar ibn Ibrahim al-Khayyami (c. 429/1039–c. 517/1123)

Omar Khayyam is the famous Persian poet who is also well known in the Western world for his poem the Rubaiyat which has been translated into many languages.[61] He was also one of the most notable Islamic scientists in the Islamic world. He was born in Naishapur where he spent most of his life and his tomb is there. To this day, people visit it from near and far. He was a famous mathematician and was called upon by Malik Shah to reform the calendar. This calendar, known as the Jalālī calendar, is still in use today in Persia and is considered more accurate than the Gregorian calendar. About a dozen works of Khayyām have survived, the most important being his *Algebra* which is the best work of its kind in medieval mathematics. He also wrote on geometry and physics as well as on metaphysical questions. His *Quatrains* translated beautifully by Fitzgerald have made him the best known literary figure of the East in the West. In the Islamic world, the influence of Khayyām was in the domain of mathematics and his philosophical position was judged by his metaphysical and philosophical writings. It could be said that Khayyām is the only figure in history who was both a great poet and a great mathematician.

Abu'l-Walid Muhammad (PBUH), ibn Rushd (c. 520/1126–c. 595/1198)

Ibn Rushd (or Averroes) was born in Cordoba, Spain of a well known family of judges and religious scholars. He became an authority in religious law and medicine, as well as in philosophy. He was a judge in Seville and Cordova as well as the personal physician of the caliph. Averroes was the greatest medieval commentator on Aristotle. St. Thomas called him "the Commentator" and Dante referred to him as "he who made the grand commentary." There are altogether 38 commentaries by Averroes on different works of Aristotle in addition to short treatises devoted to particular aspects of Aristotle's philosophy. All three of

---

[61] "A Jug of Wine, a Loaf of Bread–and Thou, beside me singing in the Wilderness, and oh, Wilderness is Paradise now."

Averroes' commentaries on the works of Aristotle, including his *Physics* and *Metaphysics*, have survived. In addition, Averroes wrote works on astronomy, physics, and medicine. In the West, Averroes is considered as the most influential Muslim thinker. Most of his works survive today in Latin rather than their original Arabic versions.

4.5 Islamic Contributions to Science

The "Golden Age" of Islam, sometimes referred to as the Islamic renaissance, generally dates from the 8th to the 13th centuries of the Christian calendar. Islamic science soon became a force to be reckoned with in the 10th and 11th centuries before beginning to fade as a driving force a century prior to the coming of the Mongol invasion. During this period, engineers, scholars, and intellectuals in the Islamic world contributed to literature and the arts, to law and industry, and finally to the sciences and technology. The fast growing Islamic civilization was becoming the most productive of all the prior civilizations in the domain of science with much activity in a wide variety of individual sciences ranging from medicine to astronomy. As such, it is important for young people and students of Islam to know the vast contribution and extensive heritage that the Islamic sciences have brought to bear in the development of the sciences in particular, and its influence generally in the development of modern science as we know and experience it today.

Industrial and Technological Development

It may come as a surprise to many people living today that Muslim engineers in the Islamic world made a number of innovative industrial uses of such things as hydropower, tidal power, steam, and wind power. The industrial uses of watermills in the Islamic world date back to the 7th century, and horizontal-wheeled and vertical-wheeled water mills were both in widespread use since at least the 9th century. Similarly, by the 11th century, a variety of industrial mills were in use in the Islamic world, including paper mills, sawmills, steel mills, sugar mills and windmills. Muslim engineers also invested crankshafts and water turbines, used gears in mills and water-raising machines, and pioneered the use of dams as a source of water power, putting to rest many tasks that previously were driven by manual labor in earlier times. Needless to say, all of these innovations had an influence on the coming Industrial Revolution.

In addition, a number of industries were generated by developments in the Islamic approach to agriculture and other industries, including early innovations for agri-business, astronomical instruments, ceramics, chemicals, clocks, glass, mechanical hydro-powered and wind-powered machinery, matting, mosaics, pulp and paper, perfumery, petroleum, pharmaceuticals, rope-making, shipping, shipbuilding, silk, sugar, textiles, water, weapons, and the mining of minerals such as sulphur, ammonia, lead and iron. To further their industrial appetite, the early Islamic centuries witnessed the development of large factory complexes and knowledge of these industries was later transmitted to medieval Europe around the 12th century. For example, the first glass factories in Europe were founded in the 11th century by Egyptian craftsman.

Mathematics

Muslims made remarkable contributions to many domains of mathematics, partly because of their love for the principle of unity that is the center of the Islamic intellectual and spiritual tradition, together with their vision of the universe, understood according to the laws of mathematics as comprehended in the traditional sense of the term. In arithmetic, the Muslims are remembered for their adoption of the Sanskrit numerals and later transformations which finally came to be known as Arabic numerals in Europe. In addition to Arabic numerals, Muslim mathematicians also carried out research in the field of number theory, decimal fractions and computation of numerical series, culminating with the discovery of decimal fractions and devices to carry out mathematical calculation by Ghiyath al-Din Jamshid al-Kashani, the author of *Miftah al-Hisab* (*The Key to Arithmetic*). In geometry, the Muslims carried on from the Greeks in furthering plane and solid geometry and systematized mathematical equations for the solution of many geometric problems, creating a relationship between algebra and geometry that would be pursued later in Europe. Trigonometry was another field of mathematics that was especially developed by Muslims. Muslim mathematicians first systematized the six trigonometric functions which bear the mark of their Arabic origin to this day. The first treatise on trigonometry that deals with the subject as an independent branch of mathematics goes back to al-Bīrūnī. The word "algebra" is of course from Arabic origin. 'Umar Khayyam, better known in the West for his love poetry, also wrote a famous book on algebra, the most perfect treatment of the subject prior to modern times.

Finally, perhaps a lesser known branch of mathematics of interest to Muslim scholars at that time was the study of Arabic and Persian music. The study of music was considered a branch of mathematics and as such often appears in the classification of the sciences. The study of music was considered such because of the close association of proportion and harmony to the study of math in general.

Astronomy

Muslims scientists developed a keen interest in astronomy, partly because of the importance astronomy plays in the Islamic religious rites, such as the timings for the prayer and finding the direction of the *qiblah*. They drew on the vast heritage of traditions from the Babylonians, the Greeks, the Persians and the Indians in creating a new synthesis that established the science of astronomy on a much vaster foundation than ever before. Islamic scientists took special interest in observation and in the development of observatories. The observatory as a scientific institution was in fact an invention of the Muslims and individual astronomers were known to observe the stars and the movement of the moon from the minarets of mosques. The first observatory as an institution was established by Nasir al-Din al-Tusi in Maraghah and others soon followed in Samarqand and Istanbul. These became the model for observatories that would later be developed in the West during the Renaissance. Muslims also distinguished themselves in the development of observational instruments, the most famous one being the astrolabe. Islamic astrolabes appeared early in the history of Islam and were put together with exquisite art, together with scientific precision to create useful instruments that were essential for navigators and astronomers alike. Finally, regarding mathematical astronomy, the Muslims studied the Indian and Persian methods of calculations of the movements of the heavens, as well as the Greek calculations. Al-Battane and al-Biruni were well known Muslims who continued to refine the mathematical astronomy of Ptolemy.

Other contributions from Muslim astronomers include Biruni speculating that the Milky Way galaxy is a collection of numerous nebulous stars, the development of a planetary model without any epicycles by Ibn Bajjah (Avempace), the optical writings of Ibn al-Haytham having laid the foundations for the later European development of telescopic astronomy, the development of universal astrolabes, the invention of numerous other astronomical instruments, continuation of inquiry into the motion of the planets, the discovery that the heavenly bodies and celestial spheres are subject to the same physical laws as earth, the first elaborate experiments related to astronomical phenomena, and the first clear distinction between astronomy and astrology, the use of exacting empirical observations and experimental techniques, the discovery that the celestial spheres are not solid and that the heavens are less dense than the air. There can be no doubt that Muslim astronomers added an entirely new dimension to the study of the heavens.

Earth Sciences

Muslim geographers began to write on geography from the 3rd Islamic century. Such figures as Ibn al-Hawqal and al-Biruni wrote major geographical works that ultimately led to the work of al-Idrisi and the beautiful maps which he drew in the 7th Islamic century at the Sicilian court of Frederick the Great, maps that expanded the knowledge found in earlier works and had much more information on the Indian Ocean. Such major discoveries as the source of the Nile River, which Europeans explored in the 19th century, were already described in these earlier geographical texts. It was also with the help of Islamic geographers that Henry the Navigator, Magellan, Columbus and other important explorers of the Renaissance were able to cross the Atlantic and go around the Cape of Good Hope. A number of Muslim scientists, including ibn Sina and al-Biruni, were very much interested in geology and studied the question of rock formation, sedimentation, the differences between sedimentary rocks, and even the study of meteors. Al-Biruni raised awareness about the tremendous changes that have taken place on the surface of the earth between the sea and the land.

Physics

Muslim physicists from earlier times would not recognize the physics of modern science; the science of physics as understood today did not have a place in the classification of the sciences within the Islamic tradition. There were, however, deeply interested in three areas of interest in what could be called the early developments of physics. Muslims made major achievements in the study of optics and light phenomena. The greatest scientist in this field outside of Euclid and Kepler was Ibn al-Haytham who wrote a book called "Optical Thesaurus", one of the most outstanding works in the field of optics, where he carried out detailed research on refraction, reflection, and the properties of various kinds of mirrors. The second field of physics that Muslims showed an interest in was the question of motion and what they achieved prepared the ground for the Scientific Revolution with the appearance of Galileo on the scene. We know that in the early 1609 work *Pisal Dialogue*, Galileo refers to Ibn Bajjah's theory of projectile motion. The third field of physics that interested Muslims was the question of weights and measures and the tradition of Archimedes concerning the determination of specific weight and the measure of the weight and volume of various objects.

Alchemy and Chemistry

Chemistry finds it roots in the Arabic word *al-kimiya*. In that sense, alchemy is actually a form of pre-chemistry and was once considered a science of the cosmos and science of the soul. It made use of minerals and studied them mostly for their symbolic significance and their relationship to the inner states of the soul. Chemistry was born from the material aspect of alchemy. The most famous Islamic chemist was Jabir ibn Hayyan who lived in the second Islamic century. He composed a large number of works dealing with many different sciences, but especially alchemy which was a respected discipline within the world of Islam. In the 3rd century, it was Muhammad, ibn Zakariyya al-Razi who created chemistry as a distinct field of science and laid the foundation by introducing an early experimental method for chemistry. Islamic scientists are generally credited with introducing precise observation, controlled experiments, and careful records. They invented and named the alembic, chemically analyzed innumerable substances, composed substances, and studied and manufactured hundreds of drugs. Alchemy, which the Muslims inherited from Egypt, contributed to the field of chemistry by a thousand incidental discoveries, and by its method, which was the most scientific of all medieval operations.

Medicine

Muslim physicians also made major contributions and significant advances in the field of medicine, including anatomy, pathology, the pharmaceutical sciences, physiology and surgery. However, the origins of Islamic medicine are traced all the way back to the Prophet himself. Certain sayings and actions of the Prophet deal specifically with health, hygiene, the care of the body and of the soul's relation to the body. Thereafter, Islamic medicine was born with the classic work of Ali ibn Rabban al-Tabari called *Firdaws al-hikmah*, in English *The Paradise of Wisdom*, a major medical encyclopedia which was written in the 3rd Islamic century. Another famous encyclopedic work soon followed called *Kitab al-Hawi* (Continens) of al-Razi, who was the most outstanding clinician and observer in the field of medicine, the discoverer of many new illnesses and the person who is said to have used alcohol for the first time as a medical antiseptic. The works of Ibn Sina are the crowning achievement of early Islamic medicine. As "the Prince of Physicians", his book *The Canon* is one of the most famous of all medical books in the history of medicine. It was taught for 700 years in the Western world and is still taught wherever traditional Islamic medicine survives in such countries as Pakistan, India, and certain areas of Persia and the Arab world. He is credited with the discovery and diagnosis of certain illnesses such as meningitis. His greatest achievement was to synthesize the vast medical traditions that went before him. The Islamic medicine developed by Ibn Sina became part of the traditional life of the Muslims which has survived down to the present day and which is still of great significance for the everyday life of many Muslims, particularly in Persia, India, Egypt and Syria. It is a holistic approach to medicine in which the treatment of the body and the soul are considered together, using herbal treatments that can cure the body without being harmful to it. Islamic medicine is one of the major achievements of Islamic civilization and to this day remains beneficial to the Muslim community.

Overall, the extent of the Islamic contribution to the development of science in general and the various branches of the sciences in particular is impressive indeed. The modern world, and modern science in particular, tends to forget the tremendous achievements of the Islamic scientists of earlier centuries when modern science was in its initial stages of evolution and development. Islamic scholars and scientists need to model their efforts on the inspiring record of their forefathers, who pursued the path of knowledge-cum-science in the living spirit of the Qur'anic revelations whose first principles, signs of nature, and elements of essential knowledge provide the backdrop and inspiration for the pursuit of knowledge that can further enhance the quality of life for present and future generations.

PART FIVE

Foundation and Pillars

5.1 The Mystery and Certitude of Faith

When it comes to understanding the idea of faith in a reality that cannot physically be seen, it doesn't matter whether you are Christian, Muslim, or Buddhist. All practitioners of the major global religions take part in this leap of mind in order to transcend the limitations of the physical world. Considering the vast gulf that exists between the mystery of faith and its corresponding certitude, we need to suspend all the automatic belief systems that we have inherited from our parents in order to arrive at the heart of the matter. Christians and Muslims are well familiar with the formal aspects of faith. Muslims, for example, profess to believe in God, His angels, His messengers and in the Day of Judgment, and we give lip service to these ideas with a simplicity and speed that is surprising. However, when it comes to actually acting on behalf of these beliefs, acting upon beliefs that we have fully internalized as second nature, we fall short of putting into practice what we profess to believe. Is there any wonder that in this day and age we fail to take benefit of the implicit blessings that accompany every act of faith? In truth, faith is a suitable companion for those with sense enough to befriend it with sincerity and trust, as we do with any true friend.

Consider life for a moment as a river whose source and destination are not fully known. The river of life flows through a landscape that does not fully explain itself and it contains for humanity a geography of secret thoughts and conflicting emotions that are never fully satisfied or resolved. We must become one with this river and fully integrated with the environment that the river serves, but we do not know how to do this exactly. We must become like the river that flows within us, a river that irrigates near and distant lands but never forgets its source. The question we must ask ourselves is how can this be accomplished as we live out our lives from day to day? The answer lies embedded within an understanding of the significance of faith in the spiritual life of a person and the role it plays in the modern world.

Needless to say, it is not easy to actively think about the meaning of faith, much less discover through words and phrases the light of faith that can clarify rather than obscure faith's essential mystery and its promise of certitude. It is an issue at once subtle, sensitive, and profoundly personal. There is nothing more precious or intimate than a human faith in a Divine Being, and perhaps nothing more fragile. It is the *mihrab* or inner precinct of the mind and heart and holy sanctuary of the soul. Through faith, the believer puts him/herself on the line and identifies with a spiritual identity that places its trust in God. It is a sacred trust whose blessing permits the individual to transcend human limitations and escape the narrow and self-serving drive of the individual ego. Through faith, the faithful can transcend their own humanity and lift the veil of the inward self in an act of self revelation that is outwardly human and inwardly spiritual. The Qur'an is enlightening in this regard. "On the earth are signs for those of assured faith, as also in your own selves: will you not then see" (51: 20)?

Central within the universe is the person of true faith, whose perspective of belief serves as a bridge between the reality of this world and the world of the universal reality. Central within the mind and heart of humanity must be a universe which is patterned on faith in the Divine Being, a faith that proclaims that God exists as the supreme and absolute Being, a faith that expands with the passing of the days into a coloration of mind and a firmament of soul, a faith that represents a knowledge of God within one's being and a willingness to act upon that knowledge throughout the course of one's life.

Knowledge of the Divine Reality lies at the heart of the cosmic universe. The desire to realize this knowledge within oneself remains the central aspiration of the inner, human universe. We rely on faith because a veil separates us since the time of Adam from direct knowledge of God; we cannot cross this solid barrier on our own terms and by ourselves. The Prophet Muhammad (PBUH) has said in a well-known hadith: "God has seventy thousand veils of light and darkness; were He to draw their curtain, then would the splendours of His Aspect (Countenance or Face [*wajh*]) surely consume everyone who apprehended Him with his sight." Also, the archangel Gabriel (*Jibril*) has said: "Between me and Him are seventy thousand veils of light." The veil of veils in this context is reminiscent of the absolute barrier that exists in the modern world between the knowledge of God and the limited scientific knowledge of humanity. This natural barrier that separates humanity by a veil from direct knowledge of the Reality has become during these times more like a steel shutter that effectively closes people off from the experience of the Reality through a human attitude that precludes any opening onto the spiritual world, much less to an understanding of the Spirit of God as the one true Reality.

Faith unites the knowledge of the Divinity with human intentions and good works in order to realize that knowledge through action and through the power and force of human behavior. Faith is meaningless without the dual elements of knowledge and action, for knowledge and action are brothers in a sacred alliance that takes us by the hand and leads us forward into a life of spirituality. Through action, through behavior and through the very personality of the faithful person, an active faith grows and nourishes within like a tree with deep roots, expanding, enlivening, and enriching the life experience of the individual with a view to the divine reality that lies at the heart of all experience. It grows solid and strong, rich and deep, and this is why the Qur'an refers to levels of faith within the human entity and emphasizes the importance of a faith that grows. "Allah has endeared faith to you, and has made it beautiful in your hearts." (49: 7)

In fact, faith expresses a dynamic range within the human being that actually begins with mystery and ends with certitude. Paradoxically, faith begins as a mystery within the human mind and enters the ground of the human soul as a certainty that harbors no doubt about its true intentions. In the earthly sphere, the *insan* (Adam as the original, prototype human being and all his descendants) is confronted with a fundamental mystery at the heart of himself, his world, his universe. In addition to the perennial questions that confront humans within the scope of this world–questions as to origin, meaning, purpose and end–there also exists within the conscious experience a fundamental mystery that is incomprehensible to the human mind on the one hand, and yet curiously accessible to the human heart on the other hand. We know that the mystery exists and virtually underlies our conscious existence. No one questions this without questioning the basic nature of human experience. As such, it is instinctive within every individual to yearn for and pursue the meaning of this mystery within his or her life and to place it within both a reasonable and understandable context here on earth. After all, the longing for the Divinity is deeply engraved within human nature as an indelible watermark of the human spirit. Therefore, faith becomes the instinctive and primary response to all that is incomprehensible and unknowable within the world. Faith becomes the operative factor within *insan* and the human resolution to life's mysterious and most valued secrets.

Faith addresses the mystery in life, but it carries with it no inaccessible secret. On the contrary, faith becomes the human confession once a person acknowledges that he/she is 'veiled' from the true nature of reality. Faith as a spiritual expression of the self is individual as well as universal, individual as a personal response to a cosmic mystery and universal insofar as faith reaches across barriers that inhibit full realization of the mysteries and lifts the veil that separates humanity from the true nature of reality. Every man and woman, from the simplest peasant farmer to the most erudite of scholars, can enjoy the blessing and certitude of a simple faith in God precisely because faith is a personal and intimate aspiration as well as a universal force field of knowledge and desire. The human aspiration of faith draws upon the knowledge of God, while the forces within the field of truth reach down from the sublime to the terrestrial, from the Divine to the human, and touch both the simple peasant and erudite man and woman with wonder and awe.

Faith lives within the individual as a field of vision whose horizon gives way to the certainty of the truth. If there is a secret associated with faith, it is a revelation rather than a mystery. Faith exists as a fundamental human impulse, a spiritual instinct if you will, because a fundamental mystery exists within the creation that a person needs a lifetime to explore and come to terms with. In return, faith resolves this mystery for mankind when the believer simply accepts in principle all that the mystery implies and all that the mystery has to offer. Faith permits the believer to absorb as it were the unknowable essence of the mystery without necessarily comprehending it in any measurable way. The mystery becomes for the believer an "intuition" of all that is possible or probable within humanity and within the world, while faith makes possible the practical experience of life lived within the reflection and shadow of the Divine Mystery.

Humanity seeks God and establishes the impulse of faith in the Divine Being precisely because there is this fundamental mystery at the heart of human existence. A person has faith and through faith unknown worlds emerge and become accessible to him. Perhaps this is why one often refers to faith as having the capacity to "move mountains". The believer is able to communicate with the Divinity precisely because God is the Divine Mystery of which all other temporal mysteries are the manifested earthly prototype. Everything, from our human origins, the origin of the earth, the laws of the universe and the magnitude of Nature, represent what is called within the Islamic perspective the secret (*as-sirr*) and what the Qur'an repeatedly refers to as the unseen (*al-ghaib*).

We are a mystery unto ourselves and therefore need God to substantiate for us the knowledge of our individual reality as well as the Ultimate Reality. Without faith in the Divine Being, the human being would be adrift amid a conflicting multitude of uncertainties concerning himself, his world, and the world. We have faith, we pray, we fast, we perform good words, in short, we attempt to spiritualize our existence and lift ourselves out of the mundane manner of our living through a faith in the Divinity, through a faith in Allah as the Supreme One, in order to cope with the inevitable mystery that pervades every aspect of life. It is as if the mysterious and the secret realms of the universe are necessary pre-requisites to faith that permit man to explore the true nature of his own being and the true nature of the world in which he finds himself as a human mystery facing a cosmic mystery. Faith makes possible the lifting of the supreme veil that exists between the world of man and the world of the Spirit.

The mystery is the divine challenge; man's faith is the human response. If it were otherwise, humans would not be human and man would not be man. The Divine Mystery is actually the Cosmic Secret of the universe. This is no more fittingly prefigured than in the night sky with its canopy of stars, a miraculous panorama that has been called the "city of God". Its infinity of space and eternity of time reaches down nightly to remind mankind of their other self that is a reflection of the Supreme Self. Human beings both men and women have the potential for faith just as the blue sky has the potential to become the landscape of God and a symbolic image of other worlds. This faith then becomes the human secret that makes the meeting between the human and the Divine possible, a secret that is embedded within the Divine Mystery as knowledge and actualized within the human being as an aspiration to meet the Divine Mystery through an instinctive impulse of faith that springs from within the individual as naturally as human breath.

We began this section by establishing a relationship between the light of faith and the basic mystery that confronts all people in this life. We will conclude with some thoughts concerning faith's certitude. We have already suggested that faith is required of the human mind because of its confrontation with the fundamental mystery at the heart of the self and the known world. Thereafter, faith begins to grow within the mind and heart of the believer who takes part in a life of spirituality and follows the path of an orthodox and God-revealed religion such as the Religion of Islam. Eventually, the full range of faith's influence invades the inner world of the believer like a starburst from heaven and enters the ground of the human soul as certitude and certainty. The mystery that inspired faith in God becomes a certitude that actually certifies within the soul the knowledge that is already there in faith's initial assent.

Faith is at first grounded in the completely mysterious as a single ray of light amid the total darkness of the unknown. It is based, of course, on the knowledge of God, but it would go nowhere without the human desire to believe. It becomes a kind of illumination through a great and generous leap of mind in which vast chasms are crossed and monumental heights are scaled and the believer arrives upon a field of vision whose scope expands the inner horizon of the mind and heart beyond all human reckoning.

Faith is based upon essential knowledge and fundamental desire. Its knowledge is based on the knowledge of God, that He exists, is One, that He creates, defines and sustains the Reality, that He encompasses all Truth, that He is the Beloved One and Sustainer of all life. Faith's desire is based on a free will that is purely human, without any echoes of the other timely or the other worldly, but like all true human desire, is founded on knowledge of the Divinity. As such, faith is of the earthly realm, temporal and pristine, purely personal and humanly intimate, the meeting of the human with the Divine. Faith's desire is strictly of this world in the sense that it actualizes the here and now, the present moment, thus making the eternal moment humanly real. It represents the sheer human desire to turn toward God and believe in Him in thought, word and deed. Like the roar of the lion and the cry of the peacock, faith's voice emerges from the human depths to reach beyond the solitude and isolation of the human entity as the voice of a single soul, alone in an unexplained world and on his own with this simple yet sacred spiritual response.

The divine mystery belongs to God, but faith belongs to humanity. As such, it becomes the summative statement of what they think is true and what they are willing to act upon. It serves as a font of inspiration and the headwaters of an impulse to act in order to understand and experience the world. Genuine faith is expressed through the human entity totally, in thought, through action, and by sentiment, emotion, and spiritual aspiration. It provides the inner structure and framework for the pursuit of the spiritual way and the pursuit of a life of spirituality. Without an abiding belief in God, there can be no real knowledge, no holiness, no salvation and above all no certitude. Faith opens the inward "I" of the human consciousness that is a panoramic window into the true nature of the one Reality.

Through faith, the believer can resolve all of the enigmas, the uncertainties, in short the mysteries that make up the fabric of this world. Life, the world and human existence all show themselves to be a weft and warp of apparent certainties and compelling uncertainties. We live in a world of shifting sands and our lives rarely exhibit any consistency or continuity. Without the vision of an abiding faith, our outer and inner worlds are a bundle of conflicting feelings and emotions that ultimately manifest themselves through isolation, doubt and existential loneliness that would be intolerable without the spiritual perspective of faith in a fully united reality. We are nothing if we believe in nothing. We are everything if we follow our true nature and place our trust in God.

Through faith, the enigmas, mysteries and uncertainties of this world can be transformed into feelings of certainty and certitude that always accompany any genuine faith in the Divine Being. The essential knowledge brings with it a desire for faith. With a desire for faith comes the experience of faith. With the experience of faith comes realization through faith. With realization through faith comes certitude. Finally, certitude brings with it its own compensation and its own ambience. Faith's certitude manifests itself as a compensation for the mind and heart because the certitude of faith only increases faith's desire. Faith's certitude thereafter manifests itself as an ambience through tranquillity of soul and a calm serenity of the peaceful spirit, these elements of serenity and peace being the very essence of what the word *islam* has come to mean and promise: "It is He Who sent down Tranquillity into the hearts of the believers, that they may add faith to their faith." (48: 4) It amounts to a circle of spirituality that moves from knowledge to desire to faith to experience to realization to certitude and back again full circle to an enriched faith fortified by experience with higher levels of awareness and spirituality.

Within the hierarchy of being, only humans have faith and express their faith as a sacred sentiment and as an active participation in the Divinity throughout the course of their lives. Faith sets humans apart from the angels, the jinn, the animals and plants in the kingdom of God, all of whom enjoy a knowledge of God and/or respond through their spiritual instincts on fundamental, supra-natural levels of expression. The angels execute the Divine Command, the jinn surrender to the Divine Being, the animals pray and praise, as the Qur'an tells us, even plants turn their faces to the light of the sun in praise of the Divine One. But only human beings actively choose the Divinity with their mind and heart through the profession of a faith in God. Only humanity chooses God, and because of that, faith is the spiritual expression par excellence of a person's most 'human' being.

Faith commences as mystery and comes to fruition as certitude. It begins as a subjective inspiration of the human mind in order to deal with the fundamental mystery, uncertainty and doubt that confront the human entity in this world. With time, faith grows into an outward expression of spiritual virtue that actually shapes the ambiance of the mind and provides the coloration of man's inner being. Through the excellence (*al-ihsan*) of spiritual virtue, ordinary faith finally develops into an inward certitude that takes part in the objective Reality of God. Through the power of faith, we as human subjects are able to experience, if not actually see, the mysterious presence of God, and this experience objectifies the Reality of the Divine Being and encourages people to worship and "fear the Most Gracious Who is unseen." (50: 33)

5.2 To Witness and Surrender

Of all the profound mysteries that confront the rational mind with their shadowy inquiry and that challenge the human spirit with premonitions of a Supreme Being as the intelligent force behind the creation, the greatest mystery of all lies in the intimate encounter between the heart of man and the Spirit of God. Within the mind, heart and soul of humanity lies an inner ground in which the bud of a universal mystery and its implicit resolution can take root and grow into a field of existential experience that ultimately leads to the fulfilment of the human spirit.

In the Islamic perspective, this unexpected awakening becomes a life-long endeavor to unfold within the human heart the spark of a divine mystery that finds its origin and source of empowerment in a sacred, revealed formula that strikes off the flint of four simple Arabic words "*la ilaha ill-Llah*", a negation of this world as affirmation of the one true reality, no god but the one God. This simple message comes down into the human domain as a sword from heaven to strike open with a single blow the proto-mystery that hovers over conscious existence to reveal within its heart the message of oneness and unity that surrounds us as the secret revealed, that penetrates our life as an existential reality, and that makes us who we are. It is the vertical sword that intersects the horizontal plane of existence at every moment with its message of infinitude of space and eternity of time. At the utterance of a single, revealed "sacred formula", the creature meets the Creator; the human being becomes one with the Divine Being.

Whether the sage be a human or a butterfly and the creation a vast stellar universe or nothing but a spider's web, the mystery of Oneness sews up the fragility of the universe with its permanence and certitude. With every utterance on the lips and with every beat of the heart, it showers its certitude like morning dew, always fresh and forever new, down upon the mystery of the universe and casts transcendence into the soul of humanity like reflected light on a shimmering bay. Its simplicity says a firm 'no' to the permanence of the world and all that it contains as a prelude to the unwavering 'yes' in embracing and surrendering to the Oneness of God.

If faith creates a bridge between seen and unseen worlds, then the acts of witnessing and surrender dig deep trenches into our lives, planting the seeds of spirituality into the ground of our souls. Witnessing and surrender represent the two sides of a double-edged sword that cuts through human illusions about reality on the one hand and rips away the veils of the seeking soul on the other, in order to expose the unity (*tawhid*) of God that the Religion of Islam has come to reaffirm. The Muslims witness the truth of the one God through a human intelligence that is cognitive, conscious and contemplative; they surrender through a human will that is powerful, decisive and free. Without the commitment of an active surrender, witnessing is just an abstract intellection or an empty word. Without the knowledge of a firm witnessing, surrender becomes merely an empty gesture and a hollow sound, a form without substance, or worse, "the letter of the law that killeth."

Every religion approaches the sacred mysteries of life from a particular perspective. Islam's unique vision lays emphasis upon the dual role played by knowledge and action, combining the knowledge from above with the activity from below, for which witnessing and surrender are the human modes of spiritual expression. The Qur'an records the moment when the primordial soul of man proclaimed its cosmic affirmation of God when He asked: "Am I not your Lord?" and the human soul responded boldly: "Yes! We witness You." The human being went on to become the human receptacle of a knowledge that would ultimately awaken a full consciousness of self in reflection of the Supreme Self.

In response to the divine inquiry, the human soul bore witness with its human response; but this was only a prelude to a cycle of recurring witnessing, as the soul hovered on the horizon of an unfolding cosmic process. The witnessing began as an instinctive and spontaneous overflow of knowledge and love between the Creator and His human creation. The cosmic question was asked and the human response was given freely and willingly. It was a direct communication between the soul of man and the Spirit of God, in which the exchange of knowledge was intuitive and immediate, resulting in a human witnessing both natural and honest. What followed was the compulsory test of man's free will and the fall from the beatitude of the primordial paradise. The prelude of the soul's courageous witnessing gave way to an interlude in which we humans needed to seek out and discover once again the essence of a lost truth. The harmony of interacting wills gave way to the human need to surrender the will to the expressed will of the divine preference through a revealed law.

Once Adam fell from the innocence of the paradise and the veils had been drawn before his vision, future generations needed the knowledge of God once again, and they needed the means to absorb and assimilate that knowledge into their beings. The witnessing of the mind testifies to the veracity of that knowledge, while the surrender of soul provides the means to assimilate and absorb it. Thus, the very concept of religion itself was born out of knowledge that descended to the earth and surrender to the source of that knowledge in God. With this knowledge, the future generations of Adam could make their ascent once again back into the beatitude of the paradise they had lost. The Religion of Islam is the religion of pure surrender, the primordial *islam* re-awakened once again and the primordial religion re-confirmed for past and future generations until the end of time.

Witnessing commences a life of the spirit that acknowledges the all-powerful God as the origin and source of all existence. Through his witnessing, the believer makes a proclamation that the substance of his faith in God is not only believable but also true. In fact, witnessing is actually the verification of the truth. The believer witnesses through his intelligence, his mind, his brain and ultimately his tongue, which repeats the great witnessing in Islam, the *shahadah* or the sacred formula that is on the lips and in the heart of every true Muslim. In addition to the words of the *shahadah*, however, the believer attempts to bear witness to the knowledge of God in every detail of his life, by following the words of the Qur'an and imitating the behavior of the Prophet, the *Sunnah*. Every word, every action, every attitude become meaningful statements that return back to God through witnessing the essential knowledge that He has sent down to humanity through revelation.

The essence of the religion, without its legal, formal and ritual aspects, can be summarized by a single divine command directed exclusively toward God's thinking creation: Surrender! This is verbalized in the sacred Qur'anic language through three letters: S (*sin*), L (*lam*), and M (*mim*). These three letters are the basic root that forms three key terms of the religion: These terms are *islam* or the concept of surrender itself, *muslim*, or the person who surrenders, and finally the Arabic word *salaam* which means none other than peace. In addition, the meaning behind this Arabic root also suggests an inner soundness that leads to well-being, just as peace leads to peacefulness, and just as surrender leads to the security within the Divine Beatitude.

Surrender and peace, uniting as they do in a single root, are the spiritual antipodes of earthly existence. They represent effort for the sake of contentment, conformity for the sake of freedom, denial for the sake of affirmation, and contraction for the sake of expansion. Through surrender to God, the believer comes to feel a peace within his soul that can only grow out of conformity to the divine norm. It is the peace implied in the awesome serenity of the night sky or the calm tranquility of a placid, moon-lit sea. All of nature underscores a mood of sober other-worldliness with the signature of peace. This feeling culminates in peace of heart that serves as a motivation for humanity and promises the soul the quiet stillness that it knows instinctively to be the rightful inheritance of the good life. Heaven, which is the realm of perfection in Islam, is referred to as the *dar as-salam*, the abode of peace, since the paradisal environment is a reflection of the inner condition of those near to God. In the gardens of eternity, "the believers will not hear any vanity, but only expressions of peace; and there they will have their sustenance by days and by night." (19: 62)

Faith expresses itself most completely in the *shahadah* or witnessing, *la ilaha illa 'Llah*, meaning literally no god but God. The sacred words proclaim the divine prerogative and oblige man to witness the substance of its necessary truth. Behind every act of surrender, however, is the meaning of the sacred formula, as the believer uses his finite will in the service of the infinite Will. Through faith and surrender, the believer is able to superimpose an absolute reality on his own relative reality, thereby lending to his immediate reality an absolute quality that represents the absoluteness of the Divinity.

Witnessing expresses the knowledge of God; surrender expresses the desire for human goodness precisely because the freedom implied by willful surrender to the divine norm is an essential prerequisite of the Good. Without free will, man would not be able to experience the subtle and intricate harmony of his witnessing and surrender, and human goodness as such would have no real meaning for him. "As a trial, We shall test you with good and with evil." (21: 36) Because man is free to conform to God's will by choosing between good and evil, his goodness, having been earned, arises out of the soul's free surrender to the moral ideal and is not the result of some kind of compulsory predetermination from above.

Surrender through the exercise of man's free will is not simply random desire, but specific and definitive wanting. "Have We not lead him along two paths?" (90: 100) These two distinct paths offer their own level of satisfaction, their own clear alternative, and their own particular destination. One is the path of human goodness that reflects the Universal Good, the other is the path of the evil alternative as embodied in the persona of Satan. On the relative plane, we determine ourselves by becoming what we do, and by doing what we *will* to do. God has said in the Qur'an: "I do not wrong My servants." (6: 29) On the contrary, man's evil originates in his own soul and he must bear the consequences of his actions. "We have wronged ourselves." (7: 23)

From the spiritual point of view, it is far better to be free and suffer the genuine limitations demanded by the Supreme Being, than to enjoy the appearances of a kind of freedom, but really suffer the illusion of a limitless possibility that can only deceive mankind, and lead him away from his true purpose. Through surrender to the will of God, humanity can participate in the Universal Norm that has been formalized on earth by the law, or *shari'ah* in Islamic terminology, but also earn all the rights and special advantages offered to those who choose the path of piety. Through this conformity and through this participation, humanity can feel and live the force of the will as being free, a limited freedom perhaps, but made whole by responding to the call of the Supreme Being to witness and surrender.

Total surrender of the human will amounts to a knowledge that has truly been carried out by the body and assimilated by the heart. God commands and humanity surrenders in an interaction of divine and human wills that are joined together in the unity of God. Abraham proclaims in the Qur'an: "Indeed, I am the first to surrender", having passed the divine scrutiny and earned his right to be the "first" among those who surrender. Every Muslim, however, wishes to claim that he is the first among those who surrender. Of course, this bold statement is not meant to be understood in its literal and quantitative sense, but rather in its qualitative one. To be the first to surrender is a challenge to the self, first of those who surrender insofar as the surrender recognizes the true qualitative nature of the human servitude. As such, every act of surrender is a reconfirmation of one's way of religion (*din*) and a proof of the sincerity of one's inner life. "I am the first to surrender" must mean that I am ready to be first by way of anticipation and sheer will power, if not always in actual fact.

5.3 Tribute to the Illuminated Book

Every spiritual tradition contains an initial spark – a miracle if you will – that becomes the smoldering ember at its heart whose perennial glow keeps the tradition alive as it finds its way into the hearts of its followers. Because this "descent of knowledge" emerges within this world from an otherworldly dimension that is "unseen", it is referred to as revelation that has taken a variety of forms down through history. Revelation reveals the secret nature of both humanity and the universe and creates pathways that make their way through the perennial mystery that keeps people guessing about their own nature and the true nature of the universal experience. Revelation touches upon primordial memories within us that exist as the birthright of our true inner nature. Between the lines of revelation, time becomes eternity; space becomes infinity; light becomes a luminous symbol that leads to a primal awakening, reminding us that we still carry a memory of some light of long ago that illuminates our source and first origin.

The Religion of Islam lays its foundation of faith on the principles of a knowledge whose origin and source take root in a divine revelation that originates with a Supreme Being Who is the First Cause (*al-Awwal*), the Final End (*al-Akhir*), the Truth (*al-Ḥaqq*), and the One (*al-Ahad*). This revelatory knowledge forms the baseline of a "science of knowing and perception" that fully integrates the outer appearances of all natural phenomena and their qualitative and numinous value into a single unified reality. In Islam, there cannot be knowledge of the outward appearance of things without knowledge of their inner reality; just as there cannot be knowledge of this inner reality without a corresponding knowledge of the outer appearance. It is the same with the Holy Book, the integrity of the revelation cannot be understood simply from its letter, from its outward literal sense; it can be understood only when interpreted by its inner meaning in counterpoint to what is stated in clear words. There is an absolute union that exists between the inner reality of a thing and its external appearance, between the natural, physical sciences of the world and the spiritual science that defines the true vision of the one Reality.

According to the Islamic worldview, a divine revelation is the vision of the Absolute from the perspective of the Absolute; a Self-Disclosure from God to man that recalls the primordial revelation and sends forth knowledge into the world of humanity from the ultimate original source. Revelation portrays the physical world as the consequence of actions initiated by the Creator and it offers the study of nature as a virtual science of signs and symbols whose intricacy and higher orders of magnitude reflect the design and intelligence of the Supreme Being. It understands human beings to be thinking beings made as the human reflection of the Divine Being, with a consciousness that mirrors the Supreme Consciousness and with a variety of higher faculties that can connect with this higher order of Reality.

The question could be asked why the Muslims treasure and love what they sometimes refer to as the Noble Qur'an. The answer must lie in many different factors not the least being that the divine revelation is like no other written earthly document. For one thing, the Qur'an addresses itself directly to the human soul rather than to the human mind, possessing an inner dimension that no literal, philological or literary analysis can set forth and explain away as a purely human document. As such, it has powers and properties that do justice to its celestial origin and from there moves into the innermost core of the human entity to give shape and coloration to the fundamental instincts that emanate out of the soul in search of its earthly expression and fulfillment. Through vibration, through sound, through letters, words and phrases that constitute the holy verses of the Book, the divine discourse enters the mind, heart and soul of the believing Muslim as a profound remembrance (*dhikr*) of the Divine Being and knowledge of the reality that Being represents.

Moreover, it is said that the Book addresses the soul directly because it overwhelms the profane and the earthly with a sense of the sacred and the otherworldly, because it casts the absolute and objective quality of the Real upon the relative and subjective aspects of the temporality of this world, because it responds to the human yearning for what lies beyond the horizon within the plenitude of the Divine Self-disclosure, and because it brings the presence of the Source and Center into the world of periphery and contingency that distinguishes the human being on its own in this world. This yearning of the mind and heart for an absolute and definitive knowledge of God is fundamental to the human soul and lies at the very heart of all earthly ambition to transcend the broad range of human limitations through the aid and benevolence of a Supreme Intelligence that not only substantiates the meaning of life; but that ultimately provides the means for the transcendence of the human condition.

Once again, the Holy Qur'an brings about the existence of another dimension within this world because it is a written as well as a celestial book, capable of being contained in the heart as well as held in the hand of the Muslims. Its exclusive quality lies in the manner in which it has become audible and visible, and therefore those who come in contact with it without prejudice, and with a traditional sensibility for the majestic and the sacred, are ready to be the human instrument that is played upon by the divine sound and the visual Arabic letters. The Qur'an is a sonorous and visual universe that enters the human mentality as forms of audible and visual art that have the power to transform the human form into a living reed, a human calamus and flute, that expresses through the physical presence and during the course of one's life the very knowledge of God. Psalmody is the first art of Islam, while the second major art is calligraphy,[62] constituting the letters and words of the Book and reflecting on the earthly plane the writing on the Guarded Tablet (*al-lawh al-mahfouz*) that is preserved in Heaven. Psalmody moderates the sound and modulation of the verses, while calligraphy is a sacred art that man carries within himself from the inception of the revelation since "He taught man with the Pen, taught man what he knew not." (96: 4-5)

The true value of the Qur'anic recitation as a form of worship is borne out by the fact that millions of non-Arabic speaking Muslims read and recite the Qur'an without necessarily understanding the literal meaning of the words. Yet, they approach the Book with a conscious reverence and a fundamental desire to worship God that transcends the literal meaning of the verses. In addition, even though the reader may not understand the literal meaning, it is possible that because of the power of a person's intentions and through sincerity of the mind and heart, God may bless the efforts of a devout Muslim with a realized knowledge of the doctrine without their having to necessarily pass through the gate of a literal knowledge.

Similarly, there is a potential danger that could arise from an over-familiarity with the text. Native-speaking Arabs who may know the linguistic nuances of the text may fall short of a realized knowledge for one reason or another, such as lack of intent or sincerity of purpose. In other words, a literal knowledge of the language carries with it no guarantee of an assimilated knowledge of the text or of the many and varied levels of knowledge and meaning that are contained therein. Similarly, non Arabic-speaking readers who struggle through a careful recitation of the text may well approximate a better and more accurate reading then a native-speaking Arab who through habit and routine may rush through a well-known portion of the text and lace the reading with multiple errors.[63] Only intention, effort, and sincerity can define the parameters of Muslim worship.

---

[62] "Calligraphy is the basic art of creation of points and lines in an endless variety of forms and rhythms which never cease to bring about recollection (*tidhkar* or *dhikr*) of the Primordial Act of the Divine Pen for those who are capable of contemplating in forms the trace of the Formless" (S. H. Nasr, *Islamic Art and Spirituality* [Albany, NY: SUNY Press, 1987], p. 19).

[63] There is a well-defined science of Qur'an recitation, known as *tajwīd* in Arabic, with very explicit rules for reading the Qur'an correctly. These rules must not only be learned, but practised systematically to be mastered properly, even by native speakers. It is not just a matter of knowing Arabic pronunciation and reading correctly. Arabic-speaking Muslims themselves require training and practice in the skill of *tajwīd* which raises the level of Qur'an recitation to a science as well as a sonorous art.

The Qur'an is a miraculous blend of sound and meaning. Obviously the Qur'an conveys a meaning upon those who understand the literal words, while intuitive meaning can be conveyed directly to the non-Arabic speaker, depending on the intentions of the person reciting the verses together with the mercy and blessing of God. However, there is no doubting the miraculous effect that the sacred sounds and word combinations have on the faithful generally, including Arab and non-Arab Muslims alike. In addition to the words, phrases, meanings, aphorisms, stories and symbolic images, the sacred text is replete with rhythms, cadences, intonations, elisions, ellipses, and sacred sound vibrations, whose stylistic intonations add up to a glorious psalmody that has a powerful, cumulative effect on the reader, who makes every effort to chant sonorously, clearly, slowly, and above all correctly, the holy phrases.[64] "It exercises its effect not only upon the mind but on the very substance of the believer, although it can do this only in its integral character, that is to say, as the Arabic Qur'an."[65] No doubt, the words and their associations have echoes and reverberations in the ear and mind of the faithful with a power that can melt hearts and stir souls. The Prophet once told his companions that "hearts become rusty just as iron does when water gets at it." When asked how this rust could be removed, he replied: "By frequent remembrance of death and frequent recitation of the Qur'an."

The phenomenon of a heightened spiritual emotion, commonly called the "gift of tears", is not uncommon during Qur'an recitation, when the Muslims inexplicably weep real tears for no apparent reason except as a kind of subliminal and cumulative effect that the overall recitation has on the mind and heart of the reciter. These tears are symbolic of the profound emotion present within the person at that time, while the emotion itself serves as a purification and release of repressed feelings and attitudes that often reside unconsciously within people. Muslims often feel spiritually refreshed after a session of Qur'anic recitation, uplifted and ready to meet the forces and challenges that they may be confronted with during the course of their day. The mind, heart, and soul have been washed clean and the sense of mental and spiritual refreshment hovers around the person like the scent of fresh soap from an early morning bath.

Secondly, there is the perennial question of the language of a text that fundamentally cannot be translated because of its otherworldly texture and its sense of the sublime. Non-Muslims justifiably wonder what it is about the text that renders it untranslatable any more than another text. The answer of course is first and foremost that the text is the word of God; to alter the text in any way, especially through the expression and form of another language is to withdraw the Presence by taking away the very words that make the text sacred, noble, and holy. In both its meaning and form, the text is sacred in character: the written

---

[64] In quantum terms, everything vibrates, even the human body as the physical manifestation of the soul.

[65] Charles, Le Gai Eaton, *Islam and the Destiny of Man* (Albany: SUNY Press, 1985), p. 78.

word as calligraphy, the sounds of the recited text as chanted psalmody, the physical presence of the book, and the message itself are sacred and liturgically important as a vehicle of blessing and grace. The very form of the book is treated with reverence by all Muslims in their homes. It cannot be touched unless a person is in a state of ritual cleanliness. When Muslims sit down to read and recite the Qur'an, they go through the ritual washing just as they do in preparation for the ritual prayer. Also, the book itself holds a special place within the household, set aside in an elevated place and never below the level of other books within a room.

For the purposes of worship, the chanted Qur'an is the prototype of all worship through sacred sound. It conveys a sacred resonance that overlays a Muslim soul with a knowledge of their origins and provides the guidance that will lead them in the right direction on their way of return to God. "The first words of the Sacred Text revealed by Gabriel surrounded the prophet like an ocean of sound as the archangel himself filled the whole of the sky. The sound of the Qur'an penetrates the Muslim's body and soul even before it appeals to his mind. The sacred quality of the psalmody of the Qur'an can cause spiritual rapture even in a person who knows no Arabic."[66] The sonoral character of the Qur'anic revelation remains central to the spiritual life of Islam. Through recitation and as a means of worshipping Allah, the sonoral and rhythmic presence is felt by Arab and non-Arab Muslims alike, including Persian, Turkish, African, Indian and the Malays of Malaysia and Indonesia, all of whom do not enjoy Arabic as a mother tongue. In fact, the majority of Muslims are non-Arabic, even though Islam is assumed to be a thoroughly Arabic or arabized religion.

The Muslim relationship with the Qur'an involves something more than establishing the facts or acquiring the knowledge it contains. It goes far beyond the knowing or acquiring of the Arabic language or appreciating the aesthetic quality and visual impact that Islamic calligraphy has on the mind. There is a harmony and a rhythmic flow to the words and verses that virtually defy close analysis. Non-Muslims who are unfamiliar with the Arabic language liken its mysterious rhythm to poetry, but it is not poetry in the normal sense of the word since its rhythms follow no poetic rules and contain a power that goes admittedly far beyond the realm of any earthly poetry. "The eloquence does not reside so much in the ordering of the words into powerful poetic utterance as in the degree of the inspiration as a result of which every sentence, every word and every letter scintillate with a spiritual presence and are like light congealed in tangible form."[67] The rhythms themselves are subtle and mysterious and do not really coincide with what is traditionally found within the great works of literature that have been written down through the ages.

---

[66] S. H. Nasr (ed.), *Islamic Spirituality: Foundations* (Edinburgh: Alban Books, 1989), p. 4.
[67] *Ibid*, p. 5

In addition, rhythmic patterns flow out of the Qur'anic images and symbols into the very soul of the believer and have the power to return them to a state of primordial bliss. These images and symbols are not the classical or literary symbols that contemporary individuals are familiar with from the great poetry and literature of recorded history. Rather, these images and symbols are archetypal in their character and universal in their message. They are basically of two kinds. One type can be called macrocosmic and are the symbols that relate to the world of nature in its grander magnitude. They are the symbols that recall the great and harmonious rhythms of the natural order that include the passage of night and day, the movement of sun, moon, and stars, the breadth of the zodiacal heavens, the phases of the moon, and the spiral movement of galaxies all ponderously swirling around a central metacosmic core.[68] These are symbolic images expressive of a rhythm and movement that touch the very soul of those reciting the verses as they sit with the book and intone the sacred words and phrases. "The Qur'an on the other hand engenders, in whoever hears its words and experiences its sonorous magic, both plenitude and poverty. It gives and it takes, it enlarges the soul by lending it wings, then lays it low and strips it bare; it is comforting and purifying at one and the same time, like a storm; human art can scarcely be said to have this virtue."[69] We touch the Book, take it to hand, read it, aspire to absorb its meaning and internalize its holy essence; in return we are touch by the very words of God.

Finally, we should not overlook the fact that the phrases and verses of the Qur'an enter the daily life of the Muslims to the extent that the rhythm and texture of life itself becomes interwoven with prayers, epithets, litanies and invocations that are derived expressly from the sacred text. "It is easy to understand the capital part played in the life of the Moslem by those sublime words which are the verses of the Qur'an; they are not merely sentences which transmit thoughts, but are in a way beings, powers, or talismans. The soul of the Moslem is as it were woven of sacred formulas; in these he works, in these he rests, in these he lives and in these he dies."[70] The Qur'an is an integral part of a Muslim life, permeating every aspect of the daily routine, shaping its parameters, providing its coloration, motivation, and ultimate goal. It is the first sound whispered into the ear of a newborn and possibly the last sound–if one is blessed with a so-called "happy death"–that is uttered as one takes leave of this world, becoming a verbal bridge into another dimension.

Qur'anic recitation also determines the very framework of the spiritual life for the person. Muslims draw on the language of the Qur'an to give a spiritual frame to their hopes, fears, sorrows, regrets, and aspirations. They use the Qur'an as a means of withdrawing for a few moments during the course of the day,

---

[68] "The creation of the heavens and the earth is greater than the creation of man." (40:57)

[69] T. Burckhardt, *Mirror of the Intellect* (Albany: SUNY Press, 1987) pp. 244-245.

[70] F. Schuon, *Understanding Islam* (New York: Penguin Books, 1994), p. 60.

whether it is in the early morning when the birds sing their own sacred verses or after the sunset prayer when the calm of dusk merges into the stillness of night. The holy recitation relieves the mind, the psyche, and the soul of those who intone the verses from the gravitational pull of this world with its implicit imbalance, disharmony and lack of peace. When the Muslims arises in the morning at the call to prayer, they have available the sacred book that contains all they need to know and therefore they possess the means to realize the knowledge contained in the glorious book in their daily lives. Small wonder then that devout Muslims turn to the Holy Qur'an for sustenance and strength on a daily basis throughout the course of their lives, with choices that pre-empt doubt and despair, leading them back to the source of their existence within the Divine Being.

At the dawn prayer (*salat al-fajr*), the shadowy rays of the saffron moon flow across the window sill. In the pre-dawn darkness, the dark plate of the night sky shines forth the light of ancient star dust with their message of eternity within time and infinity within space, before disappearing with the coming of the dawn. There is a hint of incense and musk in the air whose assault on the senses captures a feeling of sacrality that becomes a moving force within the mind and heart. Heavenly scents accompany the two angels who descend to witness the Qur'anic recitation that occurs in one place or another every morning across the crescent of the Islamic world. Having performed the ritual ablution and prayer, Muslims in various corners of the globe sit cross-legged on a prayer carpet and reach for the Noble Qur'an, the Illuminated Book, a document that is "on a tablet well-preserved in heaven", as well as a printed book held in hand. They kiss it out of profound respect, place it on forehead and heart, and then commence to recite the words and verses of the Holy Book. *Alif, Lam, Mim*, they chant sonorously the Arabic letter that commence the recitation: "This is the Book, of which there is no doubt, and guidance for those who fear God." (2: 1)

With the divine words of revelation, the Muslims forever repeat the task of planting in the ground of their soul the seeds of a divine knowledge that brings guidance and certainty to those who fear God. As the mind becomes illuminated with knowledge, when the heart is on fire with desire, when the imagination paints dreams of mystery and beauty, and when the higher emotions are brimming with devotion and love, the seeds of the divine Mystery take root and grow, giving entrance into a realm beyond legends and myths where mystical power and self renewal far exceed anything we are capable of creating on our own. Dust may settle and the early dawn light creeps cautiously across the windowpane while the outsized autumn moon sinks heavily below the distant horizon. As the words of revelation echo across the rafters and rooftops of the city in the emerging dawn, the aspiring soul becomes a staging ground of worship and praise that rises through levels of conscious awakening until it returns full circle to its origin and source in that universal consciousness radiating outward from the Mind of God.

5.4 The Art of Qur'anic Recitation

Devout Muslims live with the Qur'an, not as a book on a shelf to be perused at random, but as a miraculous presence waiting to be encountered and communicated with. Their attitude calls to mind a statement of the American transcendental philosopher Ralph Waldo Emerson when he wrote over a century ago: "Other men are lenses through which we read our own minds." In the minds and hearts of the Muslims, the verses of the Qur'an serve as reflecting lenses through which the faithful can see the truth of themselves as a mirror reflection of the Truth of the Supreme Being. The words of the book are beacons of light connecting existential truths with celestial realities. When Muslims read the Qur'an, the knowledge and light of a higher reality bursts in upon their ordinary consciousness with a revelation that supersedes the narrow, matter-of-fact workaday experience of their daily lives with the inrush of a profound and enlightening experience that is as unexpected as it is earth-shattering.

This question of the presence is crucial in understanding the true nature of Islamic worship and the spiritual disciplines such as Qur'anic recitation that form the ritual cornerstone of such worship. The words of the text are the sacred talismans of transmission. Muslims recognize that they have the words of God, words with which to speak and think and internalize the divine disclosure, words that reflect every virtue and every intimacy in life, words with which we can express sacred emotions and affinities that reside in the deepest well of our beings, words that tell us stories and sing of a primordial Adamic era when the story of the first man and woman began to unfold concerning human origins that to this day capture the imagination of the receptive mind.

By intoning through rhythmic breathing and chanting, and by establishing a rhythm of sacred vibration that courses through the body in waves of sacred sentiment, the worshipper is able to call him or herself back to a more authentic mode of being that takes root in the spiritual verities. Through rigorous discipline and an absolute adherence to the laws of recitation (*tajwid*), we are able recapture and harbor intimate modes of divine presence that accompany the verses of the divine disclosure. Through the worship of Qur'anic recitation, a person makes possible through his or her own individual effort the great awakening that takes places in the divine presence that creates the spontaneous sense of our own presence in the eternal continuum of the here and now, reminding ourselves of who we are as a conscious remembering.

Of course, I knew nothing of this sacred intimacy that could be made possible through the recitation and chanting of the sacred Qur'anic text. Armed with the primal impulses of an affirmative faith that expressed a readiness to believe and that made me a repository of hope awaiting fulfillment, I set myself as a new Muslim convert on a course to come to terms with the Qur'an and overcome any and all obstacles that may get in my way. Call it determination, decisiveness, short-sightedness, or possibly a kind of holy madness, I remember a spiritual conviction to my attitudes that were tenacious and deep-rooted, although from whence they came, why they had arrived and what form of expression they would take I had no clear idea.

    I came to Islam as a grown man who had embraced the religion as a matter of decision and active choice, but this was only the first step on a long road of acclimatization and realization of what it truly means to be a Muslim—and what it means to me—an effort of self-discovery and consciousness-raising that is personal and unique to each individual. "For every soul," according to one well known tradition, "there is an individual path to follow." As such, I knew that I had to come to terms with the Arabic Qur'an if not now then later, the Noble Book being the alpha and omega of all Islamic spirituality, its source material and its means of spiritual expression and worship. The religion began with its first descent into the mind of the Prophet in the Cave of Light in Makkah, and will come to fruition through the sincere expression of each individual Muslim life faithful to its dictates and guidance. In my childhood, I never attended a traditional Qur'anic madrasah because I converted to Islam later in life, over thirty years ago. However, like all serious devotees of the religion, I very soon set about learning the intricacies of Qur'anic recitation, without which Islamic worship in the form of prayer, which uses Qur'anic verses as part of its ritual or Qur'anic recitation, would be impossible.

    I do not like to measure these things in months and years and prefer the concept of an uninterrupted continuum of the present moment bathed in some perspective of eternity, but sometime after familiarizing myself with the meaning of the Qur'an in translation with the aid of my Sufi friend Haneef, I set myself the task of learning the basics of the Arabic script. Of course as a Westerner, even though I had a focused interest in other languages as an English teacher and spoke French and German with ease, I had great difficulty initially with the Arabic letters. Yet there was an appealing magic to the formation of the letters that radiated a whimsical quality of arabesques and changing profiles that seemed to spread across the page like untied knots, leaving behind a bold air of incoherent mystery. Once thoroughly familiar with the alien letters, however, I set about familiarizing myself with the words and phrases of the sacred text.

    Eventually, I felt comfortable enough with the letters to enable me to begin mouthing the sacred speech. It is one thing to be a child and undergo the demanding rigors of learning the basics of one's mother language letter for letter and sound for sound; quite another to be a grown adult in the throes of an alien wilderness of symbols and sounds patched together with an exact science of pronunciation (*tajwid*) with fixed rules and regulations that required the intonation of a chanted psalmody as a natural rhythm of sound emergent from within the sacred text and given life by the human voice. How was I to learn this on my own? I couldn't very well sit myself down next to the seven-year-olds of a Qur'anic madrasah; at least my state of development at the time would not have permitted such recourse. Nor could I sit myself down amid the faithful who often gather after the early morning *fajr* prayer in many a mosque across the Islamic crescent to sit in a circle around the imam or sheikh and fine-tune their Qur'anic recitation skills. Any genuine attempt to read the Qur'an at that stage would have proved to be scandalous. Somehow, I needed to develop a reasonable amount of skill and accuracy before gathering the courage to join the circle of worshippers after the dawn or sunset prayer.

The next phase in this process of familiarization with the physical demands of the text in terms of pronunciation, intonation and the rhythmic tonal qualities implicit in correct psalmody led me to the convenience of a newly developed technology at that time in the mid-70s, the walkman tape player. The Qur'an was available in its entirety on a series of tapes; some of the traditional Egyptian and Syrian sheikhs who are adept at the fine art of Qur'anic recitation are legendary. There are of course different styles of psalmody; I followed the advice of a Muslim friend and purchased the entire Qur'an recited by an Egyptian sheikh known for the quality of his "sound" and the perfection, accuracy, and clarity of his pronunciation. The entire Qur'an came to 30 different tapes that coincided with the 30 equal parts (*juz*) that the Qur'an is conveniently divided into.

After the Maghreb prayer at sunset, I would set aside a half hour's time and listen to the tape while reading aloud and meticulously following the progress of the text. In this way, I was able to detect whether I was making a mistake or not, and I read along while simultaneously listening to the Sheikh's pronunciation through earphones. Needless to say, the tonal clarity and the vibratory resonance of the sound of the human voice intoning the sacred verses rang through my head with the clarity of a resounding bell, echoing the famous comment of the Prophet when he told his wife Khadijah that when he heard the first verses of the revelation being recited to him by the Archangel Gabriel, they had the clarity of a clarion bell, and later he was to say: "It was as though the words were written on my heart." I spent a year in this process of becoming more familiar with the text until I felt that the words were written on my mind as resonant echoes from some distant, higher plane; but they were yet to be written on my heart.

One lesson had already come clear to my novitiate mind; the Qur'an is by name a recitation rather than a reading *per se*, meaning predominantly an oral tradition in commemoration of earlier revelations delivered to peoples of other time periods and recalling the universal quality of legends and myths whose knowledge and meaning conveyed truths delivered orally and intended to be transmitted orally. As such, the Qur'an is yet another manifestation in a long history of oral traditions that have been passed down through time as sacred forms of communication that are direct and immediate between people rather than being relegated only to some fixed place on a page, lying closed in and sequestered within the covers of a book. The symbolic value of an oral text conveys meaning to the mind without necessarily having the intermediary of a formal script whose practical value now serves us well but that does not supersede or enhance the intuitive directness that takes place orally. The written page contains a kind of nostalgia for the time when the words on a page were spoken as a kind of poetry or solar speech, whose meaning transcends dimensions as well as distance. These oral revelations were as intangible and invisible as the Spirit their words convey and as eternal as the Cosmic Mind out of which they were born.

I was yet another recipient among generations of humanity poured full of knowledge and blessing, but I still couldn't claim to have gotten inside the words of God any more than they have gotten inside me. In truth, as a vessel of the Divine Spirit, I felt as hard and brittle as glass, ready to be broken and shattered into pieces at the slightest whim of destiny and at the merest contingency of this world. How I needed these words of revelation to fill me up and cast me to the spirit of the wind that "bloweth where it listeth". I was gradually becoming more familiar with the formalities of the text; but its inimitable spirit and the higher consciousness made available through the intonation of the text still eluded me. Where was the "holy presence", the descent of the *sakinah*, I had read about in all the traditional books that I so eagerly devoured? Where was the beloved presence that creates within the human mind a sparkling consciousness cracking open with fresh awareness like the report of river ice in a raw winter dawn? Was I only a dense and tightly woven sieve leaving the thick film of sweet nectar behind at the doorstep of my being? I continued to search for the living reality of the book that would not come easy and without care, and I continued to work at the process of internalization of its knowledge and blessing to set me hopefully on the quickest and surest path of return to God until reaching the spiritual station of no return.

Only when I felt sufficiently comfortable with listening to the tape-recorded text did I consider myself qualified to enter, not a *madrasah Qur'aniyah* as such, but a Qur'anic circle of the type held after the early morning (*fajr*) or evening (*maghreb*) prayer in many mosques throughout the Islamic crescent for reasons that have hopefully been made clear. For one full year, I sat in a small group of Muslims with the imam of a mosque who guided us through the intricacies of learning the "science of *tajwid*" mentioned earlier to facilitate correct reading. It is a complicated reading discipline designed to enhance and stylize the forward movement of the text with well defined rules that involve correct pronunciation of each letter, the elongation of certain vowels, the use of ellipses, indications to pause and stop in the reading to facilitate breathing and to enhance meaning, to name only a few of the ritual complexities required in order to achieve correct recitation. This is not even to mention the psalmodic chanting that the voice eventually assumes, a skill that comes with practice and time. It takes diligent effort to become adept at Qur'anic recitation, but having once passed through the rigors of this well-specified discipline, it becomes an aspect of sacred ritual that every Muslim takes very seriously, not wishing to misread and badly distort the sacred flow of the text. Any interruption in the flow of the text and any misreading or mispronunciation is immediately repeated correctly to preserve the true sense of the meaning and out of deference to the integrity of the sacred text.

I discovered to my surprise that Arabs themselves have difficulty reading the Qur'an without making errors of some kind. Either a lack of habit in routinely reciting the text or perhaps occasional over-familiarity with the Arabic language and a tendency to resort to colloquial pronunciations sometimes hindered an accurate delivery in rendering the text justly. In fact, my slavish devotion to the literal text and my conscious effort at the correct reading of letter for letter gave me an edge over other native-speaking Arabs who felt lulled into a false familiarity with the classical Arabic of the text that they had not truly mastered. I took nothing for granted and worked hard at becoming adept at recreating every letter and sound with precision and accuracy.

Had I arrived at the "holy gate" of some cosmic ocean whose sonoral sound could sweep the mind and heart of our singular humanity across eternities of cosmic awareness and infinitudes of cosmic space? The answer must be a resounding "no!" to a question not worth posing with any true seriousness. One does not approach the book with the intention of shattering cosmic barriers and arriving on the shores of some vast enlightenment. It was enough for me to get the text right, taking care not to betray the integrity of the sacred speech and to fulfill the mandate of its ritualistic discipline and worship. I would leave the rest to God.

Still, I asked myself what else I could do to take leave of the borderland of an ego-entrenched psyche and climb inside the text, wrap it around my heart like a warm woolen cloak and attain the proximity as well as the warmth of its sacred presence. How could I give up the familiarity of my own human voice for the grandiloquence of the single sovereign voice of the sacred text whose power knows no bounds and whose energy contains modes of transcendence. It is a voice of a million years, the voice of eloquent silence that resounds within the cave of the heart in search of a suitable resting place. After much contemplation, I resolved to leave behind temporarily the vocalizations and verbalism of the original form and turn to the written script of the text whose calligraphic splendor and alien majesty as a sacred Islamic art called upon the sense of sight as opposed to the sense of hearing as a channel to the higher faculties of the mind, hoping that the engagement of all the senses of the body would allow them to serve their rightful function as effective instruments to facilitate the internalization and realization of the spirit within the text within the mind if not the higher consciousness of my wandering, modern-day soul.

As a prototype of language, the Qur'an itself is the product of both an oral and written tradition. As mentioned earlier, the Qur'an is primarily a recitation and the Prophet himself was instructed by the archangel Gabriel to "recite in the name of your Lord", this verse being the very first verse revealed to the Prophet of Islam. However the *sakinah* or spiritual presence is to be found in the written as well as the orally recited Qur'an. According to a Holy Tradition, God wrote with a Mystic Pen that symbolizes the Universal Intellect, the inner reality of all things that is preserved on the Guarded Tablet before the creation of the world. The Supreme Pen (*al-Qalam al-a'la*) has traditionally been identified with the Universal Intellect, while the ink is the reflection of All-Possibility and results in the possibility of the manifestation of the creation, recalling the Qur'anic verse: "And if all the trees on earth were pens and the sea–with seven seas added–[were ink] yet the words of Allah could not be exhausted." (31: 27) The Pen therefore has important significance as a universal symbol of the creation of the Word, the Logos, and the revelation, while the Guarded Tablet "preserved in the Paradise" maintains the record of universal manifestation[71] and sets the precedent for the significance of the written word.

It is one thing to passively regard the written word on the page and quite another to actively engage oneself in the writing of a particular text.[72] The experience becomes a challenge when the letters, words and phrases are derived from an alien alphabet that needs to be scripted and learned as a child learns to write. Having set myself the task, I bought a special notebook and pen to use as my calamus and blessed reed, in order to faithfully execute my sacred endeavor. I began of course at the beginning, with the 7-verse opening statement of the initial *surah*, appropriately entitled *al-Fatihah*, the Opening. I did not concern myself with the length, scope and breadth of this challenge; if I did I may have developed a fear that I was not up to the task. When dealing with the Qur'an, it does not matter whether you are occupied with the verses for a few minutes or an entire lifetime. Like a true friend, the book does not count the hours and days; it is enough to be there, together and entwined in a holy relationship that becomes a continuum of the ever-present eternal moment striking a vertical sword across the horizontal axis of earthly time. The ethereal and timeless power of the text is persistent and will not freely and easily give up its ghost. If a person is fortunate enough to partake of the sacred blessing (*al-barakah*), it reaches inside to touch the pulse of the heart and one must decide one way or another what it means and what to do about it.

Whenever I could find the time but preferably at least once a day, I sat myself down in a state of ritual ablution to copy the sacred text in the humble tradition, if not the accomplished style, of the traditional Qur'anic calligraphers and illuminists. The words and verses multiplied upon the page, the pages multiplied upon pages, as I worked my sacred reed through the contours and curves that make up the physical formation of the Arabic letters. The formation of the Roman alphabet relies predominantly on its straight and angular lines and has a forward movement from left to right down the page. The letters seem to have clearness and efficiency as their primary motivation, but they do not inspire as do the arabesque and fluid style of the Arabic script in the elaborate adornment of a written page. The letters of the Roman script do not seem to expect too much of themselves. In the traditional Islamic setting, everything commences from the right: People leave elevators from the right side first,

---

[71] Another tradition, reported by Ibn Abbas, says that "Allah created the Pen before He created the Creation." Also, "the Pen burst open and the Ink flows from it until the Day of the Resurrection."

[72] There are 6,234 verses in the entire Qur'an. Copying 12 verses a day on average would produce a completed manuscript in about a year and a half. It took me roughly 2 years of sporadic work on the project to complete the task.

greetings and salutations occur from the right and hand-writing has a forward movement from right to left down the page. Within the world of the Roman alphabet that we use today for modern English, one would look in vain for the flexible and gentle fluidity offered by noon, sheen and lam of the Arabic alphabet. While Western landscape art is full of space and light, the sonorous and calligraphic arts in Islam are full of sound and stroke.

Consider the bold, vertical stroke of the *alif*, statuesque and statesmanlike as if in commemoration of the vertical stance of *Homo sapiens*, making the solitary image of an individual person the symbolic equivalent of the human *alif*. The letters noon, ba, ta and tha–differentiated only by dots resting either above or below the form of the letter–contain all the suggestive, symbolic and sensuous curvature of a cup ready to contain the nectar of some sublime meaning. Like shapely crescent moons and spiraling galaxy clusters that harbor within their sublime forms the darkness of night and the silence of the universe, the letters spread out across the page as silent sentinels to the underlying sense of mystery that pervades all of existence, just as the trees and texture of a solemn forest or sacred veldt create a sense of sacrality within the ambiance of their existential reality. It is almost as if the symbolic images of the letters contain metaphors of meaning even before they constitute the totality of a word. In writing stroke for stroke and letter for letter, the traditional calligrapher virtually stepped inside the written text and in so doing was able to create within himself the sense of a larger presence beyond the very horizon of the self.

You enter a revelatory text through the medium of copying as you might enter into the lost valley of Shangri-la, with feelings of reverence and trepidation. In doing so, you enter a realm that transcends the limits of the individual self, taking you far beyond snow-capped mountains and the puffed elegance of the cumulus clouds that gather at their summit. It takes you beyond the trite sensibilities of the human mind, beyond the horizon of one's limited cognitive world, indeed beyond the contoured and shapely elegance of the Arabic script and the florid manner in which the words and verses of the Qur'anic text are written, beyond and into a world where the great mystery envelopes and becomes a part of us by virtue of our symbolic participation in the actual writing of the sacred words of God.

Imagine if you could walk to the very edge of the horizon, sit yourself down, and examine the broad panorama before you, revealing what lies beyond the horizon. Before your eyes and beyond your wildest dreams, there is spread out before you a wilderness landscape seemingly beyond the continuum of time and space in which the primordial spirit hovers amid gnarled millennium trees and divinely sculptured rock formations. There is a primitive aspect to the shape of the letters and their emergence as words whose primordial quality weaves arabesques of symbols and shapes that actually trace a kind of spiritual presence onto the terrain of the blank white page, a page that by filling up with verse after verse of the sacred discourse becomes a calligraphic map whose terrain veils in secrecy an actual spiritual presence.

The experience of copying the Qur'an letter for letter and word for word created a spiritual discipline within me that spilled over into untold areas in the experience of my daily life. You cannot spend days of your life writing down the words of revelation without becoming touched by some indelible mark of mystery and sacrality permeating other aspects of one's daily routine. Emotions become raw and facts become bold. There is a truth and a reality to every created thing from the atom with its elemental building particles to the spiraling galaxies with their uncounted billions of stars. Everything takes on symbolic value and therefore everything has meaning and significance, creating a kind of vibratory confluence of power and energy that makes itself known through sounding rhythms and symbolic strokes of the Arabic alphabet. Reciting the text for memory or writing down its verses becomes an intimate private encounter with the sounds and symbols that reveal the meaning of the universe. The personal ego fades away and what takes its place is the sublime experience of the truth of the Noble Book before you, with its message of the oneness and unity of the Reality, the very message and summative height of the entire religion, contained within the primordial point that commences the formation of any written word.

To step into the text you become a part of it and it becomes a part of you. In participating in the sound, the memorized texture and hand-scripted formation of the letters and words, the text then touches you with its energy and power. You and the text are one and the same for those moments that you take up the book in hand, recite the sacred verses for memory, or copy them down and fill a blank page with their extravagant beauty. The largeness of the revelation, which encompasses all mystery that is to be resolved and all knowledge worth knowing, allows you to come to an understanding of yourself that would not otherwise be accessible in our daily existence. In a strange sense, the knowledge itself is secondary: Knowledge, even if it is known, goes nowhere if it is not realized and internalized within your being as wisdom that shines out through behavior and good works. The experience of worship is so haunting and so elevating, indeed so entrancing an experience that it makes you cry sometimes in spite of your sensible, rational and modern mentality and in spite of the hard shell that surrounds the viewfinder that filters the perceptions of our minds and shapes our conscious world. There is an archaic affinity to the experience that is so strange and beautiful it also makes you feel afraid almost of being unable to live up to the moment once it passes by, revealing by hints and starts secrets and depths to the inner self that contain promise but no clear outcome. When you take leave of the Book, just as when you take leave of your prayer carpet and re-enter the contingencies of daily life, you take the experience with you because it has become a part of your being by virtue of the participation in the sacred discipline.

In this way and over the course of more than forty years as a Muslim, I have attempted to come to terms with the beloved, the holy, the noble Qur'an. I have no idea to what extent I have succeeded or failed. It is not for me to speculate on such matters and who can measure such things in any event. It is enough to know that I have grown to love the Qur'an as I have grown to love the Prophet

Muhammad (PBUH), who delivered it to humanity and can no longer conceive of living without it any more than I can conceive of living without the pulse of my heart or the ground of my soul. When I sit down after the dawn prayer, I read and recite the verses with familiarity and ease, to the extent that coming to the Book and reciting its verses feels like coming home. When I close the book and walk away from a session of worship, I feel refreshed and complete, like having visited some far distant country whose vistas put things in perspective and whose language gives voice to knowledge of the stars.

In having recited the words of God, I have invoked His presence. I have filled multiple notebooks over the years with my hand-written verses, perennially adding to and complementing the first primer that initiated my child-like attempts to get closer to the Divine Revelation by copying down the verses letter for letter and word for word. I realize now that it is not the having done but the doing the fills me with joy. In keeping with my namesake the Prophet Yahya, I have followed the guidance he was given when one of the verses of the Qur'an admonishes him to: "Seize the Book with (conviction and) strength." I have been living all these years in the presence of a revelation whose truth and light fills my advancing years with the same Truth and Light that has filled the universe since time immemorial. In remembrance of that Truth and Light, I hope to continue to "Seize the Book" until the end of my days.

5.5 Human Consciousness Rising

In addition to the blessings of the five senses, with their exotic sights and sounds, their aromatic smells and tastes, there is a sixth sense that gathers information like a ghost in the machine, without the use of reason and perceives knowledge without using the formal instruments of perception at human disposal. Like all living creatures, we are in principle sentient beings; but we are distinguished from the pack by virtue of our status as conscious beings having the capacity to know without seeing, to perceive without hearing, to appreciate without smelling or tasting and to feel without actually touching a thing. The question remains: how is this accomplished and what is the agency through which the miraculous becomes manifest to the human mentality? What has the capacity to serve as the repository and arena in which we open our minds and hearts and gain access to "the other side of reality"?

There is a point beyond which the five senses cannot lead us. Having arrived at this outer edge of experience and point of no return, we have only to take one further step in order to cross the threshold from outer perception to inner awareness. What allows us to do this incredible feat and lead us into the exotic world of inner experience? The answer is none other than the miraculous field of human consciousness. It is a world of self-identity in which we can see and become known to ourselves as worthy of respect and love, a world of witnessing in which the hidden camera of the "I" features the input of the world and all its experiences as a field of perception that we can then process with intelligence and insight, a world of heightened awareness with levels of mindfulness that take us where our inmost desires want to go. We make here a distinction between the higher faculties that humans enjoy such as reason, intelligence, and higher emotions we will deal with in a later section of this book. For now, it is enough to focus on that incredible field of witnessing and perception that we call human consciousness that has the power to open doors and raise spirits to a level of experience that would be unimaginable to the human mentality without this unique feature, reducing us once again to the level of the animals.

In coming to terms with the higher, more mysterious forces that are at play within the universe and that we would be hard put to ignore at the risk of completely misunderstanding ourselves and our true nature within the natural scheme of things, we need to consider this key component of the human condition that actually sheds unexpected light on the true nature of knowing and perception. If we have a secret sixth sense that provides us with a higher complement to the input of the five senses, then this sixth sense inevitably feeds off the direct insight and intuitions of the human intellect and finds shelter within the broad plain of consciousness that characterize the human mind.

Firstly, we must ask the inevitable question about human consciousness: What is it precisely, what true purpose does it serve, and to what end will it lead humanity? Beyond the face of modern humanity and beyond the grasp of the modern scientific inquiry lies the mystery of our knowledge of self, a universal mystery whose integrity as a perennial enigma has succeeded in preserving the defining quality of our humanness from the knife-edge of our irreverent scrutiny. Human consciousness continues to define our humanness in ways that still elude the comprehension of the modern scientific community, much less the mass population that enjoy its benefits.

We know from the religious traditions that human consciousness represents a state of mind and a higher cognitive field of awareness that raises the human being above the rest of the creation. What we perhaps do not remember, by virtue of the battle-scared offensive of modern science to reduce the mind to a mechanized analogue emerging out of the neurons of inorganic brain matter, is that in mirroring the consciousness of the Supreme Mind, human consciousness becomes a supra-sensory faculty that permits the divine qualities and attributes, identified in Islam through the 99 names of Allah, to become existential realities and virtues that characterize the humanness of humanity in the light of these higher spiritual attributes. We need to reflect upon and consider what the traditional mentality has known all along and what the modern mentality is not willing to admit, namely that consciousness is an attribute of the mind that irradiates the entire thinking process and links us directly to the Spirit that has created and given us life, not to mention the consciousness that allows us to appreciate it.

Because of the many levels and degrees that are usually associated with the faculty of human consciousness, it could be called the spectrum of the mind whose many colors and shades actually provide the prism through which we consider the machinations of the inner self and understand the reality of the world we live in. Nothing highlights more the interaction of the world of humanity as microcosm and the world of the universe as macrocosm as does the mystery of consciousness. The conscious–as opposed to the animal–mind serves as a kind of witness that transcends both humanity and the world by being a quality of thought that allows experience to be viewed through a transcending mirror that witnesses the essential knowledge of God through a reflection of the self. Because of human consciousness, only the human being participates in the transcendent principle and reflects its luminous source.

That having been said, however, it must be added that consciousness lurks as an unexplained mystery in the shadow of the human form. Consciousness at the universal level recalls the color of the rainbow with its transparent hint of miracle reaching down and touching earth before disappearing again in the mist. It reflects the wisdom behind the flight of the eagle. It remembers the perfection within the design of snow crystals and the calm within the eye of the storm. It summons the beauty encompassed within the colorful forms of a butterfly wing, and the message of order and design behind the spider's web. Indeed, consciousness synthesizes a web of intricacies that captures all of nature and places man at the heart of it all as the one observing and listening, in search of a knowledge that lies within the cells of his being as it does beyond the outer reaches of the stars.

The depth of human consciousness, according to the early traditions of Buddhism as well as modern depth psychology, reaches back to a past without a formal beginning with the entire universe as its basis, when consciousness became manifest as a conscious awakening to knowledge and to life. Consciousness became known to humanity when Adam first met himself in the dawn of his life. As a purely subjective being, he did not say: 'I am I'; but rather, as a subjective being capable of objectivity, he was able to say 'I am not I but He that is in me', as if he could gaze within the well of his own being and see not himself but the Divinity that created him. In this way, the first prototype human intelligence became reflective and objectifying, as the individual consciousness re-oriented itself away from the purely physical and corporeal world toward its luminous source in the lofty realm of the Spirit. Consciousness began long ago in the blue-white morning of the human mind. Consequently, the primordial resonance of dawn shines down through the ages as a crystalline quality of comprehensibility that characterizes the state of mind associated with consciousness, a clarity and heightened presence that provides the protocol and ambiance for all human thought.

Thereafter, the wise man of *Homo sapiens* has lived as a human entity through the power of a uniquely human consciousness. He is human rather than hominoid because of the consciousness of self and has the potential to transcend human limitations through a heightened consciousness that will lead back to the white light of eternity that is traditionally referred to as enlightenment. As the descendants of Adam have cascaded down through the millennia as a cornucopia of future generations, the ways and paths of the religions have whispered into the ear of the single requirement that makes people what they are as potential beings on earth and as universal beings in principle and by nature, namely the ability to see themselves as individual identities and to know themselves as a mirror reflection of a Superior Being. As such, we are beings who live 'self-consciously' in time but who exist 'supra-consciously' within eternity. As *Homo sapiens*, human intelligence is related to consciousness as time is related to eternity. As *Homo spiritualis*, we live in time within the context of eternity; while to be intelligent is to take part in a consciousness that transcends the human order. There exists something in humanity whose reality belongs to an order beyond time; there exists within us the consciousness of a Reality that can envisage not only time, but also its origin in eternity and its end in transcendence.

The ways of the spirit whisper to humanity at the dawn of day, in the final moments before sleep, in times of crisis, during moments of prayer. The ways of the spirit make themselves known when all the existential barriers have suddenly fallen away and the veils separating people from a direct perception of the true reality have been lifted. The way of the spirit reveals a conscious awakening of human consciousness that feels like an egg has cracked open inside and poured its revelatory contents over the surface of the mind. What it is and what it means exactly we do not know, but it recreates the qualities of awareness and consciousness within the mind that we experience as functioning human beings, but cannot adequately explain. The mindfulness of thought, the precise logic of reason, the powerful force of the human will, the prescient awareness of our surroundings, the abiding vision of the self, and the ability to conceptualize objectively and objectify our subjective experience are all the result of this outpouring of higher consciousness. Ultimately, the faint echoes of the supreme consciousness emerge and make their presence felt, recalling the primordial prototype of the perfect soul.

There is a structure associated with consciousness that we experience directly, a structure whose design is well ordered and subtle and whose power is unique and infinite. We have a knowledge within us that is encased in consciousness; it is not a thing to be studied or explained, but rather a field of awareness inward toward the inner self and outward toward others and the world to be experienced. There is mystery to consciousness, on the one hand, that leaves us questioning its ultimate meaning, and there is clarity on the other hand that answers all questions and resolves all doubt. It suggests the bottomless depths of an ancient well that at the same time has the power to lead us beyond the border of our known selves. Drop a stone into this well and you listen to its descent without ever hearing its final arrival. It reaches its pinnacle of manifestation when we sense a thing without knowing it and know a thing without consciously perceiving it. The knowledge has become realized within our being and its presence is known and felt as an existential as well as an inner reality. It is an awareness that seizes the body and reaches down to the level of the cells even. It is a mindfulness that seeps into the mind and psyche as an ethereal mist, revealing a presence that identifies who we are and a power that can change the course of our lives.

The conscious mind that once drew primitive images of men and animals on a cave wall in the south of France has been an active witness to its own historical development in a vast narrative of progression and change that has taken the modern mentality to places it will never visit in person. Through instruments of our own devising, our mechanical eye gazes many millions of light years into the far reaches of the heavens and radio ears listen to the whisperings of even more remote galaxies. With the aid of sophisticated microscopes, we are able to dissect the elements of our own being and through great particle accelerators, we can (indirectly) observe the actions and consequences of the particles of sub-atomic matter. Because of our formidable, inquiring mind and the unique character of our consciousness, we have broken through the boundaries that control and limit the rest of the creation and have reached a level of speculation and thought never before envisioned in the history of humanity.

Consciousness represents a continuum of intuitiveness and sensitivity that cannot be denied. Memory fades; imagination falters; reason deceives; logic fails. Our intelligence can fall short of the mark and our desires and emotions change with the wind. Still, consciousness is always there–like the air to the wind, the glow to the fire, the darkness to the night, the peak to the wave and the bud to the flower. It is there because it is the necessary foundation upon which we are built, a witness that sees but is not seen, a mystery that is dark and rich and enduring, and that shares in the wisdom of the universe. The mind and its all-encompassing niche – consciousness – is the one intangible reality that modern science does not fully comprehend and cannot control because it has not succeeded in measuring its elusive parameters and it does not dare to deny its existential presence.[73] Perhaps therein lies its determination to reduce it to its lowest common denominator in the ashes of purely physical matter in order to avoid the problem of coming to terms scientifically with an inviolable mystery.

The traditions do not say precisely what the mind is, or consciousness for that matter. Instead, they state what the mind–and its higher counterpart the intellect–can accomplish. The religions resort to traditional images and universal symbols to clarify the difficult but essential metaphysical concepts that everyone needs to comprehend, at least in principle in order to come to terms with their own reality. In one of the earliest traditional sources of Taoism in ancient China, Chuang Tzu, in his work entitled *The Book of Chuang Tzu*, refers to consciousness in this way: "What I mean by the expression 'having good ears' does not concern the faculty of hearing the external objects (*t'a*). It concerns only

---

[73] There is some considerable irony in the fact that what actually drives the scientific inquiry forward, namely the human mind in search of the true nature of reality, slips through the fingers of curious scientists and escapes their grasp precisely because they refuse to acknowledge its metaphysical origin and supra-natural source.

hearing one's own 'self' (*tzu*). What I mean by the expression 'having good eyes' does not concern seeing the external objects. It concerns only seeing one's own 'self'."[74] In this context, 'seeing one's own self' is a self-intuition that recalls what the Zen Buddhists call 'seeing one's [real] nature', a process that serves as a prelude and initiation to the experience of the higher consciousness that reflects not the individual self but the Supreme Self.

In the Qur'an, Allah is identified as the All-Seeing (*al-basir*) as well as the All-Knowing (*al-alim*), these being the two counterpoints, and the balance if you will, of a comprehensive and complete consciousness, namely a knowledge with insight and an intuitive vision based on the essential knowledge. In the words of Coomaraswamy, this 'presence of mind' is a 'point without extension' and a 'moment without duration', transcending time and place with its intuitive knowledge of the higher consciousness of God, of which man is a mirror reflection. The concept of both seeing and knowing reflects a vision of self and a knowledge of God that raises the context of consciousness above the earthly domain of humanity with its suggestion of a creative power greater than both itself and humanity, yet capable of being assimilated into the human being as an operative faculty of perception and self-awareness.

In traditional literature, the symbol of the "eye" has often been employed to represent the knowing Transcendent Self that extends beyond the limited 'ego' of individuals and the expression of their human 'self' in reflections of the expanding reaches of the stars. The American transcendentalist R. W. Emerson touches upon this idea in his journals: "Standing on bare ground," he says, "my head bathed by the blithe air and uplifted into infinite space, all mean egotism vanishes. I become a transparent eyeball; I am nothing, I see all; the currents of the Universal Being circulate through me; I am part or parcel of God."[75] The transparent eyeball becomes an expression to denote the experience of the miracle of consciousness that sees and knows, reflecting not the contents of thought, but the channel through which the process of knowing passes. Through vision and knowledge, humans are able to take leave of their individual nothingness and transcend themselves into vehicles of the Supreme Consciousness. Through the mind's eye, the human being can re-enact the qualities of God within the conscious mind that pass out into the world as examples of beauty, love, and virtue.

If the universal consciousness enters the entity of man through the mind, then it takes up residence in the heart, dwelling within humanity as the "eye" of the heart (*'ayn al-qalb*) and reflected within the intellect as a perfected and universal knowledge focused through the lens of the "eye" of certainty (*'ayn al-*

---

[74] Quoted in *The Unanimous Tradition*, Ranjit Fernando (ed.), Colombo: The Sri Lanka Institute of Traditional Studies, 1991, p. 51.

[75] Quoted in Loren Eiseley's *The Star Thrower*, New York: Harcourt Brace & Co, 1979, p. 211.

yaqin).⁷⁶ The Qur'an identifies three levels of knowledge that lead ultimately to a confirmed certainty of the truth itself. The first degree of knowledge is the knowledge of the mind, characterized in one Qur'anic verse as certain knowledge [*ilm al-yakin* (102: 5)]. This represents the onslaught of a certainty as the result of the normal course of logic and reasoning of the mind reminiscent of what scientists have achieved during these times in terms of scientific discovery and technological achievement. This is balanced by the certainty that results from the *eye of certainty* or alternatively translated *the certainty of seeing* [*'ayn al-yaqin* (102: 7)], in which the human being receives knowledge based on what he actually sees with his own eyes. Ultimately, the final degree of knowing results in what the Qur'an calls the certainty of the Truth [*al haqq al yaqin* (69: 51)], a certainty that lies within the "seat" of human intelligence–namely the heart of humanity–as "the conscious eye" and "certainty of truth" that cannot be denied without running the risk of giving up the innermost verification of Reality.

The traditional concept of consciousness embodies within its vision the many levels and modes of expression that the word consciousness implies. This includes a state of mind that is characteristically human rather than animal, an active and reflective thinking process that negotiates its way through all thoughts and impressions, a multi-tiered and multi-angled sense of awareness, a direct consciousness of self, a defining mode of self-expression, vast realms of imagination and emotion, the force of a free will, the living presence of mind, and the power to objectify subjective experience through the internalization of an objective knowledge. Ultimately, this "spirit of mind" arrives at the abode and resting place of a higher spiritual consciousness that is a heightened reflection of the Supreme Consciousness that created the universe because it wanted to be "known".

As the repository and focus of true knowledge, human consciousness processes all incoming knowledge within a framework of spatial and temporal events that find their extension and meaning, not to mention their actual reality, in their trans-temporal and trans-spatial setting of higher awareness. Without such a focus, the reality of this world would seem to enjoy an independent existence in its own right and have no extension beyond its physical, spatial and temporal truth. In other words, in separating the physical from the metaphysical, the reality of the physical world would have the objectivity found in the trans-substantiating quality of physical matter amounting to a dust-to-ashes approach to the philosophy of life. Instead, the power of the human consciousness promises us much more by permitting humanity to examine the contents of the mind within a framework of reality that substantiates and then transcends the three-dimensional structure of this world.

As the force field and center of objectivity, human consciousness processes incoming knowledge within a frame of reference that is independent of the reason and ratiocination of the mind. As a mode of objectivity, consciousness is

---

⁷⁶ In Hinduism, it recalls the frontal eye of Shiva.

"vertical" to the constant stream of thoughts, emotions, and desires that are mental, sensory, psychic and emotional and that provide the contents that the mind must evaluate and deal with. We are not just our brain and our mind in their sensorial and cognitive mode, for in claiming to 'know' things, the brain is an instrument and the mind a vehicle for knowing only the superficial aspect of a questionable reality that is externalized and peripheral with respect to our inmost being and with respect to experience that we know to be beyond the purely physical manifestation of life.

As the force field and pivot of transcendence, human consciousness serves as a bridge between worlds. It processes all incoming knowledge within a framework of higher realities that are based on the intuitive knowledge of God and that are experienced as sacred sentiments and higher emotions. What commences as a mindfulness of individuality that allows the mind to be aware of the self without being limited to the boundaries of the body reaches far beyond the physical organs of the brain and the mind to become a center of irradiation that opens onto the intellect that knows things intuitively and with certainty. In an external world that is full of mystery, uncertainty and doubt, our inmost being becomes our one absolute certainty whose existence and whose reality we cannot dispute or deny. Our intuitive awareness of the inner self is the absolute starting-point and *modus operandi* of our self-consciousness. It represents the apogee of our humanness and the watermark in the parchment of higher spiritual experience.

Behind the face of man there can be found an inward reality and a condition of knowability that we cannot actually measure or observe, but that we know exists by virtue of our experience of its enduring presence and the power of its consequences. I have it without which this work would not be possible; you have it, otherwise you never would have gotten this far in the reading; indeed, everyone has it without which they could not function as men and women within the world since it distinguishes who we are as human beings within a human society. We may not know what it is precisely, but we feel its "process" working within us as a higher reality descended upon our existential world, a reality that finds its origin and source in the knowledge of God. When opened to its fullest consciousness, it will ultimately turn humanity into a human revelation and a living source of knowledge.

In the end, the power of our human consciousness brings us face to face with ourselves and will lead us into the next age of humanity. Through the power of the inward 'eye' of consciousness, we can identify ourselves, not in terms of physical matter and not in a precarious alliance with a purely human reason to negotiate its way through the impenetrable mysteries of life. Only the ill-defined and unexplained presence of consciousness that lies behind the open face of humanity will give people the prescience and temerity of mind to resolve the fundamental mystery that lies at the core of the existential experience of life. Only the knowledge of the self will open the invisible doorway of our being, a doorway that once opened becomes the 'sun door' to a transcending and trans-luminescent world of unlimited dimensions. By passing through that door, humanity will advance beyond the reality that they now know, in order to arrive at a reality that they will come to know as the true origin and ultimate source of knowledge in the Spirit of God and His abiding Presence.

Without consciousness, we would not be human; with conscioiusness, we can know the Divinity and reflect His names and qualities in this world.

PART SIX

Spiritual Life

6.1 Dreams of a Forgotten Spirituality

"Feathers in the dust, lying lazily content, have forgotten their skies." (Tagore)

At the center of the innermost being of *Homo sapiens* lies three unique spiritual forces hidden away like distinctive watermarks of an ancient parchment. These inner forces serve as a distinguishing mark of all the untapped possibilities within the human mind and heart; but can become activated through the native disposition of an instinctive human spirituality that has the power to transform humanity from a mediocre and self-absorbed earthly entity into a human spirit that is both true to its inner nature and has the potential for perfection and sanctity. The Taoists refer to this archetypal persona as true man; the Religion of Islam makes reference to the primordial and ultimately perfect man (*al-insan al-kamil*).

These force fields include firstly an intelligence to explore the implications of the Divine Mystery that opens onto the plane of higher consciousness in order to discover the truth that exists simultaneously at the heart of the universe and within the heart of humanity; secondly a predisposition through faith[77] for the knowledge of God, together with an inborn desire to place oneself at the

---

[77] At the heart of the mystery of faith lies the wondrous compensation that faith has the power to resolve the Mystery, as Frithjof Schuon says, with its "existential intuition" and the "practical experience" that always accompanies genuine faith.

disposition of the Divinity in order to enter the Divine Presence; thirdly a readiness manifested as the "will to act" in order to abandon the confines of the individual ego and transcend the limitations of the purely human condition through a virtue that transforms the activity of the mind and heart into a modality of "being" that is endowed with the spirit of mystery and reflects the overwhelming presence of the truth.

The human condition has always included a latent potential for spirituality ever since Adam fell down from the beatitude of the Paradise into a terrestrial condition and state of being in which the human entity had to earn the knowledge of God through revelation and the blessings that accompany the internalization of that knowledge. With its roots in the spiritual and metaphysical dimension of existence, this process of human spirituality[78] can be understood as "movements" from outer form to inner substance, from the relative to the absolute, from the temporal to the eternal, from ignorance to wisdom, from the shadow of the earthly condition to the light and perfection of God, and from unending disparity to ultimate unity. As such, the life experience is neither all "outwardness" as it appears now during these times, nor all "inwardness" as it was for primordial man. Rather people today still need to find an equilibrium between the outward and the inward modalities, an equilibrium based on the spiritual meaning of life, existentialized by virtue of existence in "this world" and spiritualized to the extent that faithful individuals can put that knowledge and blessing "from above" into practice during the course of a life "here below".

At the heart of all spirituality lies none other than the compelling image of the Divinity, the Tao, Brahma, Jehovah, Allah, God. All human efforts, all rites and rituals, all forms of worship through prayer, fasting, meditation and oral invocation, all the spiritual instincts and all the sacred emotions have but one idea at their source and one objective at their end, namely consciousness of God followed ultimately by union (*al-tawhīd*) with the Divine Being. The goal of all human spirituality is spiritual realization leading to holiness and ultimately sanctity, through which the purely human can become the humanly spiritual, human with all the lingering imperfections that are endemic to the human condition, and spiritual through the innate ability to transcend human limitations through an understanding of self and a heightened awareness of God. The human mind, in pursuit of the Real, can be the vehicle of higher consciousness, and this is what the heart instinctively yearns to accomplish through faith. These two faculties of mind and heart within the Islamic context combine knowledge

---

[78] We include the qualifier "human" in this context partly to differentiate between a possible "animal" spirituality and/or other forms of spirituality such as the spiritual "presence" implicit in the seemingly inanimate forms of nature. An animal, by fulfilling its function and thus its vocation and by not stepping beyond its own limitations through unnecessary and uncalled for imperfections, achieves a kind of animal spirituality that is admirable and instructive to humanity. The peacock and the owl tell us something about pride and wisdom even if the peacock isn't proud as such, or the owl wise in the human sense.

and sacred emotion to lift the soul onto the true level of experience for which it is destined.

Human spirituality has as its prime objective, not the progressive development of the human being, but the human realization of God. It allows for an alternative reality far beyond the purely physical realm that modern science so convincingly objectifies for people today as the true reality of this world, an alternative reality that permits an understanding of the true nature of reality through modes of expression that actually transcend the limitations of human reason and are alien to the experiences of the physical senses. Humans are merely the venue and vehicle of this movement of return in which the human soul makes its sacred journey back to realization and union with the Divine. This journey of return begins as a conscious yearning through faith for the Truth that is both absolute and objective, a truth that not only speaks through revelation, but also listens to our prayer and hears the supplication of the faithful with attentiveness and mercy. It is a journey of discovery that eventually develops into a self-revelation that takes the form of a conscious spiritual experience through which humanity can bridge the distance that exists between the conscious, known and externalized human world and the inner, supra-conscious and mysterious realms of the Spirit.

Upon reflection, modern, contemporary people are not all they profess themselves to be: namely purely human and by extension humanistic beings, free spirits so to speak, proud of their logical reasoning, with no flights of spiritual fantasy and firmly rooted in the earthly plane, with a profound faith in their ability to "progress" on their own to the paradise that the inner being cries out for, but cannot find on the external plane. Increasingly, the image of the contemporary person is becoming blurred with a thousand different aspirations of a material nature that merely complement the purely physical explanation that science offers to the world in the guise of a secular philosophy and world-view. It offers a composite image of *Homo sapiens* that is grim and foreboding, a photo-finish of uncertainty and doubt, on the brink of an unknown future without perspective or promise. The Biblical Job ask himself the question: Does the hawk fly by Thy wisdom? The portrait of the modernite individual is an image of a humanity without a true sense of the power they have within themselves, amounting to the power of a spirituality that can transform the days of one's life and existence itself into what the Qur'an calls *the days of Allah*, with their overlay of sacredness and with the infusion into our daily lives of the Truth and the Reality that all people seek as a matter of instinct, even if they don't consciously accept such an other-worldly perspective.

Our reflections lead us at this point to ask two crucial questions that must be considered since we now live predominantly in a secular world in which it is increasingly more difficult to live a life of spirituality and to realize the spiritual potential that lies at the root of our beings. These two questions are firstly "What is spirituality?" and secondly "Is a truly human spirituality still possible within the contemporary setting and times?"[79] It may be yet impossible to fully come to terms with the true implications of a human spirituality since its meaning may vary from tradition to tradition. Nevertheless, we hope to aim at common elements within the family of religions that transcend the individual and formal manifestations of spirituality so that we can move on to our second inquiry concerning the possibility of a genuine life of spirituality during these times. We need to examine these questions, partly as an effort of spiritual renewal and partly because the downward movement toward a completely earthbound existence needs the shock of reverse thrust before the point of no return precludes any further spiritual advancement for people living during these times. The promise of a genuine human spirituality must still lie within our grasp, free and sufficient, in the same manner that a blade of grass relates and responds to early morning dew and has the capacity to absorb its revitalizing essence.

The human ability to express outwardly what lies within the inmost core must remain a viable possibility unless we want to betray the very foundations of our humanity, which during these times seems very possible indeed, given the fact that people everywhere seem more than willing to accept the perspective of a purely physical evolution combined with the elusive promise of a human progress, even though everything in today's world belies such a notion, leaving behind the stale aftertaste of what evolution and what progress. A life of spirituality is a two way movement in which outward natural forms of the divine creation can touch the inmost self and pluck a cord of the enlivening spirit within, sending reverberations through the human being with the rhythms and vibrations of a universal truth. The sound of a flute through the willows, the rays of moonlight reflected on my windowpane, the unfathomable mystery of the night sky with its pathways to the stars, the whisper of the wind through the palm trees, all these things and more are outer manifestations of the truth that have the power to project an inner reality[80] onto the surface of the soul, in which the soul can experience through the forms of the natural order the sense of the sacred and the intuition of spirituality that lies at the heart of the manifested universe.

---

[79] A third, more poignant question also comes to mind: What gives our whole being its motivation? We need to reassess what it is that fundamentally convinces us and has the power to draw us out of ourselves. The answer to this question perhaps lies embedded within the answer to the other two questions.

[80] While form is a "veil" of the spiritual world and hides the spirit within the form, it is also a symbol and sign of God as well as a remembrance of the Divinity by virtue of its very creation, existence, and implicit meaning, to the extent that a person can reach the spiritual world through the world of forms. Virgin nature as a "sign" of God and traditional art as a "remembrance" of God are two prime examples of this simple truth that form is not only a veil but also a key to the world of the spirit. The Qur'an speaks of mountains: "They will ask thee of the mountains. Say: My Lord will break them into scattered dust. (20: 105-108)

Similarly, movements from the inward to the outward rise to the surface of the inner world of spirit to manifest their essence on the external plane. The charity implicit in a smile, the profound emotion captured within a tear, the openheartedness of the extended hand, the virtue behind all good works, the promise of resurrection in the arrival of spring, the harmony of the cosmos, all these things and more contain inner manifestations of the Spirit of God that have the power to proclaim an outward spirituality by giving meaning to the external forms of the creation. We desperately need to reactivate the spiritual disposition of our minds and hearts in order to appreciate what lies within the inner as well as the external eye of our beings.

We have already mentioned that faith, as the initiatory impulse of spirituality and point of departure on the path of transcendence, helps to bridge the vast chasm that exists between God and humanity. From the human point of view, the distance between God and humanity is infinitely far, but from the Divine perspective, God is infinitely near, and He affirms this in the Islamic revelation with the words "He is nearer to you than your jugular vein" (50: 15), predisposing individuals to a spirituality that will lead eventually to sanctity, as prefigured in the journey of spiritual evolution from primordial man to fallen man to traditional man to perfected man. If we contemplate the distance between the finite and Infinite Being, we discover a profound sense of our own nothingness, as well as the inadequacy we face by being halfway between primordial man and perfected man. Yet, because of the power of faith, the separation of God and man is the thinnest of threads, the most transparent of illusions. Therein lies the implicit blessing of faith, a hope that washes through our being like a river of grace and projects its sentiments into the future like beams of light. "Allah will deliver them from the evil of that day and will shed over them light of beauty and joy." (76: 11)

In English, the root word for spirituality is generally associated with the word spirit, which originates from the word *spiritus*[81] of the Latin/Christian tradition, the luminous and pneumatic principle, sometimes referred to as the gale of the Spirit which "bloweth where it listeth." (John III.8) The Hindu tradition refers to *atman* which assumes a derivation from the root *an* or *va* meaning to breathe or blow.[82] In the context of Islamic spirituality, Arabic, but also Persian, Turkish and Urdu, are considered "Islamic languages" because the spirit of Islam and its

---

[81] The modern concept of man as being composed of body and mind has been preceded during traditional times with the concept that man possessed a body, soul and spirit, the *corpus, anima,* and *spiritus* of Hermeticism, a doctrine that has always been a part of the traditional wisdom.

[82] This coincides with the Qur'anic verse: "And I blew into him of My Spirit," in which the breath and the Spirit are polar opposites of the outer and inner worlds, the one manifested and the other beyond the sight of the eye. Also, the Upanishads contain the following question: "What is the Spirit?" That is to say, "What is this 'Self' that is not 'myself'? What is this 'Spirit' in 'me', that is not 'my' spirit?"

accompanying spirituality can be found in all of these languages. In Arabic and Persian, for example, the terms for "spirituality" are *ruhaniyyah* and *ma'nawiyyat* respectively. Interestingly enough, both terms have an Arabic root, taken from the language of the Qur'an. The Arabic term *ruhaniyyah* stems from the root word *ruh*, meaning spirit, and the Persian term *ma'nawiyyat* stems from the Arabic word *ma'na* which is the term for "meaning".

That having been said, it is also worth mentioning that the Qur'an warns of the unfathomable quality implicit in the word "spirit" with the cautionary verse: "They ask thee concerning the Spirit. The Spirit is from the command of your Lord." (17: 85) Nevertheless, with the caution ever in mind not to explore too deeply into areas that are beyond the realm of human understanding, it can be safely asserted that this term "connotes inwardness, the 'real' as opposed to the 'apparent', and also 'spirit' as this term is understood traditionally; that is, pertaining to a higher level of reality than both the material and the psychic and being directly related to the Divine Reality itself."[83] Thus, to answer the question what is spirituality, linguistic roots and the traditional perspective already point the way toward a world of inner meaning and contains elements of inwardness and a process of enrichment that identifies the mind and heart with the soul, while the soul implicitly yearns for the Spirit of God.

The term "spirituality" also includes another dimension which is crucial to the understanding of the "process of spirituality" that is at work among the faithful. "When this term is employed, there is always evoked a sense of the presence of the *barakah*, or that grace which flows in the vein of the universe and human life to the extent that he dedicates himself to God. There is, in addition, the sense of moral perfection and beauty of the soul as far as human beings are concerned. There is also a 'presence' which brings about recollection of God and the paradisal world.... The term spirituality evokes in the Muslim mind a proximity to God and the world of the Spirit."[84] This divine blessing, in addition to being within the cosmos as an actuality and within humanity as a potential, also exists within the rites and rituals that serve as the channels of blessing and grace that descend from Heaven to earth. When the Muslims pray, when they read the Qur'an, when they recite the sacred *shahadah* (the testimony of faith), they become the recipient of a divine favor that is contained within the very form of the ritual by virtue of his participation in that ritual form. Of course, beyond the forms of the religious rites and rituals lies the aspiration to interiorize the knowledge and experience of life in order to become aware of the inward dimension of reality so that it becomes a part of one's being. If primordial man was the embodiment of religion, then traditional man, namely the faithful and

---

[83] S. H. Nasr (ed), *Islamic Spirituality: Foundations* (New York: Crossroad, 1987), p. xvii.

[84] *Ibid.* This needless to say is a very strong argument for the return to the sacred forms of spirituality without which contemporary societies will continue to miss out on the channels of blessing and grace that are still available to him.

true man, is the embodiment of a process of spirituality which seeks to interiorize all aspects of life through every means possible.

Within the spiritual perspective, the spirit is not disconnected or in opposition to form as it seems to have become during these times in which there is a solid barrier between matter and spirit that many people do not even want to cross, much less believe in.[85] There is a magical quality to matter that intrigues our sensibility with its immediate objectivity and solidity; yet there is a mysterious quality to the substance of a thing that intrigues us with its unknown and potentially unknowable secret. Within the traditional perspective of which we write, the spirit resides within the form to the extent that everything has an outer dimension and an inner dimension. This is in keeping also with Islamic Qur'anic terminology in which Allah is characterized as having the qualitative name of *al-zhahir*, which refers to the outward and the external, and *al-batin*, which refers to the inwardly secret, the internal dimension. Similarly, in the Qur'an, Adam was taught the names of things.[86] This is traditionally understood by the commentators to mean that Adam was taught the inner nature and quality of every manifested "thing" in the creation. Thus, a tree has its given name and contains an impression, a meaning and a spirit that a grain of sand does not contain. Instead a grain of sand has its own function and meaning, and is not to be misunderstood or diminished because it is not a tree. The Qur'an reminds modern-day individuals that everything has its own value and meaning, from a grain of sand to the harmony of the celestial spheres.

All the spiritual traditions that have made an appearance down through the ages have attempted to convey the essential knowledge of God and the true nature of reality, together with the spiritual means to know God and to realize that reality. Much of that knowledge is still available to contemporary man and the integrity of the spiritual traditions is still intact. They can still act as sources of spiritual and thus essential knowledge and they still contain channels of blessing for those ready and willing to draw on the nectar of this sapiential wisdom and grace. It is not as if humanity does not have the knowledge and the means available to know the truth of one's own human nature and transcend the limitations that are but temporary aberrations in the soul's journey of return to union with the Divinity.

---

[85] "I gaze upon form (*surat*) with the physical eye because
There is in form the trace of the Spirit (*ma'na*).
This is the world of form and we live in forms:
The spirit cannot be seen save by means of form." (Awhadi Kirmani)

[86] "And He taught Adam the names of all things; then He placed them before the angels, and said: 'Tell Me the names of these if you are right.' They said: 'Glory to Thee: Of knowledge we have none, save what Thou hast taught us: in truth it is Thou who are perfect in knowledge and wisdom.' He said: 'Oh Adam! Tell them their names.' When he had told them, Allah said: 'Did I not tell you that I know the secrets of the heavens and the earth and I know what you reveal and what you conceal.'" (II: 31-34)

The Christian perspective is founded on the fall of Adam with its emphasis on the fallen nature of humanity. Because of this state of being, the Christian calls upon the Messiah whose suffering and death will both literally and symbolically "save" humanity from their predicament on the earthly plane. The focus of the Christian perspective is understood in light of the persona of Christ, whose mystery combines the human with the divine. Jesus Christ is the center of the Christian life, its source and end. It is for this reason that the Qur'an calls Jesus *a word from Allah* (3: 39) and further explicitly identifies the son of Mary by saying: "Allah giveth thee glad tidings of a Word from Him, his name will be Jesus, the son of Mary." (3: 45) Christ has come as the living revelation in the form of a person, while in Islam, the revelation is a Word in the form of a Book, "on a tablet well preserved." Christ marks once again the descent of a higher reality, an avatar or incarnation, to infiltrate the earthly sphere with his guidance and light.

The Islamic perspective initially identifies humanity (*insan*) as the primordial man and ultimately envisions the human entity as the perfect man, exemplified through a messenger rather than on an avatar or divine incarnation, as in Christianity. By focusing on the fallen nature of humanity, Christianity highlights the characteristics of individual man who is both fallen and sinful and therefore requiring the waters of baptism as the first symbolic gesture on the road to deliverance from the human condition. In theory, Islam portrays the human being collectively as primordial man at his inception and potentially perfected man with regard to his destination and final end. In practice, however, Islam addresses itself to "average" man who follows the "straight path" that the Muslim refers to five times a day in his prayers. He requests guidance to follow the "middle road," echoing the middle way of the Taoist. In its formal manifestation, with its comprehensible, Qur'anic rhetoric, *in clear Arabic*, and its well defined forms of worship through the five pillars, Islam makes itself accessible to anyone and everyone. In principle, everyone has the right to go to Heaven, provided that he uses his intelligence to discern the truth and uses his free will to surrender that intelligence to the Divine Imperative, both intelligence and free will being faculties that are at the disposal of every person provided that they use these faculties properly. Therefore, every man and woman have available "the middle road", an avenue of balance between extremes, with which to pursue his interests and follow a way of spirituality.

Whatever the mode of spiritual expression, the inner meaning is the same. The believers choose God over themselves; they choose the Divine Principle over human speculation; they choose the Paradise which is "promised" over the temporary and thus illusory pleasure of "this world". They place themselves at the disposition of the Divinity and in so doing take the first step in the process that calls for a separation and detachment from the world that leads to an attachment to the One (*al-Wahad*), the Only One (*al-Ahad*). In so doing, they become part of that Reality, not as a disharmony, a question or a fragment, but as a unified self in search of the Greater Self. This is the objective of the process of spirituality that always has been and still is available to individuals everywhere, embedded within the human psyche and spirit as a fundamental possibility that awaits its own expression within the Divine Design.

Perhaps it is also a "sign of the times" that while we are witnessing the degeneration and destruction of the traditional world to the extent that, with the coming of the new millennium, speculation has increased concerning an imminent "end of the world", there still exists the possibility to pursue a life of spirituality for those with the courage and insight to stand against the secular currents prevalent now in the life of our time. The spiritual disciplines of Islam discussed in the next section are still available to humanity that will allow many people to slip through a newly available corridor of spirituality with a quicker, more direct access to spiritual realization than was formerly possible. Muhammad (PBUH), indicated in one of his sayings (*hadith*) that if in the early times of the religion a person were to practice nine-tenths of the religion they would get to heaven, whereas in the "latter time", if one were to practice only one-tenth of the precepts, they would also get to heaven, a sure indication that in these latter times, every consideration and mercy will be given the faithful in compensation for having to live through this "dark age".

Similarly, it is now possible to take advantage of spiritual traditions that are not necessarily one's own, in order to draw the benefits of a universal knowledge that lies embedded within the core of each of the spiritual traditions; but that are for one reason or another no longer accessible in one's own country and culture. Martin Lings has written that because of the great loss of the traditional way of life, "there can now be, for those capable of taking it, a certain compensation in the gain of access to the spiritual riches of traditions other than one's own."[87] Through travel and other possibilities inherent in these times to live in different countries and cultures, more and more people are becoming interested in the possibilities offered by alternative spiritual traditions. Many people who travel to the Middle East are immediately impressed and intrigued by what remains of the spiritual and traditional trappings of the Islamic society that enliven the environment with a remembrance of a more traditional way of life. The call to prayer, the corner mosque, the traditional turbans and kaftans, the ever present prayer beads, the Qur'anic epithets that are threaded through daily speech, all this and more summon an immediate remembrance of a time when the remembrance of God infiltrated the daily lives of the people to create in fact a sacred and holy ambiance as a fully integrated environment within a traditional society.

It is not uncommon nowadays that people align themselves to spiritual traditions other than their own. The reason for this is partly the fact that people who do turn back towards a life of spirituality to compensate for the emptiness of purely secularized life, turn back with an intensity that leads them directly to the

---

[87] M. Lings, *The Eleventh Hour*, p. 71.

deeper, more mystic elements of a particular spiritual tradition. Thus we have witnessed in the last several decades, a profound interest in the practice of yoga and various forms of meditation,[88] in sutra chanting, in various aspects of the Taoist and Buddhist philosophies, including breathing exercises and massage techniques. People have rushed to India to sit in ashrams at the feet of yogis and adepts. Others have travelled to such places as Thailand, Japan and Sri Lanka and entered Buddhist monasteries in order to subject themselves to the rigors of austerity that promise freedom from suffering and release from the illusions of this world. Swamis travel to America and cleverly establish communities there in ways that are more suited to the mentality of people living in the West. The interest in Sufi orders and practices, which is the Islamic form of mysticism, is on the rise to the extent that there are now books in translation of such mystics as the well-known Ibn al-Arabi (d. 1240) often referred to as the Sheikh al-Akbar (the Greatest Master) and Jalal al-Din Rumi,[89] a 13th century Sufi poet who lived in Turkey and is presently buried in Konya. Among Muslims, both tombs remain to this day popular pilgrimage places for those seeking to absorb some of the spiritual influences that hover near certain sacred space, including tombs of saints.

If the modern and contemporary humanity are going to get to Heaven "by themselves", or if they are going to move down the newly available corridor of accessibility to the spiritual realities, it is still going to require major effort and struggle. The message of Islam unashamedly refers to the inner *jihad al-nafs* or battle of the soul that is required of every person, in order to achieve the inner, spiritual goal, and nothing less than this "greater *jihad*" will serve the present moment. Contemporary modernites will still have to identify themselves with a valid spiritual tradition, whose knowledge and wisdom still pass down through the arteries of the universe from Heaven to earth, and whose blessing and grace still provide the spiritual motivation as well as the implicit joy, tranquillity and peace that represent the promises of the life of spirituality. By taking part in the

---

[88] It is also perhaps a "sin of the times" that the meditation techniques of Transcendental Meditation took the Western world by storm back in the 70s. It aggressively presented itself as a form of meditation that was completely disassociated from religion to the extent that it advertised itself as a secular form of meditation. Not surprisingly and perhaps a little ironically, it was the Western secular mentality, especially in America, thirsting as it is for spiritual satisfaction, that adopted this method in what amounted to a form of anti-spirituality because it boasted of its complete break from the very sources of spirituality that the TM methods proposed to emulate, namely, the Primal Cause and Supreme Force at the heart of the universe.

[89] Among the most noteworthy of these new translations are William C. Chittick's two books, *The Sufi Path of Love* (State University of New York Press, 1983) and *The Sufi Path of Knowledge*, (State University of New York Press, 1989). In these two books, he has compiled translations and commentary of the spiritual teachings of Rumi, together with Ibn al-Arabi's metaphysics of imagination respectively. Thus, two ancient texts that deal with the very pulse of the spiritual life and the spiritual world generally have been made available to contemporary man in a style and manner that is accessible and comprehensible.

diverse modes of spiritual expression that are still living and still available to people today, modern men and women everywhere may once again light the spark of spirituality that hovers within their beings like moths seeking the light, thus making possible within these uncertain contemporary times a life of spirituality that lends the kernel of dignity, meaning and above all "spirit" to the empty shell that the modern mentality has unwittingly become.

Are we merely feathers in the dust and blown by every wind, having surrendered the beatitude that allows the birds of paradise to soar on high in defiance of the laws of gravity? Have we forgotten "our skies" and fallen down to the ground in desperation, bereft of the freedom and spirit that characterizes the mystery of the bird in flight? Are we gazing up at the stars and waiting with a patience that is infinite, while the moon emerges from behind a cloud to enlighten every leaf and blade of grass with its pale reflected light? We can fall no lower and we blind our eyes no further. The vast heavens above continue to beckon us with its mystery and its infinitude. We have nothing to lose by pursuing the life of spirituality that is still available to us as a merciful compensation to the human condition and everything to gain in coming to realize our true destiny as spiritual entitles united within the fold of the Great Spirit.

6.2 Spiritual Disciplines

The religion of Islam offers the Muslims specific spiritual methods that will lead them back along the straight path (*sirat al-mustaqim*) to God. Islam is very specific in advising the faithful concerning what the soul must accomplish in this life. The five pillars of Islam, as earthly duties, offer the Muslims a means through which they can purify themselves in this life and make ready for the next life. The earthly duties not only purify the human being on both outer and inner levels, they also create within the soul a fullness of spirit that leads to a heightened awareness of God and His continued remembrance. With the verse "Remember Me and I will remember you" (2: 152), the Qur'an reminds the Muslims of the tendency to forget "the one thing needful". It is guidance, plain and simple. In return for the faithful performance of the earthly duties, God will confer on the believer certain divine rights that correspond in blessing and grace to the effort required in performing the duties.

The *shahadah*, alternatively known as the testimony of faith in Islam, is the ultimate remembrance of God and amounts to a fusion of the soul with the spirit of God through this simple human act of remembrance. Armed with the knowledge contained within the sacred formula, the soul takes part in a conscious inner life that allows the human being to superimpose the awesome reality of God onto the surface of the human consciousness in order to expose the fragile, dream-like quality at the heart of material existence. Of course, as a new Muslim many years ago, I was like a child again on psychic and spiritual levels of perception. I knew nothing of the history or philosophy of the religion, nor had I read a single word of the Qur'an prior to my conversion. Initially, all I had to hold onto was the miracle of the *shahadah* itself, the great witnessing in Islam, but it served as a symbolic sword that had the explanatory power to infiltrate the mind and the emotive power to pierce the heart with the light of its essential knowledge and the energy of its sacred sentiment.

Eventually, I came to know that the sacred formula was actually the key to a sacred psychology of man and not just a formal doctrine of the religion. It is not just a theory and an abstraction, but a practice and a way of life. It provides the handle to a way of life and the key to a body of knowledge, the means and the method to order and integrate the entire life of a person if he or she so wills, their waking and sleeping moments, their work and their rest, and their interaction with one another.

Increasingly, I felt as if I had fallen out of a dense, amorphous cloud only to arrive at the door of my true inner self. I could finally say: Now I am myself as I was intended to be, *Homo sapiens* and the most human being of the creation, living under the protection and guidance of the Supreme Being. What I accomplish is in the name of God, I could finally affirm with conviction after years of self-doubt and uncertainty: I am my true self, without fear and without falsehood. Previously I had existed but in some strange way I didn't "happen" from inside out. On the contrary, everything happened to me from outside myself and I was confronted by people and the world itself with an insistence that could be frightening. Now, I happened to myself and to the world as best I can, armed now with the principles of the religion as my guide. I finally know that I exist as an absolute reference point to the divine Authority. Now I know who I am and who Allah is. There is authority in me because I take part in the Divine Imperative. I enjoy a 'relatively absolute' quality because I have surrendered myself to the Absolute. I affirm, witness, and worship my Creator and Lord. In return, a heightened spiritual consciousness is sufficient proof of all I aspire to.

Almost immediately after my conversion, I turned to the Qur'an which Muslims believe to be the sacred words of Allah. The Qur'an, as revelation, is the source of the religion as well as the source of all essential knowledge. "We have sent down the book with the express purpose of clarifying their differences and it is a guidance and a mercy for those who believe." (16: 64) Here is the final version, delivered by the 'seal' of the Prophets, of the sacred book of knowledge, an illuminated scripture, preserved eternally on a tablet in Heaven, that offers mankind the ultimate understanding of himself and the world as it is prefigured in its true reality. As such, it is a comfort and a healing during the course of the Muslim life. Here is the Explanation and the Criterion that every civilization must have in order to function effectively on the earthly plane. Indeed, the silence of Heaven would have been unbearable if Allah had not spoken directly and with words to mankind: The divine Speech is for those who have faith and whose hearts find a serene peacefulness in the remembrance of God. A well-known Qur'anic verse makes this promise quite explicit. "Indeed, in the remembrance of God do hearts find serenity and peace." (13: 28)

I passed my first Ramadhan discovering the secrets of the fast, which is an intense experience that engages more than just the physical aspects of the body. By taking part in this unique experience, I followed the advice of my new Muslim friends who suggested that if I really wanted to taste, with my whole physical being, that Allah exists, then fast, they told me. The fast is the bodily sacrament *par excellence*. Anyone who has ever accomplished the full course of the Ramadhan fast, in good faith and only to please Allah, realizes that the fast is really the consummate bodily experience that gives the fasting person a taste of what it means to transcend the human body through the force of one's will alone. It is worship brought to its most rigid test. One of the traditions says that "Everything has a gateway and the gateway of worship if fasting. Even the sleep of the fasting man is worship."

The most distinguishing characteristic of the Muslim life is the ceremony of prayer. According to the Prophet, the ritual prayer is "the key to paradise." Five times a day the believer puts aside his cares and worries, lays down his prayer carpet or walks to the mosque nearby, in response to the Qur'anic injunction that says: "Invoke the name of Allah or the name Rahman or any name you may invoke, they are all good names; and do not recite your prayers too loudly or too softly, but follow the middle course." (17: 110)

In Islam, the ceremony of prayer is a formal ritual as well as an intense personal communication between man and God. During the prayer, the Muslim repeats the opening chapter of the Qur'an, the Al-Fatihah, which consists of seven verses. He also goes through the motions of bowing and prostration, in which the body itself as well as the mind and soul take part in the prayer of submission to the Divine. The totality of man prays in Islam and this includes the body, mind, heart and soul.

To remember Allah and to increase our awareness of the reality of the Divine Presence that we profess to believe in requires devotion and a well-defined discipline. The ceremony of prayer serves this function very well. There must be a sacred method of remembrance; otherwise we will forget Allah once again, even if we fervently want to remember Him. To remember Allah does not come naturally to us. We are forgetful and must remind ourselves of certain essential truths. We need to cultivate the God-perception; otherwise we become completely entrenched in our own worldly affairs and forget what really should matter to us.

The meeting with Allah that takes place during the ceremony of prayer is not some remote fantasy designed to distract us from the external physical world. It is the promise of Allah that the Muslim who stands up for prayer is virtually standing in the presence of God. "Observe the prayer for the remembrance of Me." (20: 14) Prayer is the central phenomenon of all religion, especially in Islam, where it is the hearthstone of all piety. The ritual prayer is directed towards the Ka'aba in Makkah, which is the house of God on earth and the symbolic focus of the religion. Within the heart of the believing Muslim, however, the entire ceremony of prayer and all its good intentions are directed toward God through the symbolic Ka'aba of the heart, the very center of man's spiritual being and the innermost core of his spiritual existence.

Theoretically, a believer must pray. To believe and yet to refrain from prayer at the same time does not make sense. The spiritual life cannot sustain itself without the action of the prayer, and good intentions must express themselves in some way. Prayer is the elementary and necessary expression of a spiritual truth; most notably that man must come out of the limited confines of his own being and speak with the God who created him. The fact that it has been made a formal ritual in Islam and a duty of the believer only shows the importance of the prayer in the Muslim life. If we want to remember God, we must have a method to remember. Prayer is a powerful method of integration, bringing the body, mind, psyche and soul of man together in a unity of purpose and direction that opens for him the channels of blessing that are available to man from Heaven, as God has promised.

In particular, the prayer is a powerful and effective means to integrate the psyche of modern individuals, who suffer so much these days because they are essentially without a center, disharmonious and separated from the Divinity by the lack of focus in both their mind and psyche. Prayer is a shock to the totality of the human system, in which the body, the mind, the psyche and the soul of man takes part in a sacred ceremony five times a day. The believer can lay aside his cares for a few moments and interrupt the flow of daily events with this communication and this meeting with God. Through the action of the prayer, the believer can actually transcend his horizontal, earthly understanding of existence through a vertical perception that cuts across the horizontal plane and elevates him to a higher level of spiritual consciousness. He can become vertical man once again and this means not just the human animal standing upright, but also the human *alif*[90], pointing heavenwards.

"What action is dearest to Allah?" one of the companions of the prophet asked him.

"Prayer at its proper time," he replied.

If the *shahadah* signifies knowledge and discernment, then prayer signifies experience and union. The sacred formula, as God's gift to man through a divine descent, conveys a theoretical knowledge of the Reality and a practical means of discernment between the Real and the unreal. Prayer, as the human response to God and a means for spiritual ascent, translates the celestial knowledge into an existential experience of the Divine. To resolve to pray is to turn to God in one's heart; to assume a prayerful attitude is to enter into the Presence in order to reunite oneself with the Divinity; to actually recite the prayer is to communicate the human aspiration to the Divine Listener, the One Who Hears and Answers Prayer (*al-mujib*), which is one of the ninety-nine names of God. Thus God, man, the meeting and the eternal moment become a part of the human as well as the celestial reality, while the world and all that it contains including man, his

---

[90] The first letter of the Arabic alphabet, drawn as a single vertical line.

wealth, his possessions and his fame, even life itself assume an air of unreality, a passing cloud or a feather in the wind. "What is the world if not the outflowing of forms, and what is life if not a bowl which seemingly is emptied between one night and another? And what is prayer, if not the sole stable point û a point of peace and of light--in this dream universe, and the straight gate leading to all that the world and life have sought in vain?"[91]

The pursuit of an Islamic spirituality involves devotion and worship to the straight path mentioned in the opening *surah* of the Qur'an, *Al-Fatihah*. It requires much of the believer, including self-discipline, conscientious attempts toward piety, inner restraint and the exercise of the spiritual instincts of charity, love, submission, fear and hope. Gradually, the believer feels the momentum of this inner process having a profound effect; I can confirm this now after many years within the traditional, Islamic fold. There develops within the context of this Islamic spirituality a real possibility of spiritual advancement that allows the believer to lay aside the externalized world of alternatives for the spiritual world of clear choice and vision. The believer can fulfil his nature and function as in a temple or mosque. His ego is overpowered and his soul is transformed by the vision of the Whole and by the direct and existential experience of the Divine, in this life and on the earthly plane of existence.

The believing Muslim knows the secret of the heart's desire and begins the ascent and return heavenward to the primordial paradise he/she once lost. He/she is the human mosque, providing the setting for a sacred drama that takes place within his very being. Their physical shape and vertical stance make them the human minaret. Their head and shoulders form the towering porch where the call to prayer is made. The heart is the mosque enclosure itself. The soul becomes the inner sanctuary of the body and the *mihrab* or prayer niche of their inner essence. The *Homo sapiens* of 21st century man becomes the *Homo spiritualis* of the traditional person whose physical body actually serves as a pinnacle of the natural order and the living symbol of the higher consciousness and Spirit of the Divinity.

The religion of Islam itself still remains a vital and living spiritual tradition in the world today. The modes of worship such as the prayer, fasting, and the pilgrimage of Makkah are still performed as they were fourteen centuries ago, and they still have the power to heal, purify and sanctify. The call of the minaret still beckons the faithful to prayer, and the grace called down by sincere worship still has the power to transform the human soul into a perfected being. Modern individuals can still connect themselves with God's sacred Presence in the world through the human expression of their own spirituality and they can still escape the limitations of their own earth-bound ego through the realization that there is more to life, indeed more to the universe, than their own self-perception of the ultimate Reality.

---

[91] Frithjof Schuon, *Essential Writings* (Dorset, England: Elements Books Ltd, 1991), p. 444.

Eventually, the Muslim convert must abandon his status as convert and become a Muslim, which is none other than one who surrenders his 'self' to the will of God. Beyond conversion lies a vast realm of spiritual identity and spiritual experience that through effort, striving and worship continually connects man with God. After many years now being Muslim, I can honestly say that this single major theme stands out for me in profile and bears special emphasis.

The Muslim life is not one choice, but many choices. The Muslim life is not one solitary act of faith, but a mode of existence and a way of living and being in which faith continues to narrow the gap that exists between the known world and the unknown frontier that the Qur'an identifies as the mysteries of the unseen. The servant approaches the Master and the vice-gerent gives account to the King. In so doing, he can lift the veil that separates the purely human from the spiritual world that finds its center in the Divine Being. Allah is infinitely transcendent, while at the same time infinitely close to man. "He is nearer to you than your jugular vein" (50:15), a well known Qur'anic verse relates, in order to emphasize Allah's proximity to man, and reinforces this major idea in another verse: "Allah comes between man and his heart." (8:24)

The central purpose of the religion of Islam and its accompanying traditions is to keep alive in the mind and heart of the Muslims the truth of the one God as a living remembrance. Through the duties and other spiritual practices and through worship generally, the knowledge of God must be made manifest in the lives of the people and not just as a token gesture to truth. A man of faith faces the idea of God and eternity with his total being in body, mind, heart, and soul. He knows that his exterior personality is merely a temporary persona to deal with the contingencies of the external world. His behavior and his actions must reflect the inner force of a spiritual identity that will keep him on the straight path and lead him along the way of return. He realizes that he has obligations to Truth, and he fulfils these obligations with a willingness to act upon that truth.

At the time of my conversion, I had finally come to realize how difficult it really is to be a human being. It is not easy to be ourselves, and it is not easy to transcend our own limitations, especially in today's complex and fragmented world. The purely secular and materialist attitudes of the contemporary world do little to satisfy man's inner yearning. We see plainly that we come into being, the world is the way it is, and ultimately we must take our leave. Somehow, we must find an explanation in a world that does not explain itself. Thus, my perspective has taken root in a purely spiritual vision that is based on a revelation from God. However, it has also evolved from both an intellectual and an emotional process, intellectual so that thinking man can grasp the message from Heaven with his mind, and emotional so that a man of spiritual sensitivity can come to love God with all his heart. We need the God perception for such is human intelligence that it yearns for its greater counterpart in the supreme Intelligence. Similarly, we need faith, because it will lead us into the paradise and give us the peace that we instinctively hope for.

6.3 The Significance of Prayer

The Religion of Islam has formalized the human communication with God through a prayer ritual captured within a formalized ceremony of devotion and worship that emanates from the Muslim soul. In commemoration of the Prophet Muhammad (PBUH) who learned the formalized ritual of prayer from the archangel Gabriel, the angelic messenger *Jibra'il* of the Qur'anic text, all Muslims learn the formalities of the prayer ritual when they come of age, although many young children from two onwards feel at ease amid the rows of worshippers in the mosque and often mimic the movements of their elders in a spontaneous outpouring of their innocent souls. Indeed, the Islamic ceremony of prayer represents a spontaneous outpouring of the Muslim soul that reflects through prayer an instinctive faith in a Supreme Being, Allah, whose very name calls upon the Divinity and awakens the *sakinah* or Holy Presence of God within the human heart.

Devout Muslims take the prayer ritual very seriously because it is a form of worship that strikes at the heart of the Muslim psyche and gives shape and substance to the Muslim mentality. If the Qur'an represents a major descent of divine knowledge, then prayer is the "ascent" of the heart-inspired expression of one's deepest and most secret intimacies through a ritualized form of worship and praise that represents the most human expression of a person's understanding of truth and reality. In a era that values the seen over the unseen, that excludes the presence of the Mystery that permeates all of nature and seeks to explain the origin of the universe from within the natural order itself rather than from the supra-natural order that is the origin and source of its laws and harmonies, an era that understands the human entity to be the result of an evolutionary process that began as some spontaneous effusion of dead matter with that mysterious spark we know as "life" resulting from the fortuitous interplay of chemistry and lightning whose modern counterpart lies in the birth of Frankenstein, and that through a secular, pseudo humanistic worldview offers possibility and promise to the notion of a human progress through sidereal and historical time, the notion of a formalized and sacred ritual that addresses the Hidden, the Unseen and the Mysterious in life as we know it requires some explanation.

To the Muslim soul, however, prayer is the natural response to the revelatory "sword of divine knowledge" that has come down to humanity, not as a cosmic flash of lightning to shatter the serenity of the ur-darkness with the genesis of an unexplained life form, but as the wellspring and source of the essential knowledge and as the vertical wand of Heaven, intersecting the horizontal plane of earthly time with the conscious awareness of the eternal moment, this being none other than the white light of Absolute Truth. The predominant consciousness of our existence in time pulls us away from the timeless and the eternal; but the higher faculties of intellect and intelligence, the higher emotions and sentiments, the intelligence of the heart and the human soul that provides the ground of our spiritual identity do not belong to this world or to time as we know and experience it. There is nothing that our hands can hold onto that is worth having. They cannot hold a moonbeam or seize a rainbow. The beauty of an eagle in flight eludes our grasp as well as our common sense. It is only who we are in our essence, what we believe in, and the manner in which we communicate with a higher order of existence through prayer that lifts us out of the deep well of turpitude within ourselves and sets us back on the straight path, an image often invoked in Islam.

To pray is in effect to step neither backward nor forward but out of time completely for a few moments to remember our primordial origins, to infuse the "breath" of the Divine Spirit into the human soul already awash in a sea of multiplicity and afloat amid the turgid currents of a dark Kali Yuga era, and finally to recreate the optimum conditions of body, mind and heart for the ascent, not only of prayer and worship of the individual, but the awakening and lifting of human consciousness to the point that it "sees God everywhere", not with the human eye of course, but with the inner eye of consciousness that sparkles with the remembrance of God, its own light reflecting off the light of God.

In order to bring about a better understanding of life's mystery, Islam makes possible a private and possibly intimate relationship with God. The encounter between the human and the Divine is direct and immediate; there are no go-betweens such as clergy and seers in Islam as you find in other religions. The earth is God's mosque and conscious awareness fused with an instinctive faith, together with good works supported by right intentions become the warp and weft of a person's inner being just as the thread on a loom become the prayer carpet of one's dreams ready to be spread wherever one walks. While there are always parents and relatives as mentors and guides, leaders in the community who maintain the integrity of the social fabric, imams in the mosque to lead the faithful in prayer, and sheikhs and walis who set the standard of holiness and sanctity that is possible within the framework of Islamic spirituality, in the end every Muslim stands alone with his Creator. When they stand on their prayer carpet, they bring this awareness with them. This gives a sacerdotal quality to the Islamic character that makes individual Muslims virtual celebrants before God enjoined to perform their own rituals of praise and worship. When the Muslims stand on their prayer carpet, nothing comes between them and their Lord. The sacred communication is formal, direct and surprisingly real. They are in the presence of God and the presence of God is within them. For those few moments of focused remembrance of all that is sacred and true within the framework of existence, the mystery that governs the human worldview and colors it with insecurity and doubt fades away like morning mist, making the prayer ritual a bridge between knowledge and faith in God's enduring Reality.

The prayer ritual is the second earthly duty and the very heart-stone of all spirituality in the Islamic cosmos. Five times a day, the Muslims interrupt the flow of their daily routine with the formal Islamic prayer ritual. After making their clear intention, they perform the ritual ablution, which is an inner as well as an outer purification, then throw down their prayer carpet or walk to the mosque, in order to take their stand for a few minutes on the symbolic terrain of sacred ground, at the disposition of the Divine. As a matter of principle through the prayer, the Muslims turn their mind, heart and soul inward in order to communicate on an intimate level with God. The value of the ritualized ceremony lies in the fact not only of its faithful remembrance of God, but in a continuity that maintains through the phases of the day a constant remembrance of God and a heightened sense of spirituality within mind and heart. The spiritual benefits of the prayer last throughout the entire day and not just at the prayer times. Prayer is not only a communication with the Divine, but a state of mind that awakens a spiritual consciousness fully responsive to the demands of life.

The hidden dimensions of spiritual experience encourage the pursuit of traditional spirituality to deeper levels, and this is no more effectively evidenced in the Qur'an than through the meaning of the prayer. The Muslim is enjoined to perform the prayer ritual, "establish regular prayers" (17: 78) at five established times during the day. Beyond the formal and ceremonial prayer, however, lies the inner prayer of the heart. "And celebrate the Name of thy Lord in the morning and in the evening." (76: 25) The name of course is none other than the name Allah as the Name of names, but also includes the other 99 names and qualities of the Divinity mentioned in the Qur'an that characterize the divine essence. The Qur'an goes on to exemplify a more intense kind of prayer in the form of nocturnal vigils: "And part of the night prostrate thyself to Him, and glorify Him throughout the long night." (76: 26) The pursuit of the way encourages this kind of spiritual dedication and anticipates a higher spiritual station. "Soon will thy Lord raise thee to a station of praise and glory." (17: 79)

For devout Muslims, vigilance and watchfulness of soul are the keys to the way of return to God, qualities distinguished by their intimation of vision and readiness. The pursuit of the way becomes a journey through all phases of personal and spiritual identity toward a consciousness of self that finds its natural and only true complement in unity in the absolute Consciousness of God. The believer offers his/her limited individual soul in exchange for the embrace of the Supreme Self. If the beginning of this process is human aspiration to reach beyond individual limits, the destination and end is always God. The life experience of the human individual is the very heart of the way, the human offering in expectation of the divine promise of salvation in the Divine Beatitude.

Muslims recite the opening seven verses of the Qur'an,[92] the *Surat Al-Fatihah*, as the key component of the Islamic prayer ritual. The seven verses are recited a minimum of seventeen times a day throughout the course of the five

---

[92] The opening seven verses of the Qur'an are described by the Qur'an itself as seven of the oft-repeated verses (*sab'an min al-mathani*) in the following Qur'anic verse: "We have given thee (the Prophet) seven of the oft-repeated (verses), and the mighty Qur'an." (15: 87) Scholars have often referred to these seven verses as the quintessence of the whole of the Qur'an.

prayers, and this does not include supererogatory prayers related to the *Sunnah* or the practice of the Prophet–additional prayers that accompany the five ceremonial prayers at the "appointed time"–which would include even more repetitions of these seven "opening" verses. In other words, these verses are of paramount importance to every Muslim because they highlight both the doctrine and the practice of the religion, the doctrine insofar as they represent the quintessence of the entire Qur'an and the practice because they are repeated between twenty and thirty times a day by the practising faithful depending on their vigilance in following the Sunnah or practice of the Prophet. Needless to say, these seven verses have powerful associations with the spiritual dimension, and contain a symbolic value in terms of both knowledge and sound vibration that have the power on physical, psychic and spiritual levels to transform the mind and mentality of the practitioner with its clarity and light and to soften the heart with deep emotive sentiments.

It is worth highlighting the seven verses used canonically in the Islamic prayer ritual because they not only represent the quintessential substance of the Qur'an, but also because they instil within the Muslim soul the elements of the essential knowledge of God. The sacred words contain a symbolic imagery that encapsulates within a few phrases all that they need to remember in order to maintain the foundation of piety and equilibrium they need to re-establish themselves within their own center, before meeting the center of the earth at the Ka'aba in Makkah, as a prelude and personal experience of that primordial Center that exists at the heart of the universe.

"Praise be to God" opens the Islamic prayer with formal praise of God as the most fitting spiritual attitude that, not only men and women but, every living creature can offer the Divinity. Praise is the most elementary as well as necessary human response to the spiritual truth of the Divinity, especially for human beings, who must give voice to their praise through deliberate intention and prayer, unlike the other animals who praise the Divine Being by simply *being* what they are instinctively.

"Lord of all the worlds" highlights the fact that the universe is made up of multiple worlds both outer and inner, microcosmic and macrocosmic, but there is only one Divinity who is the Lord of the metacosmic universe that is inclusive of all the worlds.

"The Infinitely Good, the Ever Merciful" are alternative names of God, and express variations of His divine qualities and attributes of which the human qualities are but transparent reflections. The Muslim remembers these particular names of Allah because of their association with the *Rahmah*, or Mercy which the human being is in desperate need of. God gives us our daily bread as the Lord's Prayer has foretold and this is only one of the infinite mercies that emanate from the Divinity, our very existence being the ultimate mercy.

"King of the Day of Judgment" is one of the names of God directly identified in the *al-Fatihah*, perhaps to indicate that God is not only Lord of all the worlds, but also master of the end of finite time, with Judgement Day understood to be the most momentous and summative event in the life of the soul. We by contrast are slaves of the King, just as the relative must defer to the absolute and will ultimately disappear in the Face of the Absolute.

"It is Thee we worship and it is in Thee we seek refuge" gives shape and definition to all human duties and aspirations. Worship counterbalances the praise initiated in the opening verse. Praise is the initial, instinctive impulse as a prelude to the systematic worship of the Divine Being because "no one compares with Him." Worship recognizes God for what He is and provides us the opportunity to escape from the confines of our own limited mentality for the sake of the Beloved who becomes the object of all worship. Refuge then complements the concept of the Lord of all the worlds and is the natural response of the human lover for the Divine Beloved. Refuge is possible because of the sacred trust between the human and the Divine. God is infinitely Good and Merciful and therefore the only refuge lies in returning to that goodness and mercy.

"Guide us on the straight path" represents the systematic and saving entreaty of human beings who know their place in the hierarchy of being and know the condition of their inner being, namely as entities in desperate need of guidance along a path that is straight and direct and that leads to a clear destination. The straight path is ultimately the path of hope and the path of ascent represented by the symbolic vertical dimension that intersects the horizontal plane of existence with its projection of universal truth, thus the reference in the following verse to the path of grace.

"The path of those on whom is Thy grace" is available as part of the Divine Mercy and the overflowing beatitude that has the power to attract and draw us upwards. Humans need to open themselves up to that grace and respond with their existential affirmation of the Truth through intelligence and free will. Otherwise, they will become disposed to the path of fear and loathing.

"Not of those upon whom is Thy wrath and those who are lost:" Those people who do not pursue the path of grace and blessing are susceptible to the Divine Anger and the separation that is implicit in that wrath. By opposing the Divine Unity, they become separated into a realm of endless multiplicity and ultimately suffer damnation by virtue of the fact that they have free willingly separated themselves from the Divinity.

Needless to say, every Muslim gladly closes the verses of the *al-Fatihah* with the firm conviction to take the path of those who receive the Divine Favor and avoid at all cost the path of those who receive the Divine Wrath, while remembering the well known inscription that is said to be written at the base of the throne (*al-arsh*) of Allah: "My Mercy precedes My Wrath." The prayer concludes as in the Christian prayer with the sonorous word *Ameen*, intoned by all the faithful in congregational prayer as a means of setting the seal on their most human prayer to the Divine Being they wish to communicate with and emulate.

It is worth highlighting the symbolic imagery of both of these prayers since they play such a significant part in awakening the mind, not only to the key concepts of Christianity and Islam, but also because both traditions create a feeling and an ambience that awakens the imagination with their power for creating sacred meaning. The Lord's Prayer, replete with its sacred, symbolic imagery, can be described verse by verse in this way.

"Our Father" identifies the human mentality with the patriarchal persona of the Divine Being, resorting to familiar familial terminology in coming to terms with the concept of a Supreme Being as the progenitor of the human soul. Within the symbolic imagery of this perspective, the sacred psychology is such that God is referred to as father in keeping with the Biblical figure of the ancient and stern patriarch of which the prophets were the human counterparts. "Who art in Heaven" locates the other-dimensional and other-worldly kingdom that promises the human entity transcendence of the limitations of his earthly condition, although Christians are reminded elsewhere in the New Testament that "the Kingdom of God is within you." "Hallowed be Thy Name" recalls the sacredness of the absolute Name of God, and if it be hallowed, then it becomes the medium of man's worship and praise, thus the invocation of the holy Name becomes the basis and focal point for the prayer.

"Thy kingdom come, Thy will be done." Contingent upon the human impulse to pray is the response of the Divine Being, manifested as the coming of the kingdom and the perfection of His will. Once again, we have been told that the kingdom is within and therefore directly associated with the perfection of the human will in association and in perfect harmony with the Divine will through surrender. "On earth as it is in Heaven" links once again the created earth with the other-worldly paradise, offering possibilities and promises that the Lord's Prayer merely hints at through symbolic language without further elaboration. It is enough for the faithful to remind themselves of the immanent blessing of the "Father" and the divine recompense for the human response of their worship.

"Give us this day our daily bread" reminds the faithful of their dependence on God for their daily sustenance. Bread is of course symbolic of life itself; in Arabic the word for bread is *aisch*, which is the colloquial word for the verb "to live", emphasizing through the spoken language that bread and life are one. Obviously, humans owe their ultimate sustenance to the Divine Being, who provides the human sustenance necessary for survival, including the cycles of seasons, agriculture and weather, universal cycles that highlight the fundamental reliance of God with regard to His provision for mankind.

"And forgive us our trespasses." We need to ask forgiveness for our transgressions as a matter of spiritual routine. Because we are human, we suffer the fault of our own limitations and weaknesses. Our deliberate sins and evils take us outside the norm and alienate us from the beatitude of the divine presence. We ask forgiveness because of who we are and what we have done.

"As we forgive those who trespass again us." We cannot ask of God that which we are not prepared to ask of ourselves unless we want to expose ourselves as hypocrites. If we ask for divine forgiveness, we must be prepared to express our own humanity in light of the divine example and forgive those who trespass again us. Otherwise, on what basis can we rightfully expect that we ourselves should be forgiven?

"And lead us not into temptation" because temptation is the prelude and forerunner of all that leads us away from the Divine Beatitude. We must rely on the Divine Being to keep us out of harm's way, and that must include the way of temptation that can only lead to further separation from the Divine Being.

"But deliver us from evil." After the divine forgiveness, after the promise to forgive those who trespass against us, and after the heart-felt entreaty to keep us far from temptation, the Lord's Prayer concludes with the aspiration to avoid the evil alternative and keep away from the inclinations that will lead us into further evil. Deliverance from evil means none other than deliverance from Satan, the great corrupter, seducer and whisperer into the ears of humankind. Deliverance from evil as a heart-felt sentiment to conclude the prayer is actually a deliverance from Satan as the enemy of God and as the principle of evil itself.

Finally, "amen" is the sound word that concludes the prayer and seals the communication. Its sonorous cadence and prolonged vowelization approximates in curious fashion the utterance of a sigh and actually summarizes with a symbolic sound a concept that is equally represented in a number of languages including Arabic, Hebrew, Greek, Latin, Old/Middle English and finally modern English. "Amen" actually means "so be it" with the implication "so be it as truth and certainty" and contains within its utterance a definitive and conclusive air. Therefore, it resolves in a word the heart-felt entreaties of the prayer and brings the sacred communication to its logical conclusion. "Amen" closes once again the envelope to eternity that was opened by the commencement of the formal prayer.

The content of the Lord's Prayer and the *al-Fatihah* have interesting similarities and differences that highlight the unique character of each unique, spiritual tradition. Both prayers identify the Divinity and give Him various Names, the one paternal, the other regal and qualitative. The Lord's Prayer makes reference to the coming of the (second) Kingdom which indirectly implies a kind of day of judgement which is mentioned outright in the *al-Fatihah*. The Christian prayer mentions sustenance in the form of "daily bread" while the Islamic prayer focuses on worship and the trust between the human and the Divine. Finally, the Lord's Prayer focuses on forgiveness and deliverance from evil while the Islamic prayer highlights the imagery of the path (*tariq*), a path most notably leading in two directions, the one vertical and transcending, bound for the beatitude and blessings of the Paradise, the other horizontal and leading downward, bound for the netherland of unspeakable separation and loss characteristic of damnation. Both prayers find resolution and seal in the commemorative word "Amen", the contemporary "so be it" that recalls the proverbial and more hopeful "be it so" of traditional lore. "Amen" closes both prayers as a statement of certainty and as a confirmation of the Truth.

6.4 The Rigors of the Fast

Only the one who has tasted knows." (Sufi adage)

Nothing captures more effectively the tempting and transient quality of the sensorial world than the sense of taste. As instrument of perception, medium of pleasure and pain, and focus of all that leads us away from the inner side of the reality, our ability to taste the world and all it has to offer promises to drag us down into the depths of the earth to the extent that we are bound by its parameters without the option of ever taking wing and setting ourselves free. The wondrous experience of tasting the world we live in is like the adventure of someone who has to be brought up from the bottom of some deep well. The light is there in the distance as a peephole of promise into the reality of some alternative world; you lie there on your back and are lifted up as though pulling on some internal rope that is none other than the "rope of Allah" sent down to humanity as a blessing and a mercy. The sense of taste contains a secret that we must discover on our own and a symbolism that resembles an inverted glass, in remembrance of the well known image from the Gospels reminding us that we will experience life as though "through a glass darkly".

The sense of taste enriches not only the body, but also the mind, heart and even the soul at all levels of experience and brings people together in ways that would otherwise be unimaginable: the body through the ingestion of food and liquid, the mind as a means of appreciation for the rational and intellectual aspects of life, such as the admiration of a finely executed film or the savoring of a well written novel, the heart as an instrument of appreciation of the emotive, the subtle and the beautiful aspects of life that lift us out of ourselves and lead us beyond the threshold of our superficial world onto a high plane of creative spirit well inside the external world of words and forms, and finally the soul as the ground of an experience whose tasting verges on true insight into the intuitive realms that open invisible doors onto the direct perception of the knowledge of God.

Just as the powers of smell derive from an elaborate olfactory network of sense perception that makes it at all possible to appreciate the wide variety of smells at our disposal, so also we can thank our taste buds for their ability to perceive and communicate the broad range of the taste experience from delectably sweet to revoltingly bitter.

Taste is first and foremost a gustatory experience of great pleasure through which people nourish their bodies three times a day, not to mention the inevitable daytime snacks and midnight forays to the refrigerator. While the other senses could be called solitary senses because they are essentially appreciated on their own, either through the direct vision of seeing the sublime wonders of nature, the intimate experience of listening to rhythms and the appreciation of the harmonies emitted by every physical thing, or the unique experience of smell that introduces the essence of a thing through the chemical molecules in the air, the art of tasting is usually done in communion with others and therefore could be called the social sense. People generally feel uncomfortable dining alone, and dining alone in a restaurant can actually be a painful or embarrassing experience, singling a person out in some unexpected manner since people are not expected to eat alone, much less in a restaurant. We eat with family or friends; business meetings often take place over lunch; weddings always find their culmination in a feast with treasured guests; Irish wakes are notorious for the amounts of food and drink consumed in tribute to the dead, as if in celebration of the life that has now completed itself and passed away.

Every culture uses food as a sign of friendship, approval, celebration or commemoration. In Arab and Islamic countries, the celebration of food as a sign and complement to hospitality is a well known aspect of the Islamic culture. I have been invited into Egyptian, Emirate and Palestinian households and plied with every manner of food from *kusheri*, an exotic and layered combination of rice, lentils and pasta, topped off with a thick tomato sauce and sprinkled with pan-fried onions, to stuffed pigeons, considered not only a delicacy, but also a special offering to the expectant guest who can savor the succulent pieces of meat as they fall away from the tiny, fragile bones.

In counterpoint to fine culinary dining and the savoring of exotic drinks from fresh fruit juices to the finest wines, the Islamic traditions turn the sense of taste inside out through the Islamic fast based on the premise that hunger rather than satiation of the senses will turn the mind away from the temptations of the sensible world to the inner world of higher experience, when the eye of the heart and the intellect opens wide and the sheer experience of formal denial of the taste experience, at least for a temporary and limited time frame, will open a door to the conscious experience of a higher order. When the physical eye sees the sun, moon and stars, the inner eye witnesses the singular reality of the Creator who created the formal universe and set humanity at its very center to witness and surrender. When the Muslims set out to systematically deny the pleasures of the sense of taste, they put their surrender into an action that is the direct expression of their will to surrender to the commands of Allah. "Oh those who believe! Fasting is prescribed to you as it was prescribed to those before you so that you may learn heedfulness. (2:183)

Muslims around the world fast during the Arabic lunar month of Ramadhan first and foremost because Allah has asked them to do so in various verses of the Qur'an. When the Divinity asks, the true Muslim complies. If this were the only reason why the Muslims fast, it would be reason enough. Muslims believe the Qur'an to be the direct communication of the Divine Being to mankind, a revelation that provides the essential knowledge they need to know in order to realize their spirituality as a living spirituality within their beings. It is not, however, the only reason. The great communal gatherings that express the solidarity and friendship through the sharing of tasty food and drink are turned inside out into a communal experience of fasting with well-defined restrictions on food and drink during the daylight hours as a spiritual disciplines–and one of the five pillars of Islam–that commemorates the remembrance of Allah as the Supreme Being to whom all Muslims surrender. The Islamic fast has a spiritual significance and efficacy that ranges from purely external benefits to profoundly internal blessings. Embedded within the ritual of fasting, however, there lies a spiritual meaning, a human secret, and a divine promise that forms the rationale and purpose of the entire body experience of the fast.

In its external manifestation, the fast of Ramadhan is a well known phenomenon. Most people know that fasting calls to a halt the satisfaction of the appreciative sense of taste for a specific time period from the c call to prayer at the first light of dawn until the call to prayer at sunset. The rhythm of normal life is sharply interrupted, while the Muslims adapt themselves to the routine of self denial implicit in the fast. The fast is an intense physical experience in which the body experiences a kind of death to the satisfaction of the senses, in keeping with the traditional saying (*hadith*) of the Prophet: "Die before you die."

The fast of Ramadhan is a form of worship in which the body itself offers up its own prayer as it passes through a netherworld that denies all sense experience relating to taste. Because of its message of effort and self discipline, the fast is a most effective way of conquering the evil within us. The Prophet of Islam has said: "Satan affects the sons of Adam by pervading his blood. Let him therefore make this difficult for Satan by means of hunger." The fast denies the senses their natural satisfaction because they are the "grazing ground" of the devil. As long as the senses are fertile, the devil will continue to frequent them and as long as he frequents them, the majesty of God will not be revealed to the human consciousness." Had it not been for the fast," the Prophet said, "the devils would hover around the heart of the children of Adam when in truth the fast would have lifted their hearts unto the kingdom of Heaven." For this reason, the Prophet also told his favorite wife, Aisha, "Persist in knocking on the door of Paradise." When she asked how, the Prophet replied: "With hunger."

The physical efficacy of the fast has been well documented down through history, and most religious traditions have encouraged fasting. Even the secular societies of the West recognize the benefits of the fast and have included fasting as an important factor in the pursuit of good nutrition and health. In fact, fasting has been called "the bread of the prophets" because it is virtually a prayer of the body. Fasting helps the body to purify itself of the toxins that accumulate through over-indulgence of good and incomplete digestion. The resulting purification leaves the body in a more refined state of physical readiness and awareness. Through denial, the physical senses are actually heightened; some of the veils that separate us from the higher realities may be lifted and the remembrance (*dikhr*) of Allah is brought clearer into focus. The body itself goes through a process of fine tuning, so that a person can begin to listen to the message that the body has to convey. The celebrated poet Rumi has written: "If the brain and belly are burned clean with fasting, every moment a new song comes out of the fire."

Beyond the boundaries of the external fast lies the internal fast. Internal fasting imposes a discipline on the mind and soul. The inner self is restrained from indulging in passions and desires that go beyond the physical senses to affect one's personality and inner psyche. These are the inner evils such as lying, backbiting, envy, jealousy, anger or pride. "Cultivate within yourself," the Prophet said, "the attributes of Allah." The internal fast transcends the physical limitations of an individual and amounts to imitating the qualities of God. With its inward focus, the fast weakens the knots of the psyche, controls the negative emotions of the personality, and strengthens the human will that initiates the fast in the first place. In this way, the human spirit becomes stronger both outwardly through control over the senses and innerly by focusing the mind and transcending the limitations of the psyche. Those who do not fulfill the minimum conditions of both the outer and inner fast are the people about whom the Prophet has said, "There are many whose fasting is nothing beyond being hungry and thirsty."

Of all the earthly duties, the fast of Ramadhan is the most secret because it is strictly between the individual and God. The fast by its very nature is an act of honor and a secret pledge between man and God. The prayer rituals, the *zakat* payment and the Hajj pilgrimage are all open to plain view and subject to comment and approval by the community, whereas the fast is the one act of worship that is witnessed only by God. People who fast cannot prove their veracity and don't have to; rather they share their secret with no one but the only One, in obedience to God and for His sake only.

All five pillars of Islam have the remembrance of Allah as their fundamental motive and purpose. This is obvious in the first duty, the proclamation of faith (*shahadah*), which is the perpetual remembrance of the one God and the one Reality. According to the Prophet, the prayer is the "key to Paradise". By observing the *zakat* or giving of alms, the Muslims remember Allah through their earnings. The pilgrimage brings us back physically as well as spiritually to the center of the world, the Ka'aba in Makkah, which is also the symbol of the inward center, the heart, which is the place where the remembrance of God becomes a meeting ground and a reality. Finally, the main purpose of the fast is the achievement of a state of detachment from the world through the outright denial of the senses, in order to create a space within the mind and heart for the "remembrance" (*dhikr*) of Allah. This is the greatest and most immediate benefit of the fast, for Allah has said: "Remember Me and I will remember you." (2: 152)

The fast of Ramadhan ultimately contains a meaning, a blessing, and a promise that extends far beyond human expectations or experience. "Fasting is for Me and I shall grant reward for it Myself." In compensation for the human effort of the fast, the divine promise has both an outer and an inner aspect. The two joys of fasting are the *Iftar* or "break-fast" meal that concludes the fast and the vision of the new moon that signals the *Eid* at the termination of Ramadhan. The inner blessing is what modern psychological terminology would call a higher consciousness or "presence of mind" together with a feeling of serenity and peace that accompanies any strong effort of human will, in this case the human will in virtual surrender to the Will of God. In Qur'anic terminology, this is called *tatma'inn al-gulub*, a peace that descends into the hearts of the believers from above as a foretaste of the ultimate divine promise, namely the joy of seeing the paradise (*jannah*) after death and the beneficence of having the vision of God after resurrection.

Is it any wonder that the sense of taste ties us initially and inevitably to the sensible world that we enjoy and relate to through all of the five senses? Because taste binds us to sustaining life through ingestion and nourishment and because its first tier significance links us to the pleasures it has on offer, we may well become negligent and fall prey to the temptation of overlooking, if not actually ignoring, the inner aspect of "taste", or what the Sufis in the Islamic tradition call *dhawq*. All of life is a tasting of the supreme beatitude that has been bestowed upon us through the life experience. When we turn back away from this world in tribute to our spiritual origins and in remembrance of that Supreme Being who has created us and given us a mind, heart and soul with which to experience the world, we actually experience an inner tasting of that approximates coming into the very presence of the Divinity.

In the Islamic worldview, the body exists as a vehicle within the world of the *dunia* (this world) and as a medium for the tendencies of the soul. The body is conceived as a kingdom; but the soul is the king, while the intellectual faculties and human senses are the cohort and army in coming to terms with reality within this vast microcosmic world. Beyond taste as nourishment lies taste as appreciation on the physical, mental and psychic planes of experience. In the Islamic traditional worldview, the human mind has the capacity to ingest and appreciate–to taste if you will–intelligible, intelligent and intellectual input that comes to us from the outside world in the form of the arts and crafts and the good works that others have accomplished. To read and appreciate a great piece of literature, to bask in the vision of a work of sacred art, to absorb the visual artistry and experience the profound meaning in the utility of a well-wrought handcraft such as a traditional carpet or a hand-carved brass serving tray is to absorb the creative, intellectual and higher level spiritual experience of another person into oneself as a means of enlightenment, such as the appreciative tasting of a book, the beauty of a sacred work of architecture or a handwritten parchment of calligraphy.

We know that the senses–and especially the sense of taste–convey a kind of knowledge, but how we appreciate that knowledge and absorb its inner content will ultimately reflect upon the kind of person we are and the kind of person we will become through the manner in which we ingest and appreciate the wisdom of the senses. Are we as individuals suppose to follow the guidance of the modern, secular worldview that has tied up human reason and the experience of the five senses into an exploratory pursuit of knowledge whose point of departure is the physical world and whose ultimately destination–such as it is–lies presumably within the innumerable and infinitely miniscule particles that are found at the quantum physical level of experience, at the expense of the world of first principles and universal knowledge that lie at the heart of the traditional, metaphysical worldview. It recalls the efforts of the spider, who not only spins its own web with the materials that has been providentially laid at hand; but who also climbs up and down and across its own little universe, pinned to the experience of its own reality in the same manner and perhaps in just compensation to the way in which it meticulously traps its prey for the sake of its own lethal purposes.

What begins as a first tier experience that involves the tasting and appreciation of the physical world has the power to become a soul experience with far-reaching proportions. What begins as a tasting and an appreciation on the bodily, mental and psychic planes of experience eventually comes to rest within the ground of the human soul as an inner awakening to a higher experience of consciousness. Within the Islamic context, it is not a given that the soul partakes of an innate spirituality; rather the soul represents the summary and culmination of the human experience across a broad spectrum of good and evil inclinations, leading the soul to become a mirror reflection of all that we know and do in this life, either as victim to insatiable senses or as benefactor to what the senses may reveal. The soul is the expression of who we are. The Turkish poet Yunus Emre has summarized the concept by putting his finger on the true significance of the sense of taste and how that relates within the deep well of the soul experience:

> When I eat something sweet without You, it's bitter.
> You are the soul's taste, what else could I want? [93]

It has been said that when the hungry man sees the sight of steaming hot bread, his instinctive desire is worth the aspiration of a thousand seekers of truth. We need to feed off our hunger as an alternative experience of taste with the power to transform our soul into a mirror reflection of the Divinity. The Sufis of the Islamic tradition refer directly to *dhawq* as an experience of taste that relates to the experience of spiritual intuition that is the immediate result of the direct perception of the faculty of the intellect of the knowledge of God. Only the direct experience of the knowledge of God as the ultimate experience of taste can bring to fruition the entire range of human yearning to transcend the physical plane of experience. Ibn 'Arabi told a disciple: "If someone enjoins you to prove the existence of the 'knowledge of divine secrets', demand that they in turn prove the smoothness of honey." I think what Ibn 'Arabi was referring to was not the superficial experience of taste that comes from the sweetness of honey or the succulence of the fig. The experience of higher spiritual consciousness and its corresponding path of awakening begins with the gustatory knowledge of the world, with the smoothness of honey and the tart quality of the lemon, the sweetness of fresh dates and the soothing quality of mother's milk, partly because they give what they have to offer without exacting an undue price and partly because they have retained the taste of the paradise that is their inborn nature.

---

[93] As quoted in *Music of the Sky*, The Drop that Became the Sea, p. 73 "Music of the Sky".

Perhaps we should invoke the words of Al-Hallaj, a well-known Sufi who was put to death by crucifixion because of his unorthodox proclamations, to help us remember the inner meaning of the taste experience, when he proclaimed: "When I wanted to drink to quench my thirst, it is You that I saw in the shadow of the goblet."[94] Let us give thanks at the table of life for the provision (*rizq*) that has been bestowed upon us and appreciate it as the sweet blessing that it is intended to be. Let us lift up our cup and bowl in salute to the provision that has been sent down to us from the Supreme Provider "for many a slender beauty heaven has made into a hundred cups, a hundred bowls."[95]

6.5 Ramadhan Nights in Madinah

The approach to the mosque in Madinah arrives suddenly as my companions and I emerge onto the grand concourse of the sacred mosque of Madinah, called the Prophet's Mosque because the Prophet himself is buried in one corner, called the Sacred Chamber, in an area that originally comprised the rooms where he lived with his wife 'Aishah. The first mosque of Islam[96] was an extension of the house of the Prophet.

The sight of this magnificent edifice is overwhelming, to say the least, for its mammoth size and stately presence. For sheer bulk and size, this architectural wonder strikes awe in the beholder. The entire structure rests serenely amid an open expanse of plaza that extends perhaps 500 meters on each side of the mosque and whose surface is covered with alabaster and marble.[97] Everything about this broad setting bespeaks of openness, air, and light and provides striking views of the mosque from any angle of approach. This is the very center and heart of the city. Everything beyond the sacred enclosure immediately becomes an afterthought to the necessities of daily life. A grand avenue leads down from the mountains beyond the edge of the small city to the five grand portals that distinguish the front side of the mosque. At a glance as you approach from the grand promenade, the building seems monumental. Like a photo that simply refuses to contain the image you wish to capture, the sight of the mosque simply refuses to be contained in a single glance. You have to span your vision from left to right, right to left, to take it all in, and even then, it seems incomprehensible to fully grasp in all its magnificence.

The day is punctuated of course by the five devotional prayers of Islam and at any given moment vast crowds of people are either moving toward or away

---

[94] *Return to the Essential*, (Bloomington, Ind, World Wisdom Books, 2004), p. 5.
[95] Omar Khayyam, *Music of the Sky* (Bloomington, Ind.: World Wisdom Books, 2004), p. 120.
[96] The dimensions of the original structure were 2,450 square meters with three doors on the south side, and in the eastern and western wall.
[97] The total plaza area is 235,000 square meters and accommodates 400,000 additional worshippers. The mosque itself may now accommodate approximately one million worshippers during peak times of crowding.

from the imposing sanctuary of the mosque. As I arrive in the early morning after my night flight to greet the Prophet and extend my "Salaams" as is the Islamic custom, I find myself moving against a sea of humanity who are now exiting the holy mosque after the early morning prayer and the commencement of the fast, since it is the holy month of Ramadhan. The entire concourse is bathed in light amidst the otherwise still darkened night within the city and this light no doubt shines heavenward as a vertical symbol of human aspiration and a love for God like no other love, while grand colonnades bedecked with gilded lamps that are harmoniously dispersed across the concourse illuminate the marble-floored forecourt like silent sentinels watching over the faithful. In the distance in the eastern sky, the promise of dawn begins to emerge over the horizon behind the rocky Madinah hills just outside the city.

I intend to make my way through this magnificent place of worship deep into the inner sanctum of the original mosque, which became the extension of the family quarters of the Prophet highlighting the concept of the mosque as the logical extension of the home. It is here along the original southeasterly section of the mosque that the Prophet lies buried, together with his Companions and first Caliphs Abu Bakr al-Saddiq and Omar bin al-Khattaab. It is customary to visit the tomb of the Prophet and greet him with Salaams upon first entering the sacred enclosure of the mosque. I make my way slowly amid the multitude and savor every moment. The mosque is still jam packed with people of every race and nationality. Old and young intermingle; many are lying supine, others are gathered in groups or sitting in circles sharing their impressions. People are moving about as I am, deferring to the space of others, careful to step over those who are resting on the floor without a care in the world.

I know I am nearing the tomb of the Prophet through two pieces of evidence, the architectural change of the building which has a smaller, more crowded, and less grandiose aspect and dates back many centuries to the time of the Prophet and the early Caliphate era and by the density of the crowds of people all vying for proximity to the resting place of the Prophet. There is a section of the mosque cordoned off and positioned adjacent to the wall of the Prophet's tomb that is referred to and revered as the *al-riyadh al-jinnah*, which roughly translates as a "garden" of the Paradise. The Prophet has referred to this part of the mosque by saying: "What is between my house and my *minbar* is a garden from the gardens of Paradise." It is an area that according to the traditions of the Prophet is actually a part of the Paradise that will rise upward and return to its original home on the Day of Judgment, which in Islam is alternatively referred to as the Day of Accounting and the Day of Religion.

Many years ago when I first became Muslim, I remember quietly entering this section of the mosque and ensconcing myself on the light blue carpet distinguished from the red oriental carpets spread through the rest of the mosque. There was indeed not only a special quality of serenity and calm there that one would come to expect in the paradise, but I felt as I sat cross-legged on the carpet as if I had come home at last and that there was nowhere else I needed to go. An otherworldly fragrance seemed to unexpectedly permeate the air and I remember considering what that scent reminded me of until I had to confess that it reminded me of nothing related to this world, that it had an otherworldly quality that seemed exquisite and heavenly.

As I sat in this "garden of Paradise," my mind took on wings and I began to fly. Call it auto-suggestion of the tradition if you like, but a dream quality seemed to emerge like dawn mist over the waters of a lake. The strange, otherworldly scent began to raise my level of consciousness from the mundane to the sublime in some unconscious manner, and I felt I was entering another dimension virtually impossible to describe. Then, without warning, I felt a surge of emotion well up inside me from depths I didn't know existed, an emotive feeling so strong and satiating that I could do nothing but surrender to the power of these sacred emotions and I began to sob a welter of hot tears that fell down my face with a will of their own. At first, I did not know why I was crying, except that I realized that the place, the moment, and the overall ambiance were powerful enough to evoke such an unexpected reaction. The outburst was not convulsive or hectic; it was sheer weeping without an obvious catalyst. It was not the kind of grief caused by the death of a loved one or the loss of a valued treasure; instead it was an emotive collapse without hill or valley, a release from the rigidity that holds us together in life, vast and inconsolable at first as a child's first confrontation with the unknown. The hot tears came as a soothing balm for the trials and tribulations of my life, the frustrations and the shattered hopes, the dreams, the remorse, the failures and perhaps even the successes. I sobbed for the person I had been and the person I might well become. The sobbing slowly died within me throb by throb until a wave as cool as spring water flowed across the shore of my being and an abiding peace streamed through my mind and body. I had received the gift of tears spoken of in the traditions of Islam in which the soul uses the mind and body to free itself of certain complexes of the psyche and psychological knots of the spirit as a form of liberation from the lower self and a way of purification.

On this occasion fifteen years later, however, I had to forgo scaling the heights of such an elevated spiritual emotion that I experienced on that former occasion—or so I thought—because the section of the mosque called the *riyadh al-jannah* was simply a teeming cauldron of wide-eyed humanity all in contest for a piece in this "paradise" on earth. I therefore joined the more sober, turgid throng making its way down the aisle that passes in front of the three tombs of the Prophet and his beloved companions Abu Bakr and Omar. It was slow going indeed, and except for the occasional shove or elbow in the ribs, perhaps it was a good thing, because as one approaches the front doors of the tombs, with their silver encrusted plating covered with Qur'anic verses, the realization suddenly dawns with an expectation brimming beyond belief that one is approaching the very presence of the Prophet. Here is where he lived, where he prayed, and where he died. Here lies the man that Allah chose to receive His revelation and to deliver it as the Holy Qur'an to future generations of humanity. Through his mind passed the very words of God and from him, they passed out into the world of humanity down to the present time. Muslims spend a lifetime attempting to find ways to express their love of God, but their love of the Prophet comes naturally and spontaneously because he is the vehicle and the path through which the love of God is possible.

As I turn a corner and approach the aisle that passes in front of the enclosed rooms containing the various tombs, the dense but still orderly crowd thickens considerably. People with cupped or extended hands in an attitude of prayer are moving slowly forward at the pace of molasses and everyone proceeds deferentially, concerned for the comfort of their Muslim brothers and not wishing to create an undue stir. Then I am there and I send forth my Salaams to the beloved Prophet (PBUH). Neither the hectic throng nor the imposing and unexpected presence of military guards at the doors of the tombs can disturb the surging feeling of humility and awe that begins in the pit of my stomach and rises to the tip of my cognitive consciousness lifting me off my feet and beyond the gravity limits of this world. As I shuffle myself along as only one of a surging crowd of worshippers, I feel lost in the wave of a deep and abiding emotion and I think: We remember the Prophet Muhammad (PBUH), every day in our prayers and we invoke his name and sayings as a matter of course, but now I am here at his tomb, visiting his ancient home and place of earthly investiture. I have presented myself here in person to make my holy Salaams to the memory of his sacred person and his exemplary life. Together with all Muslims, I feel a deep and overwhelming love for the Prophet to the extent that the evocation of his memory creates a feeling of melting in the heart and brings tears to the eyes. It is a powerful, indeed an overwhelming moment. In the presence of greatness, I utter my humble prayer as intercession to God through the Prophet as I remember all those in need within the circle of my life, a dying brother on life support, my diabetic friend, and all those who asked me to intercede on their behalf.

A moment whose quality will be remembered for years to come has passed me by, just as the slow-moving sea of humanity I am part of has passed by the tomb enclosure. Before I fully realize what has happened, the crowd has deposited me outside the mosque again like a piece of driftwood thrown ashore by the restless sea. I gaze distractedly and a little disoriented at the luminous glow of light on the eastern horizon as the sun announces its arrival and bathes the eastern face of the grand mosque with its harsh light without any thought or mercy for the faithful.

Later that afternoon, I am stunned by an insistent echo as I cross the threshold of the mosque to say the evening sunset prayer and break the Ramadhan fast, "Come, come, come, sit here! *Tofaddal!*" This is the Arabic greeting of invitation to join a repast. Somebody has taken me by the arm and is escorting me through the maze of legs and feet to what seems like the sole remaining place in the otherwise cavernous and body-packed enclosure, roofed with cascading archways in descending order as far as the eye can see. I feel dazed by the sudden good fortune and glad to have a place inside the mosque where I can break the fast and say the prayer. How this was actually going to happen in the next few minutes however was anyone's guess.

As I settled myself onto the carpet in front of my place setting, I see around me that bee hive activity that has made the breaking of the fast possible in the first place. Local citizens of Madinah have commandeered the mosque to create perhaps the largest breakfast place setting in the world. Row upon row of carpets as far as the eye can see and extending across the broad concourse of the inner mosque from east to west have been equipped with food and drink so that the faithful may break their fast. Lengthy strips of cellophane have been laid lengthwise. My own place setting represents a microcosm that mirrors perhaps tens of thousands of place settings now existent throughout the mosque. There is an appetizing ring loaf of bread, freshly baked and sprinkled with tasty sesame seeds that radiate an odor of wholesome goodness in the style of true bread that one seldom finds today. There are a number of fruits, including an orange and a banana and a handful of Madinah dates at each place setting. There is a full milk cup of yoghurt accompanied by a small tray of freshly ground *zattar* that Arabs favor and like to sprinkle into the yogurt. Every place setting has a small plastic spoon to stir and eat the yoghurt. It is a magnificent if not unbelievable display of planning and forethought. Of course feeding the faithful during Ramadan is incumbent upon the Muslims and brings with it special blessings that are highly favored. Minutes before the call of the *adhan* and the momentous breaking of the fast, *Zamzam* water[98] is poured and passed along the rows from large thermo containers situated along the aisles of the mosque.

In a final gesture of generosity, I am quickly passed a small plastic cup of Arabic coffee pungent with the spice cardamom, which I set down in front of me amid the array of delicacies that await my consumption. Then I hear the piercing cry of the *adhan*. *Allahu Akbar, Allahu Akbar*, followed by the profession of faith that there is no god but the one God and Muhammad (PBUH), is the Messenger of God, magnified tenfold and cutting through the silence like a piercing cry from beyond the known world. The vast congregation consisting of some astronomical number beyond reckoning or comprehension, but certainly approaching perhaps a million Muslims, paused for a brief second as if the loud report of a bullet had unexpectedly sounded, then everyone to the individual invoked the name of God and broke his fast with water and fresh dates in the traditional manner of the Prophet some fourteen hundred years ago.

I break my fast on a date and proceed with my makeshift repast, washing it down with a shot of Arabic coffee and refreshing gulps of the beloved Zamzam water whose purity and crystalline taste cannot be matched from any other well in the world. The thought crosses my mind that saying the prayer amidst this wreckage of food and drink, orange rinds and plastic cups, could be a problem. I

---

[98] From the Zamzam well at the Grand Mosque in Makkah. The Zamzam water is transported daily to the mosque in special tanker trucks from Makkah, 430 kilometers away.

had not accounted, however, for the planning and ingenuity of those responsible for this brief repast. Within minutes, our host for this little section of the mosque and his aids descend upon the rows depositing the leftover bread, dates, and fruit into great plastic bags reserved for the task. Once done, the entire assemblage of waste is carefully gathered up within the folds of the plastic floor cloth, which summarily disappears down the row and out of sight of the worshippers. The entire mosque had been restored to an ordered cleanliness in less than the minute it took me to dislodge my aging bones from the floor and stand together with the other worshippers in well defined rows to offer our sunset prayer.

If the world and all that it contains is woven from the stuff of which shadows are made, and if man is a transient and exile disconnected from his true self–a prodigal in search of his ancestral hearth–then this journey to the holy places that begins sitting cross-legged on a carpet with a million other aspirants and breakfasting together on water and dates becomes transformed into the true journey to that final abode of which the revelation speaks. In partaking of a revealed tradition, one gains entry into a world of vision and light; it is a reality woven of the stuff of which not shadows but threads of light are made. It makes demands on us as in the discipline of the Ramadan fast, but in compensation, its promise of vision and light becomes a part of one's inner world and leads a person beyond the borders of his or her natural shadow self into a world of higher awareness.

6.6 Journey of our Time

The physical reality of the Grand Mosque in Makkah gives way to the higher reality that it symbolizes. Herein lies the very center and heart of the Islamic cosmos. This simple cube of masonry,[99] a form of proto-art that traces its roots through Abraham back to the primordial era of Adam, is the central axis where Heaven meets earth and where the Divine meets the human. Across the globe, the Islamic rites and spiritual practices, in every mosque and in the hearts of every devout Muslim, form a directional pattern that leads directly to the Ka'aba in Makkah, which is the earthly reflection of a celestial shrine, which is also reflected within the heart of man. The inherent symbolism of the Ka'aba as center of the human being and vertical axis beyond the earthly dimension creates a feeling of sacred space and sacred time, a coming into the Presence through the sacralization of space. The circumambulation of the Sacred House as a physical reality raises the consciousness of a person to a rarefied spiritual universe as the Ka'aba of the human heart meets the central Ka'aba of the Divine Reality.

---

[99] The Ka'aba is a small square building made of stones, about 60 feet long, 60 feet wide and 60 feet high. The four corners roughly face the four directions of the compass. The building, made from gray-blue stones from the nearby hills of Makkah, is covered with the Kiswa, a black brocade cloth that has the Islamic testament of faith (*shahadah*) woven into its fabric and embossed gold-lettered calligraphy as adornment.

As we entered the mosque and made our way toward the magnetic draw of the rhythmic mass of people circumambulating the Ka'aba, I was becoming increasingly alarmed. The crowds were overwhelming and I was beginning to wonder, as I wrestled with my unfamiliar and ill-fitting garments, whether we would be able to find a place, indeed some special place in the shadow of the Ka'aba, where we could say the afternoon prayer with serenity before performing the *Umrah*. Various aisles were still open to people moving in and around the sanctuary and Amr suggested that we position ourselves right there in the aisle in view of the Ka'aba when in a matter of minutes all motion would stop and the prayer would commence. In fact, the mosque was jam-packed with not a free space to be found. The heat even in November can be oppressive and I thought of those in the open courtyard under the intensity of the late afternoon desert sun. There in the shade, as I made my prostrations during the prayer (*salat al-asr*), I was sweating profusely and my heart began to beat erratically. I had been fasting since predawn with no food or water and felt a little dehydrated, dizzy, and concerned about my ability to fulfill the requirements of the rites; but the motions of the ritual prayer and the intensity of the situation, together with the presence of my friend nearby, guided me through the difficulties of the moment.

Amr's broad, respectful, village-boy smile greeted me upon the completion of the prayer. We were now to perform the sacred rituals of the "lesser pilgrimage" that date back to the time of the Prophet fourteen hundred years ago. It is interesting to note that the rituals themselves transcend the time of the Islamic Messenger and refer in their essence and symbolism to the Abrahamic era, shifting the focus of the rites beyond the inception of the religion of Islam proper to a more universal setting and significance with the patriarch Abraham as the symbolic father of the prophets.[100] Essentially there are three main duties to be performed according to the dictates of the lesser pilgrimage and these include the circumambulation seven times around the Ka'aba in an anti-clockwise direction with the Ka'aba on the left, followed by prayer at the Station (*maqam*) of Abraham,[101] and finally the *Saiy* which consists in running seven times between the hills of Safa and Marwa. We hoped to negotiate our way through these rituals together with the vast congregation of *Umrah* pilgrims and complete the *Umrah* before the sunset prayer and breaking of the fast.

With affection and open eagerness, Amr took my arm and led me through the confusion of the crowd toward the swirling orbit of people moving about the Ka'aba in a steady stream of worship and spiritual rapture. "We need to get as close to the Ka'aba as possible," he whispered urgently in my ear. No sacramental

---

[100] Indeed, it is a sad legacy that the Jews and the Muslims, who trace their Semitic line back to the great patriarch Abraham through his two sons Ishmael and Isaac and whose symbolic value still conveys a profound meaning to the world's population, are such bitter enemies in today's world.

[101] Inside the Station of Abraham is kept a stone bearing the prints of two human feet. The Prophet Abraham is said to have stood on this stone when building the Ka'aba and the marks of his feet are miraculously preserved.

dictate required us to get as close as possible to the Ka'aba, yet custom and tradition suggested proximity to the structure if possible. I also knew that Amr harbored a secret desire to kiss the black stone, said to be a meteorite fallen from Heaven that is firmly secured in a silver encasement found in the east corner of the cubic structure which marks the place of commencement of the *tawwaf* or circumambulation.

No Muslim who has made *Hajj* or *Umrah* pilgrimage will deny that the circumambulation is a physical experience that takes stamina and will power. When you view the scene from the roof of the Grand Mosque or witness the event through TV cameras hoisted on high, it gives every appearance of being a rhythmic stream of humanity flowing in sublime unison around the central axis of the world. However, the reality of being amid this throbbing, densely packed mob is tumultuous and unpredictable and yet all the while nobody seems to care about the tumult around them or complain about the crush of people. Upon entering the throng, you lose your sense of personal identity and personal space and become one with the teeming horde moving about the symbolic vision of the ancient edifice and focusing all your hopes and aspirations on the reality of the Divine Being in a state of ecstatic rapture.

Entering the ritual practice of circumambulation is like entering into the "once upon a time" of myths and folktales, *in illo tempore*. The pilgrim enters into sacred time that is actually the "real" time of the "vertical" or eternal dimension, as opposed to the horizontal, linear, and progressive time that we experience here on earth as a relentless, forward-moving machine. I fell immediate victim to this sublime transcendent state of mind as if by some remote control of heaven and felt at one with the rotating vortex of the crowd. I no longer seemed to matter as an individual entity for I had been swept away in this "first sanctuary" to a primordial time of perfection and heightened consciousness when the truth is there to behold, there to witness, and there to be known as nothing else can be known. As I circumambulate the sacred Ka'aba, I make my entreaties, I send my greetings, I pray to Allah and worship the Divinity. Soon enough, beyond all reckoning of time, I am truly swept away by a flood of emotion and higher sentiment as I become one with the wave of worshippers. Indeed, I feel myself giving up and surrendering to this moment of eternity in time and this central place that makes possible the ascent of man beyond the horizon of the rational mind and beyond the dictates of the lower self.

Amr has managed to seize a seven beaded cord resting on the wall by the Station of Ishmael along one side of the Ka'aba with which to keep track of the seven circumambulations that are required of the *tawwaf* ritual, although how he has managed this feat is anyone's guess as he grins sheepishly at me with the beaded cord. Our arms are locked together for security as we make our way round and round within the circumference of the sacred precinct. I am happy to have this fellow with me as we make the circumambulation in communion with the Spirit of God that overshadows the environment. It feels as though I have known him for a thousand years.

Perhaps it is the writer and natural-born observer in my nature, but I unconsciously take the time to notice the behavior and movement of the people around me. Everyone seems solicitous of the other's safety and comfort, although admittedly the movement around the Ka'aba is far from harmonious at ground zero. It takes effort just to keep standing and one is literally carried forward on tiptoes by the mob pressing in on every side. Still, no one exaggerates the hectic quality of the procession and everyone seems to be trying to defer to the person nearby. Of course, there is every size, shape, and color of person to be imagined in this vast horde of humanity. I see the elderly and the young, husbands and wives, fathers, sons, and daughters. There are groups of women clinging together for safety and surprisingly strong as they race past me. There are groups of men, from Iran, from Ethiopia, from Malaysia, from China, arms linked together in a chain for support. People of all races and nationalities are praying aloud, uttering in Arabic the Qur'anic epithets and litanies that are appropriately noted for the occasion, entreaties to Allah for health, for blessing, for provision, for the *hasanat* or good things of this and the next world. The elderly and the crippled are being carried in litters overhead on the hands of husky black Africans; others are being moved along in wheelchairs by family members or friends. In one shocking instance, I felt a rustle at my feet and upon looking down toward the marble floor of the enclosure, I see to my horror amid the disorder of moving legs a crippled woman crawling along in circumambulation on all fours with a look of determination and joy on her face.

I cling to my Egyptian friend Amr for stamina and support, approaching an age when I can call myself elderly and fearful of falling down and being overrun by this juggernaut of moving humanity. On the sixth round, a way close to the wall of the house suddenly opens, seemingly miraculously, for both Amr and I noticed that the agitated waters of humanity we were among have unexpectedly opened a path to give free passage to the vicinity of the *Hajar al-Aswad* or the beloved black stone, known as a sacred meteorite fallen down from Heaven during the primordial era. I think to myself that Amr and I are of one accord in our desire to touch the black stone.

Under normal circumstances, it is well-nigh impossible to get anywhere near this sacred artifact for the crowds that are clamoring to touch and kiss the holy object. Amr suddenly sees the opportunity and makes his move, veering toward the black stone and dragging me alongside with him. We are immediately engulfed once again by the teeming throng of people surrounding the stone and only footsteps away from touching the sacred object. I look up and see Amr standing by the silver frame of the black stone grinning broadly with satisfaction. I knew that he has achieved his goal and has touched the stone. I try to lean forward and extend my arm as far as possible in the direction of the blessed object, but I simply cannot move another inch forward. I am about to give up the effort and blend back into the wave when I feel a hand seize my wrist and move it down into the framed enclosure wherein resides the *Hajar al-Aswad*. It is the swift movement of Amr's powerful grip that has made this possible. For a second,

I feel the cool, electric presence of the stone run up through my arm and down into my soul and I smell the unearthly fragrance of the Paradise evoking a memory of some primal purity and perfection amid the chaos of the moment. Then, we are both summarily thrown beyond the area of the building containing the black stone by the crowd surging forward around the corner, whence we raise our right hands to greet the Divinity one last time before commencing the final *tawwaf* around the Ka'aba.

Once this sacred ritual is completed, we ease our way out from the surging mass and make our way over to the Station of Abraham where we find a small area to make the traditional two prostrations. After that, the traditions allude to the ritual of drinking and refreshing oneself with the Zamzam water, spring water that dates back to the time of Abraham. According to the Islamic traditions, Hajar, one of the wives of Abraham, was searching within the area of the Ka'aba for water for her son Ishmael. In her desperation, she ran seven times between the two hills of Safa and Marwa[102] adjacent to the precinct of the Ka'aba. She eventually discovered the waters of Zamzam flowing from under a rock and began to drink. In commemoration of this hardship, the pilgrims run seven times between the hills of Safa and Marwa[103] and refresh themselves with the Zamzam waters. Indeed, after the ordeal of the *Tawas*, which we undertook in the afternoon under the blazing glare of the relentless desert sun,[104] the waters of Zamzam were unbelievably refreshing—not to drink of course because we were still fasting, but to pour over our heads and faces.

The final ritual calls for the pilgrims to run seven times between the Makkah hills of Safa and Marwa in remembrance of the ordeal of Hajar and the infant Ishmael. To that end, the Saudi government has constructed an enclosure between the two hills in the form of a two-storied hallway adjacent to the Grand Mosque proper. It is a magnificent setting of a two-way hallway enclosure with two tracks running down the middle to accommodate wheelchairs and litters. As Amr and I undertake this final ritual of the lesser pilgrimage, we enter once again the vast crowd of pilgrims similarly re-commemorating the ordeal of Hajar and her son. It is difficult to recreate within this magisterial setting adjacent to the Ka'aba the dry, dusty terrain amid two now famous hills in which the wife of the patriarch experienced her desperation, although anyone who has lived in Saudi Arabia knows just how hot it can get in that country. Even now, several millennia later, it is not an easy task even in this sublime setting. After running a number of times through the concourse of these two hills, both Amr and I are feeling hot and tired and thirsty. Perhaps it was appropriate that we were still fasting and had

---

[102] The distance between the two hills is about 500 yards.

[103] "Behold! Safa and Marwa are among the symbols of Allah. So if those who visit the House in the season or at other times should compass them round, it is no sin in them. And if any one obeyeth his own impulse to good, be sure that Allah is He Who recognizeth and knoweth." (2:158)

[104] Most notably, the marble floor of the precinct contains special cooling metals to prevent the soles of the feet from being scorched by the intense heat of the sun.

been fasting from food and drink since before dawn because it added to the rigor and poignancy of the moment. We finally completed the tiring trek back and forth seven times in keeping with the tradition which considers seven a sacred number in the science of numerology associated with the Islamic traditions.

The final act of the pilgrimage upon completion of the *Saiy* is the cutting of the hair. The Prophet advised either shaving the head or cutting a part of the hair and to that end there are multiple barbershops ready with straight-edged razors to service the pilgrim community. Both Amr and I decide to trim each other's hair, however, for the sake of convenience. We have both had our heads shaved on the former occasion of the greater *Hajj* a number of years ago. Hot, tired, and feeling emotionally drained after the effort of the sacred rites, which have taken us nearly two hours, we obligingly snip off various locks of hair from each side of the head including the crown. We then depart the mosque enclosure in silence and climb the stairs leading up the side of the mountain encroaching upon the back side of the Grand Mosque to make our way to a nearby hotel.

PART SEVEN

The Higher Faculties

7.1 The Logic of Reason

Modern science—and the predominant worldview that provides the framework for its findings—is mind and matter bound. Scientists today are fixated on the ability of the faculty of reason to work its way through any dilemma and the need for empirical evidence to quantify—and thus objectify—their theories and substantiate their claims. Moreover, the modern mentality permits itself the luxury of a dream in which the faculty of reason is understood somehow to be transcendent, that is to say, a faculty that has the power to surpass itself beyond its natural capabilities *by its own means*; a faculty that in pursuit of its self-ordained inquiry into the true nature of reality will ultimately unearth sufficient evidence to substantiate the miracle of existence *on its own.*

The modern-day reliance on the determining powers of human beings and the absolute trust in the ability of human reason to lead us into the future of ourselves, on our own and without the aid of Heaven, tends to dominate the first tier of our inner world with its superficial line of reasoning and its closed system of thought. The mind, with its intricate thought processes, moves from the phenomenal world of the senses to the inner world of thought and abstraction and back out again into the world of created forms with an assurance that is frankly astounding and that belies the truly mysterious nature of our inner world. The question, however, lingers at the edge of human consciousness to haunt our waking moments: What lies beyond the first tier of the mind which is the ground of our normal, everyday thinking? Does anyone know how the mind really operates? Does anyone want to know?

No one doubts that the faculty of reason plays a vital role in the inner discourse of the mind; but the reality of our inner life–at both conscious and unconscious levels–goes far beyond what the faculty of reason can account for and handle. There is something happening within the human mind that leads us far beyond the literal and logical proceedings within the theater of our rational mind. Like "the wind that bloweth where it listeth," (John 3:8) our minds move in uncertain and unpredictable ways. Our imagination portrays possibilities that lead us beyond the apparent self; our understanding arises from a dimension for which we cannot fully account. Ultimately, we arrive at thoughts, ideas, and resolutions that have their own mysterious origin and that offer no explanation beyond their ability to enlighten the mind, raise our consciousness, and offer the certainty for which the human heart yearns.

What, then, are we as modern individuals to make of the faculty of human reason? What should it accomplish for modern humanity, and how and why? Is it capable of establishing the *raison d'être* of the human being on its own? Does it define human meaning according to the proclamations of the scientific paradigm of knowledge? Does it actually permit human beings to maneuver through the corridors of the mind in a way that allows them to transcend the limitations of a matter-based mind? If so, what is the ultimate source of such explanatory power and such potential illumination? Does the faculty of reason we rely on today observe, witness, and exercise awareness in the same way that the intellect and higher consciousness of the people living in an earlier, more traditional culture functioned, drawing as they did on the source material of revelation and the capacity of the higher faculties to recognize and appreciate the direct knowledge of God? Is the modern concept of reason actually the mind's "I," the self-centered ego of the 21st century personality that serves as a pale reflection of the mind's "eye" of the religions, the "eye of certainty" referred to in the Qur'anic revelation, the third eye that reflects a higher dimension, or the eye of Shiva that is symbolic of the gift of spiritual vision?

According to the prevailing scientific worldview, the only possible answer must be a resounding no, for nothing and no one today wants to play the shadow figure and be the dark afterthought to an illuminated faculty or first principle. The realm of the shadowland must traditionally be considered the domain of unreality and illusion, where a pale horse and rider pose as the real thing, when in truth they are merely phantom shadows representing the unrealities they truly are. To rely on reason alone as the mechanism to process human thought in a manner that reflects the whole person is to live in the shadowlands of the lower self and to rely on a faculty of mind that was originally intended–but no longer serves–as a bridge to the higher faculties and modes of perception.

In other words, human reason was not intended to be a one-horse rider serving the impressions of the human senses and directing them through the filter of the human ego, for this in fact only represents the first tier of humanity's inner world of awareness and perception. According to the traditional Islamic perspective, human reason (*al-aql*) serves as a bridge between the lower world typical of the mind-body relationship and the higher world of the intellect-spirit relationship; it thus takes an active part in the borderland of the spirit as a human faculty illuminated by the superior realms of the intellect and not the shadow self that it has become in today's rational and scientistic environment.

Perhaps we need to understand the traditional concept of the faculty of reason from a different angle of approach. According to traditional philosophy, we live within the rhythms of the earth and enjoy an easy familiarity with the harmony those rhythms convey. The enduring cycles of nature are reflected in the changing seasons in the life of humans. The waxing of spring becomes the waning of winter, just as the expansion of childhood and youth matures into middle age and maturity, only to diminish again in old age and finally senescence. The seasons and cycles of nature and earthly life seem to interact in ways that suggest a broad complementarity of purpose and design between the rhythms of human beings and the rhythms evidenced in nature.

So much for appearances; and yet the truth of the cosmos would be impossible to imagine if it were not more than what it appears to be. Within the harmony of the natural cosmic order lies a dark and sobering symbolic message. Everyone is familiar with the two faces of the earth. The sun casts down its light to give us the face of day, while the rotation of the earth turns us away from the sun to give us the face of night. The mystery of day and night is unceremoniously resolved in the relative fixity of the sun and the rhythmic fluidity of our planet Earth as it floats on its orbit. The message is self-evident to the casual observer, or do appearances again mislead? Is there contained within the darkness of night a lingering secret that refuses to shed its moon glow of light?

In fact, the cosmic Eye has a different perspective than the human one. The sun casts down its light upon the earth in the form of an ever-expanding ray, while the earth sends forth its night back out into the cosmos in an ever-receding shadow coming to a point before disappearing completely into the wall of infinity. The earth's day wears its pale luminescence like a mantle of blue, while the earth's night wears its conical shadow like a wizard's cap.[105]

In this way, we arrive at a conception of reason that transcends the narrow and limited framework of the scientific perspective, which invests much of its identity in the ability of matter to objectify reality. The immense intelligence displayed in nature and the timeless rhythms of the natural order are reflected as similar properties within the human mind, most notably in the instrument of human reason whose cognitive rationalism can react and claim interest in the intuitive insights and natural rhythms of a higher order. If we are not careful in the way we express our modernity, we may end up wearing the wizard's cap, sending shadows in every direction when we should be reflecting the influences of a supra-rational luminescence.

---

[105] The image of the wizard's cap is drawn from Chet Raymo's *The Soul of the Night: An Astronomical Pilgrimage* (Saint Paul, Minnesota: Hungry Mind Press, 1992).

Every object in the vicinity of an illuminating sun carries with it a cone of night whose shadow-draped stylus casts its signature into the surrounding void. Why should human nature be any different, if not the very antithesis of natural law? Human beings and their higher faculties of mind are no exception; they are the example *prima facie* of the universal norm, whether they walk across the earth in search of livelihood and fulfillment or traverse the borderlands of some inner universe. They can always count on the light of intelligent intuition to shine across the surface of their being, just as a person's physical form always casts a shadow.

In the next section, we will write more extensively about the luminosity of the human intellect as a direct reflection of the Supreme Intellect, by virtue of whose reflection we as human beings are able to transcend the limitations of the earthly realm and reunite once again with the presence of a Supreme Being. Perhaps it is no small miracle then that as rational beings, we have the use of the faculty of reason with which to traverse the inner landscape of thought and reflection in a logical and ordered manner. Like the conical darkness of the night that leaves its mark on the universal void, the stylus of our inner being can engrave its signature and leave its mark on the mystery of the individual self. Whether we use our faculty of reason as an instrument of light or darkness remains a decision that is ours alone to make, a decision that will determine the true nature of our unfolding destiny.

Beyond the question of an arbitrary reductionism that searches through the remotest elements of the natural order in an effort to comprehend the totality of the cosmic reality; beyond the questions raised by quantum mechanics concerning the true nature of physical matter; and beyond the problem of a reality based solely on the concept of matter to the exclusion of all else, lies the meaning and significance of the human faculty of reason within this speculative context. When we say that humans themselves have become the criterion of reality, we refer of course to the faculty of reason within the mind, which provides the operative framework and rational basis for establishing this objective reality. From the traditional point of view, this assumption is considered a highly questionable point of departure, suggesting that there is no higher faculty within humanity other than the faculty of reason. The modern scientific worldview makes matters worse by suggesting that reason is both *tabula rasa* and *end station* of the mind, the rarefied arena for the pre-figuration of all knowledge and the final transfiguration of the mind into the witness and harbinger of truth.

As a kind of *tabula rasa* of the mind, reason is portrayed as a neutral faculty that has its own integrity but that does not suffer the intrinsic emotion, confusion, uncertainty, and doubt that are the inevitable characteristics of the human condition. As the operative receptacle of all thoughts and impressions, reason is understood to be free of the all too familiar condition of inner turmoil that is embodied in the human ego and summarized in the conflicting emotions of our daily lives. As such, we imagine in our fantasy that the faculty of reason is unencumbered by any outside influence and unobstructed by the psychological knots or complexes that may confront the emotional and psychic systems of the mind. This, of course, must be the very stuff of a modern-day mythology. As *end station* of the mind, it sweeps away any challenge to its authority by proclaiming that there is nothing real in an objective world other than what the human reason itself can establish and process through the senses. Needless to say, what distinguishes the two philosophies of the secular and traditional worlds is the distinction that exists between reason and the capacity of the intellect to enlighten the rational mind with the first principles that form the basis of all thought.

From the point of view of traditional wisdom, reason possesses only a dialectical and not an illuminative function; it is therefore not capable of grasping that which lies beyond the world of forms. The fault lies not with its traditional ability but with its modern-day interpretation and application. The modern scientific worldview claims that reason can deal with the origin and source of our existence and our fundamental reality without opening itself to the higher levels of perception made available by the direct intuitions of the human intellect. The intellect has traditionally been understood to be the faculty through which humanity apprehends and experiences the metaphysical and eternal realities. However, modern science is not interested in these metaphysical and eternal realities. With no use for these astounding truths, the scientific establishment simply pretends, indeed insists, that they do not exist. Scientists adhere to the party line that their discipline is a rational one, just as their form of knowing resides within the physical rather than the metaphysical plane.

However, the denial of the existence of the intellect leads to a conceptual chasm between the seen and unseen realities, and this is nearly impossible to bridge in the modern world:

> The external world of matter and the internal world of mind, if you will, have then seemingly lost their connection; and this means, of course, that the universe, and our position therein, have become *de facto* unintelligible. It is the nature of reason to analyze, to cut asunder even, it would seem, what God Himself has joined; no wonder, then, that a *Weltanschauung* based upon reason alone should turn out to be fractured beyond repair.[106]

It is as if the power of observation, the cognitive abilities of the mind, and the immediacy of sensory experience have constructed a kind of "wall of prejudicial truth" that arbitrarily excludes the faculty of the intellect with its concomitant perceptions of the higher realities. From the point of view of modern science, beyond this wall of truth nothing exists; indeed, nothing is considered real unless it is measurable and can be expressed via mathematical formulation.

---

[106] Wolfgang Smith, *The Quantum Enigma* (Peru, Ill.: Sherwood Sugden & Company, 1995), p. 16.

Observational experiments can be conducted and believed in without the alleged deceptions and vague promises of a blind religious faith.

Once again, more questions emerge that need addressing by the scientific community. Was modern science then born as a form of worship of our purely sensorial experience? What precisely does modern science ask of us? Does it ask us to believe in a homogeneity of knowledge that results in the certain reduction of the qualitative aspects of nature to quantitative modalities? If so, then modern science asks us to sacrifice a good part of what is, according to the various traditions, the reality of the universe. In compensation, it offers us a mathematical schema whose major advantage is to help us manipulate matter on the plane of quantity, without however taking into account or realizing the qualitative consequences that have had such disastrous results for humanity in the modern world.

Why does modern science ask so little of modern humanity? Indeed, one could rightfully ask: why does it ask so much if it proposes to narrow the scope of a universal knowledge to the ability of reason to determine what is a valid experience through the human senses? Doesn't this attitude effectively eliminate all of the qualitative and spiritual richness of the universe, as well as the world of the spirit within us? Is the human being all mind and matter, dependent on the chemical fusions of the brain and the implicit intelligence of cellular DNA, leaving humans bereft of the benediction of the higher planes of spiritual intelligence, intuition, soul, and spirit?

After careful study of the contemporary research concerning the nature of the mind and the implicit consciousness that makes us what we are, a person cannot help but come away with a feeling of profound ambivalence concerning the modern conception of humanity because this ambivalence lies at the heart of the modern worldview and is reflected within the social norms and ethical behavior of modern society. What people today seem to want is a rational and empirical explanation that can define what a human being is and to what purpose the species *Homo sapiens* is supposed to function. Yet, for all of its advanced powers of observation, its incredible single-mindedness of approach, its miraculous discoveries, its technical powers, and its broad diversity of expression, modern science still has no clear idea about the true nature of humanity. What escape its scrutiny are the very things that define a human being's identity, that characterize individual human nature, and that ultimately establish a capacity for humanity to transcend itself.

The overwhelming question in neurobiology today is the relation between the mind and the brain. Most neuroscientists now believe that all aspects of mind, including its most puzzling attribute, consciousness are likely to be explainable in a more materialistic way as the behavior of large sets of interacting neurons. Still, it is precisely because there are mysterious aspects to the nature of the human mind, to consciousness, and to the presence of an awareness that seems to elude all physical description, that people living in today's world still remain basically unsatisfied with the scientific explanation of the mind and of human consciousness as purely a manifestation of the chemical activity of the physical brain. The irony lies in the fact that in its single-minded attempt to reduce all the miraculous interaction of the body, mind, and heart to the machinations of chemicals and neurons, science has inadvertently revealed a deeper world of mystery that is not yet ready to give up its secrets. The deeper our scientific understanding becomes of the inner world of the mind, the more profound the mystery that is revealed.

Before closing this section, it is worth noting in passing that physicists, who are perhaps most familiar with the mysterious ways in which matter actually behaves, tend to take a less mechanistic view of the world than do biologists and are actually taking the lead in articulating a new scientific paradigm that can lead the way beyond the old thinking of the classical and mechanical scientific worldview into a new age science that is less dogmatic and more attuned to the realities of nature it sets out to describe. Biologists have been steadily moving toward a hard-core kind of materialism as a result of the reductionist approach that attempts to reduce the human mind and spirit to a series of atoms and molecules. They have invested so much in the theory of evolution that for them to abandon it now would be perceived by the life science people as a form of intellectual suicide. The insistence on the spontaneous and indeed miraculous emergence of the life force within inanimate nature against all statistical probability and the discontinuous transmigration of species from a single-celled organism to sophisticated humans attests to the fact that modern scientists will go to any lengths to maintain the basis of their assumptions.

Physicists, on the other hand, have come to realize through their relentless analysis of the fundamental building blocks of matter that we do not even know anymore where a particle ends and where a wave begins, a phenomenon that lies at the heart of the quantum mystery. The true nature of matter has become indeterminate in such a way that the true nature of the mystery has finally been revealed. Some scientists are increasingly preparing themselves for the eventuality that our scientific criteria and methods of observation may have to undergo some subtle but important shift and begin to take account of certain clues that may present themselves in unexpected ways in areas of understanding that may initially seem to be beyond the scope of science *per se*, but that eventually could bring about a greater enrichment in the understanding of ourselves and our place in the universal scheme of things.

Roger Penrose, a well-known British mathematician who has written extensively on the mystery of the mind,[107] falls back from embracing a new scientific paradigm of knowledge and relies on the following comment which really summarizes the heightened feeling of ambivalence that lies at the heart of this difficult issue. He writes:

---

[107] *The Emperor's New Clothes* (1989) and *Shadows of the Mind: A Search for the Missing Science of Consciousness* (1994) are among his most respected works on the subject.

> It may well be that in order to accommodate the mystery of mind, we shall need a broadening of what we presently mean by science, but I see no reason to make any clean break with those methods that have served us so extraordinarily well.[108]

Scientists may be reluctant to realize that a paradigm shift may happen not so much as an accommodation to the mystery of the mind as an accommodation to the mystery of the scientific attitude that all truth must be reduced to a rational and empirical standard of thought in order to adjure its validity. If a real paradigm shift were going to occur, it should have happened by now giving the astounding insights we have received recently through intriguing discovering in quantum physics.

Perhaps the shift in perception will find its sufficient cause in the realization that what we know to be true by virtue of an inner experience cannot be described in the words of a determined rationalist by a top-down set of algorithmic rules and principles. Curiously enough, much of what we know and act upon is the result of what we call common sense, an inner knowledge amounting to a wisdom that is based partially on sound experience and partially on an accepted and universal perception of things which is the collective pursuit of the ages. The main failure of artificial intelligence to date has been in the common sense activities that the humblest of us indulge in every day of our lives. No computer-controlled robot can yet begin to compete with a young child in performing some of the simplest of everyday activities such as recognizing that a colored crayon is needed to complete a particular drawing. Even an ant could far surpass today's computer controlled systems in performing its daily activities. The mind, the will, and the self-awareness that we take for granted are perennial mysteries that cannot be accounted for by modern science. Common sense tells us that they exist, serve a useful purpose, and ultimately determine and define who we are in ways we may never fully understand. In fact, even if/when we do understand the mystery of human consciousness, we may not want to impart this knowledge to an ultra-sophisticated robotic man that would be on an equal footing with us.

If we could perceive and experience our lives with the unimpeded clarity of our higher, spiritual consciousness, we would be able to see and understand that no visible thing–indeed nothing belonging to the world of natural phenomena–possesses existence or being in its own right. We would see and understand that, apart from its inner dimension and its spiritual identity, matter on its own possesses no reality whatsoever, whether physical, material, or substantial. That the purely physical reality could come into being and exist on its own is a strictly modern conception that is the product of the ego-consciousness of this era and is the defining characteristic of our time.

---

[108] Roger Penrose, *Shadows of the Mind* (Oxford: Oxford University Press, 1994), p. 50.

The manner in which the faculty of reason is exercised during modern times is merely a reflection of the shadow self and not a reflection of the higher intellect that can perceive the truth directly. What, then, can lead human beings beyond the horizon of the individual self? For an answer, we must turn now to the inner world of higher intelligence in our search for a faculty with the power to transcend the limitations of the human mind. The faculty of reason, with the aid of an intelligence that finds its luminous source in the Supreme Intelligence, and with the aid of an intellect that enjoys direct access to the knowledge of God, can fulfill its role as bridge between worlds, dealing with the contingencies of this world and with the illumination of the world of the spirit. It can serve as one faculty among a number of other faculties that make the totality of the human experience possible in the first place.

If we take this modern-day reliance on reason back down into the well of our being in order to reach its source, we may be startled by what we discover. If there is a mystery at the center of our being, then we must use all the means at our disposal, including our mind, our intelligence, our reason, our heart, our imagination, our emotions and not least the sacred sentiments in order to come to terms with that mystery. The mystery that lies deep within the well of the human being is the mystery of existence itself, whose resolution can only be found in the experience of being oneself within the totality of one's true nature and being.

Ultimately, the spiritual traditions may have the final answer to the dilemma of reason as an instrument of enlightenment. They envision the faculty of reason as a two-sided face, one side illuminated by the rays of the intellect and the product of its divine reflection, the other side a dark hinter-ground of logic and causality whose self-reflection produces shadows that run the risk of actually creating an eclipse of the intellect rather than reflecting its light. In the traditional context, the faculty of reason serves as the bridge between the two worlds of logic and transcendence, giving rise to a conviction, like a lamp beckoning in the darkness of some vast prairie, that there is a knowledge whose certitude cannot be denied, whose source lies far beyond the horizon of the human mind, and whose realization within the human heart is destined to become the final emotion and the most enduring one.

7.2 The Light of the Intellect

Within the mind, beyond the first tier of human reasoning, lies a sun door that leads to the mysterious if not downright mystifying faculty of the intellect. This is the human faculty that draws into the inquiring mind, with a little coaxing, a spiritual intuition that radiates with the perennial message of the direct knowledge of God, a sublime imperative that fuels the fire of the mind with the inner glow of the infinite and the eternal. We know enough about ourselves to realize that our intelligence and its complement the mind is the prime mover of our thinking and conscious selves; but precisely what forms its contents, how it operates, where it draws its first principles from, and what enables and sustains the vital flow of its complex and subtle activity remains a mystery without resolution, particularly to modern individuals who refuse to consider the sacred paradigm of knowledge that relies on the light of the first principles emanating from a divine Intellect to define the true nature of human intelligence. The secrets of the human mind are still not forthcoming and may never be, at least not to the modern mentality long steeped within the tradition of mathematical precision and the uncompromising exclusivity of the modern scientistic approach to understanding the world.

As we hope to portray throughout the course of this work, the balanced functioning of the human mind, its native intelligence, and the consciousness that provides the driving force of the human self-awakening needs inspiration and support from a source higher than itself, for the mind on its own is a *tabula rasa* of human potential waiting to be awakened and fully expressive. Left to its own devices, human intelligence is an uncertain faculty in search of a medium of true understanding, bereft of the wisdom of the ages and deprived of the spark and afterglow of an initial first knowledge.

According to the traditions of the perennial philosophy embedded within the great world religions, the source of such knowledge originates within the vertical dimension whose axis intersects the horizontal plane of this world like a flaming sword from heaven and whose insight has perennially provided people the means to confidently navigate the dark realms that exist in the labyrinth of the mind. This first knowledge experienced within the mind as a mysterious and incisive light descends from above as the luminous source of intelligence that casts indiscriminate rays of illumination across the surface of the mind like the whirling beams of a lighthouse illuminating some stormy promontory of the mind. Every thought in the light of those celestial rays seems to have something infinite behind it. Every object seems to abide in its appointed time and place.

According to the traditional view, human intelligence exhibits a synthesizing quality that enables humans to assimilate the knowledge of all the faculties with which it is associated in order to objectify themselves to the extent that they can see their own reflection and place it within an intelligible context, that they can identify themselves with something other than themselves, and that they can know with an objectivity and a certitude that what they conceptualize is truthful and real. The coherent interaction of the faculties that come together and are summarized by the smooth functioning of an intelligent mind produces what scientists now refer to as consilience,[109] which is an explanatory power that

---

[109] Even Edward Wilson, in setting the stage for the exposition of his major work entitled *Consilience*, resorts to religious terminology when speaking of his theme, in spite of his adamant attitude toward the religious spirit. "The belief in the possibility of consilience beyond science and across the great branches of learning is not yet science. It is a metaphysical worldview, and a minority one at that, shared by only a few scientists and philosophers." p. 9.

derives part of its authority from a variety of disciplines. When the traditions accord man a central position within the cosmic frame of the hierarchy of being because of his human intelligence, this is what the traditions intend to convey: Through the functioning of the human mind, through the capacity of its intelligence, and through the practical power of reason, subjective man can objectivize himself with the criteria of a principial knowledge that is in the power of his intelligence to encompass, and thus exceed the specific and individual criteria that inevitably emerge within the human mind on its own.

In Islam, however, the faculty of reason (*aql*),[110] while displaying qualities that go far beyond the purely rational conception of human reason as the secular norm within a purely physical reality, is considered an intermediate and mediating faculty and not the final arbiter of truth that it is considered to be *de facto* in the Western contemporary worldview. There must be another, higher faculty that can transcend the inherent limitations of the faculty of reason, a faculty that has the power to witness the truth directly, and the capacity to objectify – with a final certitude – things as they are in their reality. Aristotle has written: "One does not demonstrate principles, but one perceives directly the truth thereof." This higher faculty must have the power to place in perspective the totality of the truth. Its direct insight, and the conscious experience into the true nature of reality that accompanies such insight, could then seep down through the mind, the intelligence, and the reason to become an operative certitude guiding the life of a person. Plato called this organ with the capacity to witness a transcending truth and grasp intuitively the first principles that underlie all of existence from the platform of certainty the *nous*; Islam calls it the intellect.

The line of direct perception commences with the Universal Intellect, alternatively called the Universal Spirit. According to the Messenger Muhammad (PBUH), the first thing that Allah created was the light of the Intellect. Thereafter, the Universal Intellect began to shine forth as if through a prism into multiple 'lights' and manifests upon the earth in the form of revelation or the Word of God (*Kalimat Allah*), providing humans with the objective criteria that they need to establish their place within the Divine Design. This knowledge then passes directly into the human intellect in such a way that the content of the inspiration is direct and immediate and has descended from the highest possible source imaginable, namely the Universal Spirit (Intellect), thus making humanity capable of objectivity, not by their own resources, but through the empowerment of the Universal Intellect of the Divinity in an act of consilience of the highest order of magnitude.

The revelation, which is an objective knowledge that descends from the Mind of God, allows humanity, as a subjective human being, to become truly

---

[110] The Qur'anic term *aql* keeps man on the straight path and prevents him from going astray. In the Qur'an, those who go astray are those who don't use the full extent of their reason (*wa la ya'qilun*) and thus are not able to understand what comes down to them from above.

objective. There is a direct encounter of the Divine Intellect with the human intellect, pouring into the receptive mold of the human intellect the essential contents of knowledge that the intelligence needs in order to function according to its own true nature within the created world of nature and man, touching the human mind with a magic wand that glows with the Divine Light, the *Prima Veritas*. According to the great Islamic scholar, Ibn Sina, every act of knowing involves the illumination of the mind by what he calls the "active intellect" (*al-'aql al-fa'al*) which bestows upon the mind the knowledge that it needs to know in order to function effectively and righteously. As a result of that encounter, the conscious human mind is forever cast within the aura of this supreme knowledge whose insight substantiates all thinking with its implicit light, recalling the famous phrase "light upon light" from the oft-repeated verse of light (24:35) in the Qur'an.

Within the collective schema of the descent of knowledge, the Universal Intellect is the metacosmic manifestation of the Supreme Unity. Revelation, as the exteriorization of the Divine Mind, is the macrocosmic manifestation of the Universal Intellect. As complement on the earthly plane, the human intellect becomes the instrument of direct perception of the essential knowledge of God, including the first principle of His Unicity and the truth of the one Reality. As such, the human intellect is not something cerebral in the manner that we understand the human mind to be, nor is it a specifically human faculty in the sense that we understand the reason to be. Instead, it represents the spiritual faculty *par excellence* with a modality of perception that rises above the human dimension of this world in a kind of spontaneous act of transcendence that arrives at a vision of the Sublime Reality. The intellect does not rely on the reflective thinking process or the cognitive principles of reason; rather it is a receptive and synthesizing faculty, capable of knowing directly and intuitively without any cognitive undertaking and therefore capable of transcending the individual person and his or her manner of thinking. Its revelatory power resolves the mystery underlying the source of true knowledge and its explanatory power conveys a feeling of overwhelming certitude that further verifies its objectivity and absolute quality.

If intelligence is the faculty of discernment and if human reason is characterized as discursive and rational, then the intellect[111] is the faculty of direct perception and of illumination. As the transcending faculty and the instrument of synthesis, the intellect is the highest faculty of perception that is available to

---

[111] On the concept of the intellect, Thomas Aquinas has written: "It must be said that just as to proceed *rationally* is attributed to *natural philosophy*, because in it there is observed most greatly the mode of reason, so to proceed *intellectually* is attributed to *divine science*, because in it there is observed most of all the mode of the intellect" [*Dicendum quod sicut rationabiliter procedere attribuitur naturali philosophiae, quia in ipse observatur maxime modus rationis, ita intellectualiter procedere attribuitur divinae scientiae, eo quod in ipse observatur maxime modus intellectus*. (*In Boetium de Trinitate*, q. 6, art. 1, ad. 3)].

humanity. Human reason is the faculty of the purely individual order; pure intellect is supra-individual. Without the transcending feature of the intellect, the capacity to conceptualize metaphysical knowledge would be impossible since such unique knowledge lies far beyond the range of the individual domain and is of the universal order. In fact, that metaphysical knowledge is at all accessible to the human mind lies in the fact that while we partake of the human order, we are also a manifestation of something far more miraculous. The being that we know ourselves to be in this world is also the expression of a different quality of person by virtue of the permanent and immutable principles that consecrate our deepest essence.

The intellect opens the gate of spiritual intelligence and its rarefied knowledge gains a person entry into the world of the spirit. Through the knowledge conveyed by revelation and received by the human intellect, every living person can know, with a certainty, his or her first origin and final end. The dilemma surrounding the starting-point for all cognitive processes is resolved in a higher faculty that serves as the ultimate medium between converse worlds. The point of departure for all knowledge is established in the connection of the human intellect with the knowledge of the highest Principle and is confirmed in the Pure Intellect of the Divinity. The inner life of the individual, including all the natural instincts, spiritual imagination, sacred emotions and higher consciousness, indeed the very faith humans express in the Divinity, are fully awakened and receive the direct impress of the knowledge of the Divine, thereby ushering into the higher consciousness of the mind and heart knowledge of a complete and undivided Unity.

That humans are much more than their body, more than the unique instrument of their mind, more even than the self-reflective wonder of their expansive consciousness, and that knowledge extends far beyond the inquisitive ideas and analytical concepts deduced from the physical senses and orchestrated into a symphony of theoretical speculations, is taken as axiomatic by all the major world religions and their traditions. The power of the intellect permits people to transubstantiate their inner reality from an uncertain platform of tentative theory and speculation into an objectifying reality in order to raise themselves above the level of mundane awareness to a higher plane of consciousness and a more profound level of spiritual experience. It connects people directly with the supra-natural realities of a higher dimension, a power that passes from the human intellect to the created Intellect of Revelation and back once again into the vortex of the Universal Intellect where it lies steady and fully centered within the Godhead. It is truly the premier faculty of the human mind connecting our immediate earthly world with the world of the spirit, the faculty that objectifies the subjective reality of humanity, the faculty that fully synthesizes the great disparity of this world with the Supreme Principle of the one reality of which this world is but a pale reflection and the stuff of which shadows are made.

The spiritual faculty of intuition, as the operative agent within the human intellect of knowledge that is inaccessible to normal intelligence and thus the scientific methods of investigation, takes place in full view of the mind and happens directly and unconsciously, without any seemingly formal apparatus, as a matter of spiritual instinct.[112] It enables people to perform the kind of mental tasks that they love to experience, but that they cannot account for consciously. We communicate through spoken and written words; we reason and think; we use our imagination and we dream. We plan and built cities; we farm land and feed ourselves and the world; we create literature and compose symphonies. We intuit imaginal worlds that have the power of reality and the certainty of knowledge. Mental processes are even coming to be recognized by some of the more enlightened thinkers of today as more intuitive than cognitive. Scientists themselves rely on the creative process of the mind and the imagination to initiate much of their probing, scientific inquiries. They would be loathe to admit it, but those sudden, intuitive illuminations could actually be lightning flashes of the higher intellect that permit a person to move beyond the limits of his or her own shortcomings as a special dispensation to humanity from the Divinity during the present-day modern era.

Psychiatrists who research and study human behavior are beginning to realize that people who follow their intuition through a challenging endeavor actually have a competitive edge over those who simply think their way through a problem in some straightforward rational manner, and often they cannot specifically account for how they arrived at their conclusion. Mathematicians do not believe that they are blindly following unconscious rules that they are incapable of knowing and believing in, nor do they think that their reasoning is based on some arbitrary algorithmic procedure that – unknown to them – governs all of their mathematical perceptions. "What they think they are doing is basing their arguments upon what are unassailable truths–ultimately, essentially 'obvious' ones–building their chains of reasoning entirely from such truths."[113] They use their rational intelligence to make their way through complicated mathematical equations, but their intuitive intelligence could well be recognized as the dark light through which the unconscious first principles of mathematics arrive within the human mind.

Unsurprisingly, there is a vast difference between the knowledge arrived at through the efforts of human reason and the direct knowledge arrived at through the inimitable intuitions of the intellect. The reason of modern man investigates the knowledge of this world. The intellect of traditional man participates in the knowledge of the world of the spirit. Both forms of knowledge pass through the human mind and are filtered through human intelligence as key components to the practical functioning of people in dealing with this world. Intuitive intelligence needs the practicality of human reason to cope with the apparent

---

[112] "The infallible "instinct" of animals is a lesser "intellect," and man's intellect may be called a higher instinct." *The Essential Writings of Frithjof Schuon*, S. H. Nasr (ed.), p. 115.

[113] Roger Penrose, p. 127.

existentialities of this world, whereas reason needs the bright light of the intellect to make the essential knowledge of God shine forth as a guiding star in the dark firmament of the mind.

When our intelligence is cut off from its luminous source, our knowledge, our judgment, our insight and indeed our sense of discernment will be seriously diminished during the course of life. Under these conditions, there is no way that these faculties can function to their fullest capacity, in accordance with what is true to human nature. Sadly, the modern mentality does not accord the intellect its true value as a spiritual faculty capable of direct knowledge of God. Although modern individuals still have an intellect, they do not know they have it and do not fully appreciate its vast potential. Therefore, they have nothing to effectively counterbalance the tenebrous inclination of the human mind to roam aimlessly through the dark and labyrinthine corridors of idle theory and pure speculation in search of the solid ground of certainty that only the reality of the Spirit provides the human mentality.

People today have the gift of intelligence and they enjoy its multitudinous fruits, of this there is no doubt. In today's modern world, however, we falter and hesitate in our definition of terms: What is the mind, what defines consciousness, what is the stuff of intelligence and where will our intelligence lead us? We have the duty to ask ourselves not only whether consciousness, mind, and intelligence are enough to serve our needs, but also to what end? Opinions differ on the key fundamentals that shape the contemporary worldview and yet the goal seems to be the attainment of knowledge that does justice to human intelligence: to be intelligent, to live intelligently, and to connect with the Supreme Intelligence with the golden thread of faith and desire. We need to free ourselves from an undue reliance on all speculative and ego-serving ideas whose only source is the human mind blundering on its own without the aid of Heaven. We need to turn away from the downward drift of human pride and pretension and submit ourselves to that which surpasses us. We need to surrender to the divine paradigm of knowledge and the source of all wisdom that alone has the power to illuminate the mind and lift up the heart.

A final thought leads us to reaffirm that behind the natural workings of human intelligence lies a supra-natural source whose luminosity shines down on the mind–with all of its faculties of knowing and perception–like rays of light penetrating woodland trees to reach the forest floor. If reason is in principle a *tabula rasa* whose innocent void awaits a true knowledge that will awaken a world, then human intelligence is a playing field awaiting the illuminative rays of the intellect, which is none other than the intuitive faculty within the kingdom of man around which are gathered the ministers of state in the form of the noble faculties of reason, intelligence, imagination, and the higher emotions. They all contribute to the qualitative expression of the human species; they all make humans what they truly are. It is only because intelligence is touched by the light of the intellect that individuals can reflect upon their human condition and say: I am a thinking creature created as a reflected image of the Supreme Intelligence; I am a shadow of the Divine Light; I am a soul whose ground reflects the luminous rays of the Divine Spirit; I am a subjective entity capable of objectivity because the Absolute has taken up residence within the cave of my heart as the living principle of my being.

In the end, our approach to the spiritual realities and the achievement of some measure of proximity to the Divine Throne is like roaming under the open, free space of the night sky, knowing that above the earth lies a configuration of stars that will always remain incomprehensible to the mind, yet strangely familiar to the soul. We need to go through life partaking not only of the pleasures that the five senses have to offer, but also basking in the light of a knowledge that comes to us either directly through sight, sound, smell, taste and touch, or indirectly through the inner senses and faculties of our intellect, intuition, intelligence and spiritual instincts. We need to journey across the great plain of our lives steeped in the mystery of every created thing, from the grand edifice of the universe to the intricacies of the spider's web, drifting like butterflies in search of nectar over the landscape of human experience.

There are textures to the world and patterns in life that have their counterpart in celestial realities if only we could open the door to the inner senses of perception. We go through life in terror of the unknown mystery that challenges our waking moments, when all the while we had only to see the outstretched branches of a tree reaching heavenward in order to recognize its benevolent smile. Then the vastness of eternity could be taken in through the blink of an eye and the expanse of infinitude could be reduced to a single first step as we make our way on that final journey into the interior.

> "I said to the almond tree, 'Sister, speak to me of God.'
> And the almond tree blossomed."
> (Nikos Kazantzakis, *St. Francis*)

7.3 The Modes of Intelligence

> A mind that is stretched to a new idea
> Never returns to its original dimension.
> –Oliver Wendell Holmes

The search for a more complete understanding of the human experience leads us to reflect on the faculties of knowing and the fields of perception that not only distinguish the human condition, but also represent special gifts from the Divine to the human. These inner faculties include human reason, intelligence, heart knowledge, consciousness, spiritual imagination and sacred instinct, all of which are firmly embedded within the ground of the human soul and are activated by a free will that can lead us out of ourselves and make transcendence of the human condition possible. The inner realm of the higher faculties constitutes a borderland and wilderness area of the spirit that we need to more fully explore and experience if we ever wish to understand the universal mystery that characterizes all existence. We must recognize this mystery as a basic truth of our existential reality if we are ever to achieve the knowledge of the true reality that everyone, modern scientists included, unequivocally professes to be the ultimate goal of the modern, forward-thinking individual.

One cannot help but have a feeling of entering a "lost world" when considering the characteristics of this borderland of the spirit between outer and inner worlds. The traditional world of the spirit has become a ghost from some remote past that is nearly unrecognizable in today's world except as a distant impression of a world now passed by. The faculty of the human intellect that was once capable of the direct perception of the Divinity no longer exists as a viable option for modern humanity. This open door to the Infinite seems to have been irrevocably closed to the contemporary modern mentality. The mind now relies solely on the perception of an externalized intelligence made up of brain matter that can be monitored and measured on the one hand, and a creative and fertile imagination that can produce contemporary, modern art as the expression of our inmost selves on the other, to help navigate the way through the mysteries and challenges that confront people in today's modern world. The brave, the sensitive, the intelligent and open heart of more traditional times–what we call further on "the forgotten heart"–is only a vague sentiment of its former self, a heart that once took root in the ground of the soul and could see reflected in the promise of some future world the primordial beginning of time.

One point worth mentioning is the fact that the human being does not, and never will, perceive the inner reality directly, at least not within this world. Behind all the theories of modern science and the perennial message of the spiritual traditions lies the realization that humanity will not see the Face of God and will only perceive the Reality "through a glass darkly" (1 Corinthians 13:12) or from behind a veil. Particle physics and molecular biology clearly highlight this truth by forcing scientists to observe the subatomic world of quantum mechanics through highly sophisticated devices rather than the naked eye, in order to witness the activity of the sub-atomic world of protons and electrons by suggestion as it were. The traditions highlight this truth by requiring the faithful to perceive the true nature of Reality indirectly through the words of revelation, through signs and symbols within the world of nature, and through the inner experience that characterizes the borderlands of the spirit that still exists within the lost continent of the inner being. We must rely on human intelligence to become the open door it was intended to be, giving access to the knowledge of God as a direct human experience.

We need to ask ourselves what is the true nature of this gift of intelligence and how are we supposed to act upon its hidden messages. Intelligence is the human faculty that gives to the inquiring mind a spiritual intuition that shines with the perennial message of the direct knowledge of God, a sublime imperative that fuels the fire of the mind with the inner glow of the infinite and the eternal. We know enough about ourselves to realize that our intelligence, and its complement the mind, is the prime mover of our thinking and conscious selves; but precisely what forms its contents, how it operates, where it draws its first principles from, and what enables and sustains the vital flow of its complex and subtle activity remains a mystery without resolution. This is particularly so in the modern world in which many people refuse to consider the sacred knowledge that relies on the light of the first principles coming from a divine Source to define the true nature of human intelligence.

The balanced functioning of the human mind, its native intelligence, and the consciousness that provides the driving force of the human self-awakening needs inspiration and support from a source higher than itself, for the mind on its own is an empty page of human potential waiting to be awakened and become fully expressive. Left to its own devices, human intelligence is an uncertain faculty in search of a medium of true understanding, without the wisdom of the ages and deprived of the spark and afterglow of an initial first knowledge.

Perhaps it is symptomatic of the era in which we live that modern humanity does not seem to realize that it cannot fit the totality of the human mind into a strictly rational and purely physical mold. Conscious experience is portrayed in today's world as a physical and not a supernatural phenomenon while the mind, which comprises both human consciousness in addition to rational processes, is actually considered by the prevailing materialistic outlook to be neural activity at work within the brain and nothing more. How can the possibility of a transcendent human intelligence be brought home to people for whom intelligence is nothing but a means of acting out the dictates of matter and whose search for knowledge culminates solely in the explanation of phenomena within the natural order? Are contemporary scientists, as the high priests of our rational and technological culture, willing to reduce our humanity solely to the activity of neurons and neurotransmitters as the basic building blocks in their construction of a grand synthesis of a theory of mind?

For all its technical wizardry and in spite of the reams of detail intended to substantiate its validity and its ultimate veracity, the modern, scientific viewpoint is not particularly enlightened in its approach to articulating not only the origin of human intelligence, but also its very nature and purpose. In order to somehow come to terms with the mystery and miracle of the higher faculty of intelligence, the reductionist tendency of modern scientists articulates a sequence of explanations that quickly moves downward from the lofty regions of the mind to the brain to neural activity to anatomical structure, cellular physiology, molecular biology, and ultimately comes to rest on a firm bedrock in the laws of quantum mechanics, rather than upward through the arena of the human psyche to the realms of higher consciousness, to the soul and ultimately the spirit of man that in the Islamic perspective draws its true sustenance from the Breath of the Compassionate (*al-nafas ar-rahman*).

As a consequence, thinking has become a neuro-chemical process or, as the naturalist E. O. Wilson says, "an epiphenomenon of the neuronal machinery of the brain."[114] As such, all the qualitative and profound richness of human intelligence as it was understood within the traditional world has been reduced to neuronal networks based solely within matter, which manifest as "points of energy" at source and nothing more, without reference to the creative spark, the incandescence of intuitive thought, the cold ice of cognitive reasoning, and the rich afterglow of higher consciousness of mind that forms the distinctive bedrock of our humanness and qualifies us to be both the symbolic bridge between terrestrial and celestial worlds and the human representative of God on earth within the borderland of the spirit.

Human intelligence is a conduit of knowledge and perception that everyone wants in order to enjoy the many prospects that life has to offer, that everyone needs in order to navigate their way through the challenges and turmoil of life's progress, that everyone admires when it shines forth its illuminating insight, and that no one will admit to being without lest they fail to meet the distinguishing mark of their true humanity. Nevertheless, the faculty of intelligence has created a major controversy among individuals today as regards its true meaning and import. The well-known British scientist and mathematician, Roger Penrose, in a lengthy work exploring the true nature of the mind, confesses at one point that the ultimate origin and meaning of human intelligence escapes a definitive resolution. He writes with surprising frankness:

> Perhaps we should seriously consider the possibility that our intelligence might indeed require some kind of act of God–and that it cannot be explained in terms of that science which has become so successful in the description of the inanimate world.[115]

In other words, we still have no clue what intelligence is precisely, how it functions, what its ultimate purpose is, and from where it draws its luminous coloration, including shades of brilliance that, in fact, have the power to illuminate the remotest, the darkest, and the most adamantine reaches of the human mind? Should be limit the possibilities of our native intelligence to purely physical brain matter reacting against a variety of chemical reactions and rule out the sublime intuitions and flashes of brilliance that lead us beyond the physical world.

According to the perennial wisdom of the major world religions, human intelligence distinguishes itself from all other intelligences exhibited in the world of nature by virtue of its power of discernment, this being none other than the power to *know*–without any doubt and with a certainty–the Truth, the Reality, the Absolute, and the Good in both a substantive and an objective manner, since it is the true, the real, the absolute, and the good that runs through the universe

---

[114] E. O. Wilson, *On Human Nature* (Cambridge, MA.: Harvard University Press, 1978) p. 195.

[115] Roger Penrose, *Shadows of the Mind*, p. 144.

and through humanity itself like a cosmic Ariadnean thread,[116] connecting the created universe and everything in it with its origin and source in the Creator. In addition to this higher level of discernment that substantiates intelligence and that is concerned primarily with first principles, there lies within the intelligence the more pragmatic discernment that pertains to certain existential facts here on earth. The former refers to the intuition of metaphysical realities; the latter applies to the recognition of elements of the phenomenal world and their relation to higher orders of thinking and intuition. Thus, the human power of discernment permits a person to cultivate a sense of proportion on the plane of earthly phenomena, while the symbolist and abstract discernment of the truth keeps a person focused on "the one thing needful." (Luke 10:42)

In fact, at every level in the hierarchy of being, we can witness forms of intelligence within nature that reflect the natural instincts that are required for natural phenomena to exist and function within their own sphere of experience. The message of a hidden wisdom shines forth in the corporeal intelligence that manifest throughout the human body in a multitude of cellular, chemical, and neural activity. The intelligence of the macrocosm shines forth in the vast array of heavenly bodies and the spectacular and harmonious precision that is witnessed in the celestial movement of the cosmos. Sensory intelligence identifies and appreciates gourmet tastes; olfactory intelligence recognizes a wide array of smells and responds to them on a number of levels, including memory and emotion; even the intelligence of the sense of touch knows the difference between the natural fibers of cotton and the artificial feel of polyester, as everyone who lives in a tropical climate fully appreciates.

Every living thing expresses a form of intelligence that fuels its functioning within a given domain; but only the human being knows with a prescience of mind that includes primary instinct, subtle logic, discursive reasoning, common sense, insight, aesthetic appreciation, moral value, and ultimately the defining discernment that is uniquely human to the extent that it virtually defines humanity in terms of its capacity to know. If true knowledge is there, then wisdom cannot be far behind; if morality is there, then virtue will show its sublime face; and if discernment is there, then true intelligence will shine forth as a fully formed creative power that embodies all the elements already evidenced in nature and that are reflective of a higher intelligence–the "supremely Intelligible," in the words of Frithjof Schuon.

Human intelligence is cast under the spell of a reflective consciousness that forms the backcloth of self-awareness and is charged by the heightened setting in which this intelligence functions. As such it is the fundamental and defining element of the humanity within the human being and is not a vestige or

---

[116] Theseus, the champion of Athens, walked into the Cretan labyrinth and was able to negotiate the twists and turns by unraveling a ball of thread given him by Ariadne, the lovestruck daughter of King Minos. By following the thread, he was able to retrace his steps out of the labyrinth after killing the Minotaur.

contingency of some random evolutionary process. Human intelligence–the primary manifestation of inward activity and thus the direct reflection of the inner being–becomes therefore the focal point and catalyst of how people identify themselves. Are we to understand human intelligence as a purely cognitive activity, displaying a mercurial tendency to wander in search of an equilibrium that is perfectly capable of being destabilized and carried away by waves of endless speculation or the devouring flames of an unfulfilled and possibly irrational emotion?

We marvel at the precision of the scientific mind of today, with its capacity for the exactitude of mathematics and its penchant for enduring the detail of innumerable dry facts; but we are equally concerned about its capacity for restless and unrequited movement, without ever being satisfied by the play of its formulations as it passes from concept to concept in a desperate search for the virtue of consistency and the grace of certitude to be found within the traditional conception of mind and its implicit intelligence.

The question of genuine sources for the first principles of knowledge strikes at the heart of the very definition and meaning of human intelligence. What indeed is the source of human intelligence? From where does human intelligence derive its vast array of characteristics, including its clarity and its brilliance, its knowledge and insight, its power of abstraction and reflection, its adaptability, its creativity and its vision, in short: its ability to process a vast range of conceptions, abstractions, and emotions through the medium of a self-reflective and abstract language in order to articulate in words this unique assemblage of qualities?

It is not for nothing that the litany of the mind's attributes has commenced with clarity and brilliance since the traditional view has long espoused the belief that human intelligence has an illuminative aspect that derives from a luminous source within the Universal Spirit. This is in sharp contrast to today's view which claims that human intelligence takes root in the faculty of reason, which provides individuals with the ability to think through any problem based upon an empirical method of inquiry, without independent principles of thought that transcend the limits of the human mind and the physical world. In truth, human intelligence has two sources of knowledge: it relies on intellect and reason, *ratio* and *intellectus*, to reflect upon the order of the natural world and alternatively to transcend it. The sibylline clarity of human intelligence represents an expression of mind that derives its substance and objectivity from the font of certainty that is characteristic of universal truth found within the Qur'an and the other great world religions, while its brilliance is the lunar reflection of the symbolic sun that is the Light of the universe.[117]

Far from being a one-sided and narrow faculty of perception amounting to a closed system of the mind that is exhibited within the modern scientific

---

[117] In Islam, Light (*al-Nur*) is one of the ninety-nine names that identify the qualities and attributes of the Divinity. According to a well-known Qur'anic verse (24: 35), "God is the Light of the heavens and the earth."

worldview with its emphasis on physical matter alone as the sole source (and final end) of reality, human intelligence within the traditional perspective found in Islam and other religions draws on a number of modalities that ultimately lead back to the origin and source of its illuminated insight.

In addition to bringing rational, reasonable, and common-sense factors to bear on its functioning, the *aql* of the Islamic traditions calls upon certain modalities of thought to complete the full complement of its intellective mold. Reason displays a reflective quality that brings to its line of thought all of the supportive documentation of the human emotions, the imagination, natural instinct, and a fundamental capacity for intuition that all take part in enriching the process of humanity's reasoning and in extending the human mind beyond its cognitive ability to encompass the possibilities of higher imagination, insight, inspiration, and creativity that is the very frontier of the borderland of the spirit. The full range of this intellective process can be achieved by none other than the use of the human *ratio* as a principle of coherence and the *intellectus* as a principle of transcendence as well as the source medium for direct access to the truth.

Another question that needs to be asked and that Islam answers can be framed this way: Where can we discover the origin and source of the immutable criteria upon which we rely, even within our scientific systems? What is it within ourselves that has the unchallenged right to say this is true and this is false? Who is the disembodied spirit within that whispers to the intelligence what it ought to believe as resounding truth, not based on human reason alone and the observation of the senses, but that finds its source in a knowledge that descends from an alternative world within a higher dimension. If the answer is human reason on its own, then it begs the question of the origin and source of such insight.

According to the traditional view, human intelligence has a synthesizing quality that allows humans to see themselves in the mirror reflection of archtypes of a higher order of manifestation that they can then place within an intelligible context. They can identify themselves with something other than themselves, and they can know with objectivity and certitude that what they conceptualize is truthful and real. Through the functioning of their mind, through the capacity of their intelligence, and through the practical power of their reason, subjective human beings can objectivize themselves with the criteria of a principial knowledge that is in the power of the intelligence to encompass, and thus exceed the specific and individual criteria that inevitably emerge within the human mind on its own.

In Islam, however, the faculty of reason (*aql*), while displaying qualities that go far beyond the purely rational conception of human reason, is considered an intermediate and mediating faculty and not the final judge of truth as reason is considered in the modern, scientific worldview. There must be a higher faculty that can transcend the limitations of the faculty of reason; a faculty that has the power to witness the truth directly and the capacity to objectify—with a final certitude—things as they are in their reality. This higher faculty of the mind must have the power to place in perspective the totality of the truth. Its direct insight, and the conscious experience it has of the true nature of reality, can then seep down through the mind, the intelligence, and the reason to become an operative certitude guiding the life of humanity.

The line of direct perception commences with the Universal Intellect, alternatively called the Universal Spirit. According to the Prophet of Islam, the first thing that God created was the Intellect; thereafter, the Universal Intellect began to shine forth as if through a prism into multiple "lights" and manifested upon the earth in the form of revelation or the Word of God (*Kalimat Allah*), providing human beings with the objective criteria needed to establish their place within the Divine Design. This knowledge then passed directly into the human intellect in such a way that the content of the inspiration is direct and immediate and has descended from the highest possible source imaginable, namely the Universal Spirit (Intellect), thus making human beings capable of objectivity, not by their own resources but through the empowerment of the Universal Intellect of the Divinity in an act of consilience of the highest order of magnitude.

When our intelligence is cut off from its luminous source, our knowledge, our judgment, our insight, and indeed our sense of discernment will be seriously diminished during the course of life. Under these conditions, there is no way that the faculties can function to their fullest capacity, in accordance with what is true to human nature. Sadly, the modern mentality does not accord the intellect its true value as a spiritual faculty capable of direct knowledge, and more importantly direct perception, of God. Although modern individuals are still considered to have an intellect, they do not understand its function in the same way as traditional peoples; they therefore have nothing to effectively counterbalance the tenebrous inclination of the human mind to roam aimlessly through the dark and labyrinthine corridors of idle theory and pure speculation.

People today have the gift of intelligence and they enjoy its multitudinous fruits; of this there is no doubt. In today's modern world, however, we falter and hesitate in our definition of terms: What is the mind, what defines consciousness, what is the stuff of intelligence, and where will our intelligence lead us? We have the duty to ask ourselves not only whether consciousness, mind, and intelligence are enough to serve our needs, but also to what end? Opinions differ on the key fundamentals that shape the contemporary worldview and yet the goal seems to be the attainment of knowledge that does justice to human intelligence: to be intelligent, to live intelligently, and to connect with the Supreme Intelligence with the golden threads of knowledge, faith, desire. We need to free ourselves from an undue reliance on all speculative and ego-serving ideas whose only source is the human mind blundering on its own without the aid of Heaven; we need to turn away from the downward drift of human pride and pretension and submit ourselves to that which surpasses us; we need to surrender to the divine paradigm of knowledge and the source of all wisdom that alone has the power to illuminate the mind and enlighten the heart. As the poet Robert Browning wrote nearly two centuries ago when people still responded to the lure of the spiritual: "A man's reach should exceed his grasp. Or what's a heaven for?"

A final thought leads us to reaffirm that behind the natural framework of human intelligence lies a supra-natural source whose luminosity shines down on the mind–with all of its faculties of knowing and perception–like rays of light penetrating woodland trees to reach the forest floor. If reason is in principle a *tabula rasa* whose innocent void awaits knowledge whose truth will awaken a world, then human intelligence is a playing field awaiting the illuminative rays of the intellect, the regal faculty within the kingdom of the mind, around which are gathered the ministers of state in the form of noble faculties including reason, intelligence, imagination, and the higher emotions. They all contribute to the qualitative expression of the human species; they all make human beings what they truly are. It is only because intelligence is touched by the light of the intellect that a person can reflect upon their human condition and say: I am a thinking creature created as a reflected image of the Supreme Intelligence; I am a shadow of the Divine Light; I am a soul whose ground reflects the luminous rays of the Divine Spirit; I am a subjective entity capable of objectivity because the Absolute has taken up residence within the cave of my heart as the living principle of my being.

7.4 The Cave of the Heart

"God cometh between man and his heart." (8:24)

The human heart has always held a prominent place in coming to terms with the true meaning implicit in the name of *Homo sapiens*. Because of its symbolic value and its role as a higher faculty, the heart has access to higher perceptions and spiritual insights that would otherwise remain inaccessible to the human mind on its own. Nothing captures more effectively the essential character and the intrinsic humanity of the human spirit than does the traditional symbol of the heart. As seat of the intelligence and an instrument of enlightenment, it contains latent dispositions and powers that far exceed the life-giving properties of the physical heart that lies within the breast.

Nothing in nature reveals the symbolic transparency of matter more and nothing in human nature permits people to better perceive the inward reality of things, from the inverted angle of spiritual insight as it were, as does the human heart. If the instrument of the mind relies on the penultimate faculty of the intelligence and its principal well-spring, intuition, then the heart, as the seat of the intelligence and the niche of sacred sentiment, is the quintessential organ of human perception directly influenced by the overflowing cornucopia of all the human emotions. It is a transcendent faculty that has the capacity to combine the essential knowledge of God with the heart-felt experience of the human being in order to internalize the fundamental unity that underlies all of universal reality.

The heart has traditionally been portrayed as a holy sanctuary of reflected light and a hidden cave in which there is sequestered all essential knowledge, all sacred emotion, and all intimate love in a manner that permits human beings to transcend their fragmented earthly likeness for a complete truth that summarizes the meaning of their true destiny. As such, the heart's rarefied vision of the world has an inverse application that through the filter of an intuitive knowledge literally changes the phenomenal world from the brute physical matter that it appears to be into a living reality that it is by virtue of its connection to the knowledge of the Universal Reality.

Unlike modern humanity, which attempts to take leave of its being through the labyrinthine passageways of the mind, people in more traditional cultures believed that the point of departure from the confines of the individual self lay within the affective heart rather than the cognitive mind, much less the cerebral brain, which for modern humanity is the starting point and ultimately the highest organ that justifies the implicit *sapiens* within *Homo sapiens*. More traditional societies understood their existence to be the result of the existential manifestation of a Supreme Reality in which they took part on an individual level of experience. This existence was envisaged as having its point of first origin and its ultimate source in a Transcendent Being who was the central point beyond which all existence radiated outwards. This Supreme Being substantiated the mystery of His Spirit through the creation of the universe and came to be known through a humanity that populated and animated that universe as a conscious and thinking being capable of communicating with its Creator.

The human heart establishes its signature and utters its truest word by being the symbol of humanity's spiritual center and the vertical axis upon which its knowledge and affection ascend heavenwards. As the symbolic image of humanity's true center, the physical heart lends its physiological meaning to the totality of the human being, but the force of its symbolic presence draws upon far deeper reserves within the vital essence of the human being. As such, the heart is the center not only of the bodily individuality, but also the center of the integral individuality, or the human being known and realized on both physical and spiritual modes of expression. When human beings become all heart, they express their inmost knowledge and feelings in such a way that the external world can witness the full range of their intelligence and sensibility.

Ironically, in today's world the heart that we now identify and remember as the seat of affection and sentimentality is actually the heart that forgets, while the other heart of our chapter title, the forgotten one, is actually the heart that remembers. The "heart that forgets" implies the absence of the knowledge and light that integrates the independent fragments of the human being into a synthesis of the Whole that is based on the unity and oneness of the Reality and the Supreme Identity projected into the universe by the Divinity. The other heart "that remembers" implies the presence of the knowledge and the light that illuminates the totality of the human being with the remembrance of our forgotten primordiality, when we walked with God, spoke with God, and knew

God directly with a heart knowledge that knew no barriers or veils.

Tradition relies on a number of images to qualify the heart's inner bearing, depending on the point of view envisioned and its role within the framework of particular human needs. The cave of the heart is a well-known traditional expression.[118] The Islamic tradition specifically refers to the heart as the seat of the intelligence,[119] which may be startling for a modern humanity imbued with the idea that intelligence resides in the brain as the vehicle of all conscious reckoning. The kind of intelligence referred to in this instance is one capable of pure intellection and not the kind of logical and discursive reasoning that the general public envisions when it makes reference to the word intelligence. As the seat, ground, and inner crypt (Greek: *kruptos*) of the intelligence, the heart symbolizes the sanctuary that fittingly provides the ambiance for an intelligence, not as we envision it today in its discursive and reflective modes alone, but rather in view of its far-reaching spiritual significance as a crystalline source of conscious awakening that reaches from the center of the mind and heart to the Center of the universe and whose connecting golden thread is the belief in God and surrender to His Supreme Will.

In the traditional view, the heart does not merely serve as the embodiment of human affection and sentiment, a heart that corresponds to what the modern mentality believes to be the seat of affectivity, which amounts to being a source of heat for the emotions without the corresponding light that accompanies the knowledge of God. This concept of the heart corresponds to and complements the prevalent understanding of intelligence as the expression of modern-day rationalism and nothing more. In spite of its rigid scientific approach to the understanding of a reality that finds its source–or rather proof–in physical matter, the modern mentality exhibits a curiously lopsided form of sentimentalism that considers the sentimental emotions to be the most profound expression of the human being. A purely sentimental heart, together with the rational intelligence prevalent among people today, has no patience with the view of the other heart found among people of more traditional cultures whose broad intelligence identifies with and draws its inspiration from the human intellect. Its intuitive insight cuts through the duality of this world with its direct perception of reality and transcends the narrow domain of human individuality by focusing on the knowledge of universal principles and higher realities.

As deep cave and sacred crypt of the knowledge of God and prayer niche of the most profound human aspirations, the symbolic image of the heart focuses on the idea of a place deep within where something preternatural happens, where a

---

[118] "The cave, or the grotto, represents the cavity of the heart considered as the center of the being" (René Guénon, *King of the World* [Ghent, NY: Sophia Perennis, 2001], p. 43).

[119] The Greek philosophers, including Aristotle, also refer to the heart as the seat of the intelligence.

realization of the numinous quality of life casts its glow across the field of our perceptions, where the knowledge of God burns as an inner flame and the presence of God is experienced in the heat of its afterglow. As the seat of the intelligence and the locus of centrality, the heart symbolizes an inner sanctum whose inward space offers a world without limits and a universe of infinite possibility. It is a sanctuary of knowledge tempered by feelings of love, a holy niche where our most sacred aspirations can be expressed and where an abiding intimacy with the Divinity can be experienced. As inner abode, the human heart is the place where the intelligence finds its home and where human intimacy with the Divinity makes itself felt as the ultimate expression of our relationship with the Highest Reality.

Beyond the concept of the heart as a locus of centrality and as a place where something not fully explicable happens lies the concept of the heart as an inward eye where some kind of witness sees with an inner vision, an organ of perception that has the capacity, indeed the prescience, of a conscious awakening that amounts to a vision of the one Reality. This inner eye of perception views with a lucidity what the external eye of observation and discrimination views with an opacity that recreates in the mind's eye the world of shadow-making. In its observation of the external, phenomenal world, the outer eye is able to experience a vision of God indirectly as it were through the signs and symbols of nature and through the spirit apparent in all living things. The inner eye of the heart, however, offers an alternative vision of the Divinity which is as direct and immediate as can be approximated within the human sphere of experience. As with the signs and symbols of nature, there is a unique harmony between the outer, opaque remembrance of God through the revelation of the phenomenal world, and the opalescent remembrance of God through the inner world of the heart.

The heart is the container, the receptacle, the sacred repository that is ready to receive the light and the heat that accompanies the knowledge and love of God. The alchemy of the heart is a miraculous fusion of spiritual possibility and promise, a container whose contours already has the capacity of the Presence and is waiting to be filled with the knowledge and love of that sublime Presence. Unlike the heavens and the earth whose overwhelming magnitude cannot contain the Divinity, the "heart of My believing servant can contain Me" (*hadith*). In addition, God proclaims ominously in the Qur'an, "I am nearer to you than your jugular vein" (50:16), only to add in another verse on a more intimate level, "God cometh between a man and his own heart." (8:24) The heart substantiates the promise of transcendence within humanity that perceives and understands that God reserves the prerogative to enter the human heart because humanity has the capacity to receive the knowledge and contain the presence of God within that very heart.

Human beings are vertical beings. Their thoughts, desires, and aspirations bespeak of an ascending desire to rise above themselves, to transcend their limitations, and to connect with the Intelligence, Consciousness, and Spirit that is evidenced in everything from the existence of a grain of sand to the procession of the galaxies. The Divine Being created a heart to serve humanity as its center and core. As center of the human system, the heart contains the knowledge of their primordial origin and final end, a first and ultimate knowledge that is the intuitive inheritance of the primordial heart, adequate to their spiritual needs and perfectly adapted to the vertical ascent. Because of the capacity of their heart, human beings can both know and communicate with the Divinity.

Heart-knowledge would be as nothing, however, without the higher consciousness that heart-knowledge activates. In approaching the meaning of higher consciousness, one can envision the cracking open of the universal egg and the spreading out of a subliminal and seminal "visionary awareness," a kind of ether of higher consciousness to wash over and permeate the entire concourse of the human mind and all its cognitive endeavors with this "esprit" of presence and the élan of higher awareness. Similarly, in conjuring up the symbolic image of the heart, we can envision a unique vessel whose contours are slowly filled with replenishment so miraculous and enriching that the heart becomes enlightened with the light of a pure knowledge and the warmth of an enduring love. It fills to brimming with the certitude of a universal knowledge, displays an incandescent clarity, and exudes warmth whose afterglow is as intense and satisfying as the heat of a coal fire in a remote winter cabin.

The breast is to the heart what the face is to the person, namely the face of the heart. In other words, the movement of the breast through the breath recollects the inner aspiration of the heart. The rise and fall of the human breast in response to the breath explicitly recalls a process of expansion and contraction that is symbolic of the process of denial of the truth and surrender to God that cuts to the core of the human self-image. Surrender represents an expansion of the heart, while denial of the divine possibility represents a constriction of the heart. Describing those whom God wishes to guide or lead astray, the Qur'an reveals: "He expands their breast to Islam. Those He wishes to lead astray. He constricts and closes their breast." (6:125) Ultimately, the symbolic imagery unites in the realization that the breath activates the remembrance of the heart to the extent that every breath becomes a remembrance of heart-knowledge. Both manifestations establish an inner rhythm of conscious vitality, the rhythm of the breath sustaining life and the rhythm of the pulse sending its vibratory drumbeat through the entire human system with the regularity of a metronome.

Modern science ignores the fact that humanity can conceive of things beyond the horizon of its mind, can desire to reach further than beyond, has a consciousness that is aware of itself, whose inner domain represents an objectivity and a certainty that leads ultimately to the higher archetypes that find their source and nourishment in the Divinity. Modern science is oblivious to or, even worse, deliberately ignores the fact that human beings can know themselves in ways other than through the purely empirical avenue of understanding. Modern science ignores the fact that the body without the soul does not constitute the human being and is no longer what is called a human person. It refuses to concede that human beings are made as a direct reflection of the Divine Prototype, exemplifying as they do all the qualities, attributes, and virtues that one usually associates with the Divinity and that within the tradition of Islam are identified through the ninety-nine names of God. Modern science ignores the fact that humanity has another heart, the forgotten one, in which God can dwell as a living presence and a truly felt reality.

At the heart of the human experience lies a fundamental mystery that virtually shapes and defines the way we experience the world. Similarly, at the heart of the universe lies a profound mystery that characterizes our understanding of the manifested universe and that challenges the human imagination to come to terms with the unknown quality of life. In other words, within the heart of both humanity and the world lies a veil that needs to be lifted and an isthmus that needs to be crossed, this being the fundamental challenge of the human experience. During the course of an individual life, the mystery begins to unfold, the formal meets the Formless, the thinking person meets the Universal Intellect, and sacred feeling meets the source of all intimacy in the knowledge and love of the Beloved.

The heart is to the human being what the Ka'aba is to the religion of Islam: the point of departure for the vertical ascent heavenward and the heart pulse that energizes an inner movement that commences the ascension of hearts leading along the path of return whose goal is the transcendence of self as a prelude to union with the Divinity. If there is a secret to be revealed and if there is an essential knowledge to be unveiled and realized, then there must be an abode within the human being where this secret may lie hidden and where this knowledge may nurture and grow. There must be a faculty of perception that has the power of a mind, the depth of a heart, and the prescience of a spirit penetrating enough to crack open its protective shell in order to pour into the human being its overwhelming revelation with the steadfastness of the breath and the pulse.

That abode, that cave, that "kingdom of God within you," is the human heart, not the cardiac organ that beats rhythmically within us, but the true heart that lies behind the symbolic image of humanity, in whose cavernous depths can be found our absolute center and the source of our vital being. This is the other heart of which we write, the one that remembers God and preserves Him within our lives as a living Reality and a conscious Presence. His remembrance resolves the mystery of the unknown, leads us across the lost continent of our inner being, and will bring us into the safe harbor of our future selves in the *vita venturi saeculi*, the life of the world to come.

7.5 The Power of Communication

It is not enough that we have a mind with reason and intelligence, or that we have a heart that contains knowledge and emotions that lift us out of ourselves, or a free will that give shape and coloration to the destiny of our lives. None of the human faculties of knowing and perception would amount to much without the distinctive human ability to speak with words and to communicate the meaning of one's mind to others. That the human mind can ask a question and then attempt to answer it leads us to highlight one final attribute that clearly separates human beings from all other living creatures. We refer of course to the use of human language as forms of speech that can be communicated to others and understood by everyone.

In the traditional view, language is not a survival advantage resulting from a process within the natural order or a "practice convenience" amounting to no more than "notes" on some scale of communication; on the contrary, it serves as the singular mode of communication of a conscious and reflective being whose unique faculties come together and act in unison through the synthesizing quality of the intelligence and the practical ability of the vocal cords to give voice to both thoughts and desires.[120] We speak our mind and by doing so are able to draw upon a language of the self that makes our intelligence not only audible but actually physical, uniting what we know with what we are able to put into spoken words or written form in order to communicate to the world.

Throughout the millennia, the gift of speech has always been one of the hallmarks of the traditional perspective, which distinguished human beings from the animals and underscored the very essence and meaning of their humanity. According to the Qur'an, Adam was taught "the names of things" (2:31) while the Bible says that "whatever Adam called every living creature, that was the name thereof." (Genesis 2:19) This knowledge distinguished him from both the angels and the animals because of the unique power he enjoyed to articulate, through sound symbols, the "names of things" in the form of a language that permitted him to communicate his innermost thoughts and convey their meaning. He could consciously think, know, and give voice through the gift of words to a complete and natural language system that could reason through abstract thoughts, communicate an infinite range of speculative ideas, and describe the world around him. This ability represented tremendous power and incredible prescience of mind; it was tantamount to permitting not only the person of Adam but all future generations to think about and articulate in words their own meaning of the world and their place in it.

Perhaps our intuition, intelligence, consciousness, and higher emotions highlight the essential characteristics of our humanity; yet it is language that makes us feel human. Our inner world of imaginative thinking and the continuous inner dialogue with our conscience all become known to the outside

---

[120] For some, there is no question concerning the origin of human language, although many reasonable people might wonder why this is so. "That spoken human language *did* emerge from the melting pot of hominid evolution is unquestionable. But, because of its nature, *why* or *when* it arose must remain forever the secret of times past" (Richard Leakey, *People of the Lake: Mankind and its Beginnings* [New York: Avon Books, 1978], p. 171) (italics mine).

world through words. The spoken and written word creates images, tells stories, and stirs emotions. Through language, we can articulate the sense of our own identity and make ourselves known to the world. Thomas Henry Huxley, the well-known friend and champion of Darwin, wrote in 1863: "No one is more strongly convinced than I am of the vastness of the gulf between . . . man and the brutes . . . for he alone possesses the marvelous endowment of intelligible and rational speech [and] . . . stands raised upon it as on a mountaintop, far above the level of his humble fellows."[121]

When Adam was given the names of things, he actually took possession of the world and became, as the Qur'an relates, the *khalifat Allah*, or God's representative on earth. By way of compensation, he discovered the unique dimension of the self, a world within a world that left the world of primal utterances and primitive emotive cries behind and opened up the vista of a higher consciousness and a higher form of expression never before witnessed outside the human kingdom. This represented a primordial human condition that distinguished humans from the rest of the creation and was the mental counterpart to the symbolic vertical stance represented on the physical plane of being. It represented an external sign of an inner process that went so far beyond the physical senses that the higher mind could speculate about the farthest reaches of the universe and look beyond its physical being into the past and future of itself. Through vibration, sound, rhythm, intonation, and ultimately through prayer and worship, the higher mind and heart could utter the deepest secrets of their inmost yearning. The mystery of intelligent thought and the act of the spoken and written word combined to create for humanity a language of self that would not only prove the intelligence in measurable form, but also reveal the inmost thoughts concerning the mystery of the highest reality.

Not everyone, however, holds this view of language and its origins. In fact, next to the perennial debate concerning the origin of the universe and of life itself by intelligent design or by natural causes, perhaps nothing has become as contentious as the gift of language:[122] how it originated, how it is learned, how it functions with reference to natural processes of the body and how it is rationalized into a meaningful system of communication. Is language a unique human characteristic or is it merely the extension and enhancement of cognitive capacities whose inception and ultimate source may be found among the grunts and murmurs of the family of primates or the echolocation of dolphins, bats, and whales?

In the 1874 revised version of *The Descent of Man*, Darwin wrote: "I cannot doubt that language owes its origin to the imitation and modification of

---

[121] T. H. Huxley, quoted in Richard Leakey, *Origins Reconsidered: In Search of What Makes Us Human*, p. 240.

[122] We refer here to language generally, although there exist over 5,000 languages globally to actually accomplish the job that language in principle was created to accomplish.

various natural sounds, the voices of other animals, and man's own instinctive cries."[123] Such a suggestion may seem incredible today, given the level of human achievement in the realms of art, literature, science, and technology; but dealing with these incredible abilities, not to mention the very nature of the bodily form, has given rise for over a hundred years to the conundrum associating the mystery and miracle of the human being with the mindless (yet disturbingly creative) processes of natural selection and the analogous similarities humanity shares with the animal kingdom. For example, Darwin asks if "some wise ape-like animal" might not "have imitated the growl of a beast of prey and thus told his fellow-monkeys the nature of the expected danger?" Then, in the next clause, he suggests, "this would have been a first step in the formation of a language."[124] One can only speculate if Darwin was just trying to accommodate a difficult question on the periphery of his developing theory, or whether he actually believed that only a short step led beyond the communication system of a chimp or a gorilla into the world of the human language system and the vast cognitive complexity, the abstract reasoning, and the creative heights that it entails, not to mention the prescient self-awareness that works hand in glove with the human sensibility.

Fortunately, idle speculation concerning the true nature of human language and its implications has evolved since the time of Darwin. In recent times, vast resources and enormous amounts of money have been invested in an attempt to teach chimps and gorillas the use of language in a manner that might approximate human usage, presumably to lend further evidence in support of the theory of the close proximity of humans with their simian ancestors through such a direct link as the evolution of language from primate to hominid to present-day men and women. One can only wonder what other purpose could be involved here, except perhaps the interest of the truth, to somehow justify such research on a higher philosophical level. For example, what would it mean for us to finally prove that these animals could be taught to communicate and use language in the same manner as their human cousins, the primates? Would we have to surrender our position as God's unique thinking creation and adapt to the reality of our talking cousins? Would our intelligence somehow be compromised in associating the miracle of language with nothing more than the capacity of a chimp to articulate its desires and ask for the moon? One can only speculate about the desired outcome of such speculative research rather than anticipating the awful consequences of such a fact.

The issue of whether animals can be made to talk can only be mentioned here in passing as a point of interest and can certainty not be resolved. It has turned into yet another lengthy battle surrounding the theory of evolution and its place in the philosophical worldview of modern civilization. Yet, it is worth mentioning that the results achieved to date, although remarkable in their

---

[123] Charles Darwin, *The Descent of Man* (New York: D. Appleton, 1874), p. 87.
[124] *The Creation Hypothesis*, ed. J. P. Mooreland, p. 236.

individual efforts and outcomes, do not justify the hyperbolic claims[125] that the animals studied and trained could approximate the language spoken by humans. Even infant children, who through a perfectly natural process far removed from the rigorous training that the chimps receive, are able to acquire and command the use of all the basic grammar and structures of the language.

Perhaps the most revealing aspect of the research to date highlights what the chimps and gorillas cannot do. For one thing, the apes are universally incapable of entering into any abstract thought and make common everyday associations in keeping with the linguistic ability of ordinary human children. They can only use the sign symbols and handle the immediate situation to which they had been trained to respond within a very specific context. Thus, their linguistic ability was found wanting and they were not able to apply what they had learned for other hypothetical abstractions. According to Thomas Sebeok: "That apes can be taught fairly large vocabularies of symbols has been well established. Time and again, however, reports indicate that there is only a faint resemblance between a chimpanzee's or gorilla's use of these newly acquired tools and that of humans, especially children who don't have the mental and psychic clutter of adults."[126]

Moreover, the apes displayed a complete inability to use syntactical structures of grammar, which represent the supporting skeletal bones of all languages that all normal children quickly learn and rely upon. The correct syntactical meaning between the phrase "the dog chased the car" and "the car chased the dog" would immediately be apprehended by any child. In the phrase "time eat," the chimp is trained to respond to the phrase to indicate that it is time to eat; and yet there is no way of knowing or proving that the chimp actually knows or appreciates the concept of time beyond responding to the impulse of hunger and the perceived desire to eat at that time, and not that it wants to eat because it is the appropriate time.

The respected linguist Noam Chomsky calls this aspect of language usage the "structure-dependence" principle. Children, as a matter of course, make distinctions between many grammatical categories including sentence structure as well as the role of words within the sentence, such as subject, verb, and object. The chimps can produce chained responses that they had learned by rote repetition through association and reward, but they cannot make distinctions of meaning resulting from the structures of grammar, which are embedded within the syntax of all sentences.

---

[125] The distinguished Harvard professor emeritus D. L. Bolinger once wrote that a couple of well-known chimpanzees had "matched the language ability of a four-year-old child and ... proved that creatures other than humans had the intelligence to transfer meaning and to create syntax" (*Aspects of Language* [New York: Harcourt Brace Jovanovich, 1975], p. 29).

[126] Thomas A. Sebeok and Jean Umiker-Sebeok, eds., *Speaking of Apes: A Critical Anthology of Two-Way Communication with Man* (New York: Plenum, 1981), p. 272.

This leads to another, peripheral point worth mentioning: Children learn language naturally in a communicative and functionally interactive setting through listening, association, and response. They hear, listen, observe, mimic, imitate, and eventually begin to speak in the natural setting of their homes, without much effort and as a matter of course. By the time they begin their schooling, they are already adepts in the understanding and usage of all the fundamental structures of the language. Whatever the chimps and apes have managed to learn, on the other hand, has been the result of a systematic and intensive effort of devoted and sophisticated researchers to instill a few hundred sign symbols that have been tirelessly drilled into them through repetition and satisfaction reinforcement. This is not exactly the setting of natural selection and survival of the fittest, free of all intelligent design and purpose, that evolutionary experts prefer to rely on for their explanations into the patterns of evolutionary development.

Perhaps the most revealing—and symbolic—limitation of the language-learning behavior of the apes is the fact that they do not ask questions. Beyond the inevitably complicated syntactical structures required of questions, not to mention the time factor, they simply do not seem to understand what a question is. It is as if making an inquiry is quite simply too far beyond their means, in spite of the fact that they are notoriously well known for being inquisitive animals. The telling interrogative why never became part of their repertoire and remains to this day clearly beyond their cognitive reach. Even a young child, on the other hand, distinguishes itself through the perennial nature of its inquiries, making possible the very pursuit of a knowledge that has brought us from the edge of the primeval forest to the celestial horizon of the universe

The underlying presumption of the research into the language-learning capacity of certain animals would certainty tend to debunk the traditional belief that the symbolic force of the human ability to communicate through language makes us unique beings among the creation and separates us from the rest of the animal kingdom in a manner that will never be trespassed. A modern-day assumption seems to be that if a direct link can be established between the language ability of animals and humanity and that if the only thing effectively stopping the apes from actually speaking comes from the inherent limitations of their vocal cords and not from any deficiency of their native intelligence, then a very strong case could be established to lend support to the common ancestor theory of evolution. To date, however, the gulf that exists between animal and human intelligence is absolute and convincing proof lies in the total inability of animals to learn to approximate any form of truly human language as all humans know and experience it, namely abstract reasoning, cognitive thinking, and the creative flow of language that make sophisticated forms of communication at all possible.

Language has always been linked and gives voice to the inner faculties and higher powers of the mind, as the various spiritual traditions have always maintained. It is not the natural evolution of the grunts and groans of primates, nor the primal cries and warning calls of animals in the wild that have given rise to the articulation of abstract thought, much less the great vocal skills of humans such as the talent of debating and the power of oration. Everything in nature, both animate and inanimate, emits sound of one kind or another–even a drop falling on water adds its note to the sonant symphony of the natural environment. Birds sing, but the song of the nightingale and the song of a human voice highlight, not the language acquisition capabilities of animals and humans over eons of time, but rather the vast distance that exists between the two species in terms of both vocal ability and the mental power that vocal ability represents.

The use of language is the final, external destination of the inner faculties of mind. As the ultimate defining power, language actually puts the seal on the entire range of the faculties within the inner human cosmos. Through the symbolic use of words, we can describe our inner world and create a captivating narrative of our feelings and emotions, thereby bringing to a sublime conclusion what began as a subtle intuition to take leave of the limited self. With language, we can articulate all the axioms of mathematics and ultimately invest with meaning all the thought processes that relate forms of language to the sensory impressions that are grounded in the world of sensorial experience, namely the world of science.

Through an astute manipulation of words, we can create grand works of philosophy, literature, theatre, and indeed science. Through words, we echo the Word of God uttered at the initial moment of creation[127] and revisited through every revealed word of scripture, and we worship and praise the Divinity through prayer and invocation. Nor is language the mere use of speech or the written word; it assumes a multitude of forms including verbal thought, the gestures and body language that convey meaning, and the symbolic sign language used by the deaf, in addition to the language of the genetic code that actually builds the message of the human body within the very cells of our body.

A profound relationship exists between the use of language and the human intelligence that makes the spoken word possible. Human language reflects the entire range of the human faculties and actually makes their content known to the world. Beyond our reason and our powers of logic, beyond the workings of our mind and our ability to articulate our thoughts through words, beyond all the hopes, desires, and emotions that we can make known through language, beyond all that we know and all that we think we know about ourselves and the world, lies the image of the self. This image of our true center would remain forever hidden within the depths of our being if it were not for the possibility of a

---

[127] In the Christian tradition, the *Logos* became man. The "Word of God" is personified and identified in the person of Jesus. John writes in the Gospel: "In the beginning was the Word, and the Word was with God, and the Word was God." (John 1:1) According to the Qur'an, God uttered the primordial sound *Kun*, meaning "be", and the universe came into existence and *became* a reality, whilst the Qur'an itself–like Christ–is the supreme *Logos*, the direct "Word" of God.

language of the self that emerges from within us to become the fullest expression of our spiritual identity. Without the image of the self and the appropriate language to make that self known, the true value of humanity and its ultimate worth in the eyes of God would never be made manifest and become known.

PART EIGHT

Sacred Psychology

8.1 Integral Anthropology

Once upon a time, in an era known as the Golden Age, a perfect being was created and placed within a paradisal garden to enjoy the wondrous abundance of nature, its limitless provision, and its majestic vistas. Its fruits and pathways, forests and hidden sanctuaries were so transparent, the naked eye could actually see and appreciate the inner quality of spirit that hovered within the physical forms of nature. We are reluctant to refer to this primordial being as male, for what is male in isolation without its female counterpart in complement and reflection. We know from traditional sources that the form of this androgyne[128] was created from the shadowy substances of earth and water, and thereafter was vivified into a living entity by the very "Breath of the Compassionate" (*nafas al-Rahman*) whose Eternal Spirit fused into the corporeal body a living and eternal soul, with a body that breathed fresh air as the terrestrial counterpart to the ethereal spirits of Heaven.

    This soul, in the eternal pre-dawn of the creation, was asked by God to accept its place within the universal setting of the creation when the Supreme Being uttered the words, according to the Qur'anic account, "Am I not your Lord?" The newly created, virgin soul responded in the affirmative: "Yes, we witness You", thus establishing once and for all time the principle of reliance and

---

[128] Neither male nor female strictly speaking, but a mix of the two.

trust that exists between God and His human creation. Adam[129], for such is the revealed name of first man, enjoyed an original, unique, and pure nature that complemented the universal setting of what has come to be known as Mother Nature, uncorrupted, complete to perfection and beautiful, just as a field of lilies represents a perfection of beauty just by being what it is within its true nature. As such, this soul, in the infancy of its eternal day, was ready to embark on the greatest journey that life could offer such a universal and perfected being, universal in that its consciousness was not bounded by the ages of time and the limitations of space, and perfect in that it reflected the qualities and attributes of its creator, namely the Supreme Being, the Reality, the Eternal, the One.

Having read the sacred text that lies hidden within the words and between the lines of revealed scriptures, we know what happened next in the ancient narrative of humanity. It is written within our minds and hearts as an absolute truth and within the Biblical and Qur'anic accounts of the creation and fall of the first couple that we cannot escape, no matter how hard we try during the modern era to believe in another, modern-day myth based on the suppositions of modern science and its accompanying worldview that suggests humanity emerged as an evolutionary process from ape to hominid to thinking humanity. The scriptures of the great world religions have given us an account of the fall from grace and the expulsion from the paradise that is our human legacy from the time of the Adamic first man. But even without these ignoble accounts of how the prototype human erred within his soul and betrayed the trust and confidence that God had placed within His conscious and thinking creation, we know in our heart of hearts, within that deep cavern of consciousness that we all enjoy and that no one wishes to deny, that the fall of first man is written within our very flesh and bones, a human condition that we cannot shake off like a piece of dust from the fabric of our well being. With the fall from grace came not only the consciousness of ignorance and error, together with the significance of making moral and ethical choices; but also the expulsion from the paradisal garden signifies a much deeper dilemma we need to examine more closely that strikes at the very psychology of the human condition.

The unexpected leave-taking of the first couple from the Garden of Eden must have been desperate indeed. Adam and Eve entered a terrestrial world full of hardship and uncertainty that they had no precedent for in their experience of the primordial paradise. In addition, they had no nurturing support system of an extended family to fall back upon to give them guidance and show them the way. Suddenly, they had a taste of what it meant to be imperfect, to make a mistake, to take part in ignorance, and to be weak and impatient being, all as a result of a single choice to forget the immanence of God and disobey His clear warning not to partake of the fruit of the Tree of Knowledge. But that wasn't the worst of it. The blessing (*barakah*) that humanity lost in tasting the nectar (and knowledge)

---

[129] The Hebrew word *adam* has its root in the Hebrew word *adamah*, meaning soil, making the body of man an earth creation that gives Adam his name.

of the apple far exceeded anything they could have anticipated in the primordial garden, when the first couple were permitted to see through the solidity of the physical order with the transparency of the "third eye" that filled everything they saw with the implicit meaning and spirit behind the pictorial symbols in the created universe.

In the new terrestrial order of the universe, where everything cast a shadow and time moved forward laterally with the insistence of a metronome toward some unknown finality, including themselves and the dark premonitions of their minds and hearts, they would have their first taste of what it truly meant to be a human being without the direct perception of truth and the reality. They would enjoy the inner faculties of intuition, intelligence, reason, imagination, and heart knowledge; they would make use of the instruments of the senses that not only partake of the fruits of the physical world, but that also lead the soul inward to partake of the wisdom of the inner senses of seeing, hearing, smelling, tasting, and feeling; but they would no longer "see" God, and they would no longer walk with Him through the meadows of the Paradise.

The primordial being, born with a pure and uncorrupted nature, who walked and talked with God and saw the physical creation as a transparent mirror of the spiritual world, was no longer primordial and complete in its perfection, enjoying the fruits of an eternal Paradise. Another order of experience was destined for humanity that initiated the birth of an entity that upon expulsion from Paradise emerged as a terrestrial and human being, with all the implications that the nature and character of humanity entails. The universal human prototype that partook of the qualities and attributes of the Supreme Being was now a relative earthling, subject to all the contingencies of the earthly and human condition. The perfected soul, that breathed the Breath of the Compassionate and understood things according to their true nature, was no longer perfect and now needed to breathe the fresh air of earth's atmosphere, forever in pursuit of that primordiality, universality, and perfection that was formerly a natural birth right. Thereafter, these benefits must be earned through the experience of the human condition, on a journey of return to the peace and perfection that is the promise of unity, or *tawhid* in Islamic terminology, with the Supreme Being. Something within the human soul had broken, but in breaking open had created an aperture for a new kind of knowledge, an essential knowledge based on revelations sent to humanity as the actual words of God throughout the course of history, to give shape and coloration to this new human experience and to provide guidance on how to escape from the earthly drag of the human condition.

These revelations told of something that now remained hidden within humanity, lying in wait somewhere between the knowledge of the heart and the ground of the soul, a lost thing that hibernated within us in a kind of winter sleep that we could find again if we looked carefully, to awaken into the warm embrace of its redeeming salvation, fragments on a parchment of an ancient knowledge that could never die, whose watermark was the calligraphic script of pure spirit and written with a feathered quill as a cryptic message within the human heart. Any return to the fold of the divine embrace through surrender and repentance would be accepted by the Divinity, so long as it was accompanied by sincere effort and purity of intention. Every good work, every concentrated effort, every sacrifice or smile performed with sincerity and love would reveal that secret treasure that lies within as the forgotten legacy of the primordial era. In this perspective, everything we do becomes a symbol of return. Waiting, listening, and striving, seeking one's purest dreams, all things would lead to that great awakening where peace abides and perfection reigns.

Something within humanity remains unfinished and will come to completion and perfection through the path of return to God. This is the ultimate message of the great spiritual revelations; this is the lost secret of the human condition waiting to be whispered once again into the human heart. Between the Divine disclosure poured forth like fresh milk into the soul through scripture, and the discovery of the lost secret that finds its own revelation in the living of one's life, the faithful soul may find its way back again to that primordial condition that marked the human being as a universal, true and perfected soul during the primordial or Golden Era, when humanity became conscious of and fell in love with the Beloved.

With these initial themes gleaned from the Qur'anic revelation, namely a perfect being within a primordial world with a pure and uncorrupted nature that failed the Divine Test and subsequently fell down into the human condition, an image of self identity begins to emerge that has well-served humanity down through the ages, generations of people that in principle abided by a traditional point of view that placed them within a broader context of life and experience than what the modernite person presently enjoys with the narrow perceptions of evolution, progress, self-reliance, and the infallibility of the scientific method that seeks to expose the dark mysteries of Ultimate Reality to the world on its own terms and conditions. We are no longer perfected and complete beings in the Qur'anic sense of the *insan al-kamil*, with all the weaknesses and frailties that we are well familiar with as part of the human legacy and that we spend a lifetime coming to terms with as a prelude to shedding our humanity like the dead skin of a snake before emerging back within the chrysalis of primordial perfection.

The narrative account of an integrated anthropology, together with a sacred psychology of humanity, has revealed an unfinished being that does not know its true self and has not fully reconciled its relationship with the world. It is in search of a true knowledge that could resolve its inner doubts about the nature of reality. Within the human framework, we are in search of pure forms of behavior that could bring about a transfiguration toward a perfected and complete entity, a potential that lies secreted within *Homo sapiens* as a challenge worth accepting and as a promise awaiting fulfillment. It is a quest for meaning and certitude that leads from the kind of being that we know we are not and never were, such as the anthropoid, the hominid, and the ape, to the kind of being that we are in principle and hope to become, such as the "primordial man," the "true man," and the "perfect man" of the traditional world religions. It is a central quest that takes place within the human kingdom rather than the animal kingdom, a quest that partakes of a curious inner light of unknown origin that permits us to achieve our fullest potential during the course of life, to become something that no animal has ever been or ever will be.

To negotiate our way through the vicissitudes of life, we enjoy a number of inner faculties that entitle us to the name that not only distinguishes us from earlier forms within the genus *Homo*, but that has been adopted to characterize us during the historical era when the species *Homo sapiens* emerged as a distinctive category within the genus *Homo*.[130] The human kingdom that we were destined to enter and fully inhabit came into existence and is characterized by the truly human faculties that make us what we are, not *Homo erectus* or *Homo habilis*, but *Homo sapiens*:[131] a wise human being whose intelligence is a light, whose consciousness is a mirror, whose imagination is a field, whose higher emotion is a flame, and whose virtue is a perfume, at least according to traditional symbolism.

Unlike the instinctive world of the animal kingdom, *Homo sapiens* displays an otherness in the human kingdom amounting to a singularity of soul and a uniqueness of being that no other animal comes remotely near to approximating. Certain animals may approach this kingdom and look within, such as the chimps and the apes with their physical analogies and their corporeal proximity of shape and stance,[132] but none of them have taken leave of their given domain, crossed the narrow bridge over the bottomless chasm of species (speciation), and passed through the invisible door of consciousness into the world of humanity. Indeed, even common sense suggests that they will never bid farewell to their rightful place on earth. Instead of suggesting, by way of analogy or through similarities in molecular composition, their proximity to humankind and their link in the shadows of its evolution, the apes and hominids serve as poignant reminders of

---

[130] Technically speaking, humans are classified by scientists in the mammalian order of Primates. Within this order, humans are placed alongside what are identified as "our nearest living relative," the apes in the family of Hominidae. The separate human line in the hominid family is distinguished by being placed in a sub-family, Homininae, whose members are then called hominines. It would all sound rather depressing, if not disquieting, if it were not for the fact that these speculations are actually modern-day figments of the purely secular imagination.

[131] Not everyone of course holds this view. John Gribbin, in his book *In Search of the Double Helix* (Baltimore, Md: Penguin, 1995), suggests that we put our "prejudices" aside by placing humanity, *Homo*, into a separate category on the evolutionary branch, to be called *Pan sapiens*, referring to a small still-living ape called *Pan paniscus*.

[132] Although admittedly, the stunted and bent stature of the primates can hardly compare in terms of their symbolic projection with the elegant stature of the erect human form, nor can the faces of the monkey or gorilla compare with the adorable and endearing face of a puppy, much less the glowing countenance of the human face.

what humankind is most clearly not. They have all remained at the edge of the antediluvian forest as silent sentinels, guarding the eternally closed and magical world of humanity.

According to the traditional worldview, being human qualifies us for certain entitlements, not the least being that we can leave behind the limited confines of the instinctive world of animals in order to participate in the broad canvas of the human kingdom; but that is not enough to characterize the parameters of the human condition. The Scholastics used to say: "*Homo non proprie humanus sed superhumanus est*"–which means that to be properly human, a person must go beyond being merely human, into the realm of the superhuman. The kind of instinctive knowledge and the vital, and indeed noble, actions displayed by some animals are not enough to define man's humanity. We display the significance and meaning of our humanity through the higher faculties, namely our intuitive intelligence, powers of abstract reasoning, moral sensibility, quixotic imagination, unique personality, and the complex realm of our moral, ethical, and spiritual aspirations. Still, this is not enough to fully define humanity. Unfinished man still has to undergo the completion and fulfillment of an individual destiny in order to return to that original, pristine nature (*fitrah*) that we inherited at the beginning of time and that we promised to fulfill as a human vocation through the sacred trust in God.

We have an instrument called "mind" as opposed to "brain" that reacts to the stimulus of knowledge, the faculty of reason that analyzes cognitive thinking and follows the clear line of logic, a consciousness that brings a heightened awareness to every thought and action, an imagination that envisions alternative worlds and reacts to the impulses of the soul, and a heart that denotes the inner pulse of our moral actions and preserves their goodness within the inner sanctum of our truest desires. Still, this is not enough to qualify as the Taoist "true man" or the Islamic "perfect man," a living image of the Divinity and a hieroglyphic symbol of an enigmatic creature whose inner message contains a mystery that needs to be understood on its own rather than human terms. In order to explain the most fundamental of all the discontinuities in nature, we need something more than the "pre-biotic soup" theory[133] of origins and the corporeal and cranial resemblances–dissemblance is perhaps more appropriate–to the representatives of the simian kingdom, to account for all that *Homo sapiens* finds within itself and in its relationship with the universe. Mortality is written into the very sinews and bones of our bodies and we cannot escape its logical conclusion, namely that when we die, so also dies the possibility to bring ourselves, within our given destiny, to the fulfillment and completion that we are destined for. There is a finite quality to everything within "this world"–colors fade as do the light and the

---

[133] "'Warm little pond' was how Darwin described the pre-biotic environment in which 'life' might have originated from inanimate matter in an 1871 letter to a friend", *The Creation Hypothesis: Scientific Evidence for an Intelligent Designer*, ed. J. P. Mooreland, Downers Grove, Ill: Intervarsity Press, 1994, p. 175.

day. Wakefulness becomes sleep where we roam through dreams that have no accounting and are left behind upon awakening. So also, life becomes death which itself becomes a further awakening into another dimension altogether where the soul reconstitutes itself back into its amalgamated essence.

The decisive factors within the human kingdom and the inner cosmos of which we write are the discernment of the Real from the illusory and ultimately the union of the human being with that Reality. That is why human beings have inner faculties that will lead them through this wilderness and ultimately guide them across the borders of the mind and the horizon of the self. Human beings must express the knowledge that they attain as internalized wisdom and must exhibit their behavior and actions as consummate virtues. In order to transcend the individual self for union with the Greater Self, we must transcend the limitations of our individual nature and go beyond the needs and desires of the individual self. We need to know *a priori* the source of our origins, the meaning of our life and the true nature of our final end toward which all human effort is projected and against which all the wealth of the world is as nothing.

8.2 The Spiritual Emotions

The primary dogma of modern science is that reality can only be ascertained through the objectivity of matter and the objectifying quality of human reason, whose mandate is to navigate its way through the enigmas of the world and to identify through the observation of the senses the truth and the ultimate reality of the universe. Now if we were to believe and fully accept this definitive message, how could we account for the wealth of emotions and feelings that comprise the vast, inner world of human consciousness and higher sentiments. This world necessarily includes the world of our imagination and the full range of our creative life: the realm of dreams and the activity of the human psyche with its unconscious desires and sub-surface urges, the knowledge and sentiment of an affective heart, and the grounding essence of the human soul where the existential battle of the self is fought–the greater *jihad* according to the Prophet Muhammad (PBUH)–between the opposing forces of our inner nature.

A deep, existential chasm exists between what the modern scientific worldview proclaims to be true and certain aspects of the imagination that lie outside the realm of scientific observation and yet have an air of truth about them to the extent that they are universally accepted as serious witnesses of what we perceive to be a valid and true aspect of reality. It is one thing to desire to understand the world from the empirical point of view; but that desire should not preclude the possibility of looking at the world and taking into account the sense of awe and wonder which is a part of humanity's primordial heritage when everything in the phenomenal world of nature radiated outward with a halo of inner vitality and meaning, before the world had "solidified" into a purely outward form and veiled from the power of a direct vision of the higher, inner reality.

Of special significance within this context is the role played by human feelings, emotions, and sentiments whose impression of reality cannot be denied because they are felt and experienced by virtually every human being on the planet. Like the elusive quality of the heart and soul, somewhere within each individual lies the region of the emotions. We are aware that these emotions exist because we experience them in our lives so often and so profoundly. They happen and make their presence felt, forming shadows of a truth within the soul that cannot be denied. The poignancy of their expression affects every experience in our lives and they exert a profound influence over our minds, our understanding, and our consciousness generally. In addition, true emotions and sacred sentiments reach beyond the ordinary level of human experience and touch the mainstream of human lives with the wand of stardust. In a single stroke of feeling, a window of perception briefly opens whose magical power reminds people of the dark, mysterious field of their celestial origins and has the visionary force to project people forward to their true destination.

Nothing responds more movingly and more whole-heartedly to the secret within humanity, to the enigmas of the universe and to the mystery implicit in the idea of a Supreme Being, than the broad range of experience that constitutes the inner life of human affections. A clear distinction needs to be made at the outset between sacred sentiment and higher emotion as portrayed in the great world religions, and the emotionalism or sentimentality so prevalent in today's world, which seems to have come into the forefront of human consciousness as a compensation for the lack of the true higher emotions that traditional people expressed in response to their faith in the Divinity. Human sentiment is an open door to a higher world of knowledge and experience in the light of a revelation of the objective reality and permits people to experience the world as a process of assimilation in which the best of the world passes through the best of the individual on the way to the revelation of the inner self. Emotionalism-cum-sentimentality, on the other hand, is a purely subjective condition, such as a passing mood or preference, which can distort as much as it absorbs, and where the inward and purely individual condition of a given soul in the form of an ego becomes an obstacle to a true awareness of realities within and beyond the world.

In referring to the human emotions and sentiments, we do not mean the lower emotions that frequent the passageways of the human psyche or the romantic and affected sentiments that have come to be the defining experience of modern, humanistic life. At best, these mundane emotions help moderate the vast wealth of impressions that people must deal with in their daily lives and channel those feelings into a comprehensible mode of expression. At worst, this elemental sentimentality comes to be understood as the most profound and elevated expression of the modern psyche, offering up the heat and perhaps inner turmoil of the moment without the supporting light of the intelligence. Instead, we are referring to the higher emotions and the sacred sentiments that combine the most enlightened aspects of knowledge with the highest and most substantive modes of feeling of which the human being is capable, and that virtually define the nature of the spiritual experience. In the words of Frithjof Schuon: "Knowledge is beyond sentiments; but sentiments can be modes of indirect knowledge."[134]

People living in more traditional times witnessed this mystery of God everywhere, in keeping with the Qur'anic verse: "Wherever you turn, there is the Face of God." (2:115) From the existence of a grain of sand to the sublime procession of the celestial galaxies spread across the night sky, God is witnessed as the "Creator of the heavens and the earth," (14:19) Because more traditional people acknowledged the rare ability of the unknown quality within phenomenal nature to lure the human psyche out of itself and tempt it beyond its limited perspective, they were able to respond with a full spectrum of emotions ranging from curiosity to interest to awe to reverence to a profound fear and a far-reaching love of the Sublime that they saw evidenced throughout the natural order of the universe. Nothing stirs the human emotions more fully than the astonishing miracles of ubiquitous Nature, capitalized here to encompass the full manifestation of the phenomenal world in memory of what was once referred to as Mother Nature. Its perennial mystery, its savage wildness, its innocent quality of enchantment, and its revelatory messages have permitted people of earlier and more traditional times to come to an understanding of themselves and their surroundings in such a way that they could combine the knowledge embedded within the phenomena of symbolic nature with the sacred emotions and holy sentiments that symbolic nature inevitably arouses within the human heart.

The human sentiments and emotions represent another modality of perception that supports the activity of reason. Sentiment is not knowledge precisely, although it contains knowledge within the fullness of its expression, and it is not precisely a manifestation of free will either, although it contains a force whose source can be found within that will. How, then, are we to envision the true significance of human sentiment? What is its actual role within the repertoire of human faculties and modes of perception and what exactly is it seeking to accomplish in this world?

In a manner of speaking, human sentiment could be likened to the first layer of the soul or the open face of the soul to the world. If the soul is the ground and bedrock of the individual entity, the true composite of the human being's essence and the summary of the inner person, then the emotive sensibility comprises the first layer of earth in the ground of the soul where the initial yearning for the greater Self takes root. The higher sentiments of compassion, generosity, charity and the corresponding virtues all lead a person out of and beyond the individual self in a translation of creative thought to higher emotion that ultimately becomes a love of the Divinity and the desire for union with the Beloved. The process may be the adoration of the Sovereign Good and the final goal may be union with the Sovereign Being, but its heart-felt reverberation begins with the initial experiences

---

[134] Frithjof Schuon, *Logic and Transcendence* (New York: Harper Torchbooks, 1975), p. 163.

of higher emotions and holy sentiments as they are felt within the human being and as their effect extends out into the world.

True knowledge, in particular any knowledge associated with the principial knowledge of God, is objective, discerning, and contemplative. As such, it is the expression of an intellectual reality that is definitive and absolute. Sentiment, on the other hand, is emotive rather than discursive and is the human expression of an emotional subjectivity that arises within the human being as an existential reality to the extent that the emotions exist, are truly felt, and therefore cannot be denied. Sentiment takes the knowledge of God and internalizes it within us as a subjective reality that can first be experienced as a prelude to becoming fully internalized. As such, it is the expression of an emotional reality that is simple, direct, spontaneous, freely expressed and genuinely felt.

Knowledge serves as a kind of internal skeleton within the emotive vista of the human being. It provides the skull and bones of our understanding of ourselves and our surrounding world and permits us the luxury of placing ourselves and our world within a universal framework that has meaning and makes sense. The corresponding sentiments and emotions that arise and are taken on by us as a result of the revelatory and essential knowledge of God also act as the flesh and blood of the internal noetic system, the substantive heat and life force of a knowledge that allows us to be ourselves and leads us toward the future of our manifest destiny.

Human intelligence, free will, and holy sentiment represent individual worlds that interact and ultimately unite within humanity to create a spiritual dimension that serves as an essential component in understanding the true nature of the human being and the universe. The intelligence contains the knowledge of God and this then generates desire. Thereupon, free will inspires the mind to act on behalf of its intelligence and evokes the feelings of higher sentiment. The emotions awaken the inner being to the possibility of a departure from the closed system of the individual ego and beyond the edge of knowledge for the sake of an experience of supreme awakening as a prelude to union with the Divinity.

As the universal first principles of all human endeavors, principial knowledge and higher sentiment serve first and foremost to accomplish union with the Divinity. The purpose of knowledge is union through intellection and insight and the purpose of sentiment is union through aspiration and love. Their objective is the same, but their manner of expression and modality of approach are different. One is the path of a universal knowledge which synthesizes the entire body of the cognitive, intellective, and discriminatory fields of vision within a framework of objectivity based upon the revelation of the Absolute Being; the other is the path of human love which, as the summative and quintessential expression of the higher emotions, summarizes the sentient, affective, and emotive fields of vision within a framework of subjectivity based upon the human revelation in view of the Beloved. Curiously enough, these two paths exist within us and configure our spiritual effort with a blessed combination of knowledge and love. Knowledge without love would be like a principle without its complementary action. Love without knowledge would be a reaction and a consequence without its first principle and primal cause. Together, they steer the course of our inner life to its final resolution in "the one thing needful," namely unity with the Divinity.

We cannot expect to live effectively in the world without the sacred emotions that the heart offers and we cannot expect to understand the world without the knowledge that life demands. Indeed, who in their right mind would even want to, for that would be tantamount to preferring the eternally frigid darkness of the night sky to the rich warm blue within the dome of the heavens. Certainly, the vast dome of the empyrean, with its flash of eternal blue spread across the daytime sky, summons otherworldly instincts and holy emotions that are drawn into the profound depths of humanity through feelings of wonder, mystery, and awe. The blue firmament recreates in one striking, symbolic stroke the primordial paradise that lies within the inner landscape of humanity as a latent memory and potentially future reality. The eerie panorama of the night sky, on the other hand, with its plate of eternal darkness accented by the cold light of distant stars, without the symbolic knowledge that must accompany such a universal image, contains no comprehensible message that can relate to humanity's immediate experience and harbors no human feeling that could be recognized within that cimmerian,[135] icy, and silent void. As a sacred and symbolic architecture, the dome of heaven contains for us the message of darkness and light, the message of light serving as the perennial remembrance of the knowledge of God and the message of darkness serving as the perennial warning of the absence of the Divine Presence, amounting to the hopelessness and chaos that characterizes the supreme alienation of the damned.

Principial knowledge combined with human sentiment is therefore vital to human beings. *Homo sapiens* would have disappeared long ago if they had persisted in living in a world of dreams rather than known realities and in a universe of precarious moods and whims rather than the higher emotions and sacred sentiments that characterize the defining quality of this humanity. More traditional societies than today's pursued their life in a world of reality that was revealed, natural, observable, symbolic and thus meaningful, a world in which they existed and whose forces they used in order to survive; but they lived that life by virtue of an inner field of perception whose higher emotions and holy sentiments permitted them to understand the objectivity of their knowledge through the subjective experience of their own being. A melody is built on the foundation of notes, instruments, and the hands or breath of the person who creates it, but the temper of the soul awakens these facts of music to another level of experience and allows a person to perceive inwardly the spirit of the music. The blue color of the sky or the arrangement of particular notes on the musical scale represent a configuration of facts and figures that mysteriously leave an

---

[135] A people from Greek mythology described by Homer as inhabiting a land of perpetual darkness.

impression on the mind that the technical facts alone cannot begin to approximate.

Emotion exists as a complement to human intelligence and the powers of discernment, and not as a sentimental and subjective burden clouding the reality of the moment. Therefore, feelings are important in coming to terms, not only with the objective world in which we live, but also in understanding and interiorizing the principles of metaphysics that overlay all of existence. While these principles of knowledge may appear in many instances to be purely abstract and remote, they in fact have the power to confer upon the soul feelings of certitude, serenity, peace, and joy as a complement to the substance, the knowledge, and the meaning of a given truth. These sentiments serve as modes of perception that can actually deepen our comprehension of truth and lead in turn to the practice and development of the virtues.

To say that man is endowed with sentiment capable of objectivity means that he possesses a subjectivity not closed in on itself, but open unto others and unto Heaven; in fact, every normal man may find himself in a situation where he will spontaneously manifest the human capacity for compassion or generosity, and every man is endowed, in his substance, with what could be called the "religious instinct."[136] Knowledge leads down the path toward wisdom; but generosity, compassion, love and the other higher emotions lead down the path toward virtue.

8.3 A Sacred Science of Mind

The human persona of humanity, whether it is body, mind, or soul, inspires interrogatives: Who is man? What is the significance of his human nature? How has he come into being? Why does he exist and what is his purpose here on earth? Yet, beyond these perennial enigmas of origin, center, meaning, and final end lie the profounder and more disturbing factors that strike at the core of our conscious existence. Is the human being merely a physical being that is the accidental product of spontaneous and chance contingencies as modern science would have us believe, a being who has evolved through a process that appears to be a straight line leading from nowhere and heading into oblivion, as modern science would have a believe? Is man the symbolic image of a primordial first man of the Paradise who, through a slow process of spiritual evolution and the experience as fallen and traditional man, comes to rest full circle as the perfected being within a paradisal garden outside the envelope of time and space referred to in the traditional religions?

---

[136] Frithjof Schuon, *The Play of Masks* (Bloomington, IN: World Wisdom Books, 1992), p. 1.

Modern psychology[137] represents the study of humanity from the purely human point of view, rather than the metaphysical point of view set forth as a perennial philosophy at the heart of the great world religions. It seeks solutions to the problems of modern civilizations by an analysis of human nature and psychology, through the humanities in general, and through the sciences such as anthropology and sociology by drawing upon universal truths, rather than man-made, terrestrial facts. In particular, modern-day psychology and the other social sciences are supposed to provide an insight into the very concept of man and his human "nature", without the authority of Heaven so to speak, and without the knowledge through revelation that the words of the Divinity provide. The rebellion of man against Heaven that began during the Renaissance in the Western world has reached its logical conclusion during these times in modern-day individuals who have invested everything in the power of human reason to sift through the data measured by the human senses, in order to provide the definitive norm of what is real and what is not.

It seems that modern psychology represents the study of man through the judgement and reasoning of man himself and projects a conceptualization of the human being that excludes that which is most essential to the human condition, namely, the unifying principle of God and all that principle implies. A sacred psychology of man, on the other hand, represents the study of man based solely on knowledge of God that descends to humanity in the form of revelation and is made up of divine truths that are enduring and universal, rather than human theories that often fluctuate with the ideological fashion of the times. Traditional man, who understood himself to be basically a spiritual being, worshipped the Divine Being with a faith and vigilance that implied inward seeing with the "eye of the heart" (*'ayn al-qalb*), a direct and convincing vision if there ever was one because this concept unites pure vision with pure emotion in order to produce a higher form of sacred psychology. In the present time cycle, however, as we prepare ourselves psychologically to move into the new millennium, we act as if we were purely psychological beings who define ourselves and find our meaning through human reasoning, memory, and imagination.[138] In the contemporary

---

[137] Jung is considered the "father" of modern psychology and *the* major influence in its development. He is sometimes credited with drawing upon the themes of sacred psychology in the traditions, but he was perfectly capable of making statements, such as the following: "Psychology...treats all metaphysical claims and assertions as mental phenomena, and regards them as statements about the mind and its structure that derive ultimately from certain unconscious dispositions. It does not consider them to be absolutely valid or even capable of establishing a metaphysical truth" (C. G. Jung, *The Portable Jung* [London: Penguin Books, 1976] p. 481). To call metaphysical truths "unconscious dispositions" must represent a frustrating and groping-in-the-dark attempt on his part to find words to characterize a framework of ideas that have an otherworldly source.

[138] No one understood better than Jung, possibly the most respected of 20th century psychiatrists, the limitations of modern psychology and the dilemma of the

view, the psychological aspect of our lives is reflective of a purely mental process which is in fact an extension of physical energies rendered profoundly mental somehow through machinations of neural phenomena interfacing somehow with the human psyche.

According to the major religious traditions, human nature identifies *Homo sapiens* as man 'as such'. In principle, the Muslim, Buddhist, or Christian is not contemporary or psychological man, primitive or modern man.[139] The traditional man is man as such in essence and principle, a being that abides by the human nature he has been endowed with by the Supreme Intelligence. The faithful identify themselves according to an inward nature that is based upon the knowledge of God that has come to humanity through multiple revelations. Because of the manner in which they identify themselves and who they understand themselves to be, they have the ability to transcend their earthly limitations and identify themselves as the Christian primordial man, the Taoist true man, the Buddhist universal man, and ultimately the perfected man (*al-insan al-kamil*) of the Islamic tradition. In other words, according to sacred psychology, we are "man as such",[140] capable in essence of rising above our earthly and contingent selfhood in order to know the true nature of reality. Our nature reflects totality and is satisfied only with the Total. We are the mirror in which are reflected the names and qualities of God.

"The study of fragmented behaviour without a vision of the human nature which is the cause of this behaviour cannot itself lead to knowledge of human nature. It can go around the rim of the wheel indefinitely without ever entering upon the spoke to approach the proximity of the axis and the Center. But if the vision is already present, the gaining of knowledge of external human behaviour can always be an occasion for recollection and a return to the cause by means of the external effort."[141] The revelation offers an essential knowledge of who God is and who man is, including their respective natures. In addition, this knowledge clarifies man's position in relation to God and the other beings such as angels, devils and jinn within the universe so that man can understand his place within the great hierarchy of being. Islam, and more specifically the *Sunnah* and *Hadith* literature featuring the sayings of the Prophet, offers behavioral knowledge that amounts to being a sacred psychology of man. It allows humans to be most truly

---

modern-day psychologist. The object of psychology is the psychic; unfortunately it is also its subject (C. G. Jung, *Psychologie und Religion*, p. 61). This would be tantamount to saying that traditional man could understand the workings of his soul only by means of his own soul without the support of Heaven. For the psychologist, Jung confesses, the soul "...precisely belongs to the psychic and to nothing else" (*ibid*).

[139] Nor is he evolutionary man, Marxist man, or Freudian man.

[140] Man 'as such' departs from the Creator and Source as an individual and unique soul creation. *Mankind! Fear and have reverence for your Lord, who created you from a single soul.* (4: 1)

[141] S. H. Nasr, *Islam and the Plight of Modern Man*, London: Longman, 1976, p. 5.

themselves as they were intended to be, and provides a psychological basis through which human beings can transcend the limitations of both themselves and their own limited knowledge in order to achieve the perfection of soul and salvation of spirit in paradisal reality that the human entity in principle is destined to achieve.

This is not to say that religion is *de facto* a sacred psychology, but it contains the elements of a psychology of man inasmuch as the religion reveals a concept of man that identifies his nature as primordial, permanent, universal and complete. In the Islamic perspective, man is his own priest and therefore in a sense his own psychologist, permitting a sacerdotal role for every person that brings the sacred psychology of man into the routine of daily life, thereby uniting the individual with the universal even on the most mundane level of daily existence, thereby sanctifying it. In addition to a metaphysical doctrine, the Qur'an also offers the Muslims a spiritual identity. They understand themselves to be fully equipped with intellect and free will to respond to the principial knowledge of the revelation.

The form of the religion contains the structural framework and offers a methodology of action with which man can discipline himself, come to know himself, and ultimately transcend the limitations of his personal consciousness without compromising the expansion of a heightened spiritual awareness. Once again, a famous saying of the prophet–"He who knows himself will know his Lord"–already emphasizes the truth that man must look within toward his own human nature in order to understand both himself and his Creator,[142] otherwise he would never advance along the line of a true spiritual evolution, nor could he achieve ultimate transcendence of his individual nature toward the universal truth, but rather would commence a spiral descent into the netherworld of psychological turmoil and spiritual darkness that is the genuine prelude to damnation of soul.

The question concerning the spiritual identity of man and his true inward nature–who is man?–is a question that modern psychology cannot rightly answer; whereas the spiritual perspective need not necessarily raise the question for the very reason that it so readily provides a coherent meaning for man and a corresponding spiritual identity that, while being individual, is universal and complete. It is true that man's "supra-natural" nature is not as immediately apparent as are objects in the physical and natural world that can be verified by the efficiency of scientific observation;[143] but human nature is perfectly

---

[142] Similarly, the *Tao Te Ching* (XIX) states: "Realize thy Simple Self. Embrace thy Original Nature. Goal of man, knowledge of self, and who he is in reality." In another section of the *Tao* (XXXIII), we read: "He who knows others is wise; He who knows himself is enlightened." Socrates likewise daringly proclaimed: "Know thyself." and to quote a medieval Western contemplative: "If the mind would fain ascent to the height of Science, let its first and principal study be to know itself" (Richard of St. Victor).

[143] According to F. Schuon, the "sacred sciences" such as revelation and

comprehensible, unlike the purely physical world which in reality offers no fully comprehensive explanation.

Human nature is nothing short of a hidden disclosure consisting of four crucial elements that lend color and shades of meaning to the conceptualization of the human identity. These elements serve as open doors to the perception of the true nature of humanity, thus leading to an understanding of the nature of reality itself. Based on the Qur'anic revelation, but also conforming to the other monotheistic spiritual traditions, human nature or *fitrah* is traditionally characterised as primordial, permanent, theomorphic, and universal, thus lending substantial depth to the concept of human nature with its inborn disposition toward the life of the spirit and not just the temporal pleasures of this world.

The word *fitrah* in its Arabic root can be understood to refer to the human "norm" from which, according to the Qur'an, humanity has fallen away through weakness and ignorance. Having been fashioned from the creative "hand" of God, primordial man was innocent, pure, true, free, righteous, virtuous, and understood his place in the great hierarchy of being. The Qur'an is quite specific in its references to man's inner nature "So set thy face steadily and truly to religion, Allah's handiwork according to the nature on which He has created mankind. No change (let there be) in the work (wrought) by Allah: That is the standard religion, but most men know it not." (30: 30) It reveals that nature of man has been patterned on the nature of God (*fitrah Allah*) in terms of its original inception, and this of course cannot be altered in any respect.

Natural man, then, is already perfect man in principle, even if perfection does not come naturally to man because of the consequence of the fall from the paradisal garden. It is in this sense that we have identified ourselves here on earth as "unfinished beings". Before his fall from grace, Adam was considered primordial because he already enjoyed the perfection inherent within man's nature and he saw and understood the world "from within". In other words, primordial man was the embodiment of a living spirituality.[144] Modern individuals can still claim a primordial nature in so far as they continue to enjoy the same

---

symbolism need not adjust themselves to the modern scientific approach in the verification of objective knowledge. "The realm of revelation, of symbolism, of pure and direct intellection, stands in fact above both the physical and psychological realms, and consequently it lies beyond the scope of so called scientific methods. If we feel we cannot accept the language of traditional symbolism, because to us it seems fanciful and arbitrary, this shows we have not yet understood that language, and certainly not that we have advanced beyond it" (F. Schuon, "No Activity without Truth,' Studies *in Comparative Religion*, Autumn 1969, Vol. 3, No. 4).

[144] Schuon emphasizes the importance of the primordial man within the modern man: "...to realize the 'Ancient' or 'Primordial' man means to return to the origin which we bear within us; it means to return to eternal childhood, to rest in our archetype, in our primordial and normative form, or in our theomorphic substance" (Frithjof Schuon, *Understanding Islam*, D. M. Matheson (trans.), Penguin Books, 1972, p. 102).

inner nature that Adam exemplified in principle, once this nature is coupled with the aspiration to return to the original purity that people today are still capable of because of who they are in principle.

Primordiality already adds a spiritual dimension to the human being that modern psychology does not even admit to as a matter of basic premise. Modern psychological man is understood to have an "infra-natural" origin, arising as he does from "below", while traditional man was always understood to be "supra-natural" in nature, descending as he did from "above". Needless to say, it should be noted that neither the Qur'an nor the sayings of the Prophet offer us a flattering picture of human nature within its "fallen", earthly setting, nor does the existential experience of living in today's world help us to understand man as primordial, pristine, and pure. The psychological challenge in today's world, as it has always been down through the ages, is to conform to what we are according to our true nature, however much this may elude our grasp within the existential, earthly reality.

Beyond the concept of human primordiality, which retains and still represents an ambiance of infancy and first origins, lies the permanence of man's true nature, a nature which is unchanging in its basic construct since the beginning of the primordial era witnessed during the Golden Age. Human nature partakes of permanence which began in the primordial era of the Garden of Eden and which the soul takes on its journey of return to God. This idea also sharply contradicts the prevailing evolutionary concept that man has somehow "evolved", not only as a physical form but presumably also in the psychological and psychic capacity within his human nature, from a lower to a higher species. However, this runs counter to the spiritual perspective that admits only of a descent from higher to lower levels and not vice versa.

In this view, the religious perspective understands humanity to be characterized as "extra-spatial" and "extra-temporal" in nature, in which people contain elements that are constant and permanent, and this is none other than an aspect of the *fitrah Allah*. In other words, the human norm is characterised by permanence. Thus, the goal of all human spirituality is to recognize and to return to that norm, to humanity's permanent and original nature, to the *fitrah*. The question of who man is and how he identifies himself begins with the consideration of the characteristics that the revelation identifies man's human nature to be.

In addition, human nature is considered to be theomorphic in the spiritual perspective because it originates in God and is distinguished by the qualities that God has imbued humanity with. We can be a mirror of the divine attributes and qualities because of his theomorphic nature, which asks us to be and to behave in accordance with who we truly are. Our theomorphic nature requires us be to be true to ourselves *according to our true nature* and requires us not to forget our "original" nature. An important aspect of our theomorphic nature is the fact that we have been given a knowledge that the angels don't partake of. The Qur'an teaches us that Adam learned "the names of things" (2: 31) which must mean that he understood implicitly the inner nature and quality of things in their essence. Even though we tries to float on the surface of our being, far from our own center, being made in the image of God reminds us that we are the theophany of God's names and qualities, a reality that lies at the center of the human condition.

Finally, to say that our nature is universal means to imply that it is based on a prototype of humanity that transcends time and space and provides the balance to the eternal aspect of human nature. Universal man is both the true man of Taoism and the perfect man of Islam, true in so far as he reflects the qualities and attributes of the primordial man and perfect in so far as he reflects the nature of the prophet and the nature of the Divine Being. Muslims imitate the Prophet both outwardly and inwardly, so that they can model and identify their own individual nature with the human nature of the Prophet. Thus, they have the potential of knowing themselves and enjoy a full conceptualization of the human being by imitating the prototype of human nature as exemplified in the Prophet, who in the Islamic context is the perfect man (*al-insan al-kamil*). It is said that to enter into the mold of the Prophet's personality through the *Sunnah* and the *Hadith* is to enter into the very mold of the Qur'an, since his nature was the nature of the Qur'an.[145] In this way, the nature of man can approximate the nature of God, through the revelation implicit within his own being, through the words and the example of the Prophet, and through the revealed knowledge of the Qur'an.

8.4 The Paradox of Free Will

According to all the great spiritual traditions of the world, the defining characteristic of the human species is the quality of human-ness, for want of a better term. Humanity is considered "human" because they enjoy a number of higher faculties that distinguish the species from the rest of the animal kingdom and place it at the pinnacle of the creation as a being created in the image[146] of God. One characteristic of our humanity that gives us our unique psychological nature is the fact that we can make choices because we have a faculty called free will. This is the faculty of action, direction, and movement that all the religions unanimously identify, not as a human will unbounded by any qualifying adjective,

---

[145] It is part of the immense impact of the Qur'an that considering our 'fallen nature', it "restores to us the condition of *fitrah*. It gives back to the intelligence its lost capacity to perceive and to comprehend supernatural truths, it gives back to the will its lost capacity to command the warring factions in the soul, and it gives back to sentiment its lost capacity to love God and to love everything that reminds us of Him." Eaton, *Islam and the Destiny of Man*, p. 78.

[146] An image not necessarily in the sense of a pictorial form but in the sense of a reflection or shadow. Since God is not a form but a Spirit, any likeness or symbolic image must refer to God's inner qualities and attributes rather than to any physical properties.

but as a human will set free to roam within the set parameter the Creator has established for humanity.

The qualifying adjective "free" is crucial to the discussion of a traditional, sacred psychology. Of all the faculties and modes of perception that we have reflected upon, perhaps the most controversial and problematic is the concept of free will. Down through the millennia, religious scholars and philosophers have addressed the question of free will as a paradox. They understood free will to function as a complement to the other higher faculties of people whose destiny was written before they were born and in a world that has been preordained down to the smallest grain of sand by the Divine Being. Every appearance seems to indicate to the modern mind that the faculty of willing is not free within the traditional perspective, at least at the surface level of appearances where the modern scientific mentality stakes its claim in the pursuit of what is real. It is a paradox that the modern mentality loves to highlight in its attempt to discredit the spiritual point of view. How can a person possess a will that is free, many modern-day skeptics like to ask, when everything is written in advance and the destiny of humanity is cast from a divine mold and predestined from eternity?

To that end, we need only ask ourselves what human behavior would be able to accomplish if its beloved will were not free. The answer would be as absurd as the question is fantastic. If humanity did not have the faculty of free will and therefore the means to put into effect that which the mind had construed, the logic of a rational mind demands that it would be acting under some kind of constraint rather than freely, like a chained animal or a caged bird, whereas the image of a free flying bird is a symbol if ever there was one of the unbounded soul. Even the wind "bloweth where it listeth." In such a strange scenario as the human experience bounded by a pre-determined destiny and without the beatitude of a free will as the empowering complement to a conscious mind, the word liberty would not even be part of the lexicon, much less form the basis of the human self-image! On the other hand, to say that humans have free will does not mean to imply that they enjoy absolute freedom in the sense that people today would like to imagine as part of the bold fantasy of their self-image, namely as a complete and total freedom, like some kind of god might possess.

The kind of freedom that the modern psyche envisages for itself would actually make no sense on the human level and for obvious reasons: If people were not determined in some manner and could assume the mantle of a complete freedom, as many modern sophisticates would like to believe, then they could break the mold of natural law and make themselves into whatever image they wanted. Individuals could change their race, color, or station in life according to their will; and yet this is clearly not within the realm of human possibility. It is a spiritual as well as an existential impossibility and one that no sane person would attempt to deny. On the contrary, we are predestined to be born within a certain condition of time and place and nothing, and especially no amount of desire or wanting, can change that fact. Frithjof Schuon has put it quite succinctly: "The truth lies between the two extremes, or between two absurdities."[147] We must deal with the existential reality of our destiny and can do so with the faculty of a free will that can put into motion and give direction to the impulses of our mind, without pretending to aspire to the kind of absolute freedom that would place us beyond the need to eventually give an accounting of ourselves before our Maker.

Differences of perspective between the traditional and modern attitudes toward free will and the true nature of our freedom lie in a proper understanding of human limits and in the recognition of certain realities about the human being. Human limits defer to the nature of human destiny in which a person understands that they will never be able to alter certain parameters of their existence, namely the condition and circumstances into which they are born such as their race, color, birth date, or the genetic makeup of their DNA. Still, those limits contain a liberating as well as a demanding reality, in which individuals not only have the right and the freedom to make their own individual choices during the course of their life, but also the duty to meet the moment with the truth that every moment contains. Humility demands that we acknowledge certain realities, while intelligence allows us to know our place within the course of an individual destiny and to fulfill the role in which we find ourselves with a sense of calmness and grace.

Does God know the destiny of an individual soul? Only the bold curiosity of a human being could have the temerity to ask such a question. The answer must be and is in the affirmative since God is omniscient and knows all things, otherwise He would not be God. Does God's knowledge somehow compromise our free will and our ability to choose? The answer must be and is a resounding negative since a predestined and discretionary knowledge that exists outside the envelope of time and space has no affect whatsoever on the power of an individual will and the force of its action. What makes the difference in understanding this seemingly opaque paradox is the point of view and the angle of vision. "Man is subject to predestination because he is not God, but he is free because he is made 'in the image of God.' God alone is absolute freedom, but human freedom . . . is not something other than freedom any more than a feeble light is something other than light."[148]

From the human point of view, no one can take our freedom of choice away from us, least of all the All-Possibility of a Supreme Being who has bestowed upon His thinking creation the power to create a life of their own making to the extent that they will be called upon to give an accounting of their intentions and actions on the Day of Accounting. God's knowledge does not touch upon or compromise in any way the human thought process and the strong force of the human will to act within the parameters of its own insight and perceptions. If it did, there could be no question of responsibility within the

---

[147] Frithjof Schuon, *Stations of Wisdom* (London: John Murray, 1961), p. 81.

[148] Frithjof Schuon, *Understanding Islam* (Bloomington, IN: World Wisdom Books, 1994), p. 2.

theater of human actions and no question of an accounting either during or at the end of life.

Free will is real and not compromised by the knowledge of God, otherwise it could not take part in the existential reality of this world, nor could it take a decision and act upon it in a manner that goes contrary to the knowledge of God. The proof that the will is free, if proof be needed, lies in the fact that humanity can deny the very existence of the Divinity, as well as the knowledge and grace that are the evident manifestations of a Supreme Being. What could be more characteristic of the principle of freedom than the ability to affirm or deny the very origin and source of human existence?

The significance of free will takes on an added dimension within the intellectual climate of the modern world, partly because people have never before denied the existence of a Supreme Being to the extent that they do today in virtually every aspect of life, and partly because people have never before taken such a vested interest in searching for the clues to their own identity within such a narrow scope of self inquiry, limited that is to the purely physical plane of existence. Perhaps it is the folly of the modern mentality thoroughly adapted to the secular ambiance of the scientific worldview; but in this post-modern era, the society itself is forever scrutinizing and redefining itself, questioning and probing, especially now in light of the astounding findings of modern biology and physics down to the smallest quantum detail, in an effort to find an answer to life's mystery and particularly the mystery of the self, a search that will be arrived at on its own terms and will suit the demands of its mentality. There is danger as well as wisdom in such self-scrutiny, a kind of modern-day paradox that serves as a mirror image to complement the paradox of free will that has haunted the mind of humanity down through the ages.

Unlike lower creatures who act without question and are locked within the safety of their own particular natures, people today think they possess a kind of freedom without restraint; but whose true nature and meaning is as enigmatic and challenging as the debatable freedom portrayed in the traditional paradox of free will. Awash in the wave of modernity, people follow the lead of scientists who define the meaning of the human being and write their own conception of self based on the findings of the various fields of modern science such as biology, chemistry, and paleontology. Members of the scientific establishment search within the depths of the physical entity and probe the vast expanses of the universe for answers to the abiding questions of our time; they have the stamina, determination, and freedom to do as they like within the must-resolve and can-do ambiance prevalent in the world of research and development. Indeed, the luxury of a perceived freedom and its liberating quality is perhaps the greatest feature creating a sense of progress within the contemporary setting. In short, the supposedly expanded and liberated mind of today, both among scientists and laypersons, attempts to see things purely from the human point of view, whereas the traditional mentality was accustomed to seeing things from the revelatory point of view in which the self-disclosure of God established the norm and set the prerogative for the faithful to follow. Perhaps the greatest paradox of all in today's world is the human perception of a liberating freedom based on the narrowest approach imaginable to the understanding of the true nature of reality.

In addition, the concept of an unlimited freedom, because of the lowering of the threshold of accountability brought on by the modern-day denial of the Day of Judgment, creates more problems than it eliminates and raises more questions than it resolves. What, for example, is the object of such freedom, in what direction does it lead us, and to what end will it bring us? These are ominous questions indeed that strike at the heart of the modern approach to ethics and morality, not to mention concerns about identity, purpose, and final end. Will this search and the freedom this search engenders give wing to a perennial search for the knowledge of the individual self, or will post-modern individuals eventually realize that the definition and identity of the true inner person have taken on a coloration that is in fact infra-human and more bestial than any of the lower animals, who merely obey their predetermined nature and live harmoniously by using the God-given instincts to function naturally and harmoniously within the phenomenal world.

As an existential reality, the human being is an open door to a transcendent reality. The spiritual instincts and a heightened spiritual imagination have taught us that much about ourselves. Our free will can close the door to the Infinite, and we can begin our journey through life via another entrance if we so choose.

The dilemma facing people today is as existential and real as it is perennial and fraught with consequences. The truth is that there is a fundamental ambiguity at the heart of the human condition that keeps us guessing and clouds the true object of our desire. It is the ambiguity of this true objective that draws us into the darkening shadows of our mind even though the emerging light is there to behold in the firmament of our mind. It is the perennial doubt concerning the true nature of reality that leads people to believe in the evidence of the finite world they can physically sense rather than the infinite world of the spirit that they recognize through intuition and spiritual instinct. It is the uncertainty implicit in the cosmic veil that separates human beings from the direct knowledge of God and only permits them glimpses of the Eternal to the extent that they make efforts to lift the veil that separates them from the truth. Through free will, we have the freedom to deny the promise of another world after death and to affirm the illusions and the sensory appeal of this world instead. It is the temptation to seek the fulfillment of one's desires in the promise of an immediate satisfaction within the realm of the tangible and the visible rather than in the enduring vision of union with the Supreme Being.

Needless to say, the freely choosing human being is compelled to exercise free choice; therefore, the paradox returns to haunt us. If people make a choice that leads in the direction of disequilibrium and disharmony–conditions that are difficult to deny since they are everywhere apparent in this world–they must bear this in mind as a consequence of their choice and invite the misery and unhappiness that must inevitably accompany the wrong desire and the wrong choice. The force of the will can also recreate a sense of balance and equilibrium through the right desire and the right choice. Every thought, decision, and choice pave the way for a change in the perception of the self, while the will represents the faculty of measure and balance, of forward direction and of arrival at a state of equilibrium in this world as a prelude to the transformation of the soul in the next world.

We do not want to regret in retrospect what we should have become by virtue of the nature of the human condition. It is a condition of life that we live in accordance with the dictates of our given nature as human beings within the context of a genuine understanding of the true nature of reality. At stake here is the knowledge of who we are and what our place and role is in the design of the universe. That is why it is virtually a mandate of the human condition that people need to take a stand concerning what they believe in, for they must give an accounting of what they have accomplished in their life. That is why the vast resources of the entire scientific community have set themselves the goal of identifying the true nature of reality and seek to develop a theory of everything that will describe that reality. That is why we have free will and the concomitant power of free choice, because in choosing what we think and what we believe, and what we actually accomplish, we are creating and recreating ourselves anew at every moment in time, a participation of self that anticipates the timeless moment within every moment through the light of the mind and the empowering force of the will.

Essentially, knowledge of the truth obliges a person to choose the truth. As different as the great world religions are in their formal aspect, they all agree on the need for us to live our life wisely and well. This may not come easy and mistakes will happen; at some point, every person must trip and fall, only to pick themselves up again and continue on their way with the knowledge of the truth to guide their footsteps forward. To live life wisely is to live in accordance with the knowledge of God, Who sets the parameters for the reality we experience in this world. To live life well is to forsake one's weaknesses and limitations, to choose the good and reject the alternative of evil, to make every effort to perfect oneself in this life, and ultimately to transcend the individual world of the self for the liberating dimensions of the Higher Self. "The purpose of freedom is to enable us to choose what we are in the depths of our heart."[149]

In order to *choose* what we are, however, we must *know* what we are. Can post-modern society assert the privilege of freedom without the individuals of that society understanding their true inner nature and the limitations that accompany the reality of their existence? The dark power of free will lies within the modern sensibility and finds its underlying roots in its conception of self. No matter how deep the secular, scientific establishment digs into the atomic realms

---

[149] Frithjof Schuon, *To Have a Center* (Bloomington, IN: World Wisdom Books, 1990), p. 38.

of the body, no matter how far down it explores into the nether regions of the unconscious, no matter how persistently it attempts to reduce the human image as a shadow-image and reflection of God into the elementary particles of the subatomic world, no matter how long it searches for the ultimate description of life and the final proof of humanity's true reality, it will never arrive at a convincing portrait of the human self image and it will never fully appreciate the knowledge of the human revelation that enjoys in principle a luminous intelligence and mediating will and that serves as a link between the two worlds of Heaven and Earth.

8.5 Wisdom of the Senses

Finally, before taking leave of this part of the book, it might be appropriate to make a few comments about the five senses that we enjoy as the hallmark, in one way or another, of the human experience. Modern science sets great store in the ability of the five senses to definitively establish a credible objectivity when it comes to understanding the true nature of reality. Is the physical realm real by virtue of our ability to see, smell, hear, taste and touch through the portals of experience. Do they have the capacity to rule out the reality of experiences that cannot be verified through the instruments of the five senses alone?

Strange as it may seem, a complete narrative of the five senses is a story that has yet to be fully told. We rely on our senses as the anchors of sentience in order to perceive and understand the world we inhabit. We use our senses as vehicles of pleasure to heighten, if not our complete happiness, then at least our random and nominal enjoyment of that world. They raise us up to the heavens where eagles soar and streaks of lightning move like arrows across the heavens. They cast us down with their insatiable desires into the deepest subterranean well where the sky becomes a reflection of distant light and dreams of soaring mountain peaks are forgotten. Scientists throughout history have relied on the senses as the instruments of knowing and perception, as well as the filter through which the world around us can be objectified as a categorical truth as well as an existential reality. Because of the senses, we have the ability to know, experience and respond to the world around us and take part in the life it has to offer. We take in, internalize, and become a true reflection of the mysterious world we encounter thanks to the immediacy of the senses. One question remains, however, that disturbs the serenity of our initial inquiry: Is that enough? Is it enough that we can meet the world on our own terms with these unique instruments of perception, anchors as it were that can ground us in the reality of "this world"? Hopefully, it is a question worth pursuing throughout the course of this endeavor, one that may reveal an unexpected and surprising outcome.

Just as the four elements of earth, air, fire, and water represent the *materia prima* of the natural order, these solid, aerial, fiery, and fluid modes of manifestation have communicated their sacred quality to the five senses down through history, senses that in themselves also partake of a sacred and inner quality that transcends their literal and outward experience. Throughout the millennia, humanity has relied on the open receptivity of the five senses to capture the essential form of an object and in so doing create the sense–for want of a better word–of the reality of a thing as the initial step in the understanding of the reality of the world and the surrounding universe beyond that world. The five senses are the first tier of experience in a range of faculties and modes of perception that we have available to us in a great adventure in pursuit of an understanding of the reality we live in without knowing its true meaning and significance.

Beyond the five senses lies a myriad of human faculties including intuition, intelligence, reason, imagination, and the holy sentiments that help us make our way through a labyrinth of mystery that confronts us in this world. In addition the higher faculties support the attitude of faith and the force field of the human will to embrace the higher knowledge of a traditional worldview in which to believe, followed by the actions, disciplines and good works that make up the human manifestation of these universal principles in this world. None of the apertures of perception and experience can have any true value without the opening of the heart, which in a number of traditions including the Religion of Islam, is the "seat of the intelligence" as well as the cave of the higher human sentiments. In other words, what we see, hear, smell, taste and feel enters the senses, passes through the filter of the mind, explores the enlivening realm of the sacred human emotions, only to find their true place within the consciousness of humanity through the portal of the heart which is not contained within space, but that has space enough to contain the mystery of all we see, hear, smell, taste, and touch.

In the wake of an epic, perennial struggle to differentiate a true understanding of the role of both matter and spirit in resolving the mystery of the human identity in its confrontation with the Supreme Being, we have brought the search for the true nature of reality during the post-modern era to its logical conclusion with the scientific worldview that matter serves as the ultimate reality, and that anything that does not abide by our three dimensional world and the input of our five senses simply does not exist. Of course, the ancients thought otherwise and took inspiration from the words of Christ when he is reported to have said: "I shall give you what no eye has seen and what no ear has heard and what no hand has touched and what has never occurred to the human mind."[150] People who partook of a more traditional environment knew and appreciated that the convention of form is transcended by the largesse of spirit, just as the flicker of a flame gives way to the incandescence of light. The visionary impulses of their mentality laid claim to a third eye, fifth dimension and sixth sense whose inner door opened onto the open skies of an invisible, indeed a spiritual world, much like air and breath open the door to life itself, but lies beyond the

---

[150] "Eye hath not seen nor ear heard, nor hath it entered into the heart of man." (1 Corinthians. 2:9)

dimension of sight, that ultimately comes to a pinnacle as a single, universal reality known throughout the ages as the Transcendent, the Absolute, the Beneficent whose Spirit "hovers over the waters", but that is universally understood by the name God as Supreme Being. Unless the five physical senses and various human faculties[151] "catch fire" as it were, the Transcendent Reality cannot be experienced and the Presence of God cannot be known. All else becomes as a fireless smoke amid the smoldering ruins of human spiritual aspiration.

The soul is never satisfied until it uncovers the mystery contained within forms and it will never be truly content until it finds its final abode in the spirit that substantiates and ultimately transcends all natural forms. In terms of sheer functionality, the import and significance of the senses play a major role in experiencing the world of forms. Beyond the literal and formal input of the senses lies the wisdom of their true meaning. The five senses dutifully record what they see, hear, smell, taste and touch; but beyond their formal and functional aspect lies a visionary wisdom that intuits the inner meaning of things, that listens to the echo of a universal revelation that comes down to humanity in a variety of forms through nature, messengers and scriptures, that arouses memories and histories and dreams of a deeper truth than the physical forms that on their own give lie to a higher essence contained in the form. When we see the early morning rooster, we await the sound of its awakening call; when we see the owl perched on a tree limb at night, we imagine its eerie hoot sounding its audible waves through the stillness of the pines.

> Amidst the notes
> Of my koto is another
> Deep mysterious tone,
> A sound that comes from
> Within my own breast.[152]

What the inner spirit yearns for and therefore relies on the inner nature of the senses to proclaim is to listen to the cock when it has not yet uttered its cry, to feel the reverberations of a bell before it has been struck, or to intuit the unique wisdom of the owl's hoot without actually listening to the sound.

Every human sense contains a deep well of knowledge and insight that reveals to the unsuspecting mind what lies beyond the physicality of the world. This knowledge through forms and images and sounds creates impressions of what lies within an experience and emerges upon a plane of higher consciousness for what lies beyond the horizon of the known world. Enclosed within all the sensations that cannot be verified, the thoughts that cannot be resolved, and the

---

[151] In Sanskrit, *vijñāna*, or the eight consciousnesses, all sentient beings possess: sight, hearing, smell, taste, touch, and three different operations of the mind.

[152] Yosano Akiko, *One Hundred More Poems from the Japanese* translated by Kenneth Rexroth (New York, 1974), quoted from *Music in the Sky*, ed. by Patrick Laude & Barry McDonald (Bloomington: Ind: World Wisdom Books, 2004).

dreams that cannot come true lies the spirit of an ancient, primordial reality that is never wrong and can never fade away. From these outermost instruments of human perception flow rarefied knowledge and sensory experience that sink down into the innermost depths of our nature where their impressions and insights nurture and grow until we awaken toward a feeling of mystery as a prelude to a higher consciousness of truth, just as surely as we awaken to the new day with the sound of the birds and the patter of rain. What the inner aspect of the senses conveys is not knowledge or wisdom precisely and is almost impossible to categorize. Buried deep within the human being lies an inmost presence, a witness if you will, that knows everything that needs to be known, in a place where mystery and intuition unite to give birth to an instinctive faith in the Unseen; but how this primordial presence is stirred to consciousness to give shape to a disciplined mind and a devotional heart requires great discipline in the appreciation and use of the human senses.

We have all experienced the mystery of the senses without coming to terms with their inner power and wisdom, inspiring William Blake to remark, "A fool sees not the same tree that a wise man sees." As compensation for their loss, the blind man may see an inner light that leads to a road seldom traveled; the deaf man hears the vibratory frequencies that form the texture of a universe that escapes ordinary, human ears; but leads him effectively to his destination. Animals use the power of scent as a source of knowledge and guidance, while many a simple smell, from the perfume of flowers to the smoke of burning autumn leaves, can arouse an evocation to memory and recreate the heart of an experience that we hold dear. What some people see as the curtain of night appears to others as a milky way of stars. We listen and see; but we do not hear the voice of lightning, trace the music that lies behind the movement of the eyes, or smell the sweet fragrance of the spoken word. The glow of a color or the fragrance of a scent can never come of their own power; but are instead the reflection of some greater miracle. When we say that we see the light and hear the music, language itself fails especially when it comes to conveying the inner meaning of an experience. We could just as easily refer to the fragrance of the color and the glow of the scent to arrive at a meaning that conveys its true miracle, well beyond the lateral thinking of the mind. When we refer to the music of light or the vision of sound, are we speaking in meaningless terms or are we perhaps arriving through another door to the inner meaning of an experience that cannot be contained through the literal meaning of words; but that transmits an alternative meaning through the linguistic magic of suggestion and innuendo. To cite a poem of Daitō, a Japanese poet who lived from 1282-1337:

> When one sees with ears
> And hears with eyes,
> One cherishes no doubts.
> How naturally the raindrops

>   Fall from the leaves!¹⁵³

Isn't sound itself the absence of silence; while silence constitutes the absence of sound, acting as if the sheer power of the void were listening from some region beyond the auricular dimension altogether. There is a curious interpenetration when the eternal soundlessness actually penetrates the world of sound with its ethereal and everlasting quality of suggestion; while the sound in its living reality inspires the eternal soundlessness that is the hallmark of inner peace. A flowered landscape is as beautiful as the golden embroidery of a silken brocade and has a life of unknown mystery that is proclaimed by its existence; but it is the singing of the birds and the buzzing of the bees that would bring this portrait to life with the promise of an eternal soundlessness that lies with latent power beyond the utterance of sound.

There is a power to the senses that calls to mind the birth of a river in the appearance of a bubbling stream or that witnesses the design of a flower in the emerging rose bud. When we see the mountains, do we ask ourselves when they were laid upon the earth or what they mean in terms of stability and strength; when we hear the roar of the oceans or the howl of the wind, do we wonder about the sacred voice behind the creation of these things; when we witness the night sky, do we wonder who has scattered those distant stars across the field of night like diamonds on black velvet and do we witness the sky-blue vault of the heavens as the formless infinitude that it really is? We can easily be deceived by the magic of a name and the suggestion of its meaning, but we can never touch the inner substance of a fact without moving beyond the outer experience of the senses.

>   To listen to the music of the Sky;
>   And then to realize: the Song was I.¹⁵⁴

Such is the mystery and the wisdom embodied within the physical world of the senses that the messages they convey allow us "one foot in Eden", according to John Muir and from that vantage point give us insight from the "other land" into the world of time, of history, and of the sensory input of "this world". We only begin to awaken to this reality when we realize that the material world, the world of space and time as it appears to our outer senses, is nothing but a sign and symbol of the mysterious spirit that transcends these wayward phenomena.

There must be more to the five senses than insatiable desire or a pseudo objectivity that explains away universal reality by reducing it to the sub-atomic world of atoms and molecules. In the profound darkness of the night, the time when people perennially turn inward in search of something more than the

---

¹⁵³ Quoted in *The Buddha Eye: An Anthology of the Kyoto School and Its Contemporaries*, ed. by Frederick Frank (Bloomington, Ind: World Wisdom Books, 2004), p. 7.
¹⁵⁴ "The Song", Frithjof Schuon, *Road to the Heart*, (Bloomington Ind: World Wisdom Books, 1995).

surface experience on offer to the senses during the daytime, myths give rise to meaning and legends are born that people can listen to if they have sense enough to recognize the benefit of silence and see darkness as an opportunity for inner light. In the evening, sit under the stars and see what the universe has to offer. The stillness of the night is full of the most varied voices, sounds and whispers if you choose to listen and the black velvet of the night sky is perforated by specks of light as though the light of some eternal universe were hidden behind its plate of darkness. In truth the distant stars are but elegant fire flies that speckle the night with their phosphorescent beauty. The darkness itself contains sights and smells that come from everywhere to assault the senses with their mystery and their promise, from behind the tree, from under the ground, from the depths of the sky. During the daytime, the senses take up the cup of sweet pleasure and drain it dry. They smell the aromatic odors of the world; they delight in the provocative visions the natural world has on offer; they taste the nectar of every edible vegetable and fruit; but behind the formal structure of eyes, ears, nose, mouth, and skin lies a frightening array of sensations in the form of visions, silences, smells and experiences of taste and touch that have the power to rock our inner worlds with the secrets they contain and the wisdom they reveal.

To open your mind and heart to the true messages of the senses is to cross a mythic threshold and find yourself on the front line of spiritual experience. Nothing prevents the natural interaction of the physical world with the higher world of the spirit. There are no compromises, no stages of development, no pretending. There is only the perennial battle to lift the veil that separates us from the direct vision of the Divinity, to see the invisible, to hear the inaudible, to taste the intuitions of the mind with their direct experience of the supernatural and to bask in the feelings of certitude that shower upon the soul that is receptive to the influences of the spirit. The on-going battle of the soul that Islam proclaims as the ultimate challenge of the human condition takes place first and foremost within the life of the senses, as knowledge of the senses becomes wisdom with the power to transform the life experience into a journey toward transcendence of the human condition. The richness and diversity of the world is not experienced in purely physical, palpable, tangible and visible forms, but in view of its symbolic significance that all traditional people imparted to every river, mountain and star.

We go through life witnessing the world through the blessing of sight and we take wing and fly toward the vision of the Divinity witnessed through the "eye" of the heart. We listen to the sound vibrations of every created thing and incorporate their rhythms into the harmony of our waking moments, enriched by the sound of the cricket and the fluttering of the moth, enchanted by the cry of the peacock and enthralled by the thunder and lightning of heaven. We make our way through the world smelling the essence of things from the clove of garlic to lilies in a pond and thus become privy through aromatic smells to the very essence and soul of an object. We occupy our days with the requirements of eating and drinking to sustain the physical body, but even the mundane moments within our everyday lives can take on the magic and mystery of some untold secret if we taste the world through the intuitions that the human mind makes available to us.

It is incredible to think that we rely on the senses in so many ways without ever tapping their true reserves and without ever realizing their full capacity to reveal the inside story of our experience of the world. We eat, drink, smell the flowers and reach out to others without ever waking up to the secret import of these experiences and their effect on psyche and soul. We listen to music, for example, and what do we hear but pleasant melodies that make us smile or move us to their rhythm and beat; but the act of creative love generated by the creation of a beautiful and moving melody and the manner in which the music transports us to other realms are soon forgotten, if never fully realized. We live in the age of communication and are supposed to appreciate the power of words and their ability to communicate meaning and message; but the power of sound to reflect sacred harmonies and to transport us through the resonance and vibratory qualities of sacred revelation, for example, are lost on our busy mentalities.

We hear the sound of life's melody; but we are not truly listening to the music much less appreciate its alluring mystique. Just as the inner faculties of reason, intelligence, heart knowledge, consciousness, spiritual imagination and sacred instinct, all lead us out of ourselves and make transcendence of the human condition possible, so also the five senses and the complementary sixth sense are sentential instruments of knowledge and perception that we need to more fully explore and experience, if we ever wish to understand the universal mystery that underscores all existence. We must recognize this mystery as a fundamental truth of our existential reality, if we are ever to achieve the knowledge of the true reality that all men, scientists included, unequivocally profess to be the ultimate goal of the modern, thinking individual.

Imagine the finger of God upon our sense of touch, the hand of God upon our hands. We could do no wrong and everything we might accomplish with our hands would contain the signature of the Divinity. Imagine seeing and smelling the world through God's eyes and all on behalf of a mutual love between the Divine and the human with which nothing can compare. Imagine the presence of the Divinity taking up residence within the human heart in fulfilment of the promise that the human body is the temple of the spirit and that "the Kingdom of God is within you." The Qur'an tells us explicitly that "God is with you wherever you are" and perhaps a little more ominously that "Allah comes between man and his own heart." There is perhaps no limit to what humans can accomplish, provided our works are measured against the relationship we have with God. The human journey can become a spiritual adventure without taking leave of the reality of this world, by understanding the human senses and the ubiquitous sixth sense, not as instruments to verify the objectivity of the physical world, but rather as portals to a higher world of understanding that attempts to describe the presence of God in the world as well as in the human heart.

We are the bell that when struck resounds with the harmonies of a true reality that binds us together into a seamless whole. We are the reed flute that when blown upon by the "breath of the Compassionate" creates the voice and the soul of the virtuous man. When the human being plays its own delicate instrument and becomes its own reed flute, the sentient portals of the body, like the apertures of the flute, become capable of whispering of God's mysteries. The senses have a story to tell and it will be told. They have a music to play whose reverberations will echo across the wide open spaces of a life well lived. They have a song to sing and it will be sung, so long as the earth abides and humanity is there to experience and absorb the wise messages the senses have to offer.

PART NINE

Ethics and Morality

9.1 Living the Ethical Life of Islam

The principles of ethics and morality, and the modes of thinking and behavior that these principles shed their light upon, lie at the heart of all true spirituality. The Qur'an represents a descent of the essential knowledge of God to humanity. Prayer and the other duties (*arkan*) of Islam serve as spiritual rituals and disciplines to bring us back from the brink and center us again in the remembrance of God as the one, true Reality. The concept of morality and the precepts of the ethical life, however, are specific signposts and clear guidance meant to give shape and coloration to the way we live our lives and interact with the community around us.

In the modern world, we are confronted with the question: Do these artifacts of the traditional and spiritual world penetrate the heart of our human nature as modes of thinking and behavior that are truly a part of our "second nature", or are they merely tolerated as quaint sayings of a former time that bear no relation to the present era. Either we wear these concepts like an old suit of clothes, ready to throw them in a heap when they do not serve our purposes, or we treat them like treasured flowers that we preserve within our hearts as the signposts of the good and happy life. During the course of our day, when it comes time to draw upon their weight and influence, we find that they are dead, dried up concepts that at best we hardly know what to do with and at worst ill-suit our innermost and passionate desires.

The spiritual life echoes with the rhythms and vibrations—not to mention the strict codes of conduct—of ethics and morality. We use these words in conversation as if we know what they actually mean and put them into practice in our lives. Even when we do know what they mean and wear them like a cloak of many colors for the world to see and take note of, we invoke their memory as if we systematically apply them to our lives, when in fact, their true meaning and significance escape us at the very moment when we most need their inspiring influence on our thinking and behavior. We scold each other like naughty children to "be good", "be patient", or "be wise", without fully realizing just how much effort and presence of mind is required to resurrect the virtues of patience and wisdom from the subterranean currents of our lives where they lie buried like some ancient treasure that may never be discovered. The idea of patience and modesty and sincerity float through our minds like white pillow clouds and make us happy with the thought that these virtues are waiting to shower down upon us like blessed drops of rain; but whether they come down to earth or rise up from the ground of our being to touch the world around us as a virtuous mist remains a possibility worth exploring and an experience worth waiting for.

Two other distinct problems emerge from the shadows when we consider the forces at work behind the workings of ethics and morality. We make mistakes and commit indiscretions even at the best of times, when we profess to know what is right and wrong and want to live the good life as a matter of conscience and personal preference. We act as if our weaknesses and mistakes happen in spite of ourselves and our good will. In other words, we have good intentions, but the forces of "human nature" and the human passions and lower emotions lead us in the wrong direction and make us forget "the one thing needful". Secondly, we may commit sins and errors without fully knowing that they are wrong. In this case, it is a question of sheer ignorance and a lack of presence of mind that leads us in the wrong direction. Even if we didn't fully know or understand the wrongful nature of a given behavior or action, we still end up suffering the consequences of that action by virtue of the laws of cause and effect that are always at play within the human setting. We cannot avoid the fact that wrong-doing leads back and has an effect on us, either in body, mind, or soul, no matter how much we would like to pretend otherwise.

The American Transcendentalist Ralph Waldo Emerson, in an essay entitled "Experience", has a short sentence that could easily be overlooked, but that actually serves as a hidden pearl shining with the gleam of an evanescent light before it loses its luster in the chronicles of another age. He wrote: "The man is only half himself, the other half is his expression." The epigram touches upon an idea that has been bothering me now for some time. We are in a sense an "unfinished" creation or only half the person that we should be according to the potential of our human nature. The Breath of pure Spirit lives within us that animates our being and whose eyes and ears we have the capacity to see and hear through, recalling the Islamic saying (*hadith*) of the Prophet Muhammad (PBUH): "I am the hearing that you hear and the seeing that you see." An unanswered question, however, lies deep within our being that follows us around like a lost specter with its haunting mystery: Is it enough to know that we are drawn from the mold of the Divine Image and given life with the "Breath of the Compassionate" (*al-Rahman*)? Is it sufficient to have the essential knowledge of God woven as though with golden thread through the tapestry of our minds with the imprint of the knowledge of the true reality, giving us the ability to behave in a good and wise manner, as we act out our lives as the truest expression of the best of ourselves? Is our physical self, our identify, our accomplishments and successes, our professional vocations and our services to humanity only half the story, as Emerson seems to be suggesting, the other half being the fullest expression of the inmost self, representing all the goodness and love of the individual soul as a natural outpouring of the highest emotion the human being is capable of, so that our "fullest expression" becomes the reflection of the qualities of beauty, goodness, and truth that is the implicit message behind all the principles of ethics and morality?

In the same article, Emerson goes on to suggest another thought enclosed within his typically compressed 19th century pastoral style: "Man is a golden impossibility. The line he must walk is a hair's breadth. The wise through excess of wisdom is made a fool."[155] It is an amazing thought, like many of his well-crafted insights, that echoes well with the lingering questions of ethics and morality that confront us in today's fast-paced world. The miracle of the human being would be an "impossibility" without the creative Hand of a Supreme Intelligence; the great divide that exists between the traditional and modern worlds would amount to nothing more than a hair's breadth impossible to cross; all the advances of modern science would add up to nothing more than the "wisdom of a fool" without the higher principles of ethics and morality to guide us through the insecurities and hardships that life presents us with. Between the Supreme Principle of a universal knowledge and the way we express ourselves in our thoughts and actions through the course of our lives in this modern world lies a fine line indeed, recalling the sword bridge of Islam–thinner than a hair and sharper than a knife–that spans the abyss of Hell and across which all true believers must somehow successfully pass in order to enter the Paradise.

We will not only walk the sword bridge on the Day of Judgment. In a manner of speaking, we walk the sword bridge over the abyss every day of our lives when we are confronted with the great questions of ethics and morality that we must find answers to. We are constantly called upon to make choices, to give shape to our desires, to set goals that will fully represent who we are, and to make our dreams realities that we want to represent us in our lives. To behave according to the moral and ethical precepts of the religion is like walking the hair's breadth between good and evil, similar to crossing the sword bridge over the abyss of hell in order to gain entry into Heaven. There is a wise saying that really sums up what we need to remember every day of our lives. "What you are

---

[155] *Essays,* (Boston: Houghton, Mifflin and Company, 1891), p. 59.

is God's gift to you. What you make of yourself is your gift to God."[156] In other words, we are given our human nature as a divine gift; but the kind of person we are and what we are able to accomplish become the "other half" of our expression, our gift back to God as our truest expression and the best of ourselves, the golden impossibility that Emerson made reference to over a hundred years ago.

According to the Book of Deuteronomy in the Bible (30:14), "the word is very near you; it is in your mouth and in your heart, so that you can do it." Ethics and Morality are "big capital letter words" in our mouth and in our minds that we use with ease; but they are words that we rarely fully understand and they are not necessarily in our hearts. They are every bit as big as other such "capital letter" words as Goodness and Evil, Conscience and Consciousness. We hold these words in effigy in our minds only to lose them by the wayside in their journey into the deep cavern of our hearts. For example, do we always have clear answers to how we should treat one another and is there a "golden rule" that applies to all and everyone, the doctor, the street cleaner, the lawyer, the teacher, the tea boy? What is right and what is wrong; and do we know the difference between the two when we need to know how to act. Islam provides clear guidance through the Qur'an and the example of the Prophet clearly stated throughout his accumulated sayings (*hadith*); but do our passions and desires, the expressions of the *nafs al-ammarah* [12:53] (the soul that blames) that the Qur'an ominously reminds us of, lead us away from our true selves and drag us downward into further ignorance and wrong-doing when they are not held in check against the evil temptations of the world working on the frail duality of our human nature that wants to be good, but that leans toward evil in spite of itself?

Before moving any deeper into an analysis of more particular principles of the moral life, let us first define our terms. The term morality serves as the grand principle of right and wrong and characterizes in a word all that is good and evil in the world. As mega-principle, it represents a way of life, the coloration of thought processes, the sharpness of a decision and the great field of our behavior and actions that end up determining the quality of our lives and defining who we are with reference to the truth. Morality fills the grand tapestry of our lives with its colorations, woven with the threads of the principles of ethics and all the virtues that distinguish and shed light on all that we think and do. Morality is the grand symphony of the good life; while the principles and rules of what we call ethics comprise all the individual instruments that give coloration and sound to our actions and behavior, its vibration and its rhythm.

Ethics, on the other hand, represents the standards and particular principles, the threads of the tapestry as it were or the instruments of sound in a masterpiece of music, that we use in order to make judgments and interpretations based on the over-arching principles of morality. For example, abortion may be considered

---

[156] Kathleen Finneran, *The Tender Land* (Boston: Houghton Mifflin Company, 2000), p. 3.

a moral or immoral action based on ethical judgments that arise from the principles of morality being applied within the context of an individual situation. As such, it is not unusual or unthinkable to realize that different societies and cultures might end up having different ethical judgments on a given issue, depending on the principles of morality that they based these judgments on and the cultural and societal context within which these principles are put into action. The Islamic traditions are quite specific about the precise time of the commencement of what we call human life within the fetus, beyond which it is considered murder to terminate the progressive development of the infant embryo, but this may not be the same and hold true within different cultures.

For practical purposes, ethics can be conveniently subdivided into three basic categories in order to deal with the issues that arise within the specifically modern context. After all, life within the modern world is a unique expression of the human enterprise with its ever-emerging new technologies and narrowly restricted scientific attitudes based on the model of the physical world as the only reality, far different from the life of earlier peoples with their more traditional point of view and spiritual way of understanding themselves and the world.

Within the Islamic context, there exists a meta-morality representing principles of a higher order of magnitude cleared presented (revealed let us not forget) in the Qur'an that accounts for the origin and source of the moral principles that drive and give direction to our lives. These mega-principles clearly lay out a moral and ethical system of thought and action that is indisputable and clear. Some people may not fully agree with it; but that does not degrade its absolute and original quality with its particular coloration, not to mention its comforting certitude. Normative ethics find their basis in the principles that regulate and guide human conduct, principles that are well identified in the Qur'an that clearly indicate what is right and what is wrong.

Applied ethics represents the study of particular problems or precise issues with the application of moral ideals that are laid out as principles within normative and specific questions of ethics. Applied ethics cuts across all aspects of life from the political to the legal to the social, and provides humanity with a standard and a principled foundation upon which to base ethical behavior and human actions generally. "What do we mean by the good?" would be a meta-moral concern. "What should we do to be good?" would be a normatively ethical concern. "Is abortion or capital punishment moral" would be a specifically applied ethical question.

9.2 Ethics through History

For our limited purposes here and to give some historical context to the discussion, we can trace the early stages in the development of attitudes concerning ethics and morality back to the Greek philosophers since they have set the stage for what followed in terms of the development of what we refer to as Western civilization, from the Greeks to the Romans and then onward with the rise of Christianity and finally Islam with its unique brand of morality fully summarized within the principle of unity at the heart of Islam.

Socrates (c. 469 BC – 399 BC), a classical Green Athenian, was one of the first Greek philosophers to encourage both scholars and common people to turn their attention from the outside world toward the inner condition of humanity for the purposes of living the good life. He emphasized the importance of self knowledge and considered it to be an essential good that would lead to success and happiness, the two most important motivating forces of humanity within the prevailing Greek philosophy of the time. "Know thyself" was a phrase that was written over the portico of the temple at Delphi and was later repeated within the traditions of Islam in which man himself (the Qur'anic *insan* [humanity]) serves as a "human revelation" that needs to be discovered and understood within the earthly context. A self-knowing and self-aware person will act completely within his or her capabilities, while an ignorant and unaware person will make mistakes and not fulfill the naturally human ambition for success and happiness. Socrates suggested that people would naturally do what is good, if they know what is right. Evil was considered the result of ignorance. If a criminal were truly aware of the mental and spiritual consequences of his actions, stripped naked of all his passions of ego and psychotic complexes of the mind, he would not commit those evil actions. Anyone who truly knows what is right will automatically act in a righteous manner, according to Socrates. In other words, he associated knowledge with virtue, while he understood that virtue led to happiness. The wise man knows what is right and acts in keeping with that knowledge. This is what makes him wise. So far as it went, it was not a bad philosophy and served him well in his own life.

Aristotle (384 BC – 322 BC), a student of Plato and teacher of Alexander the Great, developed an ethical system that was based on self-realization. In Aristotle's view, when a person acts in accordance with his true nature and realizes his full potential, he will perform good actions and be happy. At birth, a baby is a potential person awaiting further development. It is only when the true potential of the child is realized that it becomes a moral and ethical person. Unhappiness and frustration are caused by the unrealized potential of a person, leading to lack of success and further unhappiness. In his view, happiness was considered to be the ultimate goal of life and sought after to the best of one's ability. All other things, such as community life or wealth were merely a means to an end and not the end in itself. Self realization, the awareness of one's true nature, and the development of a person's talents and abilities were considered to be the surest path to happiness in this world.

Aristotle wrote that the human being had essentially three natures: comprising the vegetable or physical, the animal or emotional, and the rational or mental. Physical nature can be expressed through exercise and care of the body. Emotional nature could be expressed through the expression of the instincts and natural sentiments or emotions that course through our lives like rivers of feeling and sensation. The mental nature could be expressed through the precise calculations of human reason. Rational development was considered the most important faculty and uniquely human, distinguishing humanity from the animals. Moderation was encouraged and all extremes were considered low level and unethical. For example, courage was considered a moderate virtue between the extremes of cowardice and recklessness. It is not good enough to simply live in smug ignorance of potential goodness, well-being and virtue, but to live well with conduct governed by the enveloping sense of virtue and seasoned with the exotic spices of the individual virtues. This was not considered easy, because virtue means doing the right thing, to the right person, at the right time, in the right manner, and for the right reasons.

Two other movements within the historical records of the ancient world are worth noting in this context. Hedonism was a movement whose principle ethic was the maximizing of pleasure and the minimizing of pain. There were several schools of Hedonist thought ranging from those advising the indulgence of every momentary desire to those teaching the pursuit of spirituality. In consideration of consequences, the Hedonists advocated self-gratification regardless of the pain and/or expense to others or perhaps without undue worry about its ripple effects. The broader health and well being of the society was not a major concern. In general, they thought it important to maximize pleasure and happiness in this life for most people. Obviously, this expression of ethics was very limited and superficial and does not address the essential dilemma of what evil and over indulgence mean and how these things can affect the quality of a person's life, not to mention the greater society and civilization that people live within.

Another movement was called Epicureanism, established by an ancient Greek philosopher named Epicurus (341 – 270 BC). He rejected the extremism of the Hedonists, believing some pleasures and enjoyments to have a negative effect on human beings. He observed that pursing every enjoyment sometimes resulted in negative consequences, a concept that we are most familiar with now in the modern world with all the different problems we experience now, such as pollution and ill-health that are the direct result of too much pleasure. Some experiences were rejected by the Epicureans out of hand and some experiences could be endured in order to ensure a better life in the future. The main idea of this movement was prudence through moderation and caution. Anything done to excess was considered bad, such as overeating.

Finally, the ancient Greek world witnessed a movement called Stoicism. The Stoic philosopher Epictetus (55 AD – 135 AD), whose teachings were written down by his pupil Arrian in his *Discourses*, developed a philosophy that considered the greatest good to be contentment and serenity. Peace of mind was thought to be the highest value and self-mastery over one's desires and emotions would lead to spiritual peace. We can see that this movement was completely different from the Hedonist and Epicurean approach to life and represented an ethical philosophy that valued self-control, discipline, and balance. It encouraged control of the emotions, such as anger and hatred, together with freedom from material attachments, unlike the Hedonists who focused on the pleasures attainable in this world. If a person should die, then those close to him should hold to their serenity because the loved one was made of flesh and blood destined to die like us all. Epictetus said that different problems in life should not be avoided, but rather embraced as something that would make a person stronger. It is interesting to note that these movements arose in view of the absence of clear guidance from the religions that existed at that time in what is called the classical period of the Greek and the Roman eras. It would take entry into the coming millennia for people to realize that they need to come to terms with their own philosophy of ethics and morality and realize that they must make active moral and ethical choices regarding their behavior and actions in life.

9.3 Modern Ethics

We would be negligent in the expression of our theme if we did not make at least a superficial reference to the idea of modern and contemporary morality and various points of ethics that support that morality. Needless to say, it needs no elaboration to confirm that the modern psyche, indeed the modern soul of humanity, places its trust in three basic components of thought that not only define and shape the very nature of modern-day thinking, but that also inadvertently lay the foundation and groundwork for a grand philosophy of morality and ethics that bears virtually no relationship to the principles of ethics and morality that form the backbone of traditional, religious, and spiritual guidance down through the ages from ancient times. We are referring to the modern scientific worldview, the theory of evolution now considered a proven scientific law, and finally the notion of progress that is the inevitable by-product of the scientific worldview and evolution, its ultimate hope and its fatal attraction, all leading to the illusion the humanity can somehow "figure it all out" on its own without the aid of heaven and without the perennial guidance contained within the world revelations.

We have noted elsewhere within this book that the modern scientific outlook and its supporting worldview virtually dominate the intellectual thinking of the modern world with its insistence on physical reality as being both starting and end point of an inquiry into the true nature of reality. Needless to say, this notion conflicts seriously with the traditional point of view that commences in the Spirit of God and will find its end-station and resting point back in the Spirit of God having traversed the grade circle of life. According to modern science, no such inquiry into the true nature of Reality can be made without first making the assumption that reality itself is grounded in the physical plane of existence. While not a proven fact, it is a given, a foundational premise upon which the entire philosophy of modern science is constructed. No self-respecting scientist, philosopher or rational thinker in the modern era genuinely entertains anything else in his heart of hearts than the secular, materialistic and matter-bound process of inquiry that has taken hold of the Western mentality during the present day, a mentality that is spreading fast into a global mentality that will soon be impossible to challenge with any credible alternative. Today's scientific worldview is based on the principle of matter as the overriding "ground" of reality, and the scientific method of inquiry, through the rigors of logic and mathematics, the established physical laws of the universe, and the power of reason and physical evidence through the scientific method of observation to arrive at a clear notion of the reality.

Do we belabor the point? Perhaps we do at the risk of sounding pedantic, but why not state things clearly as they are meant to be understood. If there is a body of knowledge to be internalized and a "grand divine" to be crossed between two systems of belief that amount to the traditional and modern worldviews, then people have a right to be presented with and understand the true nature of the choice to be made. When it comes to understanding such issues as the true nature of humanity, the life and destiny of the soul, the significance of the natural order set within the scope of a vast universe that bespeaks of eternity and infinity, modern-day individual have the right to know the issues involved and the consequences that are at stake when it comes to making vital choices that will affect the very destiny of their lives here on earth.

In the scientific worldview that most people today live in the shadow of, even if they profess to believe in and follow the path of one of the great world religions, members of the grand species *Homo sapiens* are regarded as autonomous entities without any internal connection with the universe beyond the purely physical one. They exist as it were apart from God and apart from any kind of force that could be characterized as spiritual, other-worldly, or blessed in the knowledge of God. They have not been created by God and they will not return to God, in contradiction to the simple, yet eloquent Qur'anic verse "We come from God and to Him we shall return." (2:152) The human being is considered to be nothing more than an individual and finite creature that has a particular moment in time and will eventually disappear back into the energy of the cosmos as dispersed particles (of dust), nothing more and indeed nothing less, since this is portrayed to be enough to support the inner desires and instincts of the human entity. He/she enjoys a faculty called reason, a faculty that is most notably cut off from both Revelation and the Intellect which belongs to the supra-human level of reality that science denies, yet the modernite individual professes to believe that reason alone somehow illuminates the human mind through a light of its own making. Human reason has become a virtual idol or mini-god today because it is regarded as the sole instrument that can navigate its way through the sea of universal mystery and that can lead people to a destination they know not where, but secretly hope will represent some kind of "progress" from the world they now live in. Anything that transcends the faculty of human reason is treated quite simply as non-verifiable knowledge or worse, as the sub-product of an over-ripe and misguided imagination.[157]

---

[157] There are some scientists who want to reduce man to his lowest common denominator and render him not much more profound than a simple, well oiled

The modern scientific worldview asserts that life, consciousness, and self-awareness—among many other faculties that represent the inner life of the individual—are nothing but manifestations of complex arrangements of inanimate particles that have evolved in a fortuitous way to result in the phenomenon of thoughts and desires within the human mind and psyche. Modern science proclaims the existence of the phenomenal world that constitutes a universe as an independent reality of its own that can be studied and known in an ultimate sense, without any reference to a higher order of magnitude and without knowledge of a universal Creator. Space, time, matter, motion and energy establish the parameters of the physical world and thus are expressed and believed-in realities that are independent of any higher order of being and are cut off from the power and influence of a Supreme Being. The physical world is portrayed as a mechanical world that is the subject of mathematics and strict rules of quantification. Anything in nature that does not fall within that rubric and is in essence non-quantifiable is irrelevant to the study of modern science or the modern individuals who lay out the parameters of that science. Faith in the veracity of these suppositions serves as the lodestar for modern civilization and as a guiding light for the evolving, modern worldview.

The theory of evolution, which today is understood to be a *de facto* law of evolution, completely dominates the intellectual and psychic horizon of our time with its insistence on a transmigration of species that began with a single cell, progressed through the amphibians and reptiles to the sweet-singing birds of the air, only to have the monkeys and baboons climb down from the trees to enter the savannah as Neanderthals in search of an avenue of escape from their brute minds into the cognitive world of *Homo sapiens*. The theory of evolution is based on the premise that biological mutations take place, not only within species (referred to as micro-evolution), but also across species (referred to as macro-evolution), amounting to a grand parade of mutative development that migrates across species. It is actually a theory by analogy, in other words, what takes place within a species, such as the development of the horse for example, can take place from one species to another, as in the scenario that the fishes developed legs and walk onto the land. Regrettably, the hypothesis of evolutionary trans-species mutation lacks even a single convincing thread of evidence that would substantiate the hypothesis into a more credible theory. The entire architecture of

---

machine. Richard Dawkins, an aggressive proponent of numerous "evolutionary tales", has suggested in his book *The Selfish Gene* that we can think of ourselves as "survival machines," invented through evolutionary tinkering by ancient replicators, snippets of DNA. In speaking of "genes", Dawkins has written: "Now they swarm in huge colonies safe inside gigantic lumbering robots, sealed off from the outside world, communicating with it by tortuous indirect routes, manipulating it by remote control. They are in you and in me; they created us, body and mind; and their preservation is the ultimate rationale for our existence. They have come a long way those replicators. Now they go by the names of genes, and we are their survival machines." Oxford University Press, USA; 30th Anniversary edition (May 25, 2006), p. 20.

modern science in coming to terms with the true nature of humanity has been built on the theory of evolution, a theory that not only affects the development of living things on the biological level, but that is also speculated upon with reference to the molecular constitution of the human brain. As a result, the theory of evolution also shapes and gives color to the human understanding regarding the development of human consciousness, verbal and cognitive, not to mention, the emotional capacity of humans and their ability to express emotive intelligence. In other words, the theory is now far-reaching and remains a major component of the modern scientific worldview that no one openly denies without risking ridicule and rejection from mainstream, intellectual thinking.

Finally, the idea of progress has taken hold of the imagination of modern-day scientists, thinkers, and philosopher to the extent that progress is now considered an elemental part of the modern philosophy of life. After centuries of philosophical, anthropological, sociological and scientific development, the conclusions we have reach from our observations of the human being and his world are: Mechanism, materialism, secularism, evolution(ism) and a firm belief in progress as the ideological counterpart of evolution. In other words, we live for things and the pleasure they promise and we live for ourselves and the pleasures we experience. We reflect the mechanism implicit in the theory of evolution and we glory in the efficiency of the machine by becoming machines ourselves. We have abandoned the spiritual perspective together with the knowledge and wisdom that has shaped the mind and life of traditional man down through the ages. We blindly aspire to a philosophy of human progress and development, even though everything within the chaos and deterioration of our existing world, including the absence of morality and the sub-standard ethics of the mass population, point to a fundamental regression of the human entity. The value system that people pretend to uphold belies the myth that humanity is advancing forward, much less upward toward higher principles of virtue and morality. The field of technology is the one area of advancement that truly astounds. Even there, however, the advancement is so spectacular and swift that the human mind still has not been able to fully accommodate its implications or develop the *raison d'etre* and true purpose of these technical achievements, beyond of course their principal monetary value. The primary efficacy of science lies in its technical applicability, while it remains indifferent, if not antagonistic, to the spiritual dimension of reality. Instead, the primary thrust of modern science is to explain away the spiritual dimension by simply denying its existence.

I have used the collective "we" in the previous paragraph in order to align myself with the contemporary "we", the vast collectivity identified as contemporary man, for we cannot pretend to live in the modern age without being modern ourselves, no matter how much we wish to abide by our spiritual heritage. Yet somehow, in spite of all the incredible technological advances in molecular biology, medical science, and genetic engineering, we maintain a superficial approach to investigating the true nature of reality. We as a civilization maintain and encourage a literal and purely analytic approach to the unknown mystery that surrounds us, together with a stubborn unwillingness to expand beyond the particularized, quantitative and exacting search for a knowledge that proposes to enrich us and make us happy. In spite of ourselves, we cannot overlook the fact that we are influenced by this world and are the products of such a world. We live now in the 21st century, on the threshold of a new millennium; but we cannot deny the fact that the reality of our existing environment and the prevailing secular and materialistic ambiance of our world affect our bodies, our minds, our attitudes, our sentiments, our emotions, and ultimately our souls.

Under the influence of misguided notions of the philosophy of modern science and its related worldview, the ever-present theory of evolution, and the idea of progress in humanity's development, we have arrived at and try to utilize within our lives a kind of "experimental ethics" based on notions of morality that have no clear basis in the well-established principles of the traditional religions. In a sense, it is "every man for himself" when it comes to knowing what is right and what is wrong, since the traditional religious viewpoints are no longer the guiding light that influences and shapes the mind and behavior of humanity and no longer provide the grounding principles that were traditionally the origin and source of the moral life of earlier times. Basically, the post-modern viewpoint is heavily theoretical, follows a fragmented, anti-authoritarian course and falls between the two cracks in the wall of narcissism and nihilism, narcissism being none other than the preoccupation of the individual ego with itself and no one else, and nihilism being a philosophy of nothingness that places no real and enduring value on the life of this or any world.

Applied ethics has become a discipline of philosophy that attempts to apply ethical theory to real-life situations, such as bioethics, business ethics, or engineering ethics. Most of us are now familiar with applied ethics when determining questions that come up in the public domain and that concern the society at large. "Is abortion immoral?" "Is euthanasia immoral?" "What are human rights, and how do we determine them?" Without these questions, there is no clear way to balance law, politics and the practice of decision-making. In fact, there would be no common assumptions of all participants. Other kinds of questions that come into play include such things as "Is lying always wrong?" and "If not, when is it permissible?" Needless to say, applied ethics can run into serious problems of credibility and sustainability in its implementation when the universal principles found within the great world religions no longer serve as the basis in establishing human morality and ethics across the civilization.

9.4 Islamic Ethics

Wisdom's journey through the life of a Muslim is nothing less than a journey beyond this world, traveling toward a supreme certainty in which Muslims become true travelers embarking on a maiden voyage beyond the realm of fact and fiction, a journey to the very limits of the way we imagine our world to be, a journey beyond known borders into the tempting allure of the Unseen and the Unknown. It commences with trust in the certitude of the s*hahadah* or testimony of faith in Islam when the Muslim acknowledges his or her place in the Divine Plan with a mental, psychic, and spiritual surrender to the Will of the Supreme Being, a surrender that ultimately becomes physical through the full prostration during the prayer ritual when the Muslims arrive in close proximity with the Presence when their foreheads meet the ground. The wisdom implicit in this surrender takes the road of virtue in order to make itself known within the life of an individual through thoughts, words and actions that weave personal destiny into the fabric of their lives. It is a road of virtue that has no true limit because its final destination is truly unattainable, at least within this world, but remains as a goal for all to work towards. Wisdom's journey is as perpetual as the river of life until it merges once again into the sea of universality that Islam identifies as the Spirit of the One (*al-Ahad*).

Within the Islamic perspective, when God created man, He endowed humans with an intelligence that is both integral and intuitive, a will that is both powerful and free, and a soul that is both radiant and translucent. In consequence, these three divine gifts allow Muslims the possibility of a faith (*iman*) that is enlightening as well as total, a submission (*islam*) that is both courageous and liberating, and a moral and therefore virtuous life that is both innocent and perfecting. Virtue brings about the full realization of the knowledge of the *shahadah* and the certainty of faith, thereby bringing to near perfection human intelligence, faith, and willful surrender to God. Intelligence reflects a mode of thought and perception; free will reflects a mode of choice and of action; virtue reflects a mode of living and thus a mode of being. Because of the human excellence expressed through virtue, the Muslim soul can participate in the perfect equilibrium of knowledge and love through actions that become refined by means of virtue and the individual virtues. In return, the benefit of the virtues is that they generously lend their sweet aura of innocence to the formal modes of knowledge. In other words, knowledge finds its purpose in action, action finds its purpose in virtue, and virtue confirms what knowledge sets out to proclaim.

Faith is a secret alliance between humanity and God. Surrender is a proclamation of the faithful who identify themselves as Muslims, as a formal religious posture. Virtue, however, is the definitive statement of the soul as it sheds its colors and aspects and spreads across both the inner and outer life of the seeker. Through virtue, the human aura glows.[158] As such, it requires a heightened presence of mind and a devotional piety that goes well beyond the standard norms of the faith and surrender required of every believer. To see the Unseen (*al-Ghaib*) with the "eye of the heart" is not one of God's gifts, but rather

---

[158] The visualization of spiritually harmonized forces is common to the religious traditions. The halo is a common feature of the Christian tradition, whereas Buddhism assigns a similar manifestation to the entire body in the form of a spiritual aura. Muslim traditions refer to the light on the face of the believing servant of God.

one of His challenges. As we have already suggested, faith may be a mode of thinking and surrender may be a mode of living, but virtue is a mode of being. Like happiness, the sustained effort to achieve a life-long spirituality behind the face of virtue is very difficult to achieve, much less maintain. Most people are fickle, inflexible and weak and find it difficult to maintain balance and harmony within the 24/7 of their lives; they need the rituals and spiritual disciplines of the religion to liberate them from their inherent limitations. Still, if happiness is the motivation, then virtue is the means through which holy sentiment is expressed in a happy and balanced soul.

Virtuous actions are direct references back to the Divinity, when a person becomes their own proof of the existence of God by virtue of their reflection of the divine light. More than anything else, virtue expresses the best of a person as he or she is summarized within the soul. It remembers most directly the primordial condition of the paradisal man and woman, who enjoyed a natural state of virtuous innocence that reflected and complemented the primordial environment. The object of knowledge is Truth or the Reality that projects that Truth. The object of the will is to choose the Good and reject the evil alternative. The object of virtue is to love God in such a way that the full range of the virtues becomes apparent. Essentially we make shadows in this world; something else beyond the horizon of the known universe shines down its light upon us.

Virtue comes to light and makes itself known within humanity most specifically through the individual virtues, which are the endlessly varied modalities of the principle of virtue, just as the colors of the spectrum are the subtle variations of the one light. Each of the virtues is an individual key that unlocks the latent perfections of the soul. They are attitudes and modalities of the mind that become imprinted on the soul as qualities and beauties once they have passed through the heart of the believer as intelligence and through a person's behavior as virtuous actions. The individual virtues enter the soul and find their place gradually over the course of a lifetime. As in moving from darkness to light mentioned in the Qur'an, they slowly uproot and supplant the imperfections and darkness that are polar opposites to the perfection and light of the virtues.

Virtue cannot lie and still be what it is. Genuine virtue draws its substance and its meaning from knowledge and presentiment of the Divine Reality that underlies everything in life. Whatever knowledge people possess about the ultimate reality will shine through their thoughts, words, and virtuous actions. The more the Muslims yearn to become virtuous, the more they will develop the means to attain the divine names and qualities that differentiate the virtues. In of compensation, the believer can experience the benefits of the divine names and qualities as real once they are firmly fixed within the soul through the virtues.

Thus, the human expression of an Islamic spirituality finds its most comprehensive statement in the combined effects of the Muslim's faith, surrender, and virtuous soul. Faith becomes the human expression of the mind's intelligence as it identifies itself with the intelligence of the Supreme Being. The free surrender through conformity to God's law becomes the true expression of the heart's desire and proclaims the witnessing in thought, word, and action. Finally, virtue, with its ethereal fragrance and its aura of latent luminosity, becomes the outward expression of the soul's essence. The knowledge of God and the choices of free will unite to form a beauty and a nobility of soul that share in the rays of the divine light. "Some faces that day will beam with beauty and light, as they gaze on their Lord." (75: 22)

Virtue lends brilliance and depth to the human face that reveals in the sculptured texture of flesh and bone a radiance of soul that only the human being can achieve. Radiance that is reflected as a message of the human face comes about through a presence of mind that embodies faith and an effort of will that projects complete submission to the truth. This radiance of soul is none other than the soul's fulfilment of an obligation it has borne throughout earthly time: To project into the face of the world the true radiance of the Face of God.

Virtue comes to light and makes itself known within humanity most specifically through the individual virtues, which are the endlessly varied modalities of the principle of virtue, just as the colors of the spectrum are the subtle variations of the one light. Each of the virtues is an individual key that unlocks the latent perfections of the soul. They are attitudes and modalities of the mind that become imprinted on the soul as qualities and beauties once they have passed through the heart of the believer as intelligence and through his behavior as virtuous actions.

The individual virtues enter the soul and find their place gradually over time through the repeated imprint of their quality. As in the movement from darkness to light mentioned in the Qur'an, they slowly uproot and supplant the imperfections and darkness that are polar opposites to the perfection and light of the virtues. Humility represents a quality of soul, for example, when the believer fully recognizes his or her true position as one of utter dependence on the beneficence and mercy of God. Humility elevates one's nothingness to the level of sincere awareness, often called the greatest of the virtues because it ultimately implies a denial of the ego and the assertion of the soul in the Spirit of God.

The concept of morality, contrary to modern-day and contemporary moral concepts, centers on certain basic principles and beliefs within the Islamic worldview. Among the main beliefs is the credo of belief in the one God as the Creator and Source of all goodness, truth, and beauty. Humans are is the *khalifah* of Allah and God's noble representatives here on earth. The entire created universe is placed at the service of humanity so that people fulfill the destiny of soul that they were created to pursue, God does not expect the impossible from humanity or hold people accountable for anything beyond their power. In addition, people may enjoy the good things of life, but must exercise moderation, practicality and balance as the safeguard of high integrity and sound morality. Everything is permissible in principle as long as it doesn't violate the laws of the natural order and unless it is singled out as forbidden in the Qur'an and *hadith*. Divorce, for example, while frowned upon in Islam, is clearly identified by the Prophet as the worst among the permissible, and is allowed in certain situations.

The dimensions of morality in Islam are far-reaching and comprehensive, unlike in today's modern world, in that the religion deals with all facets of life. Islamic morals deal with the relationship between man and God, man and his fellow men, man and the other elements and creatures of the universe, man and his innermost self. Muslims need to guard their external behavior and actions, their words and thoughts, feelings and intentions within the framework of the Islamic spiritual framework. The Muslim should champion what is right and condemn what is wrong, seek what is true and reject what is false, appreciate what is beautiful and avoid what is indecent.

Basically, truth and virtue are the ultimate goals of the human individual. The overriding attitude between man and God is a relationship characterized by surrender and love, complete trust and thoughtful service. In the relationship with one's fellow man, the Muslim must show kindness and concern for the neighbor, respect for parents and the elderly and compassion for the young, care for the sick and support for the needy, sympathy for the aggrieved, cheerfulness for the depressed, patience with the misguided, tolerance toward the ignorant, and forgiveness for the wrong-headed. In short, we must internalize all of the qualities and virtues that are modeled on the Supreme Being through the ninety-nine names of God, qualities and attributes that we must reflect within our character and personality as the personal components of the moral life.

When God prohibits certain things, it is not because He wants to deprive humanity of anything good or useful. It is because He means to protect people and allow them to develop a good sense of discrimination, a refined taste for the better things in life, and a continued interest in higher moral values. To achieve this, good care must be taken of the mind and spirit, soul and body, conscience and sentiments, health and well being, physique and morale, provision and wealth. To show that all prohibitions are acts of mercy and wisdom, two Islamic principles are worth mentioning in this context. First, extraordinary circumstances, necessities and emergencies allow the Muslim to do what is normally forbidden. Secondly, God has inscribed for Himself the rule of mercy: Individuals who do evil out of ignorance, but thereafter repent and amend their conduct, will be forgiven since "God is Merciful and Oft-forgiving." (6:54)

The Qur'an is full of verses that guide Muslims toward the moral life, leaving little doubt how to lead the moral life. The challenge lies in fulfilling the mandate of the Islamic way of living (*al-din*) by actually living the Muslim life. The Islamic morals are unique in their nature and address all circumstances with common sense, tolerance, and flexibility. They are meant to help individuals to develop their personality and cultivate their character in the most wholesome manner possible, to strengthen their bonds with others and consolidate their associations with God as the source of all Goodness. If Muslims are wronged or oppressed, they have the free choice either to resist and retaliate in an equal measure, although preference is to forgive and entrust God with the results of the evil actions of others. These are the principles that form the basis and foundation of all moral behavior within the Islamic framework.

9.5 The Individual Virtues

The term *taqwa* comes repeatedly in the Qur'an, so much so that the Muslims must begin to wonder what it really means in terms of their behavior; not to regard it only as a concept written on the page of a book, but rather as a concept that is written upon the mind and heart. It lies there as a virtue within the treasure chest of the human faculties ready to be called upon for awakening when people need its service. Piety is none other than knowledge and awareness of God's reality, reverence and awe in the face of God's truth in the same way that we feel reverence and awe in the presence of royalty on this earth, fear and trembling as when we feel the power of nature through thunder and lightning or the forces of an earthquake or tsunami. Piety as an internal attitude speaks of a knowledge of the Unseen (*al-ghaib*) which lies at the heart of the religion and is the core secret of all spirituality. We are able through piety to transcend the limitations of this world for the world of the spirit that the virtue of piety responds to.

The virtue of piety focuses the human self on the Divine Self. It creates an implicit awareness within the soul of the believer he is and who God is. Piety represents an appreciation of the knowledge of God and a feeling for one's true level in the spiritual hierarchy of being. The pious man walks cautiously along the path of return, with his consciousness of God in his mind and a sense of the presence of God in his heart. For the pious man, life is sacred and God is everywhere, in keeping with the Qur'anic verse: "To God belongs the East and the West. Wherever you turn, there is the Face of God." (2: 115)

The Qur'an clearly identifies the pious Muslim as one who is firm and steadfast in the performance of the prayer ritual five times a day and those who spend of the provision that Allah has provided them. This represents moral actions that reconfirm their awareness of the reality and what should be important in their lives. The pious person also has a clear belief in the Qur'an as the revelation and words of God and a firm belief in the Hereafter as the bottom line of their virtuous actions. Obviously, those who believe in the Hereafter also believe that there will be a Day of Accounting, which is alternatively called the Day of Religion in Islam (*yawm al-din*). All of their actions are moral actions by virtue of the fact that there will be a scale and a balance to everything they do and their actions will be weighed in the balance on the Day of Judgment.

The virtue of sincerity, on the other hand, complements piety's consciousness with truthful sentiment. In other words, sincerity feels internally what piety comes to know externally. Sincerity fills the believer with an ever-increasing presentiment of the Truth. The Muslim turns toward God with a truthfulness of purpose that overlays all worship and spiritual devotions with frank honesty. Sincerity opens wide the door of the heart for the arrival of the Divine Presence. Eventually, sincerity flowers into an increased awareness that animates all worship and all action with a profound sense of the sacred and of the truth that underlies all things. The Muslims have been commanded to be sincere in all their thoughts and actions, but especially in their intentions. Without sincerity, everything that we think and do becomes in effect a lie. The words that we use, the ideas that we communicate, and the sentiments and feelings that we convey to others are all lacking the fundamental component of sincerity. "Which is better;' he who sets his foundation on piety to Allah and His good pleasure, or he who lays his foundation on a sand cliff ready to crumble to pieces?" (9: 109) Piety heightens the consciousness of the believer, while sincerity heightens understanding and feeling for the Divine. These two virtues act as a coloration of soul for all spiritual devotions, and reward the person with feelings of certainty and love that become the very foundation of further worship.

Humility represents a quality of soul when people fully recognize their true position as one of utter dependence on the beneficence and mercy of God. Humility elevates one's nothingness to the level of sincere awareness and can be called the greatest of the virtues because it ultimately implies a denial of the ego and the assertion of the soul in the Spirit of God. The counterpart to humility is arrogance and pride. No one likes to deal with an arrogant person. Such people have an inflated opinion about themselves that does not correspond to reality. Most arrogant people are impossible to deal with and unpleasant to be with. It is the humble person that fits in anywhere and no one is offended with his or her presence. On the contrary, humble people add an extra dimension and quality to their relationships that is truly admirable.

Charity recreates the denial and affirmation that rests within the heart of the Islamic witnessing (*shahadah*). Charity effectively denies the individual through the giving of the self, for the sake of a greater whole represented through the society at large. Charity leads to greatness of soul because it allows a person to take leave of the self in a practical way and put oneself in the place of others, thus enlarging a person's perspective and softening the heart to the needs of others.

Truthfulness represents truth on the practical level through the power of the word. Humans can only fully identify themselves through speech, so that the truthfulness of their word is the truth within themselves. Watchfulness holds its breath in conscious introspection and waiting. The watchful person is an aware one, who restrains him or herself through the sheer joy of inner self control. Watchfulness partakes of attention to detail, together with supreme vigilance against negligence, or worse, extravagance. Watchfulness transfers to the waiting soul a presence of mind that calls the believers back to the remembrance of the Divinity. As such, it makes the present moment a moment of true remembrance.

Similarly we need to mention patience as a premier virtue worth cultivating. Patience is the sweetest of the virtues in its sapiential benefits to the soul. It is the virtue most difficult to achieve, the virtue most in demand in the course of one's practical life. Life demands patience and often draws on the reserves of patience to see a person through. Indeed, patience requires an inner self control and an outer physical discipline that can often border on the superhuman. Even with its rigor, however, "patience is beautiful" as the Qur'an remind us." (12:18) It focuses inwardly toward the inner self, so that a person has the strength to bear with equanimity the reality of his/her unfolding destiny. Similarly, patience focuses outwardly toward mankind and the world with an equanimity that offers a frank visage of calm understanding to the eccentricities of one's fellow man.

Righteousness (*birr*) is another moral attitude that features highly in the Qur'anic lexicon of virtues. In fact, there is no doubt as to its meaning and intention, clearly stated within the following Qur'anic verse (2:177): "It is not righteousness that you turn your faces (in prayer) towards the East or West; but it is righteousness to believe in God and the Last Day, and the Angels and the Book, and the Messengers; to spend of your wealth, in spite of your love for it, for orphans, for the needy, for the wayfarer, for those who ask, and for the ransom of slaves; to be steadfast in prayer and practice regular charity; to fulfill the contracts which you have made; and to be firm and patient, in pain and adversity, and throughout all period of panic. Such are the people of truth, the God-minded."

This verse clearly paints a picture of the righteous Muslim who should obey all the regulations and should make as a sincere motive the love of God and the love of the Prophet. There are four clear elements worth highlighting: Faith should be pure and sincere, we must be prepared to show it in deeds of charity and kindness to our fellows, we must be good citizens by supporting charitable institutions and social organizations, and we must be steadfast and unshakable in all circumstances. Clearly righteousness is built upon a clear faith in God and belief in what the Qur'an proclaims through its verses. Ultimately, when the Islamic principle of righteousness is firmly established, it provides the individual with inner peace in all circumstances, the society with security on all levels, the nation with solidarity and the international community with hope and harmony, a far cry from what we now have in the world with all of its problems and conflicts among nations. What can be more reassuring than faith in the merciful Creator? What is more honest than the fulfillment of commitments and the preservation of a clear conscience? What is better than the maintenance of honesty and integrity in all dealings? What is more spiritually joyful than being righteous in all things as a matter of course for the love of God?

A word needs to be said clearly at this point on the Islamic concept of sin. It needs no convincing that one of the greatest problematic areas in human existence is the problem or sin and the presence of evil in the world. It is commonly believed worldwide that sin began with Adam and Eve in the Garden of Eden when they disobeyed their Maker and ate of the apple from the tree of knowledge. Islam has taken a unique position on this issue of initial and subsequent sin, a position that is not necessarily shared by the other religious. We know from verses in the Qur'an that Adam and Eve were directed by God to reside in the Garden of Eden and enjoy its provisions as they pleased. They were warned not to approach a particular tree so that they would not run into harm and injustice. Satan tempted and caused them to lose their joyful state. They were expelled from the Garden and brought to earth to live and die in anticipation of the judgment on the Last Day. Having realized what they did, Adam and Eve felt shame, guilt and remorse. In repentance, they prayed for God's mercy and were forgiven their transgressions.

The Qur'anic story reveals that humans (*insan*) are imperfect; but making a mistake does not necessarily corrupt the human heart or stop moral growth. On the contrary, humans have a unique "nature" (*fitrah*) that is original and pure, according to the Qur'an. Human beings have the sensibility to recognize their evils and shortcomings through self-reflection. In addition, they know where to turn in repentance. God is ever prepared to respond to the sincere calls of those who seek His aid. According to the Qur'an (30:30), the human is born in a natural state of purity or *fitrah*. Whatever becomes of the soul after birth is the result of actions and decisions made during the course of life. Life is full of contingencies and circumstances that force us to give shape to our personality and lives. This brings about the formation of the human personality and the moral character of the person. The constant movement between the forces of good and evil represents the supreme struggle in this life. To seek to perform the moral life is to create a life that is interesting and meaningful, all under the shadow of the supreme truth in light of God's true reality.

Although we commit sin through human weaknesses, this is because it is part of our limited nature within the context of this world as imperfect and fallible beings. The true sin is to embrace the evil alternative as a matter of intention and free choice, rather than to live the moral life and seek the perfection that is the true aspect of our human nature created by God as original to humanity and pure. In Islam, all sins are forgivable if the sinner sincerely repents and seeks forgiveness. The Qur'an states clearly that God does not forgive the sin of *shirk* in the form of polytheism, pantheism, belief in a pantheon of gods, etc. because that denies the unity and oneness of the Divinity. However, if the polytheist or atheist comes back to God with true surrender, this sincere repentance will be forgiven. Sins are not inborn; they are avoidable, and are not necessarily inevitable; but they are sometimes committed by the person within the context of this life through ignorance or weakness. If a person does something caused by natural instincts, physical drives, and uncontrollable urges, then such acts are not sins as such in Islam. God demands of Muslims what lies within the human possibility. God does not ask more from an individual than what he/she can bear.

In conclusion, Muslims can thank Allah for the blessing of universal principles based on the Qur'anic revelation and the traditional sayings (*hadith*) of the Prophet, principles that lay the foundation, offer clear guidance, and provide the guiding path toward the ethical and moral life within the context of this world. Not a day goes by in the life of an individual that he or she must make an ethical choice of one sort of another, a choice that will not only directly affect the character and personality of the person, but also lead into the future of one's life with the consequences of one's rightly guided or evil actions. The angry word, the untruth, the broken promise all give evidence to who we are and set the stage for future thought, compounded by the evil of our actions and mistakes.

It has been suggested in the Qur'an (19:71; 37:23) and *hadith* of the Prophet that there is a sword bridge (*sirat*) that all must pass in order to enter the Paradise, a bridge most notably that crosses over the fiery depths of Hell. Implicit in this knowledge is the sword bridge that we cross every day of our lives, through our actions, through our decisions, through the choices that we make that can only lead in one of two direction, namely the path of the humble, the sincere, and the righteous, or the path of the proud, the weak, and the cowardly. Where we end up regarding our destiny depends on the choices we make within the context of a moral and ethical life. The promise of Allah is directly linked to the consequence of how we live our lives and what we are able to accomplish within our destiny.

Are we prepared to cross the fabled sword bridge that will lead us over the hell-fire into the Paradise? Are we ready to meet the challenge that this life has to offer with a challenge of our own to meet the moment that is given us? Are we willing to bite the bullet, as we say in today's vernacular, and live the moral life that our true nature demands of us? The answer to these and other questions will determine the kind of people we will become and shape the unfolding of our future destiny. In commemoration of the small community of Companions close to the Prophet Muhammad (PBUH), whose hearts were on fire with their rejection of this world as an end in itself and whose surrender to the idea of the One God became the very ground they walked upon, we hope to emulate their zeal, imitate their passion, and recreate their commitment with faith in the knowledge of the one God and surrender (*islam*) to His supreme and abiding Will. Are we ready to meet the strength of their memory and the force of this challenge of the modern world? The answer lies with the coming of tomorrow.

Epilogue

Challenge and Crisis

Rhetorical questions can be like boomerangs. They are sent out into the void of this world only to come back to us with surprising answers from another world that haunt our waking moments with their persistent message. A book such as this should ultimately answer rather than ask timely questions. We have ended this work on an unexpected note, however, by asking rather than answering one final question that echoes across the pages like the melancholy sound of a solitary horn recalling distant memories and forgotten sentiments.

We ask it because the Religion of Islam avoids no questions that have a right to be asked, but we cannot answer it without betraying the mandate of every individual to expose the meaning of their lives in light of the Mystery of the Unseen (*al-ghaib*) that confronts people every day of their lives. Certain questions are not answered by the brain, but are lived and experienced in the heart. Indeed, we carry all such questions within us as a remembrance of the perennial mystery that lies at the heart of the life experience. The answer lies not in words but in life itself. Great ideas begin with the human mind; great societies begin with a worldview that makes sense on simple levels; great worldviews begin with individuals attempting to come to terms with the mystery of life, involving people that are willing to follow a path of return, such as we find in the Religion of Islam, in order to reach their true destination and final end in the light of God's truth.

In many ways, the writing of this book has been like taking a journey up to the threshold of a door, to the edge of the world, "through the unknown, remembered gate"[159] that leads to a renewed understanding of time, of nature, and of humanity, in order to uncover the essential knowledge of God in a variety of forms of revelation that must be the natural consequence of who we truly are.

While there appears to be a broad chasm separating the two dominant perspectives of traditional Islam and modern science during the modern era, the

---

[159] T. S. Eliot, "Little Gidding," *The Four Quartets*.

paradigm of modern science and the Religion of Islam have much in common upon which to build a new consensus of opinion that could reflect both the outer and inner aspirations of the vast majority of the contemporary people across the globe. These worldviews are, in a sense, two halves of the same truth and two sides of the same horizon; the venue of science being the outer, externalized and fully manifested world of nature, namely the lower order of the creation; the venue of traditional religion being the inner, internalized and fully spiritualized world of the supernatural, namely the higher order of the creation and the metaphysical principles associated with that creation.

If we are ever to achieve an intellectual revolution that can reach both the minds and hearts of the vast majority of modern and contemporary individuals, it must emerge from the cooperation and interaction of both modern science and the great spiritual traditions of the world. It will never come to pass if individuals who are in a position to influence the prevailing, contemporary thinking remain entrenched with a rigid and formulaic bias and take part in an intellectual framework that refuses to allow influences from other spheres of perception, to shed light on the perennial and universal mysteries that follow us like our shadows.

Perhaps the identity crisis that the modern world faces is nothing more than a challenge to meet the moment with true intelligence and heart knowledge grounded in the higher instincts and emotions of an enlightened spirituality. Beyond the threshold of this new millennium there may well exist a completely new scientific paradigm of knowledge that could be identified once again as a "sacred science" based on universal principles that would project a considerably different worldview from the one we have today. It wouldn't necessarily exclude the rich and enduring knowledge of the world religions, including their social and cultural traditions, their philosophy of life, and their sacred art, and it would definitely include the scientific facts that have been "proven" on their own level and according to the strict norms of the scientific method. The religions need a science of nature, a sacred science if you will, that could faithfully apply its metaphysical principles within the realm of nature, in order to understand the natural order in the light of the revealed truths that religions such as Islam protect and preserve. Similarly, modern science needs a philosophy of knowledge which could provide the conceptual and religious framework within which a natural science of phenomena could operate and flourish.

Sacred history has repeatedly warned that the decline and death of great civilizations has happened before and can happen again unless modern societies can bring themselves to combine the metaphysical principles of traditional knowledge with the rational discoveries of scientific knowledge. An enlightened being would learn to integrate the available knowledge of both worlds in order to develop certain potentialities and foster certain virtues in the spirit of a true evolution of consciousness that doesn't negate the defining qualities of humanity. This higher consciousness would cultivate the human potential to achieve knowledge of self and to realize this knowledge by living in harmony with our true nature and the natural world in which we live.

Is this possible? Who can say what the future will bring? The Divine Plan will make itself known, as it has always been made known, without the help or hindrance of ambitious and arrogant people here on earth. On the contrary, modern individuals need the mercy and blessing of the Divinity and rely on His sustained munificence, both now and in the future, to lead humanity toward an uncertain future and guide all seekers of true knowledge through the deepest mysteries of the universe.

Two final considerations bear mentioning within this context before we finally take our leave. Firstly, modern science need not necessarily close itself off from other levels of perception that may shed light on its professed objective to find a "theory of everything" that can serve as a universal knowledge to identify the true nature of reality. The knowledge that modern scientists seek in the distant regions of outer space and the answers they endeavor to find within the cellular life of the human body may lie, not in the mirage of distant galaxies and swarming microbes, but in an alternative medium that lies outside the spectrum of a purely physical reality.

Secondly, in the pursuit of a scientific inquiry since the time of the Renaissance, the scientific community has developed and brought to a rarefied level of expertise the five human senses through which scientists have explored nearly every aspect of nature, uncovering along the way the very seams of the world. Mankind sees and listens, but such seeing and listening do not encompass merely the physical plane of existence. There also exist extended perceptions that transcend the purely physical and corporeal experiences for a higher intuition that begins as faith and ends in certitude.

The call of the world and the call of the Spirit are the two halves of a single truth that cannot find their truest expression as isolated parts separated from the Whole. The open gate of the inner faculties, the feeling of expectation, of a hidden inner voice, of promises to be fulfilled and hopes to be realized are all there, in a sacred niche within our consciousness that we preserve as the expression of our inmost selves. It is the higher faculties of humanity that receive the essential knowledge of God and perceive the meaning of the one Reality in order to create an external life that reflects the inner person who lives it. The passing of days, the change of seasons, the success of people, the construction of all the churches and mosques across the earth, the accumulation of friends, money and fame are one and the same within the context of the world. They happen, they have their place, and then they crumble and are forgotten. The world endures and continues to turn on its axis.

From beginning to end and from periphery to center, the time-place continuum of the world is a boundary of God's prerogative and not man's. Plants and animals experience the gift of life within certain limits, but they do not know

God. We share the life of the senses with all animals and we share the experience of our bodies with the minerals and plants. We have other qualities and faculties that we share with no one beyond the human species, namely an intelligence that can envision the Supreme Intelligence and a consciousness that can respond to the lure of the Absolute and know the Divinity. The more we fail to attune ourselves to the knowledge of God and His unique Reality, the more we begin to think we can live a life that is sufficient unto itself and without the aid of Heaven. The more we fail to recognize, indeed the more we actively deny, the forms of the eternal wisdom that are embedded within revelation, within the world of nature and within man, the more we confine ourselves to the intellectual, psychological and sentient modes of perception, and the more we become the victims of a fragmented intelligence, a fanciful imagination, a wealth of unstable emotions, and a subjective perception of right and wrong, true and false, illusory and real.

We have written this book for the modern individual within each of us, transforming ourselves once again into the spiritual beings that we are in principle and are destined to be in truth. People today live in the world now as if they will live here forever, without realizing that the world we live for will terminate and we will be forgotten. What we need to live for and defend against all odds is the world of the Spirit in which all things are possible and where all mystery is resolved. It is a world in which the intellect receives a higher knowledge and intelligence sends forth its light, a world in which reason casts a shadow and the human heart burns with the emotions of higher sentiment. The world of the spirit contains the source material for the broad range of higher conscious experience. It makes use of spiritual imagination that is the search instrument of the soul in its endeavor to expand the horizons of the mind and in its quest to internalize the essential knowledge of God.

As the ultimate spiritual treasure, the spark of knowledge that inspired human faith in God becomes an internalized knowledge that will erase personal history and return the human soul to the primordial self. The wise person embedded in *Homo sapiens* will finally realize that he is not alone, that there is meaning in holy intimacy, that he has lived according to the truth of his given nature, and that the truth he has always searched for and finally found has made itself felt as the experience of the one Reality, in this world as well as in the paradisal world that is promised. This and much more is a message that came to a desert Bedouin over 15 centuries ago in the black hills of Arabia Felix, a message that echoes in our ears to this day and will continue to reverberate through future generations until the end of time.

ACKNOWLEDGEMENTS

My thanks to the students of the Petroleum Institute, Abu Dhabi, United Arab Emirates and others interested in the subject of Islamic culture and spirituality who read through some of these materials and gave me invaluable feedback that helped shape the themes and substance of this work. Also, I should acknowledge my good friend and colleague, Dr. Abdullah al-Shami, professor of Islamic Studies at the Petroleum Institute, who provided the inspiration, motive and driving force in building the key components for a suitable introduction to Islamic culture and spirituality. Finally, I would like to thank Farman Ullah Saleh, my friend and confidant, who continues to provide moral guidance and practical support during the writing of this work. He reminds me to pray in the mosque at the appointed time, as well as the "prayer of the heart" that the writing of this book has become. Without this variety of support and input over the last five years, this book would never have been started, much less brought to completion.

BIOGRAPHICAL NOTES

JOHN HERLIHY was born into an Irish-American family in Boston, Massachusetts and educated at Boston University and Columbia University in New York City before converting to Islam in 1974 when he was a lecturer in Academic Writing at a university in the Middle East. Twenty years after his conversion, he began to write about his experiences as a Muslim and the pursuit of an Islamic spirituality in an anti-spiritual world. In addition to writing for such traditional journals as *Sacred Web* and *Sophia*, he has written a number of works, including *Borderlands of the Spirit* and *Wisdom's Journey,* published by World Wisdom Books. He also edited World Wisdom's publication of René Guénon's writings, *The Essential René Guénon*. His most recent book, *Holy Quran: An Intimate Portrait*, has been published by Ansar Books in 2014. He currently works as a Visiting Academic teaching academic writing at Qatar University in Doha.

INDEX

A

Abraham · 38, 39, 40, 56, 59, 61, 62, 113, 168, 169, 171
Abu 'Ali al-Husain ibn Sina · 96
Abu Bakr · 66, 67, 68, 73, 74, 164, 165
Abu Hamid Muhammad, al-Ghazzali · 97
Abu Nasr al-Farabi · 95
Abu Raihan al-Biruni · 96
Abu Yusuf Ya'qub ibn Ishaq al-Kindi · 95
Abu'l-Fath Umar ibn Ibrahim al-Khayyami · 97
Abu'l-Walid Muhammad · 97
active intellect · 183
adab · 8
Aisha 163
Ali 66
Adam · 14, 38, 44, 46, 49, 62, 69, 71, 72, 105, 106, 111, 129, 137, 141, 142, 159, 168, 200, 201, 207, 208, 220, 222, 252
Aisha · 159
Alchemy · 101
al-dīn · 12
al-Fatihah · 124, 147,154-, 157, 173
Al-Ghazzali · 97
Al-Hallaj · 163
al-riyadh al-jinnah · 164
Anglican Church · 43
Arabia · 4, 7, 39, 47, 58, 59, 60, 61, 62, 63, 65, 72, 76, 77, 172, 259
Aristotle · 21, 95, 98, 183, 196, 240, 254
Astronomy · 99

B

barakah · 12, 36, 39, 81, 124, 141, 208
Bedouin · 59, 62, 259
Bhavagad Gita · 50
Bible · 22, 38, 39, 41, 86, 200, 238
Big Bang · 20, 21, 22, 78

bn al-Arabi · 144
Brahman · 50, 51, 56
Breath of the Compassionate · 24, 190, 207, 209, 236
Buddha · 50, 52, 53, 84, 231
Buddhism · 11, 17, 50, 52, 53, 55, 57, 79, 84, 129, 246

C

C. G. Jung · 217, 218
Charles Le Gai Eaton · 33, 84
Chemistry · 101
Chet Raymo · 176
chosen people · 37, 41
Christ · 37, 38, 40, 42, 44, 45, 51, 52, 61, 142, 205, 228
Christianity · 4, 6, 10, 11, 38, 42, 43, 44, 46, 52, 53, 57, 60, 61, 62, 79, 84, 142, 155, 239, 252
Chuang Tzu · 131
Classification of Knowledge · 4, 90, 102
Confession · 45
consciousness · 13, 15, 20, 24, 25, 28, 30, 31-34, 39, 48, 50-54, 65-66, 70-75, 80, 84, 108, 111, 114, 119, 120-129, 130-137, 146-149, 161-162, 165-169, 174-182, 185-194, 208, 211-213, 219, 228, 230, 233, 238-244, 250, 257, 258
Coomaraswamy · 131
culture · 7, 9, 56, 84, 92, 93, 143, 158, 175, 189, 254, 260

D

dar as-salam · 112
Darwin · 201, 202, 206, 212, 234
David · 9, 31, 38
dawn prayer · 118, 126
Descent of Man · 202
dhikr Allah · 71
Divine Command · 66, 76, 109
Divine Presence · 70, 136, 147, 216, 250

Divine Source · 27

E

Earth Sciences · 100
Edward Wilson · 182
Egypt · 39, 40, 41, 42, 46, 90, 101, 102
eleventh hour · 28
Emerson, R. W. · 119, 131, 236-37, 254
empirical science · 20
Epictetus · 241
Epicureanism · 241
Epicurus · 241
ethics · 8, 38, 40, 71, 95, 97, 225, 235, 236, 237, 238, 239, 240, 241, 244, 245, 254
European Renaissance · 7
evolution · 6, 7, 15, 21, 24, 35, 36, 42, 51, 86, 102, 139, 140, 179, 200, 202, 204, 210, 211, 217, 220, 241, 243, 244, 245, 254, 257
exodus · 41

F

Face · 32, 41, 83, 105, 154, 188, 214, 228, 248, 250
first cause · 22, 29, 79
First Cause · 22, 38, 84, 113
fitrah · 11, 14, 16, 40, 49, 211, 220, 221, 222, 252
fitrah Allah · 220
five senses · 7, 11, 12, 16, 92, 127, 128, 161, 162, 187, 227, 228, 229, 231, 233
Francis Bacon · 15
Frithjof Schuon · 17, 118, 136, 149, 185, 191, 214, 217, 221, 223, 224, 227, 231

G

Gabriel · 47, 63, 64, 65, 66, 67, 68, 69, 83, 105, 117, 121, 124, 151

Garden of Eden · 41, 208, 252
Golden Age · 79, 93, 94, 98, 207, 221
Golden Era · 14, 46, 49, 210
Gospels · 44, 157

H

hadith · 9, 14, 24, 26, 31, 32, 63, 69, 93, 105, 143, 159, 195, 198, 236, 238, 248, 253
Hadith · 8, 219, 222
hajj · 14, 49, 61, 173
heart · 6, 7, 8, 11-19, 35-39, 43-50, 53, 56-80, 91-93, 104-, 121-129, 132, 136-139, 141, 144-166, 168, 175, 179-188, 192-199, 225-238, 242, 246-252, 256-260
Hedonism · 240, 254
Hinduism · 11, 39, 50, 51, 57, 79, 132
Hira' · 63, 67
Holy Eucharist · 45
Homo sapiens · 33, 40, 125, 129, 135, 136, 138, 146, 149, 179, 195, 210, 211, 212, 216, 218, 242, 243, 259
Homo spiritualis · 129, 135, 149
human nature · 11, 16, 40, 106, 176, 179, 186, 194, 195, 217, 218, 219, 220, 221, 222, 234, 235, 236, 237, 238, 252
Huston Smith · 43, 54

I

Ibn Hisham · 64
Ibn Sina · 96, 97, 101, 103, 183
ihsan · 12, 36, 109
insan · 26, 33, 40, 106, 142, 210, 218, 222, 234, 239, 252
intelligence · 8, 16, 23, 24, 33, 34, 59, 80-84, 110-114, 127, 129-136, 150-155, 180-211, 214, 215, 216, 222, 224, 227, 228, 233, 234, 244-248
Isaac · 38, 169
Islam · 6
Islamic art · 123
Islamic science · 6, 7, 90, 93, 94, 96,

98, 102, 103
Isma'il · 38, 61, 64

J

J. P. Mooreland · 202, 212
Jabal al-Nur · 63
Jabir ibn Hayyan · 94, 101
Jahiliyyah · 60
Jalal al-Din Rumi · 144
Jerusalem · 37, 61
jihad al-nafs · 13, 48, 145
jinn · 79, 91, 109, 219
John Muir · 231
Joseph · 43
Joshua · 40
Judaism · 4, 11, 37, 38, 39, 40, 41, 42, 46, 53, 56, 61, 62, 84
Julius Caesar · 42

K

Ka'aba · 59, 60, 61, 62, 148, 154, 160, 168-171, 173, 199
karma · 51
Khadijah · 65, 121
King Henry VIII · 43

L

Lao Tzu · 54, 56
Laylat al-qadr · 46
Light · 5, 63, 72, 85, 120, 127, 181, 183, 187, 192, 194, 205
Logos · 12, 85, 124, 205
Luther · 43

M

Madinah · 5, 60, 61, 63, 67, 68, 73, 95, 163, 164, 166, 173
Maghreb · 8, 46, 121
Makkah · 28, 47, 59, 60, 61, 63, 65, 67, 76, 120, 148, 149, 154, 160, 167, 168, 171
Martin Lings · 143
Mary Magdalene · 44
materialism · 8, 15, 59, 179, 244
Mathematics · 99
Maurice Bucaille · 24
Medicine · 96, 101
mihrab · 28, 105, 149
missing link · 24
Modern science · 16, 17, 23, 80, 81, 87, 174, 199, 243
morality · 8, 42, 70, 71, 97, 191, 225, 235, 236, 237, 238, 239, 241, 244, 248, 254
Moses · 38, 39, 40, 41, 42, 62, 84
Muhammad · 9, 11, 14, 26, 31, 37, 42, 46, 47, 48, 49, 53, 59, 63, 65, 66, 69, 75, 83, 101, 105, 126, 143, 151, 166, 167, 183, 236, 253
Muslim life · 6, 13, 14, 48, 49, 69, 118, 120, 147, 148, 150, 172, 249
mystery · 6, 16, 19-24, 26-31, 34, 35, 39, 44, 45, 47, 50, 55, 62, 65, 69, 70, 71, 76, 84, 104-113, 119, 121, 125-139, 142, 145, 152, 176-181, 184, 187-189, 196, 199, 200-202, 211-216, 225, 228, 229-233, 236, 243, 244, 256, 258

N

Nature · 7, 9, 22, 26, 27, 81, 84, 86, 87, 107, 190, 208, 214, 219
New Testament · 40, 44, 61, 156
Nikos Kazantzakis · 187
nirvana · 54, 55
Noam Chomsky · 203

O

Omar bin al-Khattaab · 164
Origin · 19, 24, 28, 31, 32, 70, 79, 89
Orthodox Church · 43

P

perfect man · 136, 142, 210, 211, 220, 222
Physics · 19, 98, 100
pillars · 6, 142, 146, 159, 160, 172
Plato · 95, 183, 234, 240
primordial man · 137, 140-142, 210, 218, 220, 221, 222
primordial nature · 11, 221
progress · 7, 15, 18, 37, 93, 121, 138, 139, 151, 190, 210, 225, 241, 243, 244, 245, 254
prophethood · 65, 72
Psychology · 5, 8, 95, 207, 217, 234

Q

Quantum mechanics · 18
Qur'an · 4, 8, 11-15, 26-29, 32, 35, 38-41, 46-48, 57, 59-96, 102, 105-127, 131-135, 138-142, 146-154, 159, 165, 183-184, 192, 198, 200-206, 219-222, 233, 235, 238-239, 247-250, 251, 252, 253
Quraysh · 60, 61, 62, 67

R

Ramadhan · 5, 64, 147, 159, 160, 161, 163, 164, 173
Reality · 9, 16, 25, 27, 31, 32, 51, 62, 69, 70, 71, 75, 78, 79, 81, 84, 90, 91, 105, 107, 108, 109, 114, 126, 129, 132, 138, 140, 143, 145, 148, 150, 152, 160, 168, 184, 188, 191, 195, 196, 197, 200, 208, 210, 212, 229, 235, 242, 247, 258, 259
reason · 8, 12, 15, 16, 21, 24, 27, 29, 31, 33, 45, 58, 79, 80-84, 91, 92, 95, 115, 116, 127, 130, 133, 134, 138, 142-144, 159, 162, 174-188, 192-194, 200, 205, 209, 211-214, 218, 220, 228, 233, 240, 242, 258
Religion · 4, 10, 11, 14, 15, 16, 21, 26, 28, 34, 37, 46, 73, 76, 107, 110, 111, 113, 136, 151, 164, 172, 218, 220, 228, 250, 256
revelation · 7, 9, 12, 16, 17, 20, 21, 26-33, 36, 39, 42, 44-52, 57, 59, 61-69, 72, 74, 76-77, 82- 85, 90-95, 105, 106, 111, 113-127, 133, 134, 137-142, 145, 147, 150, 159, 165, 167, 175, 183-184, 189, 193, 197, 199, 206, 209-210, 213, 215, 218-222, 227, 229, 233-234, 239, 250, 253, 256, 258
Richard Leakey · 200, 201
Roger Penrose · 180, 186, 190
Roman Empire · 43
rope of Allah · 157

S

sacraments · 43, 45
sacred psychology · 8, 71, 146, 155, 210, 217, 218, 219, 223, 234
sacred science · 7, 20, 79, 80, 81, 82, 83, 102, 257
sakinah · 122, 124, 151, 173
seal · 9, 11, 14, 34, 37, 42, 46, 47, 49, 66, 72, 76, 147, 155, 157, 204
seat of the intelligence · 195, 228
secularism · 8, 244
Seyyed Hossein Nasr · 32, 70, 83
shahadah · 11, 12, 13, 14, 48, 49, 71, 111, 141, 146, 148, 160, 168, 245, 246, 251
sign of the times · 143
Socrates · 220, 239, 254
Solomon · 40
soul · 6, 10-17, 27, 32, 36, 37, 40, 43-48, 51-57, 62, 64, 66-69, 70-76, 83, 85, 86, 95, 101, 105, 106-120, 123, 126, 130, 137-142, 145-157, 160-162, 165, 171, 178, 187, 188, 190-199, 207-226, 229, 232-238, 241, 242, 246, 247, 248, 249, 250, 251, 252, 258, 259
Spirit · 2, 13, 17, 18, 23, 24, 45, 48, 50, 51, 69, 92, 105, 107, 110, 111, 122, 128, 129, 134, 138, 139, 140, 141,

145, 149, 152, 170, 183, 186, 187, 192, 193, 195, 196, 198, 207, 222, 229, 236, 242, 246, 248, 250, 258, 261
spirituality · 6, 7, 8, 9, 11, 31, 39, 61, 73, 76, 81, 84, 91, 105, 107, 108, 109, 110, 120, 136, 137, 138, 139, 140, 141, 143, 144, 145, 149, 150, 152, 153, 159, 162, 172, 221, 235, 240, 246, 247, 249, 257, 260, 261
Stephen Hawking · 26
straight path · 63, 142, 145, 149, 150, 152, 155, 183
Sunnah · 8, 13, 29, 48, 111, 153, 219, 222
Supreme Being · 6, 7, 11, 12, 27, 31, 38, 39, 45, 51, 69, 76, 80, 84, 91, 93, 109, 112, 113, 114, 119, 146, 151, 155, 159, 161, 176, 196, 207, 209, 213, 224, 225, 226, 228, 243, 245, 247, 249
Supreme Mind · 128
Supreme Pen · 85, 124
surrender · 10, 12, 14, 49, 59, 66, 74, 75, 76, 84, 109, 110, 111, 112, 113, 134, 143, 156, 159, 161, 165, 187, 194, 197, 198, 202, 209, 245, 246, 247, 248, 253

T

T. H. Huxley · 201
Tablet · 85, 115, 124
tajwid · 8, 77, 120, 121, 122
tajwīd · 68, 115
Tao Te Ching · 54, 219
Taoism · 11, 50, 54, 84, 131, 222
tawhid · 11, 14, 17, 29, 49, 72, 79, 83, 91, 93, 110, 209
Ten Commandments · 38, 41, 42, 53
Tetragrammaton · 39
The Book of Chuang Tzu · 131
Thoreau · 9
Throne · 28, 61, 84, 187
Tibet · 54
Titus Burckhardt · 118
Torah · 39, 40, 56

Tower of Babel · 41
Transcendental Meditation · 144
true man · 33, 136, 141, 210-211, 218, 222

U

Umar · 67, 73, 74, 99, 103
ummi · 64
Umrah · 168, 169
Unity · 11, 24, 29, 91, 155, 184, 185
unseen · 11, 16, 31, 47, 65, 78, 81, 107, 109, 110, 113, 150, 151, 178
Uthman · 67

W

William C. Chittick · 144
Wolfgang Smith · 22, 24, 178
worldview · 7, 9, 14, 16, 20, 24, 25, 26, 28, 29, 30, 31, 33, 35, 49, 54, 58, 62, 79, 80, 82, 92, 94, 114, 151, 152, 161, 162, 174, 175, 177, 179, 182, 183, 186, 192, 193, 194, 202, 208, 211, 212, 225, 228, 241, 242, 243, 244, 245, 248, 254, 257
Worldview · 4, 10, 28, 35
worship · 12, 31, 32, 42, 59, 60, 68, 71, 76, 109, 115, 116, 117, 119, 120, 123, 126, 127, 134, 137, 142, 146, 147, 149, 150, 151, 152, 154, 156, 157, 159, 160, 164, 169, 170, 172, 173, 178, 201, 205, 250
wu wei · 55, 56

Y

Yunus Emre · 162

Z

Zamzam · 167, 171
Zayd bin Thabit · 66, 67

www.ingramcontent.com/pod-product-compliance
Lightning Source LLC
Chambersburg PA
CBHW070837160426
43192CB00012B/2225